Windows® 2000 Professional

Walter J. Glenn

SAMS
A Division of Macmillan USA
201 W. 103rd Street
Indianapolis, Indiana 46290

Visually in Full Color

How To Use Windows® 2000 Professional

International Standard Book Number: 0-672-31711-7

Library of Congress Catalog Card Number: 99-65590

Printed in the United States of America

First Printing: **February 2000**

02 01 00 4 3 2 1

Trademarks

All terms mentioned in this book that are known to be trademarks or service marks have been appropriately capitalized. Sams Publishing cannot attest to the accuracy of this information. Use of a term in this book should not be regarded as affecting the validity of any trademark or service mark.

Warning and Disclaimer

Every effort has been made to make this book as complete and as accurate as possible, but no warranty or fitness is implied. The information provided is on an "as is" basis.

Acquisitions Editor
Jeff Schultz

Development Editor
Damon Jordan

Managing Editor
Charlotte Clapp

Project Editor
George E. Nedeff

Copy Editor
Kelli Brooks

Indexer
Eric Schroeder

Proofreaders
Tony Reitz
Mary Ellen Stephenson

Technical Editor
Bob Correll

Team Coordinator
Amy Patton

Interior Designers
Nathan Clement
Ruth Lewis

Cover Designers
Aren Howell
Nathan Clement

Copy Writer
Eric Borgert

Production
Stacey Richwine-DeRome
Ayanna Lacey
Heather Hiatt-Miller

Contents at a Glance

Table of Contents

7 Using Internet Email and Newsgroups *116*

8 Protecting Your Files *136*

9 Changing Windows 2000 Settings *150*

10 Using the System Tools *180*

11 Installing New Software on Your Computer *196*

A Installing Windows 2000 Professional *208*

About the Author

Walter J. Glenn is an independent writer, editor, and networking consultant. He is a Microsoft Certified Systems Engineer, Internet Specialist, and Certified Trainer. He has been part of the computer industry for about fifteen years, working his way from PC repair, to programming, to networking and has extensively written about networking and the Windows operating environment. He lives and works in Huntsville, Alabama, with his wife, Susan, his three-year old son, Liam, and his new daughter, Maya.

Acknowledgements

First off, I want to thank the team at Sams Publishing, including Jeff Schultz, Amy Patton, Damon Jordan, Mark Taber, George Nedeff, and the production team. Thanks also to David and Sherry Rogelberg and Neil Salkind of StudioB for their guidance and support.

Dedication

For my son, Liam, who spent too many nights without Dad around while I was working on this one.

Tell Us What You Think!

As the reader of this book, *you* are our most important critic and commentator. We value your opinion and want to know what we're doing right, what we could do better, what areas you'd like to see us publish in, and any other words of wisdom you're willing to pass our way.

As an Executive Editor for Sams Publishing, I welcome your comments. You can fax, email, or write me directly to let me know what you did or didn't like about this book—as well as what we can do to make our books stronger.

Please note that I cannot help you with technical problems related to the topic of this book, and that due to the high volume of mail I receive, I might not be able to reply to every message.

When you write, please be sure to include this book's title and author as well as your name and phone or fax number. I will carefully review your comments and share them with the author and editors who worked on the book.

Fax: 317-581-4770

Email: `office_sams@mcp.com`

Mail: Mark Taber
Associate Publisher
Sams Publishing
201 West 103rd Street
Indianapolis, IN 46290 USA

How to Use This Book

The Complete Visual Reference

Each chapter of this book is made up of a series of short, instructional tasks, designed to help you understand all the information that you need to get the most out of your computer hardware and software.

Click: Click the left mouse button once.

Double-click: Click the left mouse button twice in rapid succession.

Right-click: Click the right mouse button once.

Pointer Arrow: Highlights an item on the screen you need to point to or focus on in the step or task.

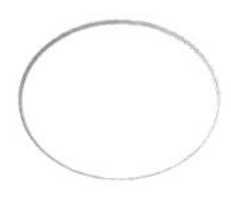

Selection: Highlights the area onscreen discussed in the step or task.

Click and Type: Click once where indicated and begin typing to enter your text or data.

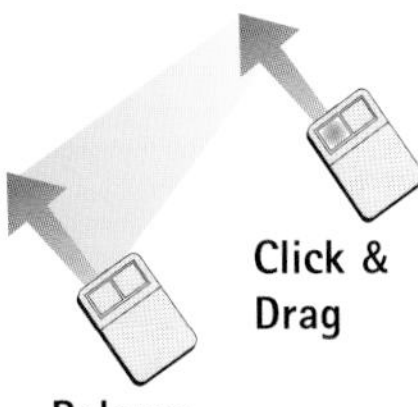

How to Drag: Point to the starting place or object. Hold down the mouse button (right or left per instructions), move the mouse to the new location, and then release the button.

Key icons: Clearly indicate which key combinations to use.

Each task includes a series of easy-to-understand steps designed to guide you through the procedure.

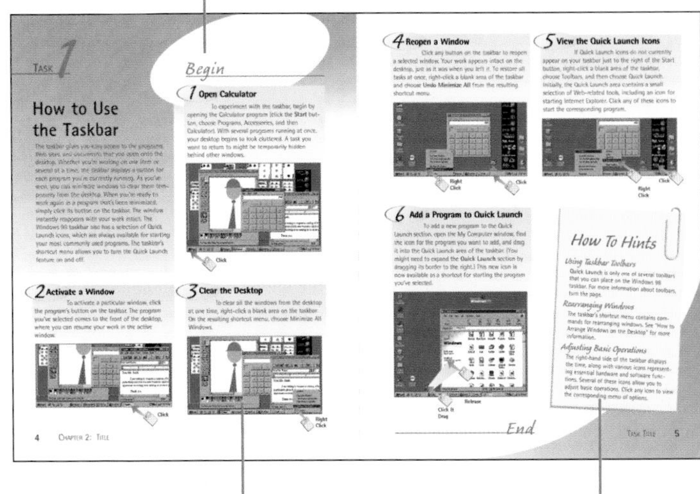

Each step is fully illustrated to show you how it looks onscreen.

Extra hints that tell you how to accomplish a goal are provided in most tasks.

Menus and items you click are shown in **bold**. Information you type is in a `special font`.

Continues

If you see this symbol, it means the task you're in continues on the next page.

Introduction

Let's face it. Most of you have better things to do than becoming a computer expert, and a complex operating system such as Windows 2000 Professional, can be pretty intimidating when your boss or administrator plops it on your desk and says, "This is what you'll be using from now on." Fortunately, Windows is designed to be easy to use, and this book is designed to make it even easier. Whether you are completely new to Windows, or feel at home clicking your way through all those dialog boxes, you are likely to have questions:

- ✓ How do you search for a file when you don't know its name?
- ✓ How do you install a network printer?
- ✓ How do you manage documents that are waiting to print?
- ✓ How do you work with files on the network?
- ✓ How do you set permissions on a file?
- ✓ How do you change the way your mouse works?

How to Use Windows 2000 provides easy-to-follow, step-by-step, and visual instructions for performing all of the common (and not so common) tasks. This book uses actual pictures of the Windows 2000 Professional screen to show you what you'll see at each step of a task. With each picture, a written explanation shows you the details of performing the task in simple, jargon-free language. Using the pictures with the text is a great way to learn and accomplish the tasks the first time. Later, you can refresh your memory by simply scanning the pictures.

Each task described in this book is a specific action you will use in Windows 2000 Professional, such as changing the volume on your computer, or backing up files. A task is described in no more than seven steps. Many tasks also include special "How-To Hints" that show you information related to the task. Finally, tasks are arranged into the following groups, making it easy to learn related sets of skills without hunting through the book:

- ✓ Using the Windows 2000 Desktop
- ✓ Working with Files and Folders
- ✓ Printing
- ✓ Working on a Network
- ✓ Working When Away from the Network
- ✓ Working on the Internet
- ✓ Using Internet Email and Newsgroups
- ✓ Protecting Your Files
- ✓ Changing Windows 2000 Settings
- ✓ Using the System Tools
- ✓ Using the Command Prompt
- ✓ Installing New Software and Hardware
- ✓ Installing Windows 2000 Professional

Whatever your level of expertise and for whatever reason you use Windows 2000 Professional, you will find this book a useful tool. Whether you read it cover to cover, or set it aside for reference when you come across a specific task with which you need help, this book has been carefully designed to provide you the information you need to complete the task and get on with your work. Enjoy!

Task

PART 1

Using the Windows 2000 Desktop

The Windows desktop works much like its real-world counterpart—it is a place where you organize files, run programs, and coordinate your work. When you run a program or open a folder, these items open in a window on the desktop. You can keep multiple windows open at once, arrange them how you like, and switch between them easily.

In this chapter, you will explore some of the basic features of the Windows desktop—features that you will make use of daily. You will learn how to log in and out of Windows, how to use a mouse, how to run a program, and how to get help when you need it. You will also learn techniques for arranging windows and switching between open programs. Finally, you will learn the proper way to shut down your computer.

TASK 1

How to Log On to Windows 2000

Windows 2000 is a very secure system. When you first start a computer, you must log on (supply a username and password) so that Windows knows who you are and what things you are allowed to do on the computer and on the network. If your computer is on a network, your logon information is supplied by your network administrator. When you install Windows 2000 on your own computer, you supply the information during setup. The first time you log on after installing Windows 2000, you must log on using the administrator account. See Appendix A, "Installing Windows 2000 Professional," for more details.

Begin

1 Press Ctrl+Alt+Del

To get to the main logon screen, you must press the **Ctrl**, **Alt**, and **Del** keys all at once. This informs Windows that you want to enter a username and password.

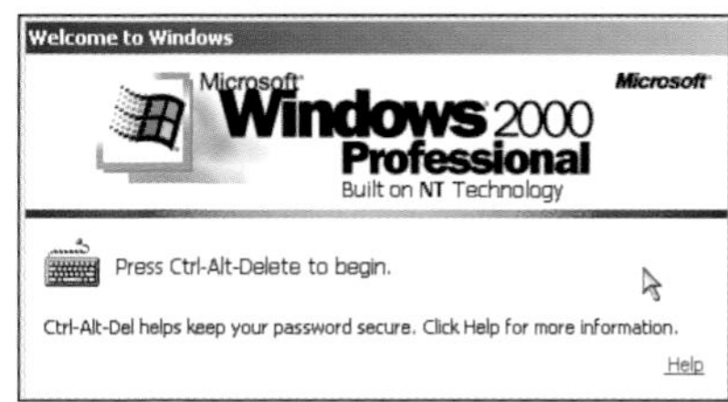

2 Enter Your Username

Enter your username.

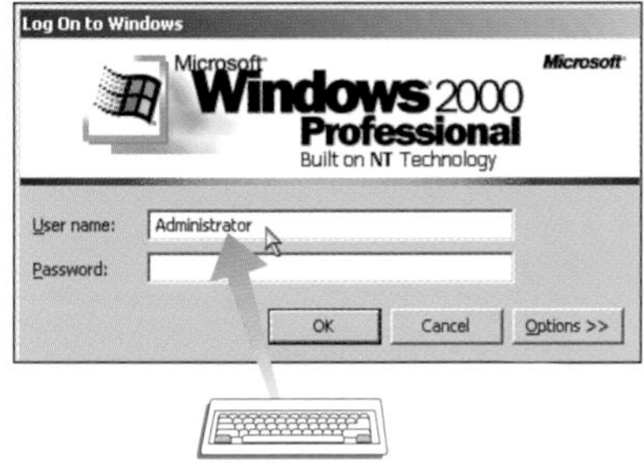

3 Enter Your Password

Enter your password. As you type, the characters you enter appear on the screen only as asterisks. This keeps people from discovering your password by looking over your shoulder. Passwords are case-sensitive. You must enter the correct combination of upper- and lowercase characters and numbers.

4 Show Extra Login Options

Most of the time, a username and password are enough. However, you can click the **Options** buttons for more choices.

5 Log In to a Different Domain

If you are on a network with multiple domains, you can choose the domain to which you want to log in. You can also choose to log in to the computer only, which lets you perform tasks on the computer as usual, but does not allow you to access any network resources, such as shared printers and folders.

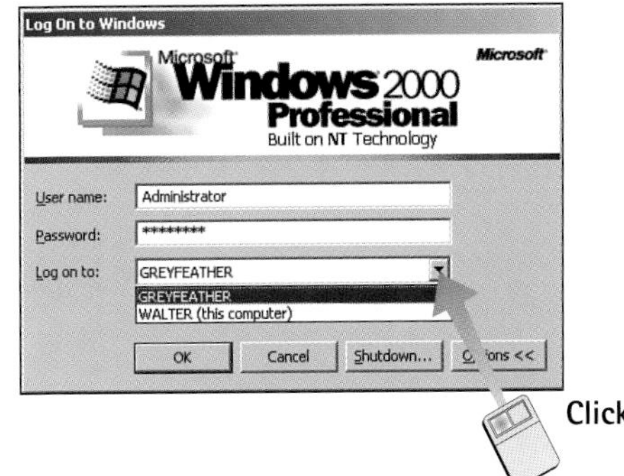

6 Use Dial-Up Networking

If your computer is configured to connect to a network using a modem, you must use dial-up networking to connect. For more information on using dial-up networking, refer to Chapter 4, "Working on a Network."

7 Shut Down

You can also shut down your computer from the logon screen. Clicking the Shut Down button opens a dialog that lets you choose whether to shut down or restart the computer. This is great when you need to shut down the system but don't want to wait through the logon process.

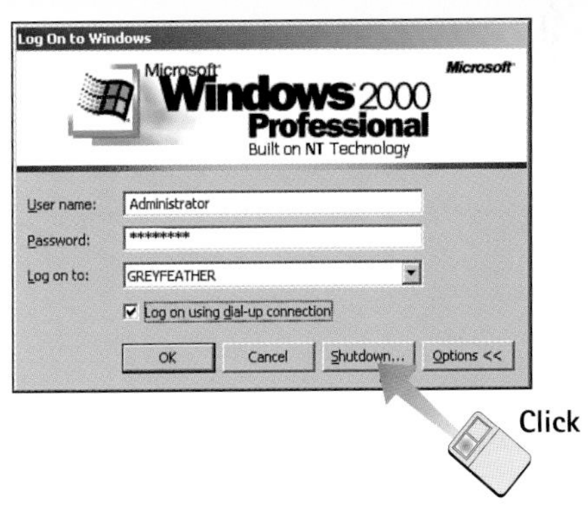

End

TASK 2

How to Use Your Mouse

Your mouse allows you to get many common tasks done more quickly than with the keyboard. Sliding your mouse on your desk moves the pointer on your screen. The pointer usually appears as an arrow pointing up and to the left—just point it to the item you want to select. The pointer shape changes as you move over different areas of the screen—a vertical bar means a place where you can enter text, for example. The shape also changes to indicate system status. An hourglass means Windows is busy doing something. An hourglass with an arrow means Windows is working on something, but you can continue to do other things in the meantime.

Begin

1 Point to an Object

An object refers to an item on your screen, usually an icon, that represents a program, file, or folder. You can point to an object by sliding your mouse so that you place the tip of the pointer arrow over that object.

2 Click an Object

Clicking your left mouse button one time selects an object. When you select the object, it becomes highlighted with a dark background. You can then perform some other action on the object, such as deleting it.

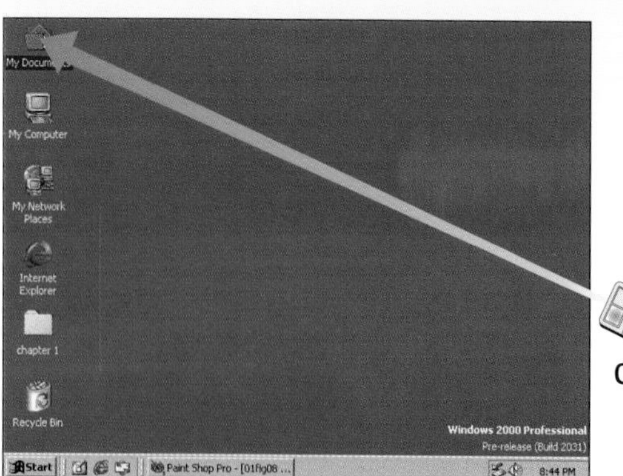

3 Double-Click an Object

Double-clicking means to move the pointer over an object and click the left mouse button twice in quick succession. Double-clicking an object on your desktop *launches* it. Double-clicking a folder opens it; double-clicking a program runs it.

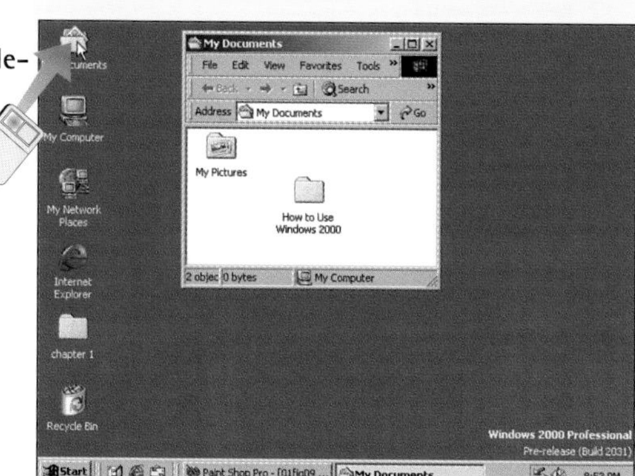

4 Right-Click an Object

When you click once on an object with your right mouse button, a shortcut menu pops up that lets you perform various actions associated with the object. The command in boldface is the action that would be performed by double-clicking the object.

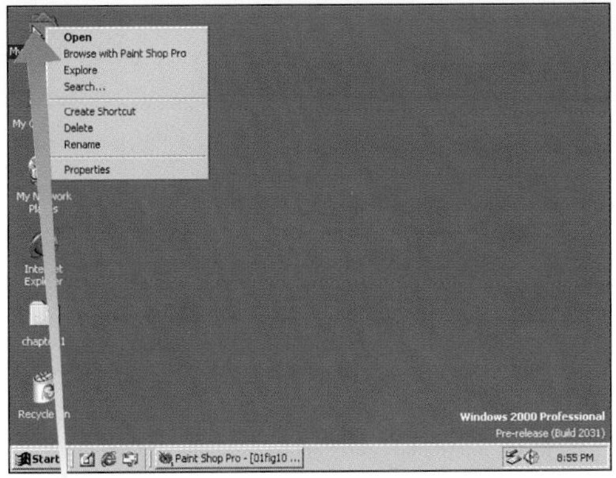

Right-click

5 Drag an Object

To drag an object, point to the item, click and then hold down the left mouse button while moving the mouse to reposition the item. Release the mouse button to drop the object. This is the way to move files to new folders and move whole windows on your desktop.

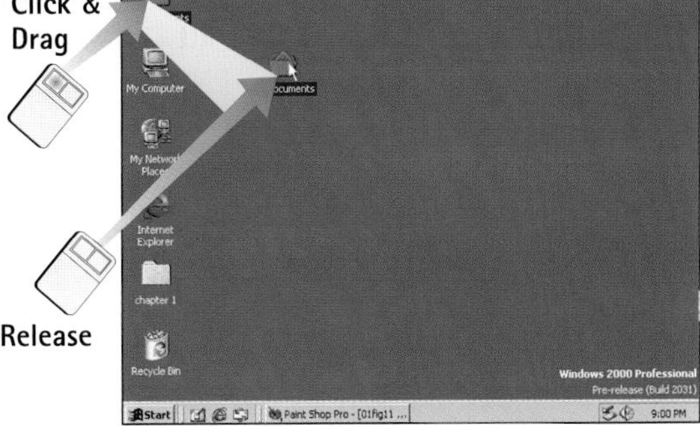

6 Open a Menu

Many windows, such as open folders and programs, have menus that provide access to different commands for working in the window. To open a menu, just click on the menu's name once.

7 Select a Menu Command

After a menu is open, you can click any command on the menu once to have Windows perform that action.

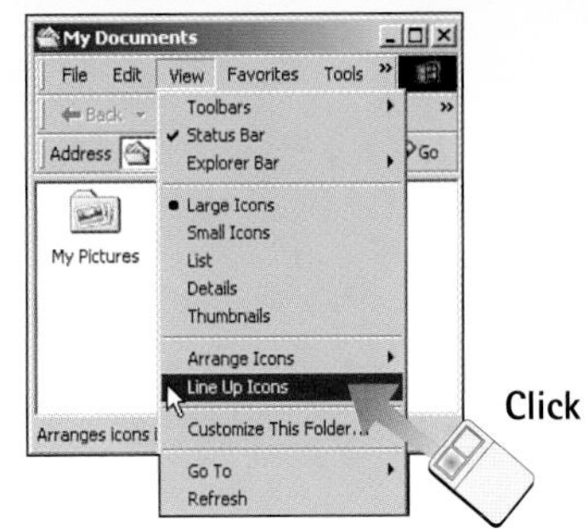

End

TASK 3

How to Use a Program

The real reason you bother with Windows is so that you can run programs that let you get your work done (and play an occasional game of Solitaire). Windows 2000 provides several ways to run your programs. To begin with, all of your programs are conveniently located on the **Start** menu. This includes some simple programs that come with Windows (like a calculator and a notepad) and any programs that you have installed.

Begin

1 Click the Start Button

Click the **Start** button to open the **Start** menu and move your pointer to **Programs**. All of the programs you can run are listed in the Programs folder. Some might be listed in folders within the Programs folder—just point to a subfolder to open it. Windows shortens long menus automatically. A small double arrow at the top or bottom of a menu indicates there is more than is initially shown. Click the arrow or just wait a moment and the full menu is shown.

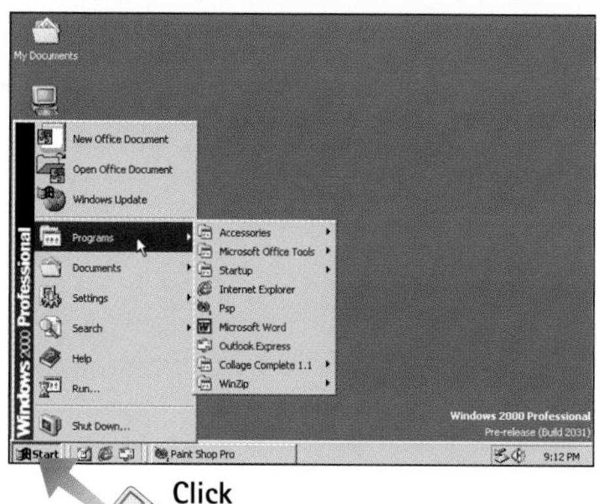

Click

2 Choose a Program to Run

After you find the program you want to run, click it once to launch it in its own Window.

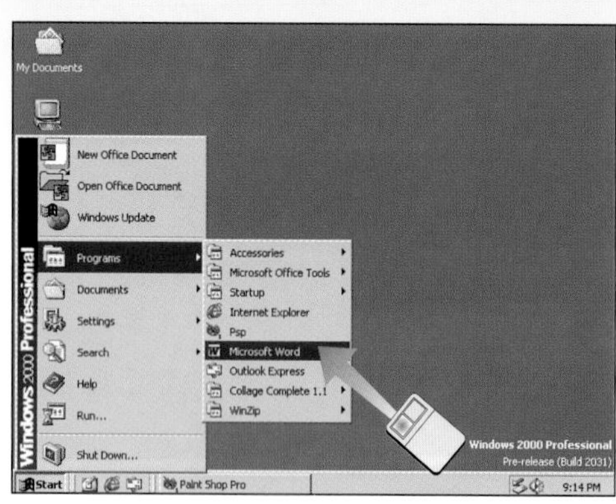

Click

3 Click a Quick Launch Shortcut

Some programs have shortcuts on the **Quick Launch** toolbar, just to the right of the **Start** button. Click any of these shortcut buttons once to launch the program.

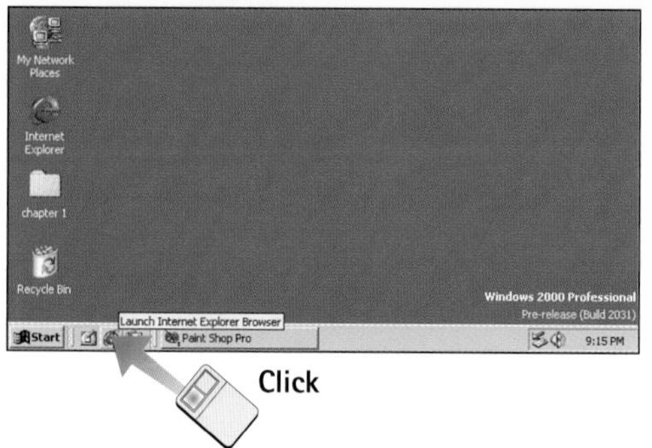

Click

4 Maximize a Program Window

Click the **Maximize** button to make the program window take up the whole screen except for the taskbar. This might be necessary to see all you need to in a window.

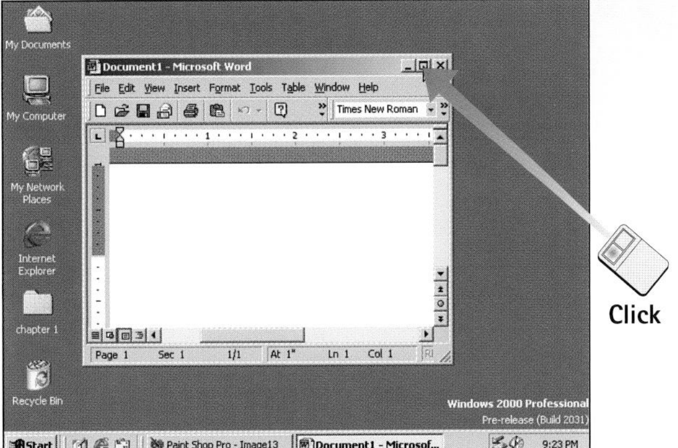

5 Restore a Program Window

After a window is maximized, the **Maximize** button turns into a **Restore** button. Click the **Restore** button to shrink the window back to its previous size.

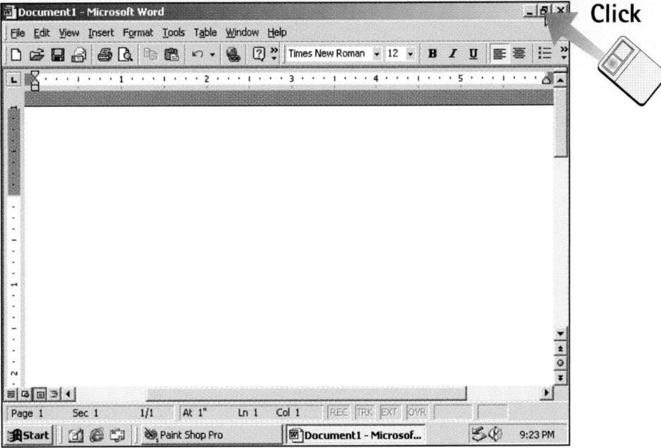

6 Minimize a Program Window

Click the **Minimize** button to remove the Window from the desktop but leave the program running. You can tell the program is still running because its button remains in the taskbar at the bottom of the screen. Click the taskbar button to restore the window to the desktop.

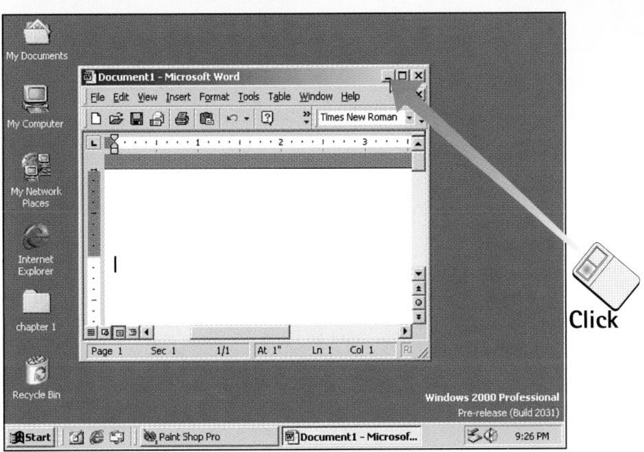

7 Close a Program Window

Click the **Close** button to end the program and remove its window from the desktop. The program offers to save any unsaved work before it closes. You can also close a program by choosing the **Exit** command from the **File** menu.

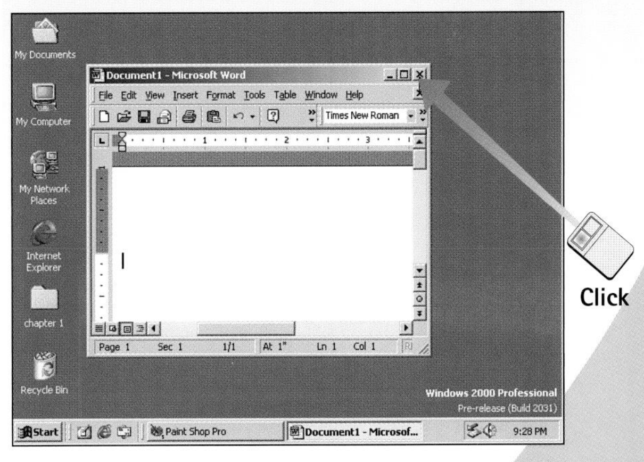

End

TASK 4

How to Arrange Windows on the Desktop

Windows offers the ability to keep many windows, whether program windows or folder windows, open at the same time. Although this provides the ability to easily move between tasks, using multiple windows can become confusing. Fortunately, Windows offers some clever tools for working with and arranging windows on your desktop.

Begin

1 Resize a Window

When you move your pointer to the outer edge or corner of a window, the pointer changes into a double-headed arrow. When the pointer changes, click and drag the edge of the window to change its size.

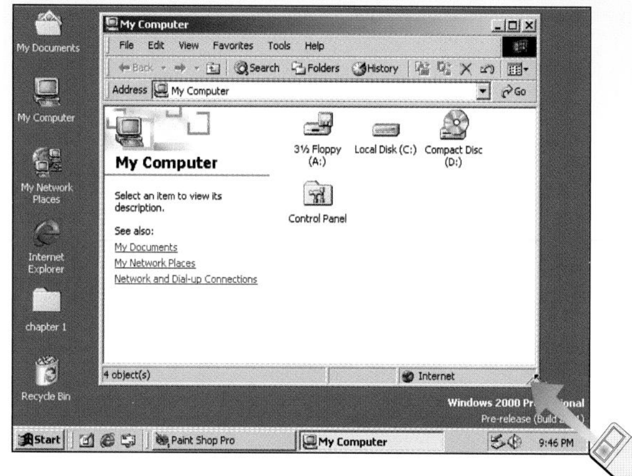

Click & Drag

2 Move a Window

You can move an entire window to a different location on the desktop by dragging its title bar. You can even move the window off the edges of your display.

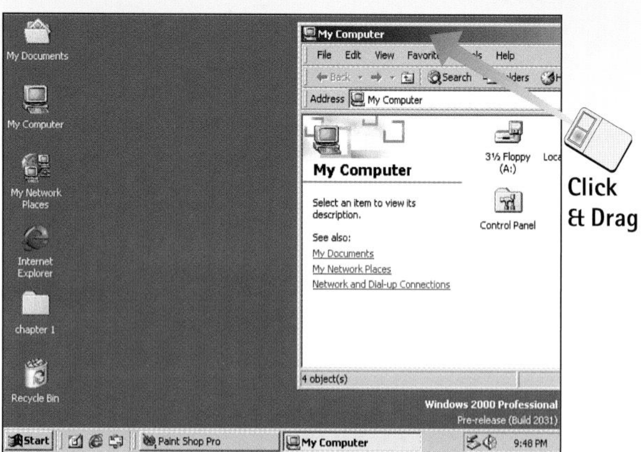

Click & Drag

3 Cascade Windows

When you have a number of windows open at once, you can line them all up in a cascade by right-clicking the taskbar and choosing **Cascade Windows** on the shortcut menu.

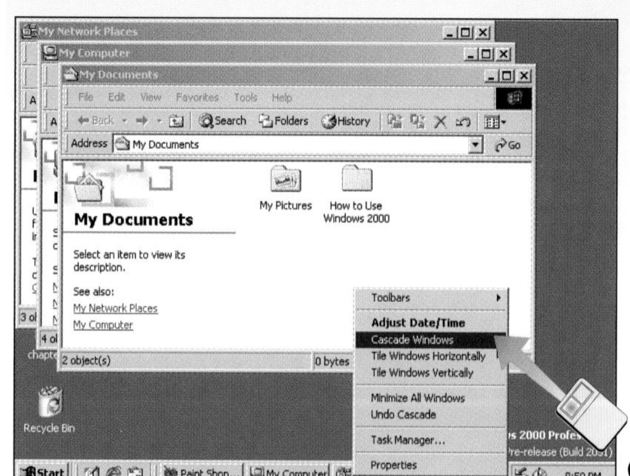

Click

4 Tile Windows Vertically

Another way to arrange multiple windows on your desktop is to tile them, which means that Windows tries to fit them all on the screen at once. Right-click the taskbar and choose **Tile Windows Vertically** to arrange them from left to right on your screen.

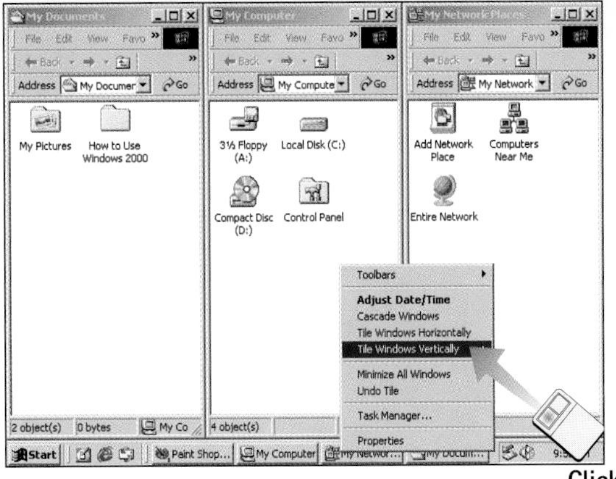

5 Tile Windows Horizontally

You can also tile windows horizontally, meaning that Windows fits them all on your screen from top to bottom. Just right-click the taskbar and choose **Tile Windows Horizontally**.

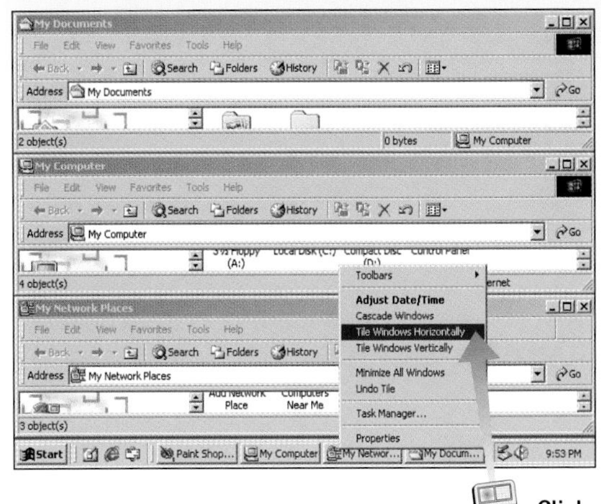

6 Minimize All Windows

You can minimize all open windows on your desktop at once (and thus clear them from your desktop) by right-clicking your taskbar and choosing **Minimize All Windows.** This is a great way to get to your desktop quickly.

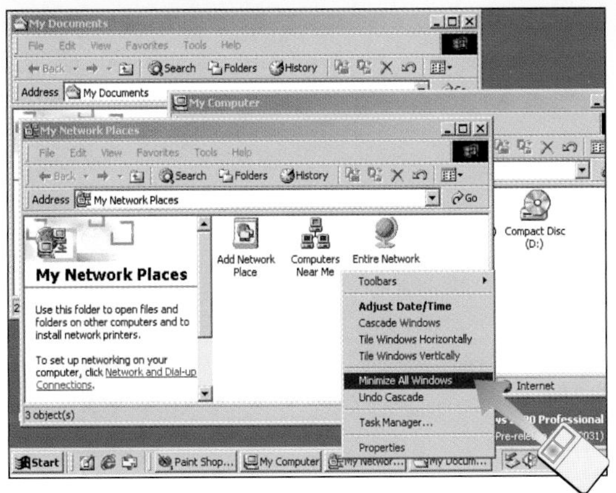

End

How-To Hints

Show Desktop

A better way to get to your desktop quickly instead of using the **Minimize All Windows** command is to use the **Show Desktop** button on the **Quick Launch** toolbar. This effectively minimizes all windows, even if some windows are showing dialog boxes (something **Minimize All Windows** can't do). Just click **Show Desktop** again to reverse the action.

TASK 5

How to Switch Between Programs

When you run several programs at once, you must be able to switch between these programs easily. Windows offers three great methods for switching between open applications—two using the mouse and one using the keyboard.

Begin

1 Click the Program's Window

The easiest way to switch to an open program is simply to click on the program's window, if it is visible. Inactive windows have a gray title bar and look dim. Clicking anywhere on an inactive window brings it to the front and makes it active.

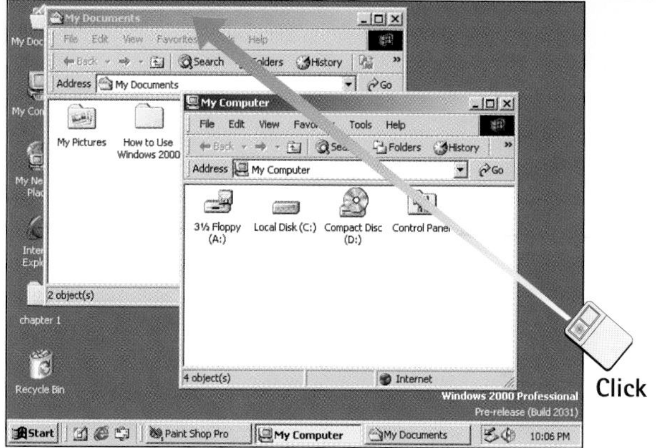

2 Click a Program's Taskbar Button

When you can't see the window you want to get to, the simplest way to switch to it is to click that window's button on the taskbar. This brings the window to the front of the desktop in whatever state (size and position) you left it.

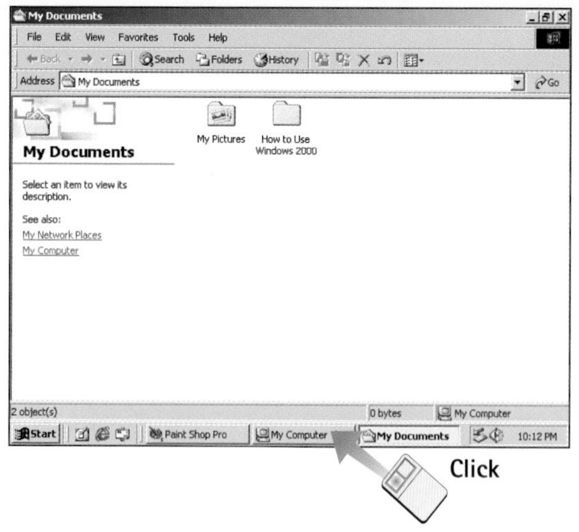

3 Resizing the Taskbar

When there are a lot of open Windows, the buttons on the taskbar might get too small to be of much value in determining which window is which. You can hover your pointer over a button to see its full description, or you can drag the edge of the taskbar to make it bigger.

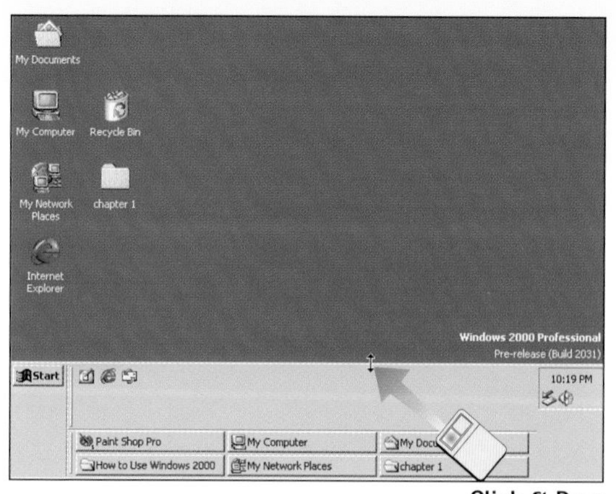

4 Press Alt+Tab

You can also switch between open windows using your keyboard. Press and hold the **Alt** key and then press the **Tab** key once (without letting go of the Alt key). A box appears displaying icons for each window. Click **Tab** to cycle through the windows. When you get to the window you want, release the **Alt** key to switch to it.

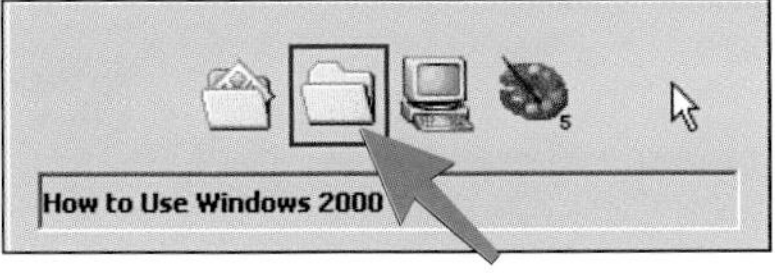

End

How-To Hints

Getting Out of Alt+Tab

If you use **Alt+Tab** to open the box that lets you switch between windows and then decide that you don't want to switch, just press **Esc** while you're still holding down the **Alt** key. The box disappears and puts you right back where you were.

TASK 6

How to Browse Your Disk Drives

Your disk drives hold all of the information on your computer—all of the files, folders, and programs, as well as all your documents. The **My Computer** window gives you access to these drives, whether they are hard drives, floppy drives, or something else. **My Computer** also provides a shortcut to the Windows Control Panel, which is discussed more in Chapter 9, "Changing Windows 2000 Settings."

Begin

1 Open My Computer

Double-click the **My Computer** icon on the desktop to open the **My Computer** window.

2 Select a Disk Drive

The **My Computer** window shows any drives present on your computer. Click the icon for the drive you want to investigate. Your floppy drive is usually named **A:** and your main hard drive is usually named **C:**. Information about the capacity and free space on any selected drive is shown to the left.

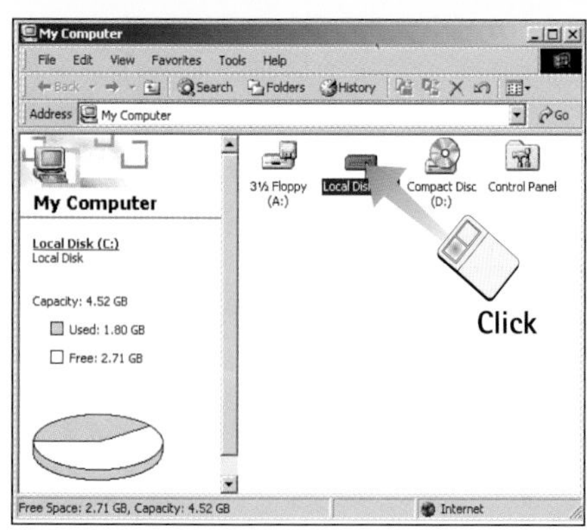

3 Open a Drive

Double-click the drive icon to open that drive.

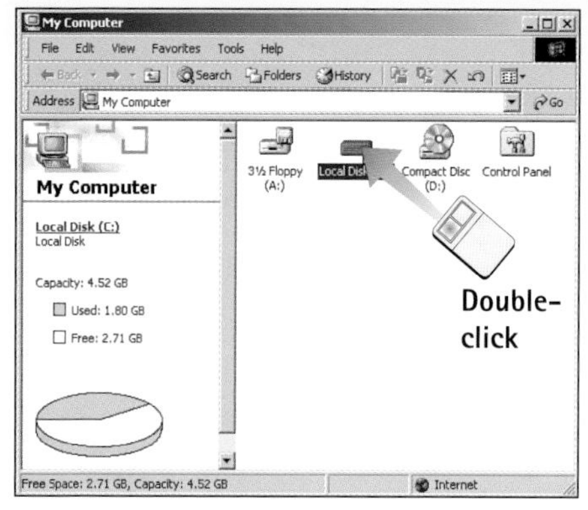

4 Open a Folder

Objects on a drive are organized into folders. Folders can contain both files and other folders. Double-click a folder to open it.

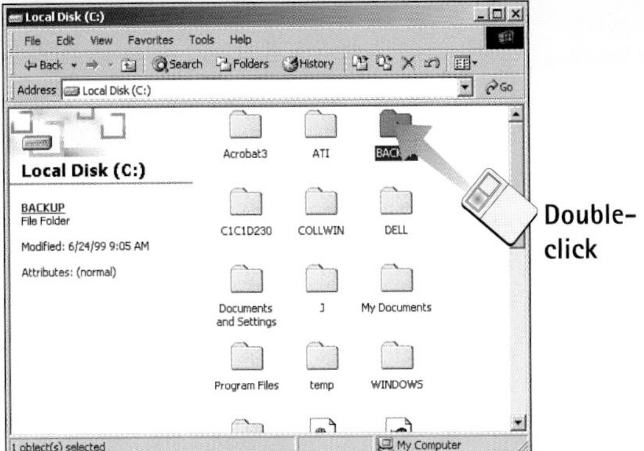

5 Open a File

When you select a file, a description of that file appears on the left side of the window. Double-click a file to launch the program that created the file and open the file within that program.

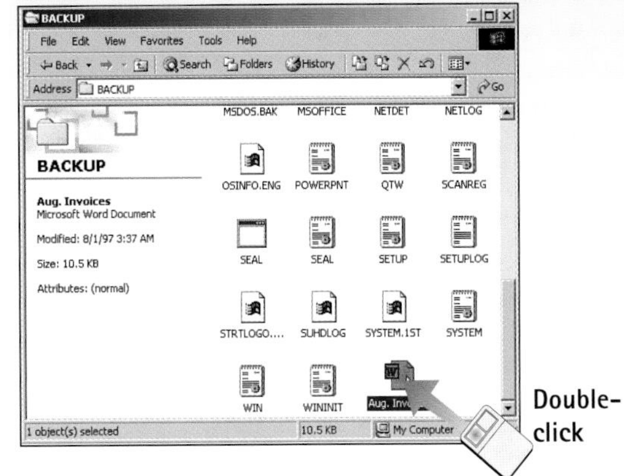

6 Navigate Folders

Click the back arrow button to go back to the folder you just came from. Click the down arrow beside the back button to view a list of previous locations you can jump back to.

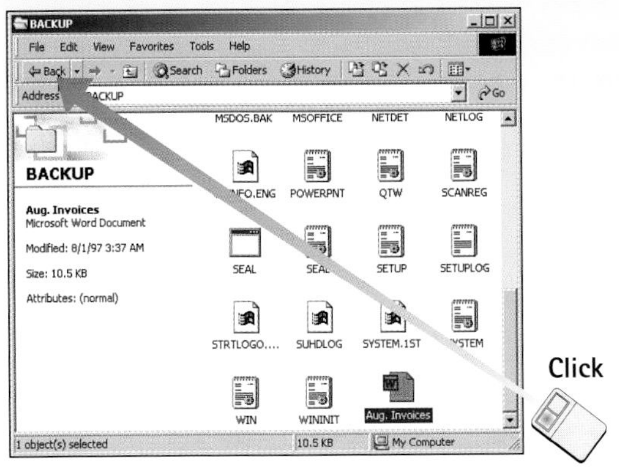

End

How-To Hints

Browsing Your Computer

Open the Address drop-down list just beneath a window's toolbar to browse a hierarchical list of the drives and open folders on your computer.

Go Up One Level

Use the Up One Level button (it looks like a folder with an arrow pointing up) to go to the parent folder of the folder you are presently viewing.

Program Associations

Some files may not have a program associated with them. In this case, you'll be given the chance to choose the program to open the file with. See Chapter 2, "Working with Files and Folders," for more information on this topic.

TASK 7

How to Get Help

Windows 2000 boasts a comprehensive help system that lets you get details on Windows concepts and performing specific tasks. You can browse the contents of Windows Help, search for specific terms, or even ask plain English questions.

Begin

1 Open Help

To open Windows Help, click **Start** and then click **Help**.

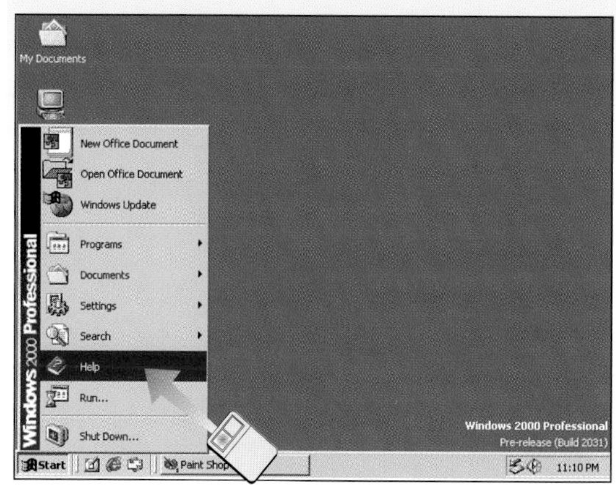

2 Find the Topic You Want

The Windows Help window has two frames. The left-hand frame lets you browse through the help contents. Book icons represent categories. Page icons represent actual help pages you can view. Click any category to open it and click a help page to open it in the right-hand frame.

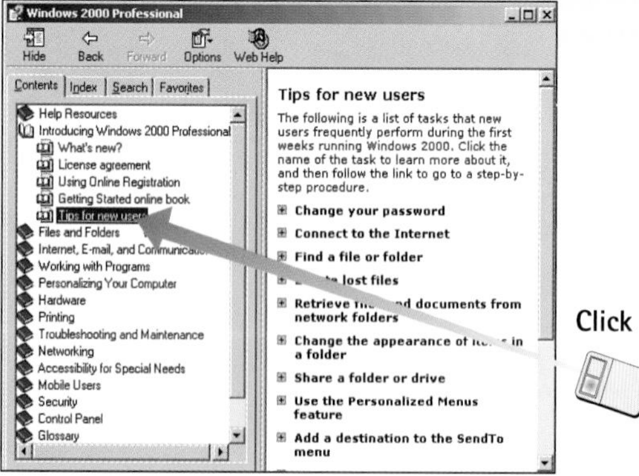

3 Read the Help Text

Use the scrollbar on the right to move down through the contents of a help page. Often, a page has links (blue and underlined text) to other help pages with related topics. Click a link to jump to that page.

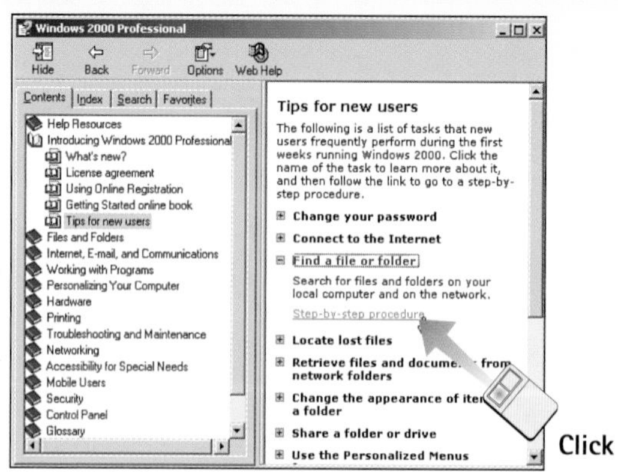

4 Click a Shortcut

Sometimes, a help page includes a shortcut to a folder or dialog box in Windows itself. This is particularly true if you are viewing a procedure for doing something in Windows. The shortcut looks like a link, but also has a small icon with an arrow just before it. Clicking the shortcut opens whatever part of Windows the help page is discussing.

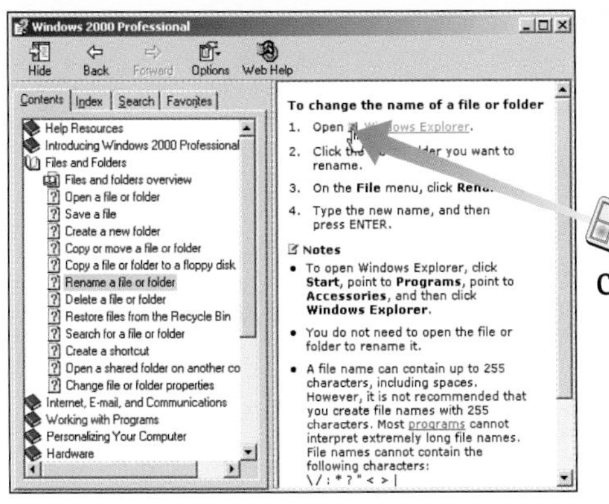

Click

5 Look Up a Topic

Click the **Index** tab to look up a specific topic in Windows Help. In the text box, enter the topic you want to search for. The list of topics changes as you enter the topic. Select any entry in the list and click **Display** to show a list of help pages related to that topic.

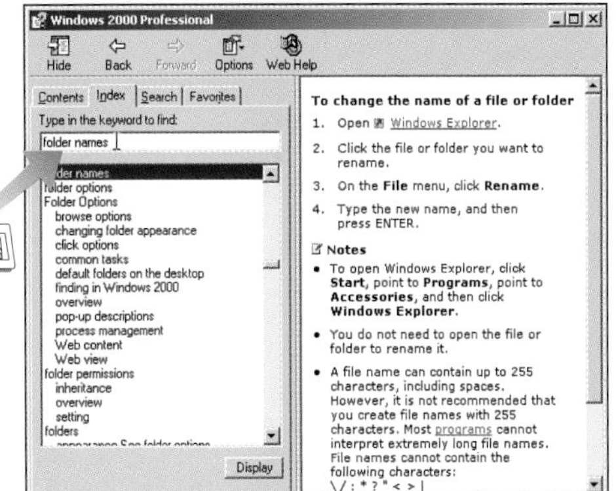

6 Add a Favorite Topic

Click the Favorites tab to add a help page to a list of your personal favorites. Click **Add** to add the current page to the list. Select any favorite and click **Display** to show that page.

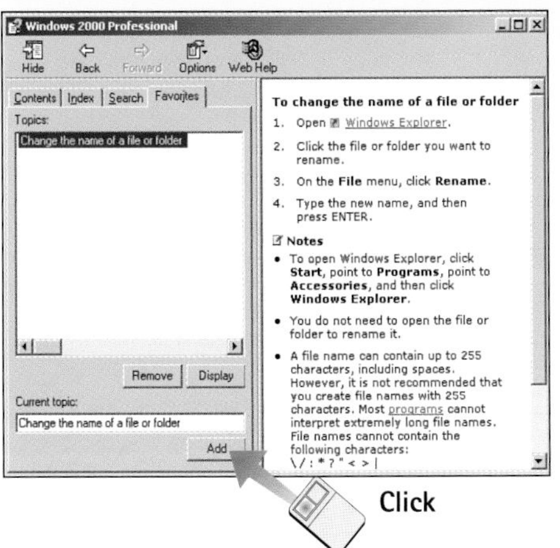

Click

End

How-To Hints

Using the F1 Key

Press the F1 key at any time while using Windows to open a help page related to your current activity. Many programs also support this feature.

Searching for a Topic

The Search tab in Windows Help works a lot like the Index tab. However, Index only includes a pre-generated list of topics. Search actually lets you search the help pages themselves for keywords.

TASK 8

How to Use the Recycle Bin

You can delete files, folders, and programs from your computer at any time. However, when you delete an item, Windows does not immediately remove it from your computer. Instead, the item is placed into the Recycle Bin. You can restore an item from the Recycle Bin later if you decide you would rather not delete it after all. When the Recycle Bin becomes full, Windows deletes older items permanently to make room for newer items. You can think of the Recycle Bin as sort of a buffer between your files and oblivion.

Begin

1 Drag an Object to the Recycle Bin

The easiest way to delete an object is to drag it to the Recycle Bin from the desktop or any open folder.

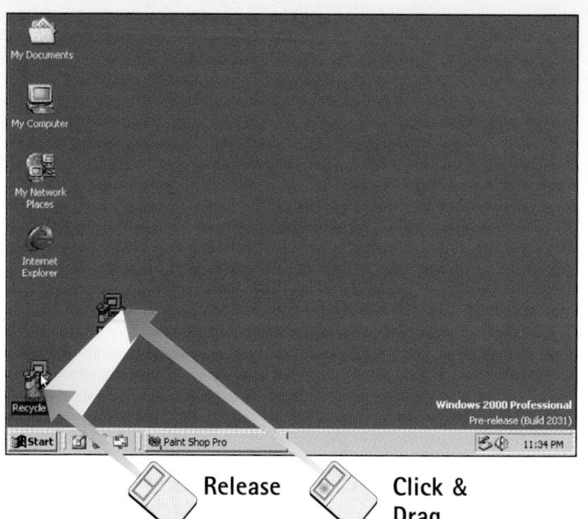

2 Confirm the Deletion

When you try to delete an object, Windows asks you to confirm that you really want to delete it. Just click **Yes**.

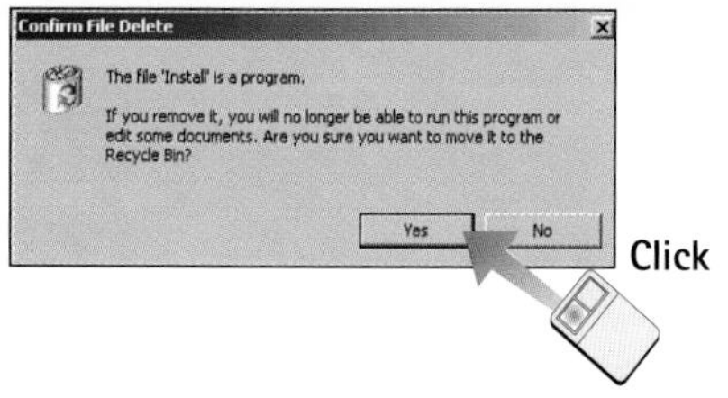

3 Open the Recycle Bin

Double-click the **Recycle Bin** to open it. All files inside are listed with their original locations and the date they were deleted.

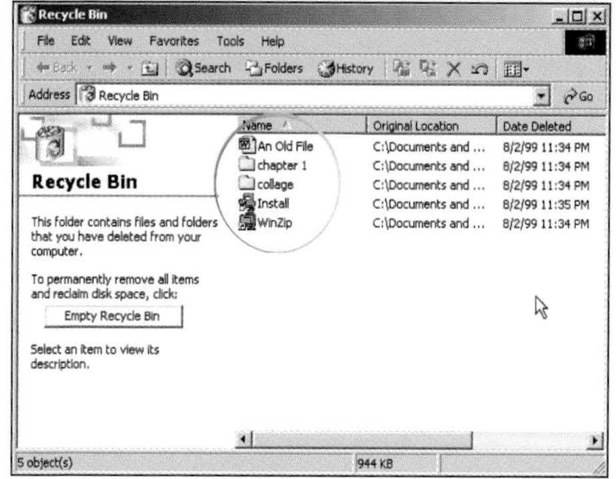

4 Restore Files

To remove a file or group of files from the Recycle Bin and restore them to their original locations, select them and click the **Restore** button that appears on the left.

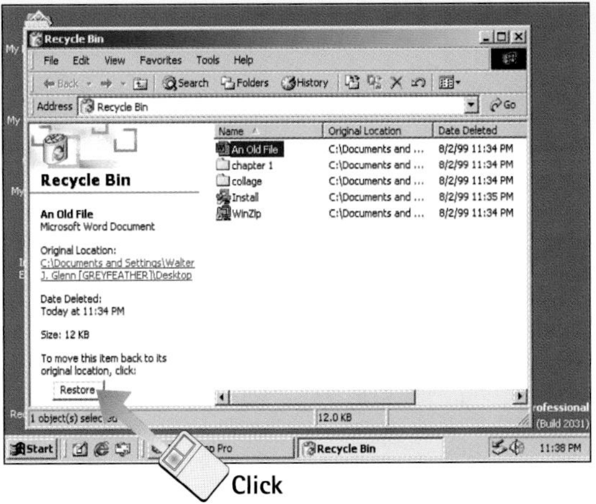

5 Delete Files

Right-click a file in the Recycle Bin and choose **Delete** from the shortcut menu to permanently delete that file.

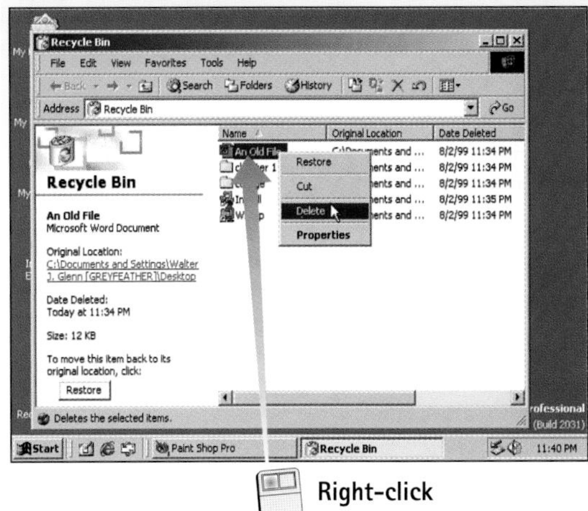

6 Empty the Recycle Bin

To permanently delete all files from the Recycle Bin, make sure that no files are selected and click the **Empty Recycle Bin** button on the left.

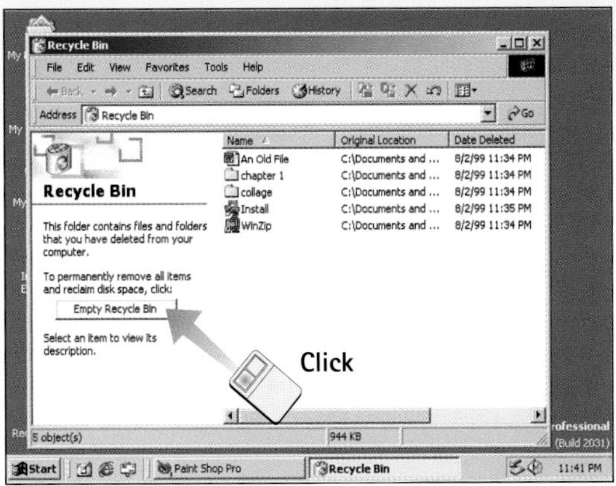

End

How-To Hints

Another Way to Delete Files

You can also delete a file by selecting it and pressing the Delete key.

Another Way to Empty the Bin

You can empty the Recycle Bin without opening it by right-clicking it and choosing Empty Recycle Bin from the shortcut menu.

TASK 9

How to Log Off Windows 2000

When you leave your computer unattended for any length of time, it is best to log off so that others cannot access your files while you are away. To get back to the desktop, you have to log on again, as discussed earlier in this chapter. Though this can be a bit inconvenient, it is better than leaving your system open for all to see and is company policy in some places.

Begin

1 Click Shut Down

Click the **Start** button and then click **Shut Down**.

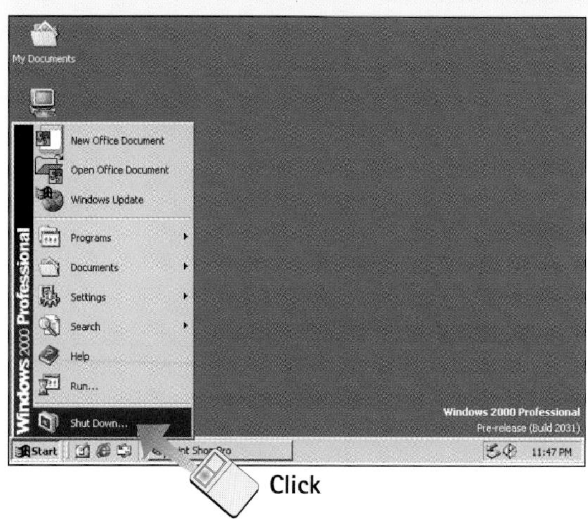

2 Choose the Log Off Options

From the drop-down list, choose the **Log Off** option and click **OK**. This logs you off.

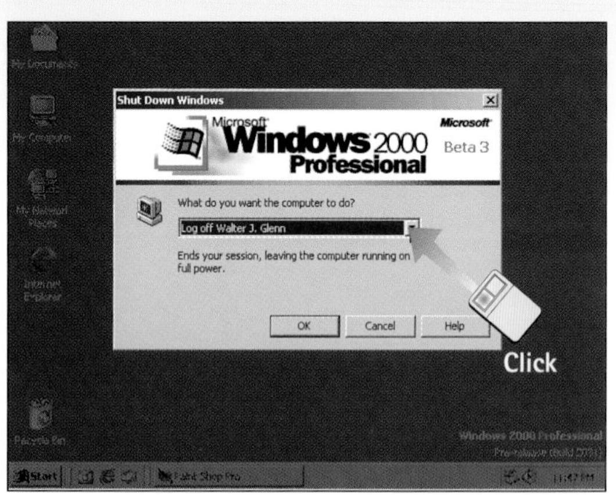

3 Press Ctrl+Alt+Del

Another way to log off is to press the **Ctrl**, **Alt**, and **Del** keys all at once. This brings up the Windows Security Window. Click **Log Off**.

4 Log On Another User

As soon as you log off, Windows presents the logon screen. You can now log back on as discussed earlier in this chapter.

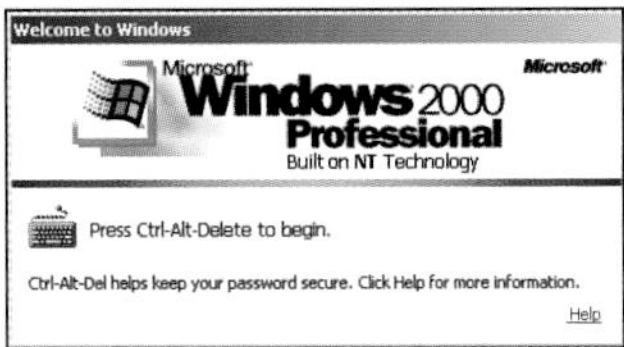

End

How-To Hints

Locking Your Computer

If you are only going to be away from your computer for a short time, you may want to lock your computer instead of logging off. You must still enter a password to regain access. When locked, your personal settings are retained and do not have to be reloaded, speeding the process. For more, see Chapter 8, "Protecting Your Files."

Using a Screen Saver Password

Screen saver passwords let your computer automatically lock itself whenever the screen saver activates. For more on this, see Chapter 8.

TASK 10

How to Shut Down Your Computer

While running, Windows keeps a lot of its information in its system memory—memory that is not sustained when the computer is turned off. For this reason, you should never simply turn your computer off using the power button. You should always use the Shut Down command to allow Windows to gracefully shut itself down.

Begin

1 Click Shut Down

Click the **Start** button and then click **Shut Down**.

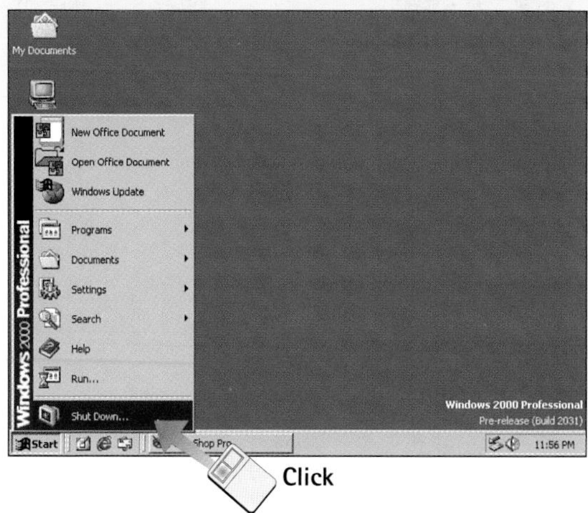

2 Choose the Shut Down Option

From the drop-down list, choose the **Shut Down** option and click **OK**. Windows closes all open programs (giving you the opportunity to save unsaved documents) and tells you when it is safe to turn off the power.

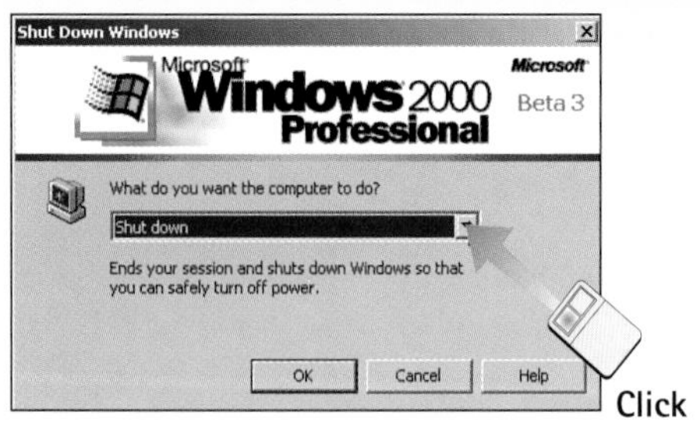

3 Choose the Restart Option

Choose the **Restart** option and click **OK** to have Windows shut itself down and then automatically restart the computer. After the computer is restarted, you can log on to Windows again.

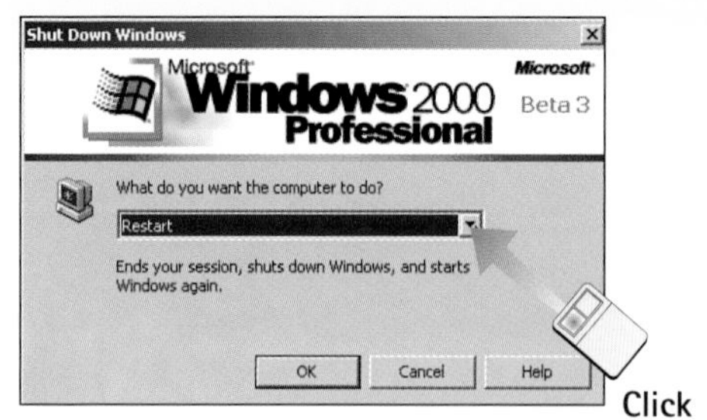

4 Save Any Open Files

If you attempt to shut down Windows while programs are running with unsaved documents, you are given the chance to save those documents before shutdown proceeds.

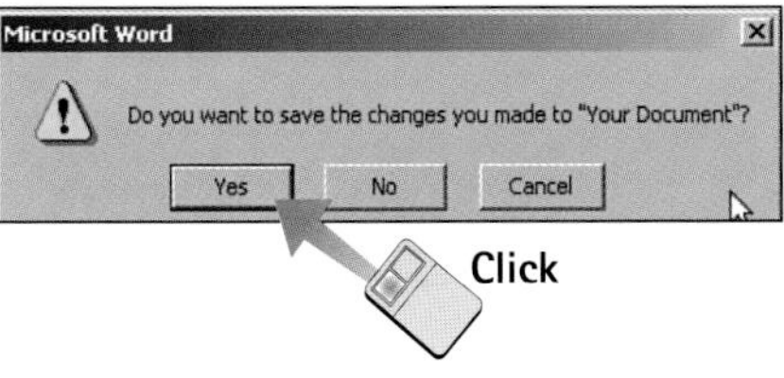

End

How-To Hints

Quick Restart

If you want to restart Windows without restarting your computer, select the Restart option and hold the Shift key down while you click OK.

Task

Part 2

Working with Files and Folders

Everything on your computer is made up of files on your hard disk. Windows itself is really just thousands of different files that all interact with one another to present what you've come to know as the Windows desktop. All of your applications are also collections of many files that interact with one another and with Windows files. Finally, all of the documents that you create are themselves files that are loaded by the applications you use to create them. For example, when you save a document in Microsoft Word, that document is saved as a file on your disk.

On your disk, files are organized into folders. Like its real-world counterpart, a folder is really just a place to keep things. In Windows, a folder can contain files and other folders. For example, your desktop contains a folder named My Documents, which in turn holds a folder named My Pictures, which in turn holds a file named **`Sample.jpg`** (a picture file). The name of a file can be up to 256 characters long and usually also has a three-character extension (the three characters after the dot) that identifies the type of file it is. **`.jpg`** is a type of picture file called a JPEG. By default, extensions are not shown for files of types that your system knows about.

In Windows, the full description of the location of a file somewhere on a drive is called a *path* and includes the name of the disk drive, the names of each folder, and the name of the file—each name separated by a backslash (\). For the Sample.jpg document mentioned earlier, the path would be **`C:\My Documents\My Pictures\Sample.jpg`**.

TASK 1

How to Use Windows Explorer

Part 1, "Using the Windows 2000 Desktop," explained how to use the My Computer window to browse through the folders and files on a disk drive, and, in truth, you can use the My Computer window to get to any file on your computer and do anything you want with it. However, Windows offers another utility, named Windows Explorer, that you might find more useful. It's really a matter of personal style.

Begin

1 Open Explorer

You run Windows Explorer just like any other program. Click the **Start** button, and select **Programs, Accessories, Windows Explorer.**

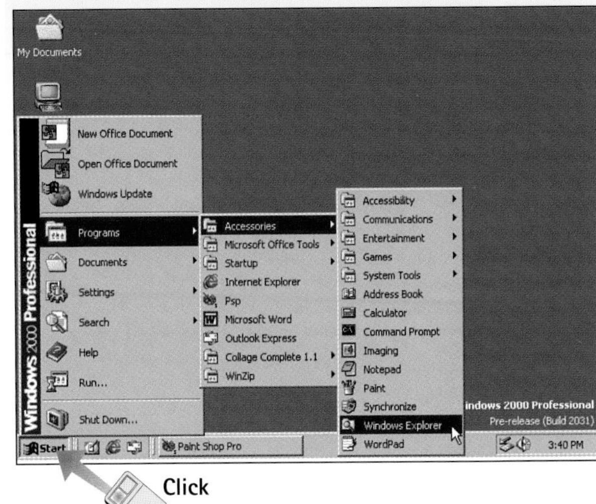

2 Browse Folders

The left-hand pane of Explorer shows a hierarchy of all of the drives, folders, and Desktop items on your computer. A drive or folder that contains other folders has a plus sign to the left. Click the **plus sign** to expand it and see the folders inside.

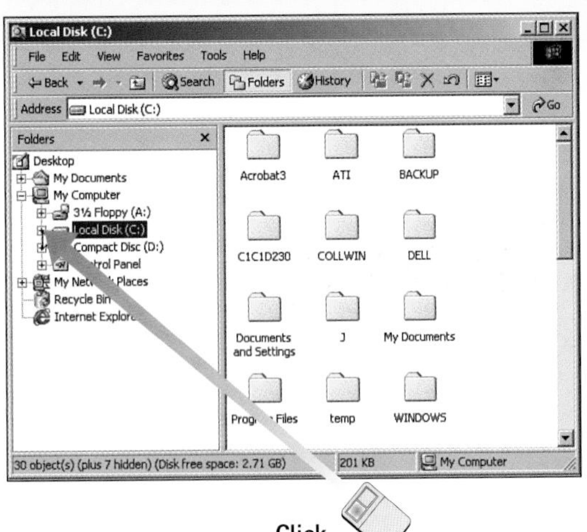

3 Open a Folder

Click on any folder in the list and all of the files and folders in that folder are shown in the right-hand pane.

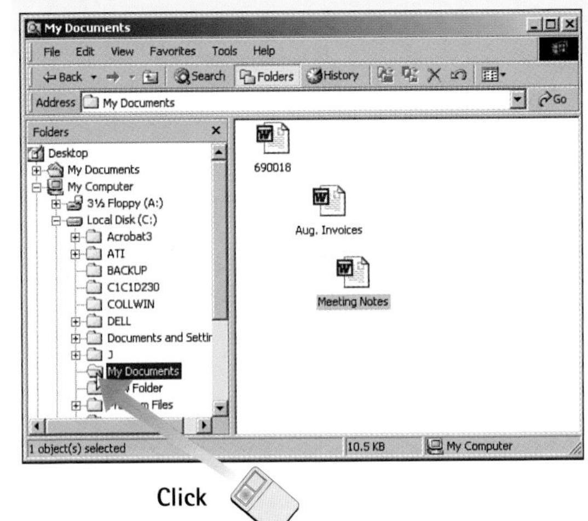

4 Open a File

The right-hand pane works the same as the My Computer window. You can double-click any file or folder to open it.

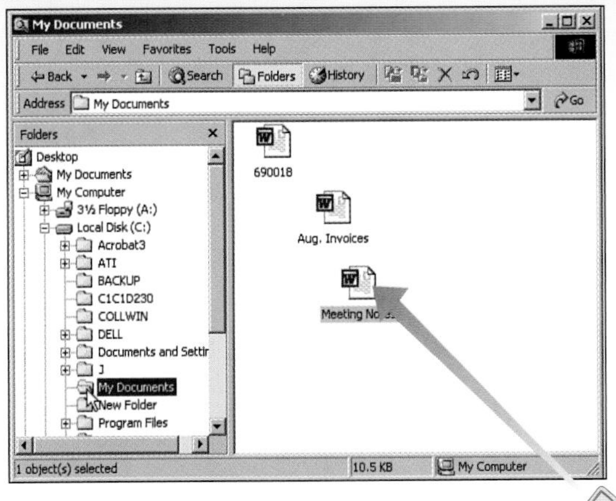

5 Move a File to Another Folder

One of the advantages to using Explorer is that you can easily move a file to any other folder on your computer. Drag a file in the right-hand pane to any folder in the left-hand pane to move it there.

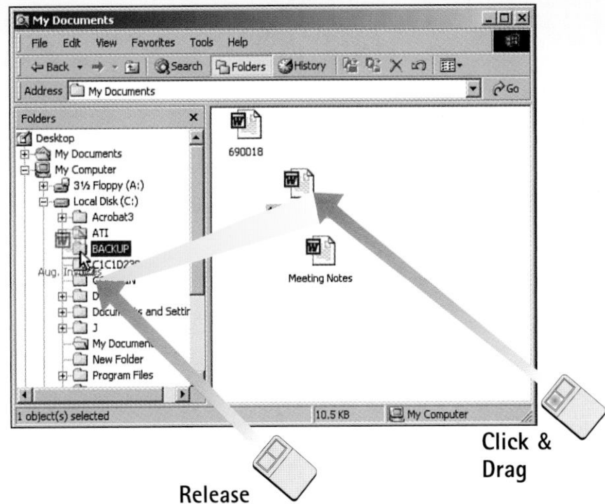

6 Copy a File to Another Drive

Copying a file to another drive is as easy as moving it. Just drag a file from the right-hand pane to another disk drive (or a folder on another drive) to copy it there. Notice that the icon you are dragging takes on a small plus sign to let you know the file will be copied.

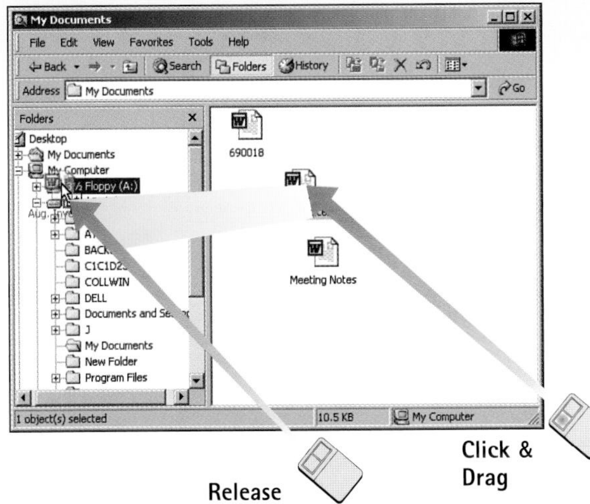

End

How-To Hints

Auto-Expanding

When you move a file to another folder in Explorer, the folder doesn't have to already be visible. While dragging the file, hold the cursor over a plus sign for two seconds to automatically expand that folder.

Auto-Scroll

While dragging a file, hold your pointer at the top or bottom of the left-hand pane for two seconds to automatically scroll up or down.

TASK 2

How to Search for a File or Folder

Using Windows Explorer is great if you know where the file or folder you want is located. Sometimes, however, it's hard to remember just where you put something. Fortunately, Windows has a great search function built right in that lets you find files and folders. You can search for folders by all or part of their name, text they might contain, or their location. You can even search using all three of these at once.

Begin

1 Open the Search Window

Click the **Start** button, and select **Search,** and select **For Files or Folders**. You'll also find a Search button on the toolbar of most windows that performs the same function.

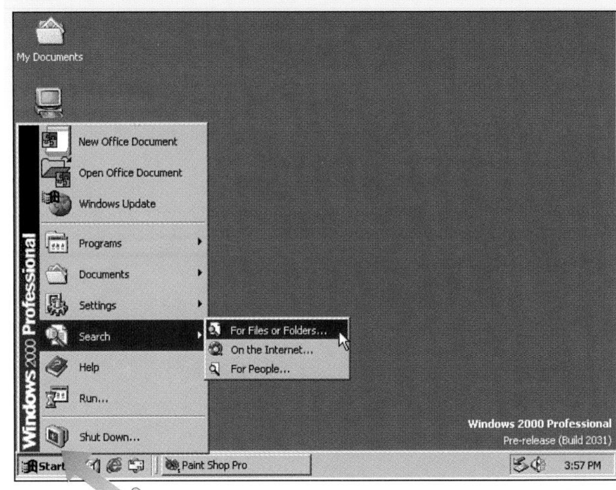

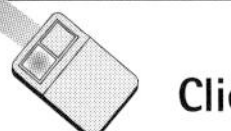

Click

2 Enter the Name to Search For

Enter part or all of the name of the file or folder you want to search for in the first text box. When you search, Windows shows all files and folders that contain the text you enter.

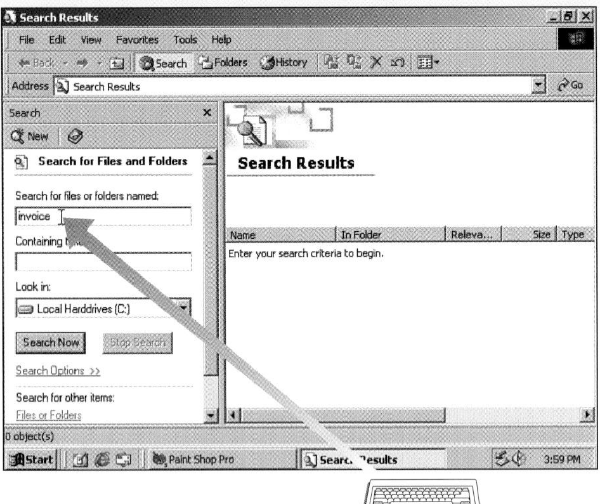

3 Enter Text Content

If you know that the document you are looking for contains certain text, enter it in the next text box.

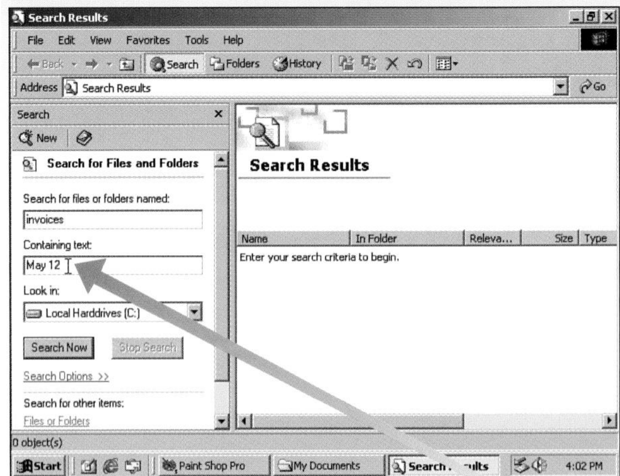

4 Select a Drive

By default, Windows searches all of the hard drives on your computer for files matching the criteria you've entered. You can limit the search to a particular hard drive or folder, if you want. Just click the drop-down list to choose.

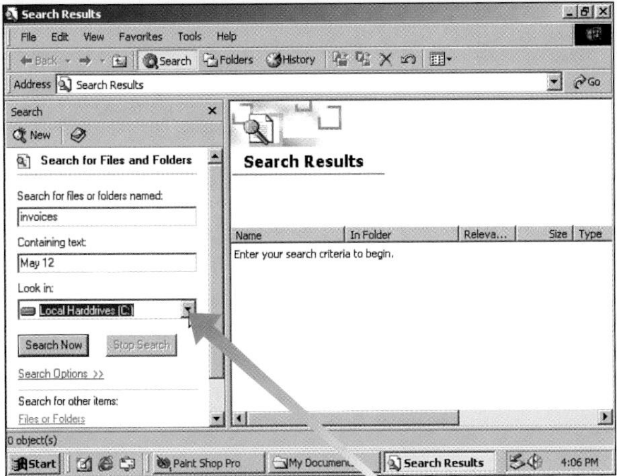

Click

5 Click Search Now

After you have entered your search criteria and location, click **Search Now** to have Windows begin the search.

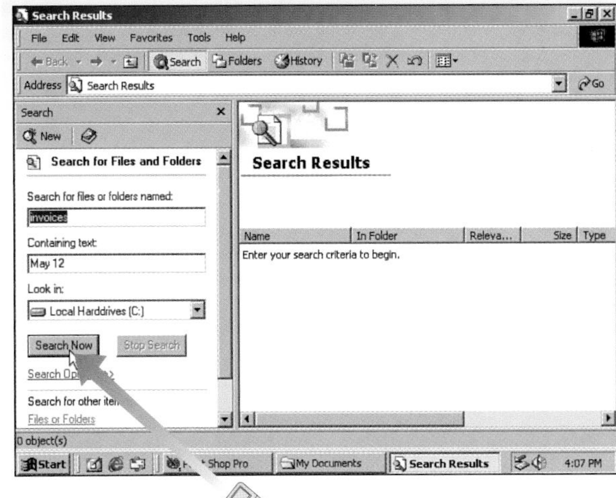

Click

6 View the Results

The results of your search are displayed in the right-hand pane. You can double-click a file to open it right from the search window.

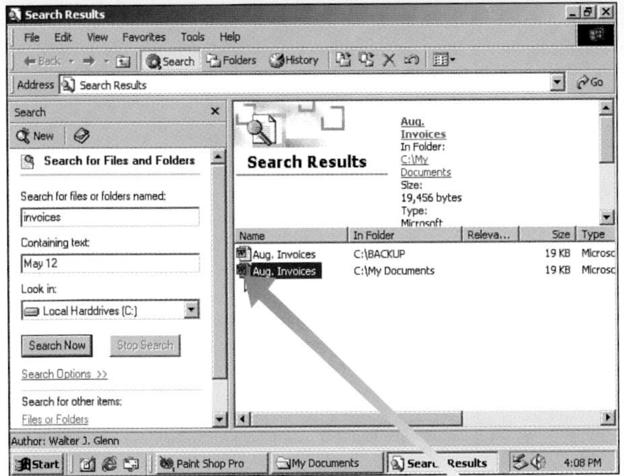

Double-click

End

How-To Hints

Advanced Search Options

Click **Search Options** to open a window that lets you specify additional search criteria, such as the dates files were created or modified, the size of files, and the type of files to search for.

Quickly Open a File's Folder

You can quickly open the parent folder of a file you've found by right-clicking the file and choosing **Open Containing Folder** from the shortcut menu.

TASK 3

How to Create a Folder

Folders help you organize your files. You create a folder using the My Computer window or Windows Explorer. You can create a folder in any existing disk drive or folder or on the Windows desktop itself.

Begin

1 Find the Place to Make the Folder

The first step in creating a folder is to decide where you want to create it. Use the My Computer window or Windows Explorer to find the place you want to be.

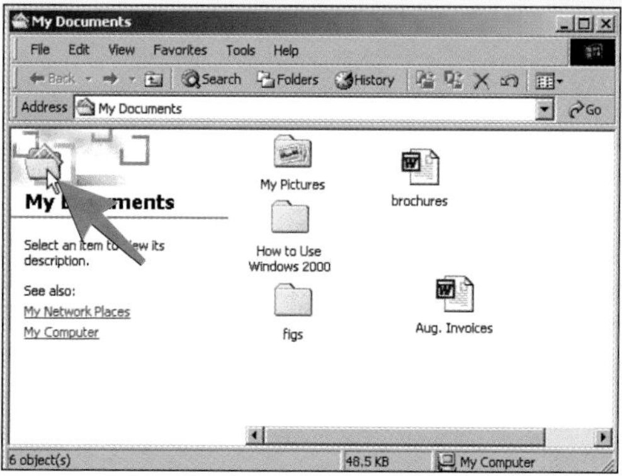

2 Create the New Folder

Select **File, New, Folder**.

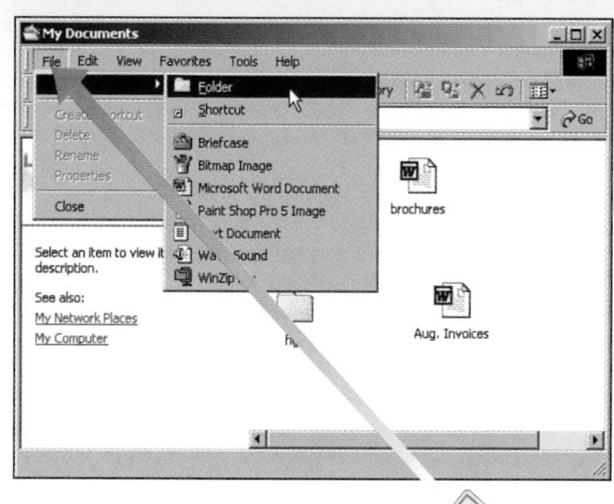

3 Rename the Folder

The new folder appears and is named New Folder by default. The name is already highlighted and you can rename it Personal Folder. You can also rename the folder later by selecting it and choosing **Rename** from the **File** menu.

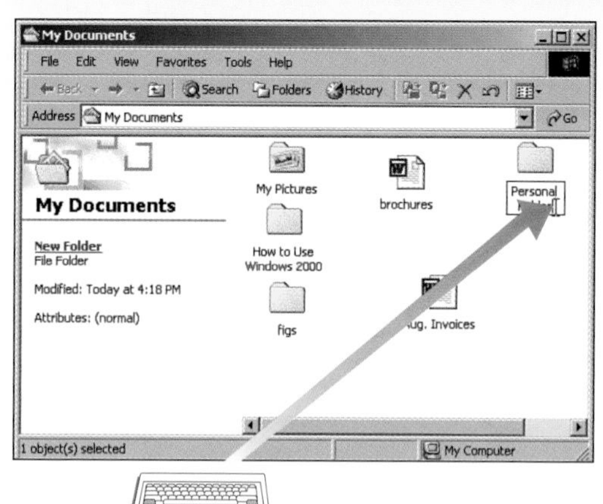

4 Create a Folder on the Desktop

To create a new folder directly on your desktop, right-click any empty area of the desktop. Point to **New** on the shortcut menu and then choose **Folder**.

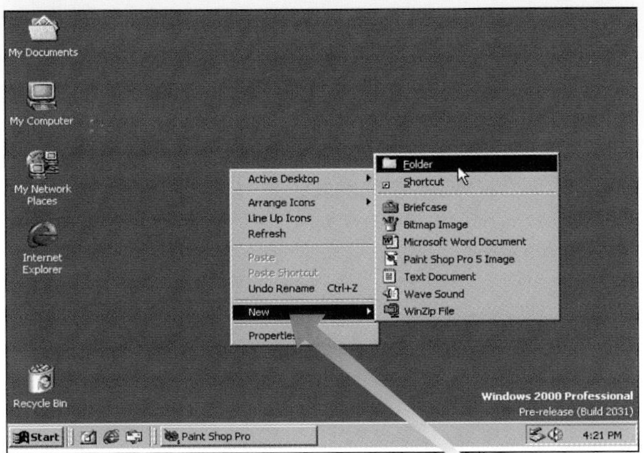

Right-click

End

How-To Hints

Saving a Document

Some programs let you create a new folder right from the same dialog box you use to save a document. There is usually a button named **Create New Folder**. Just click it, name your folder, and open it to save your document there.

Creating a Folder in the Start Menu

The Start menu is really a folder on your hard disk, and you can create new folders in it to help organize your files. Right-click the **Start** button, choose **Open** from the shortcut menu, and create the folder in the window that opens. The new folder now appears on your Start menu. For more on customizing your Start menu, see Part 9, "Changing Windows 2000 Settings."

TASK 4

How to View Items in a Folder

Normally, both the My Computer window and Windows Explorer show you the contents of a folder as large icons that represent other folders and files. This is a friendly way to view folders, but not always the most useful, especially if a folder contains large numbers of files or many files with similar names. You can also view the contents of a folder as small icons, a list, a list with file details, or even thumbnails.

Begin

1 Open a Folder

First, you need to find a folder to view. You can do this in either the My Computer window or in Windows Explorer. Notice that the regular large icon view looks pretty cluttered.

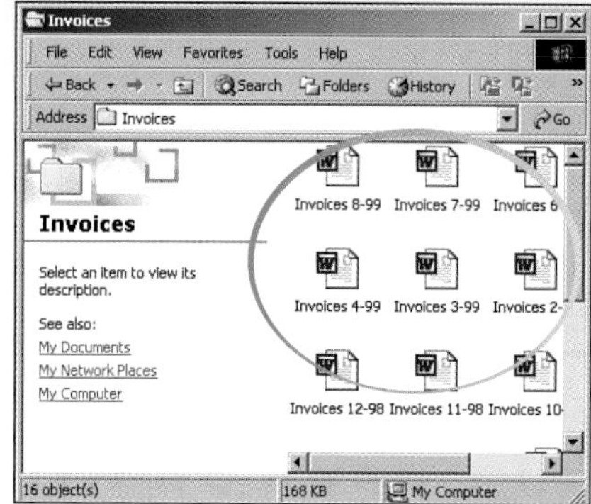

2 Change to List View

Select **View, List** to view the folder contents as a list. The contents are listed in alphabetical order. You can also use the View button on the toolbar to change views.

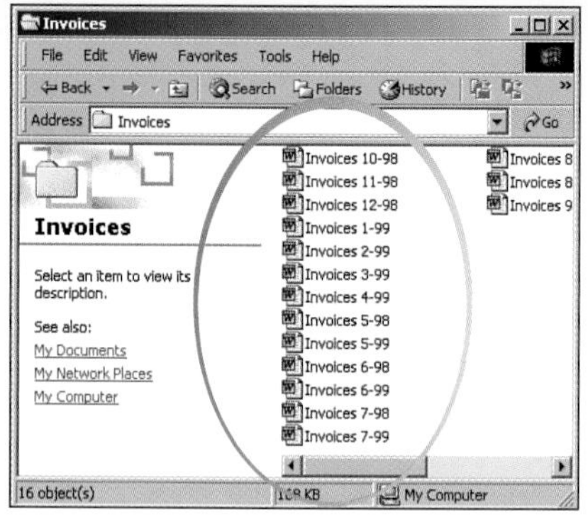

3 Change to Detail View

Detail is perhaps the most useful way you can view a folder. Just click **View, Details.** Contents are presented in a list with columns that include file details, such as the size and type of the file and when the file was last modified.

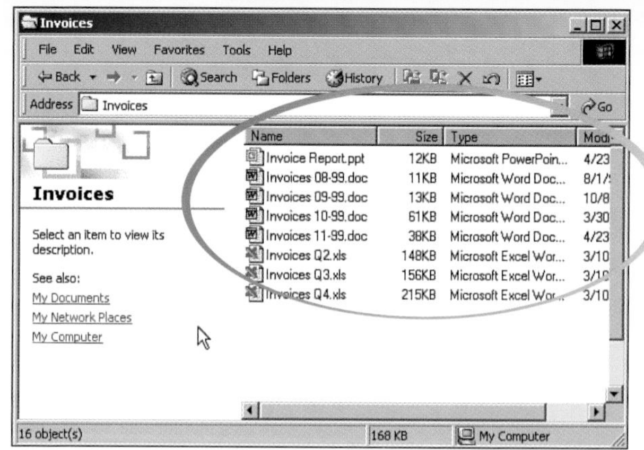

4 Change to Thumbnail View

Thumbnail view presents the contents of a folder as small thumbnails, or previews, of the actual documents. Only certain file types, such as JPEG images, support this type of viewing.

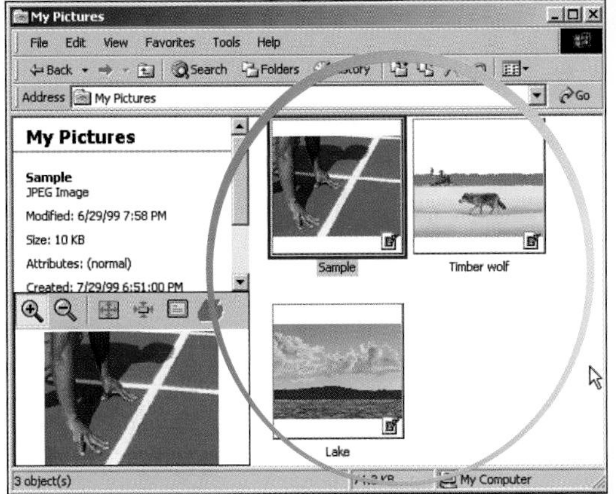

5 Arrange Icons

In addition to choosing how to view the contents of a folder, you can also choose how those contents are arranged. Click **View, Arrange Icons** and then click **by Name**, **by Type**, **by Size**, or **by Date** to order the contents of the folder.

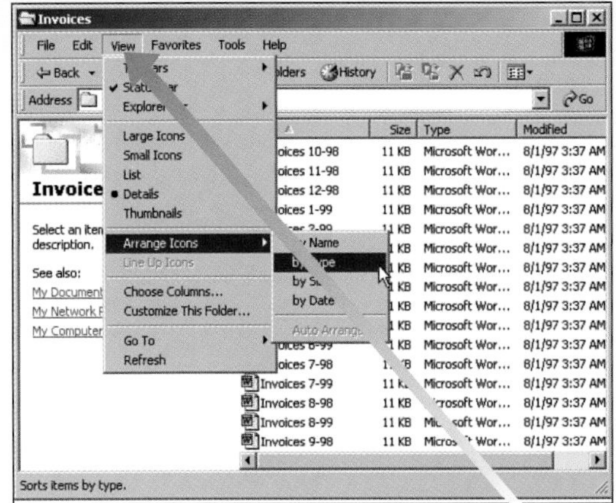

Click 

End

How-To Hints

Arranging in Details View

You can easily arrange a folder in Details view by simply clicking the column heading by which you want to order the contents. For example, click the **Type** column heading to group files in a folder by type.

Choose Your Columns

You can choose the columns shown in Details view by clicking **Choose Columns** on the **View** menu. A window opens with lots of different choices for columns to display. Just check the ones you want.

TASK 5

How to Create a File

Most of the time, you will create new documents from within a particular program. For example, you usually use Microsoft Word to create a new Word document. However, Windows does offer the ability to quickly create certain types of documents without opening the program at all. This can be quite useful when you are creating a large number of new documents that will be edited later.

Begin

1 Locate the Parent Folder

First, you need to find the folder in which you want to create the new file. You can create a file directly in any folder on your computer.

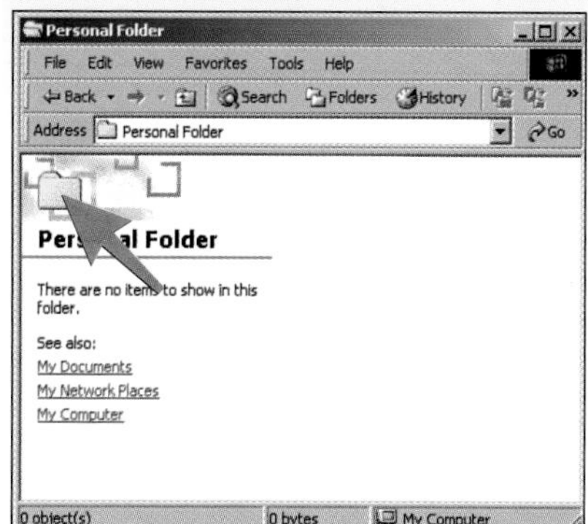

2 Create the File

Click **File, New**, and then click the type of file you want to create.

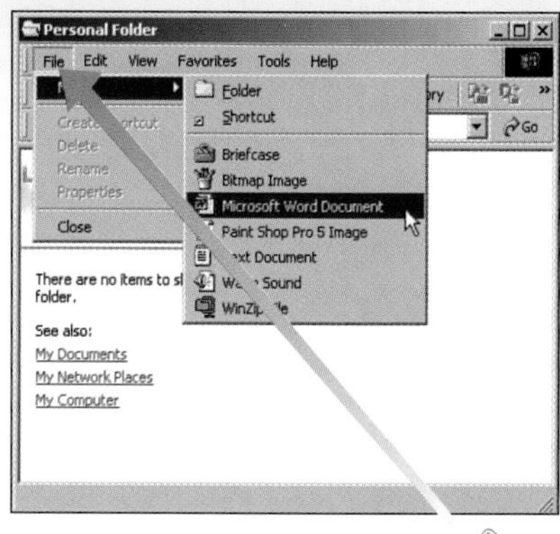

3 Locate the New Document

The new document appears in the folder with a generic name, such as New Microsoft Word Document. If you don't see it immediately, use the window's scrollbars to find it.

4 Rename the File

The new file appears with the name already highlighted. Just start typing to enter a new name.

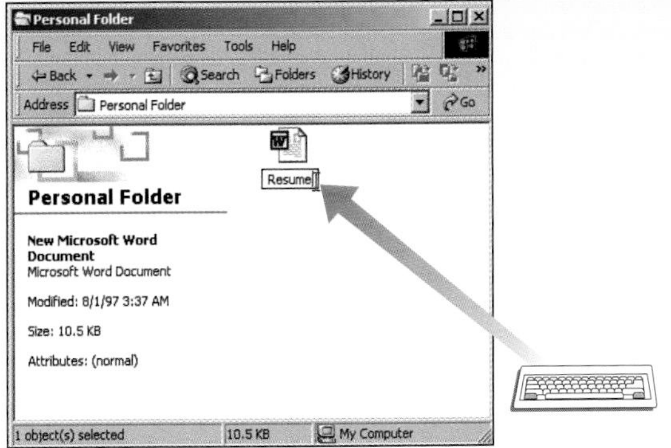

5 Open the File to Edit

After you have created and renamed your new file, just double-click it to launch the appropriate program and open the new file with it.

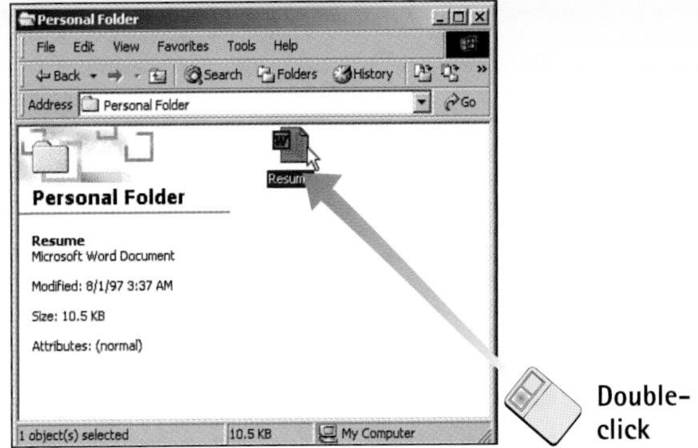

End

How-To Hints

Renaming Files

Files can have names of up to 256 characters, including spaces. There are several special characters you cannot use in your file's name, including \ / : * ? " < >

Preserving the File Type

When you create a new file, Windows automatically gives it the right three-letter file extension (the three letters after the dot) to indicate the file type. If your Windows settings allow you to see the file extension (by default, they don't), be sure you don't change it. If you do, the file won't open with the right program. Windows warns you if you try to change the file extension.

TASK 6

How to Open a File

There are several different ways to open a file in Windows. One way is to locate the file in the My Computer window or Windows Explorer and open it from there. You can also open a file from within the program that created it. Windows even keeps track of the files you have opened recently, and you reopen these in one simple step using the Start menu.

Begin

1 Double-Click the File

Find the file you want to open by using the My Computer window or Windows Explorer. Double-click the file to launch the file's program and open the file with it.

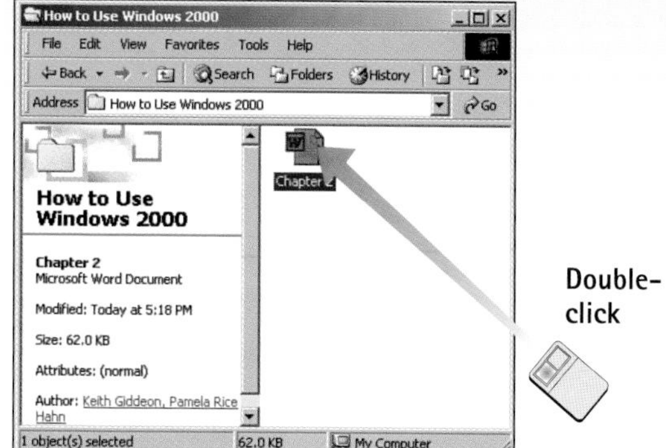

Double-click

2 Open a Recently-Used File

Windows keeps track of the 15 documents you have opened most recently. To open any of these documents, click the **Start** button, point to **Documents**, and then click the document to open.

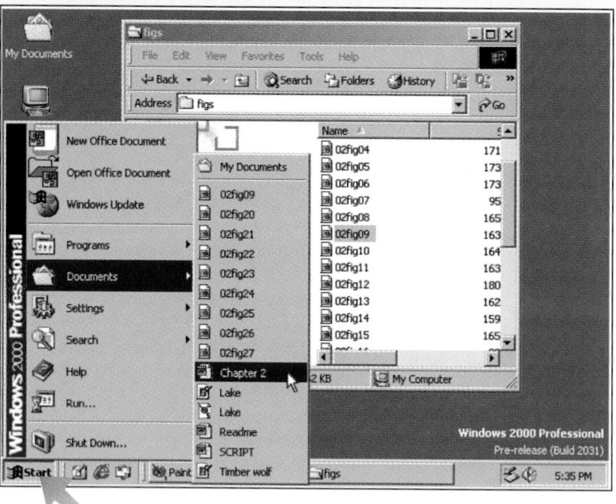

Click

3 Run an Program

Yet another way to open a file is from within the program that created it. The first step is to run the program. Click the **Start** button, point to **Programs**, and click the program you want to run.

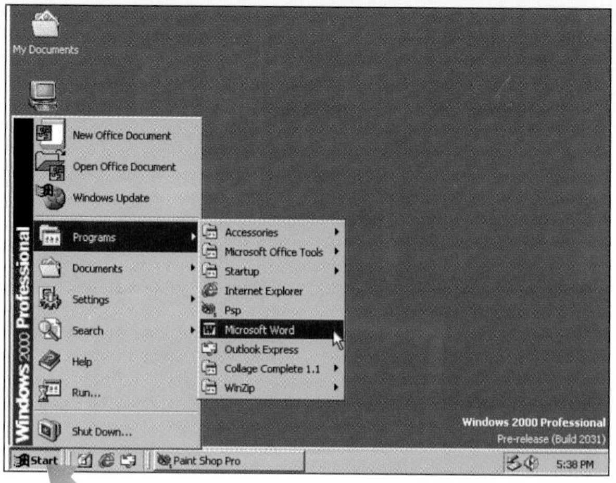

Click

4 Choose Open in the File Menu

In the program, click the **Open** command on the **File** menu.

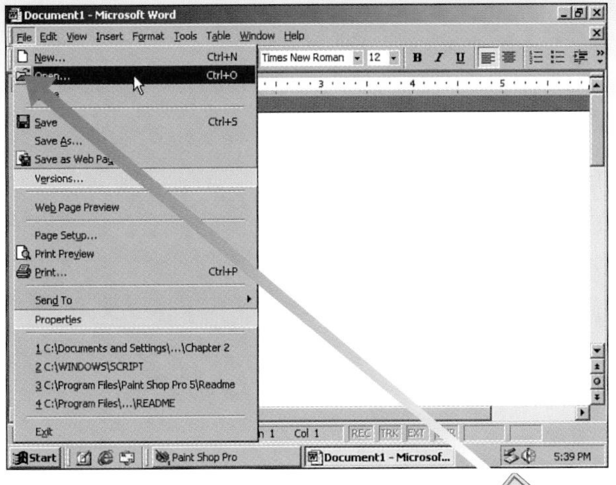

5 Find the File to Open

The Open dialog box for most programs works a lot like the My Computer window. Find the file you want to open, select it, and click **Open**.

End

How-To Hints

Removing Recently Used Files

You can clear the list of recently used files from the Documents folder by right-clicking the taskbar and clicking **Properties** on the shortcut menu. Click the **Start Menu Options** tab and then click **Clear**.

Searching for Files

When you search for files using the Search command on the Start menu, you can open any of the files you find just by double-clicking them. For more, see "How to Search for a File or Folder" earlier in this part.

TASK 7

How to Save a File

Saving your work is one of the most important things you'll do on your computer. After all, if you don't save your work, what's the point of doing it in the first place? Saving a file is always done while you are working on it within a program. There are two save commands in most programs. Save As lets you choose a location and name for your file. You must use this option the first time you save a new file. Save simply updates the file using its present location and name.

Begin

1 Open the Save As Dialog

If you want to save a file using a particular name or to a particular location, click **File**, **Save As**.

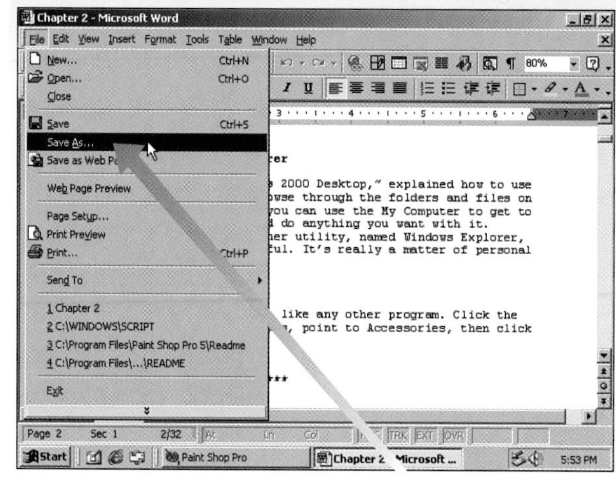

Click

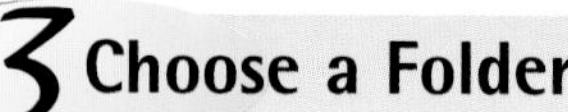

2 Choose a Location

The Save As dialog box works just like the My Computer window. Choose the disk drive you want to save to using the **Save in** drop-down list.

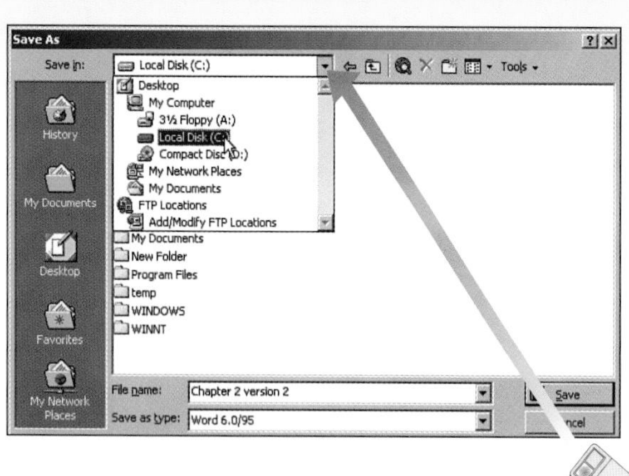
Click

3 Choose a Folder

Double-click any folder to open it.

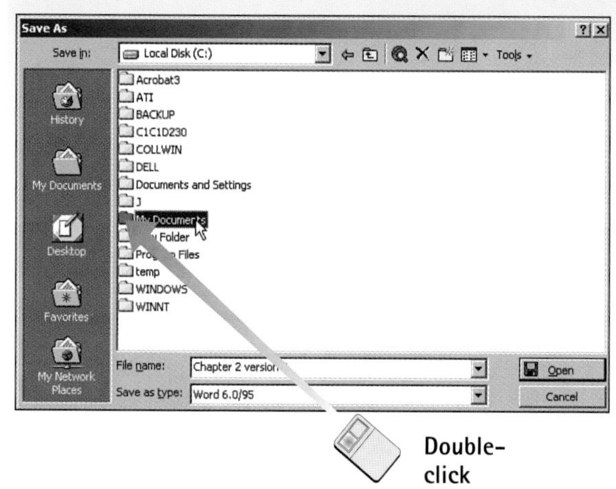
Double-click

4 Create a New Folder

Click the **Create New Folder** button. Enter a name for a new folder.

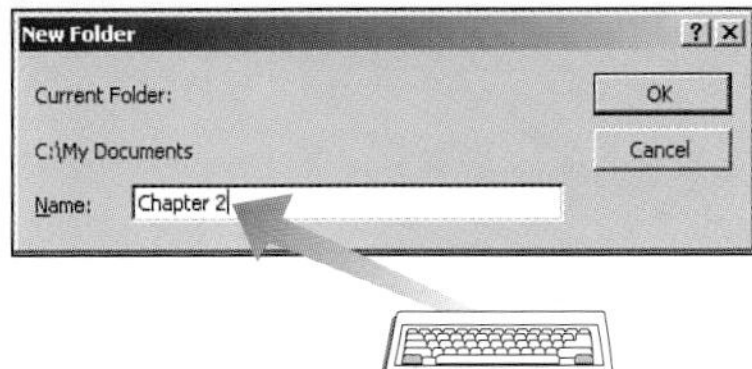

5 Name the File

Enter the name for the document in the **File name** box.

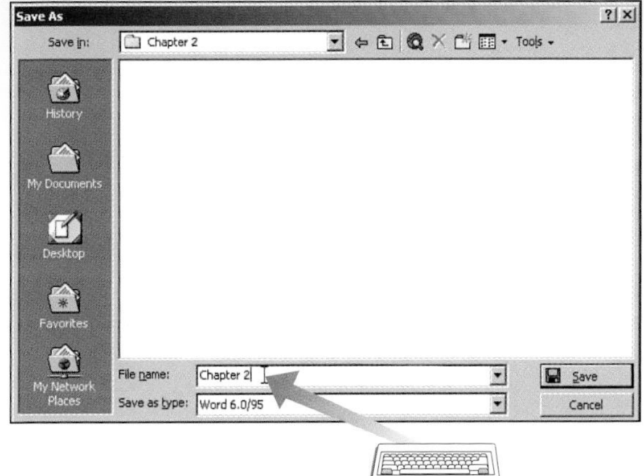

6 Save the File

Click **Save** to save the new file in its new folder.

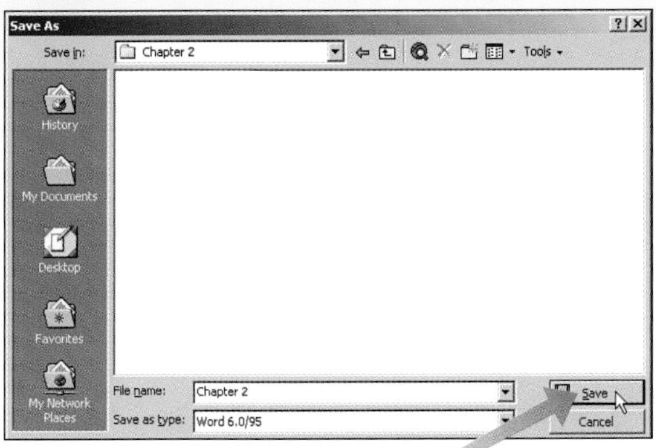

Click

7 Save the File as You Work

Periodically as you work, save any changes to your document using the Save button on the toolbar (or the Save command on the File menu). If you click Save and it is the first time you are saving a new document, the Save As dialog box opens. Otherwise, the file just saves.

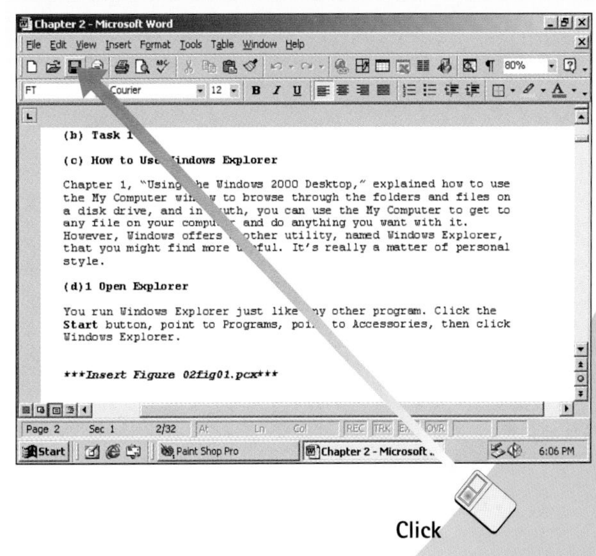

Click

End

TASK 8

How to Create a Shortcut to a File or Folder

A *shortcut* is an icon that points to a file or folder somewhere on your computer. The shortcut is merely a reference to the actual object and is used to access the object without having to go to the object's location. For example, you could place a shortcut to a frequently used document on your desktop. You could then double-click the shortcut to open the file without having to go to the folder where the actual file is stored.

Begin

1 Open Windows Explorer

The first step in creating a new shortcut is to use the **My Computer** window or **Windows Explorer** to find the file or folder you want to make a shortcut to. To open Windows Explorer, click **Start**, select **Programs, Accessories, Windows Explorer**.

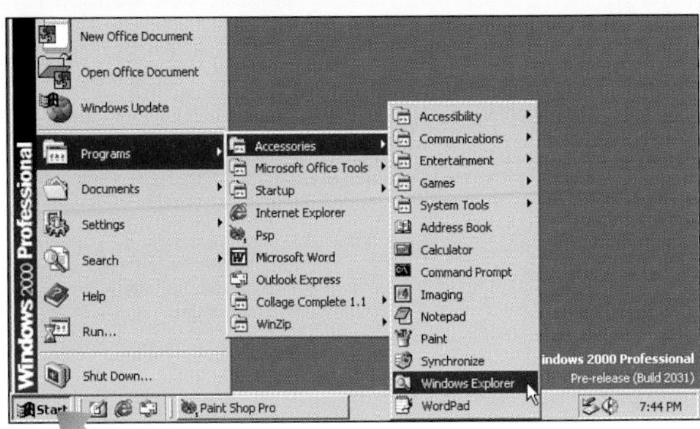

2 Select a File or Folder

In Explorer, find the object you want to make a shortcut to.

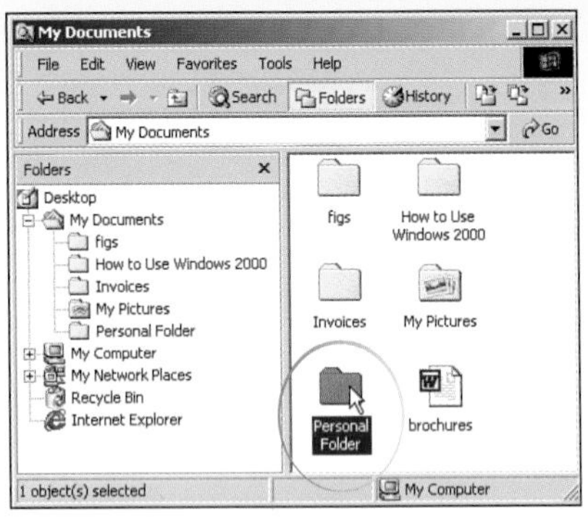

3 Drag the File to Your Desktop

Click and hold your *right* mouse button and drag the object to a blank space on the desktop. Release the right mouse button.

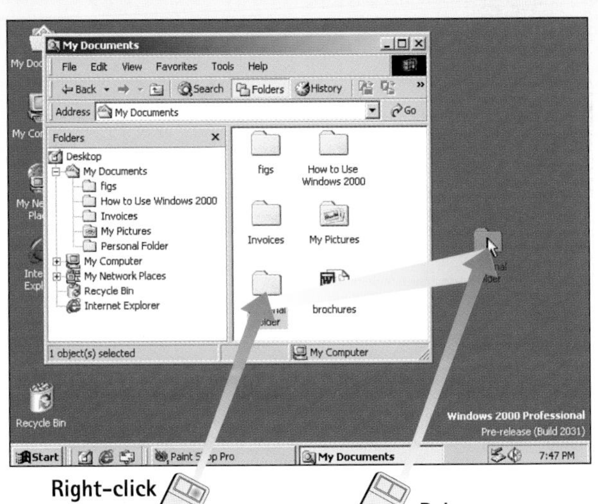

4 Choose Create Shortcut Here

When you release the right mouse button, a shortcut menu appears. Click **Create Shortcut(s) Here**.

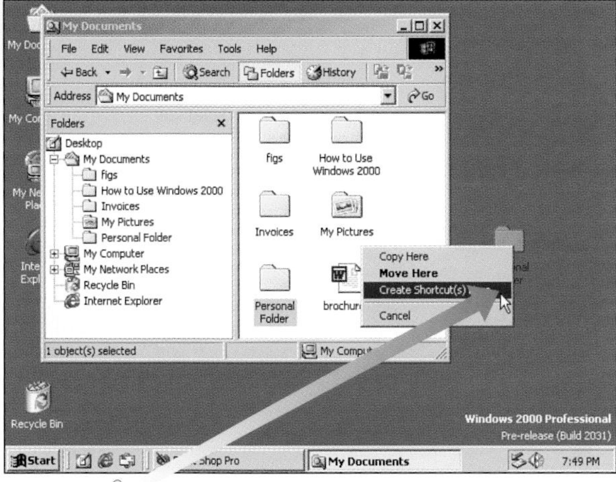

Click

5 Rename the Shortcut

Notice that the shortcut icon has a small arrow on, indicating that it is a shortcut. You can rename the shortcut to anything you like by right-clicking it and choosing **Rename** from the shortcut menu.

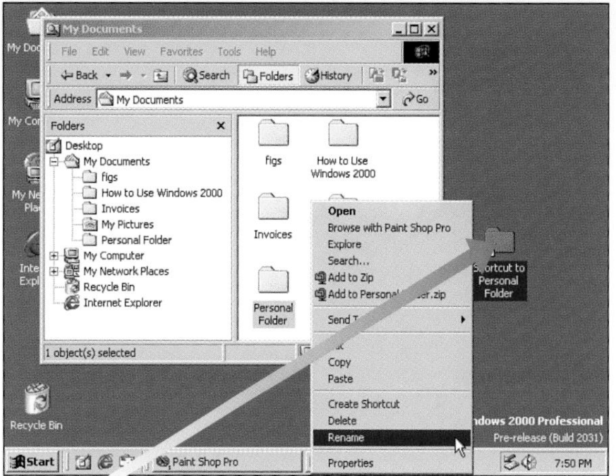

Right-click

6 Double-Click the Shortcut

To open the original object to which you made the shortcut, just double-click the shortcut icon.

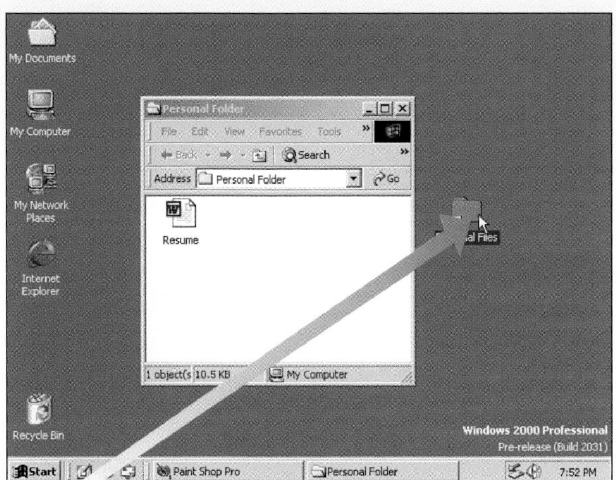

Double-click

How-To Hints

Finding Out a Shortcut's Target

If you find a shortcut for which you can't remember what object it's pointing to, just right-click the shortcut and choose **Properties** from the shortcut menu. The Target text box tells you the path to the original object.

End

TASK 9

How to Rename a File or Folder

In Windows 2000, you can name files or folders just about anything you want to. Names are limited to 256 characters, including spaces, and there are a few special characters you are not allowed to use, including the following: \ / : * ? " < >. Also, you should be very careful to only rename files and folders that you created in the first place. Windows and Windows programs are composed of many folders and files that have special names. Changing them can often cause a program, or even Windows itself, to not function.

Begin

1 Select the File

To rename a file in the My Computer window or Windows Explorer, first select the file with a single click.

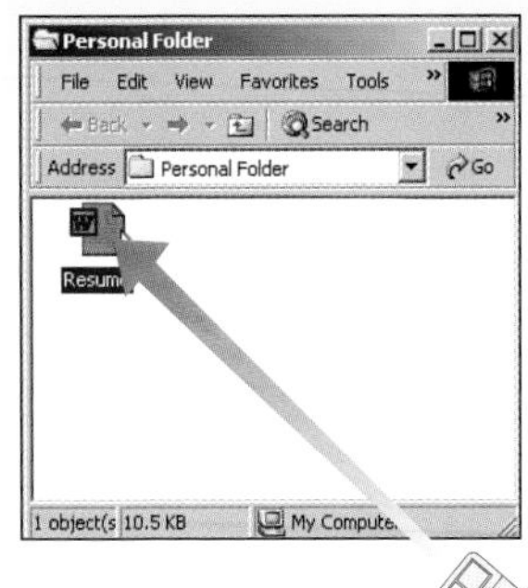

2 Choose Rename from the File Menu

Click **File, Rename**.

3 Enter a New Name

Type a new name for the file.

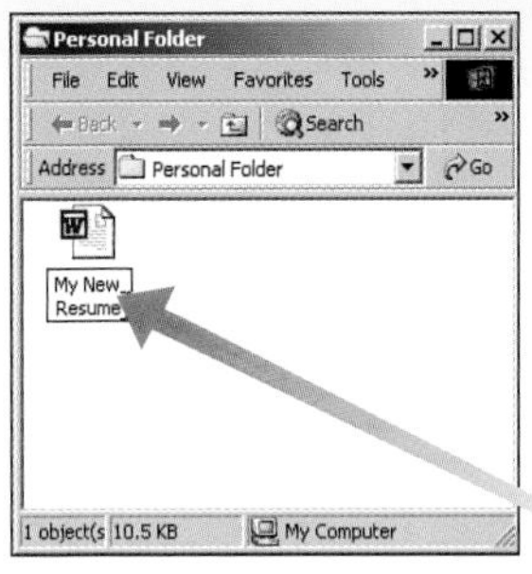

4 Click the Name Twice Slowly

A quicker way to rename a file (and one that works on files on the desktop) is to first select the file with a single click and then click the name of the file a second later—not so fast as to suggest a double-click. You can then type a new name.

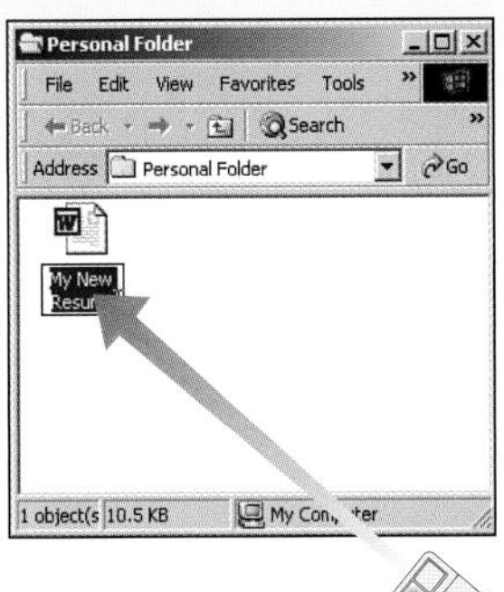

Click

5 Right-Click the File

Yet another way to rename a file is to right-click the file and choose **Rename** from the shortcut menu. You can then type a new name.

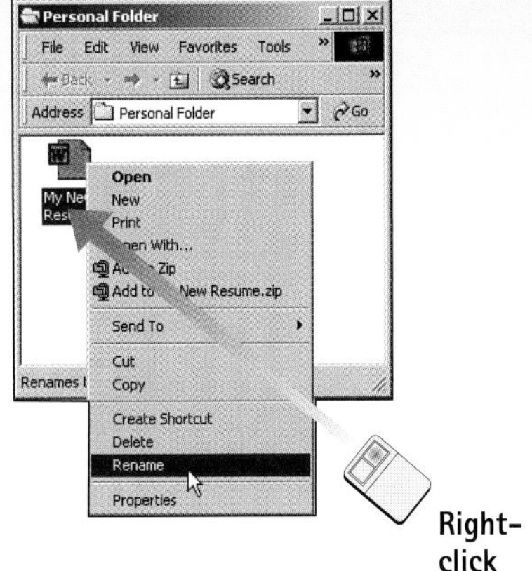

Right-click

End

How-To Hints

Keep Names Simple

Though you can create very long filenames in Windows, it is usually better to keep them pretty short and simple. The reason for this is that when you view the contents of a folder, filenames are often cut off after the first 15 to 20 characters so that you can view more files in the folder.

TASK 10

How to Delete a File or Folder

When you delete a file or folder in Windows, the object is not immediately removed from your computer. First, it is placed into the Recycle Bin, where it is kept temporarily before being permanently deleted. This allows you to easily recover accidentally deleted files. For more information on using the Recycle Bin, see Part 1. There are a few ways to delete objects in Windows, including dragging them to the Recycle Bin or deleting them directly using the keyboard or Windows Explorer.

Begin

1 Select a Group of Files

Place your pointer in a blank spot near a group of objects you want to delete. Next, click and hold the left mouse button while dragging the pointer toward the objects. A dotted rectangle (named the *lasso*) appears behind your pointer. Drag this lasso over all of the intended objects to select them all at once.

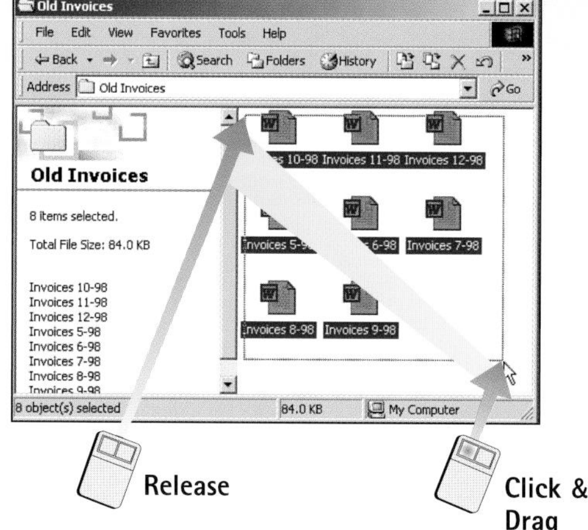

2 Drag the Files to the Recycle Bin

After a group of files is selected, drag them to the Recycle Bin by clicking any single selected file and holding the mouse button while you drag the pointer over the Recycle Bin.

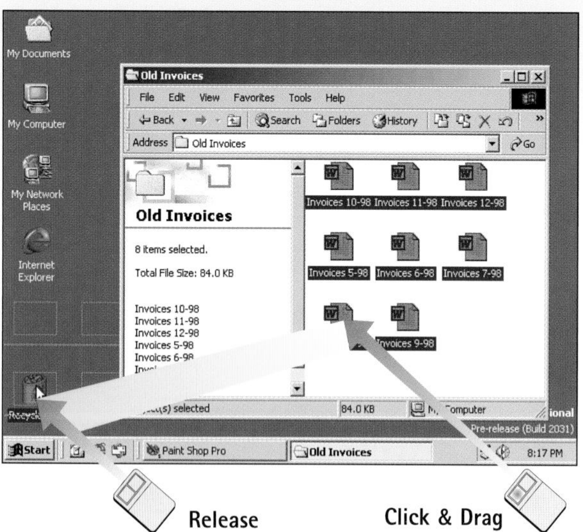

3 Select a File

It is also easy to delete files without using the Recycle Bin, which is helpful when you can't see your desktop. First, select the file you want to delete by clicking it once.

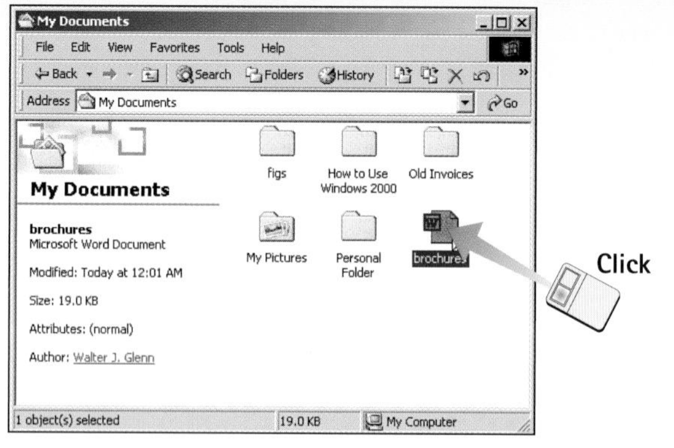

4 Use the Delete Key

Press the Delete key to send any selected file (or files) to the Recycle Bin.

5 Choose Delete from the File Menu

After a file is selected, you can also open the **File** menu and choose **Delete** to send the file to the Recycle Bin.

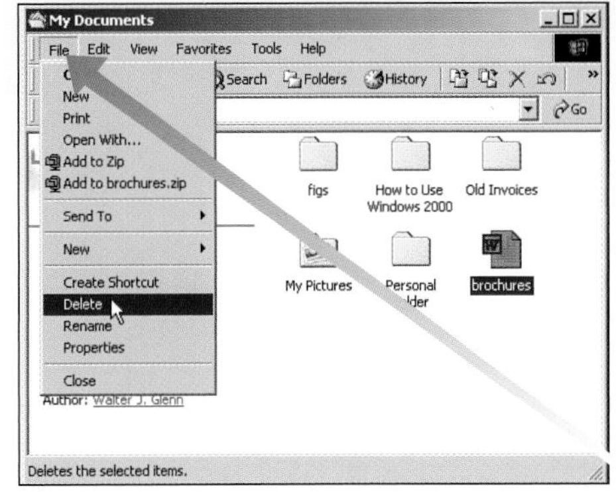

End

How-To Hints

Disable the Recycle Bin

If you would rather not use the Recycle Bin, right-click the **Recycle Bin** icon and choose **Properties** from the shortcut menu. Select the **Do not move files to the Recycle Bin** option. Be careful, though. When this option is selected, files that you delete are permanently removed from your system.

Change Your Recycle Bin Settings

There are several ways that you can customize the operation of your Recycle Bin. For more information on this, see Part 9.

TASK 11

How to Move or Copy a File or Folder

Most people move objects around from folder to folder by simply dragging them using the left mouse button. This usually works fine, but might not provide exactly the results you want. Depending on where you drag an object to, the object can be moved to the new location or it can be copied. For better results, try using the right mouse button instead of the left when you drag files to a new location.

Begin

1 Open the My Documents Window

Double-click the **My Documents** icon on the desktop to open it.

Double-click

2 Locate an Object

Locate an object you want to move. This can be a file or a folder.

3 Drag the File to a New Location

Place your pointer over the object, click and hold the right mouse button, and drag the object to the target location. Release the right mouse button.

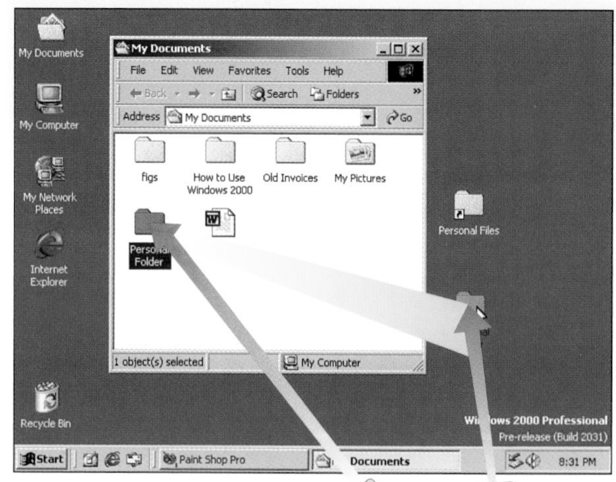

Right-click & Drag

Release

4 Choose Copy Here

When you release the right mouse button, a shortcut menu appears. Choose **Copy Here** to place an exact copy of the item in the new location and keep a copy in the old location.

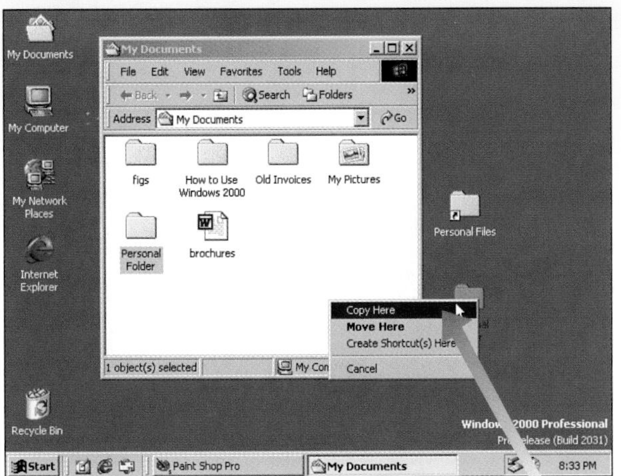

5 Choose Move Here

Choose **Move Here** from the shortcut menu to move the object to the new location and remove it from the old location.

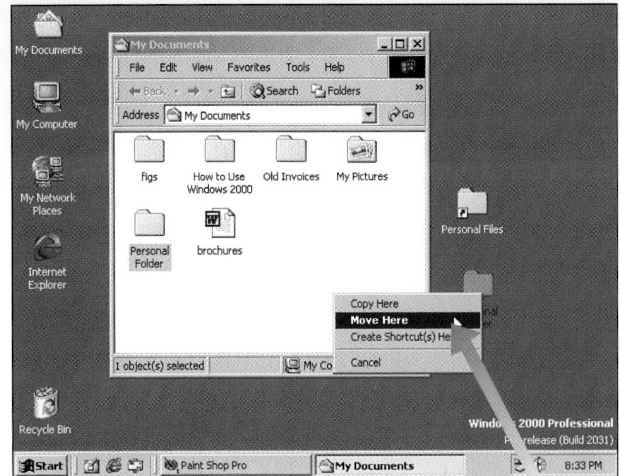

End

How-To Hints

Left Dragging

When you use the left mouse button to drag a file, the icon that you drag changes to reflect what action will be performed. If the icon has a small plus sign on it, the file will be copied when you release the mouse button. If the icon has a small arrow, a shortcut will be created. If the icon has nothing extra on it, the object will be moved.

TASK 12

How to Send a File to the Floppy Drive

Floppy disks are often used to back up files or transfer files to another computer. In Windows, the floppy drive is always labeled A: in the My Computer window and Windows Explorer. As with most other tasks, Windows offers a couple of different ways to send files to a floppy disk.

Begin

1 Open My Documents

Double-click the **My Documents** icon on your desktop to open the **My Documents** folder.

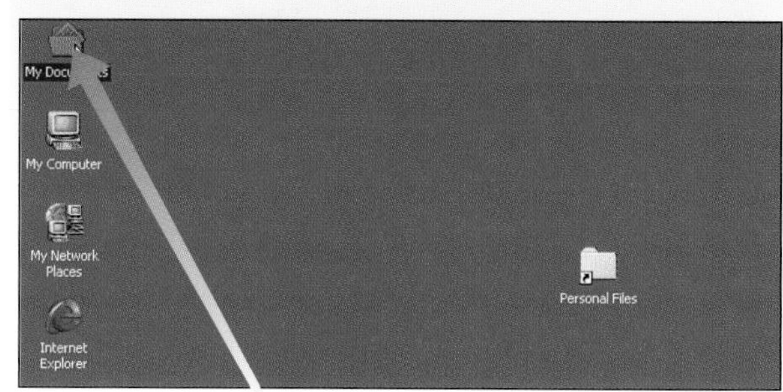

2 Open My Computer

Double-click the **My Computer** icon on your desktop to open the **My Computer** window.

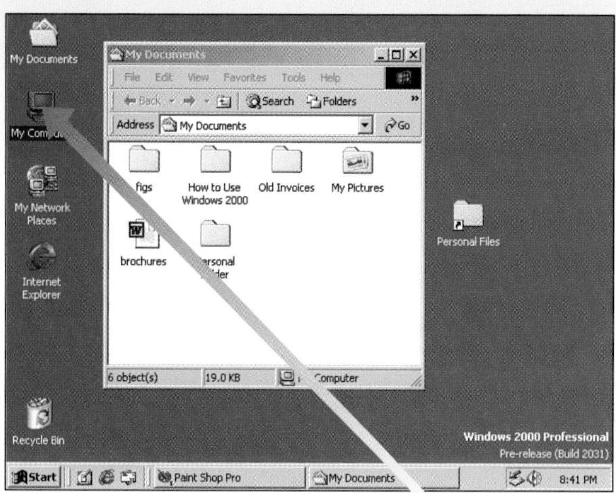

3 Tile Your Windows

Right-click your taskbar and choose **Tile Windows Vertically** so that you can see both the My Computer and the My Documents windows at the same time.

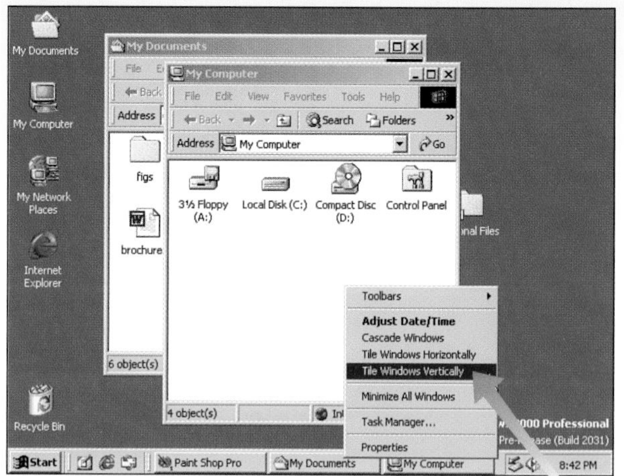

4 Drag the File to the Floppy Drive

Place your pointer over the file in the My Documents window that you want to copy. Click and hold the left mouse button while dragging the file to the floppy drive icon in the My Computer window.

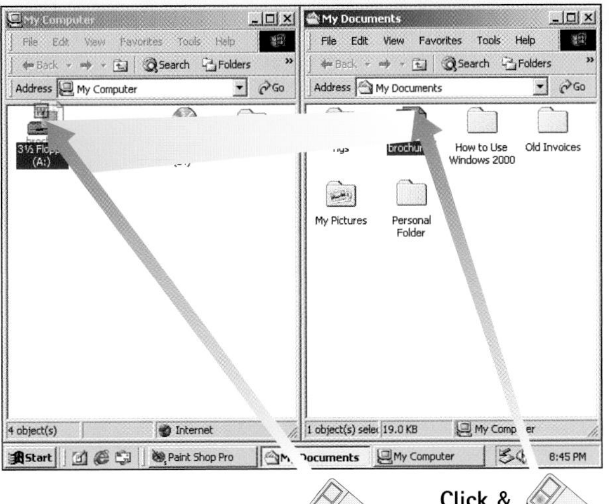

Release

Click & Drag

5 Copy the File

Release the left mouse button to copy the file to the floppy drive. Make sure a disk is in the drive, of course.

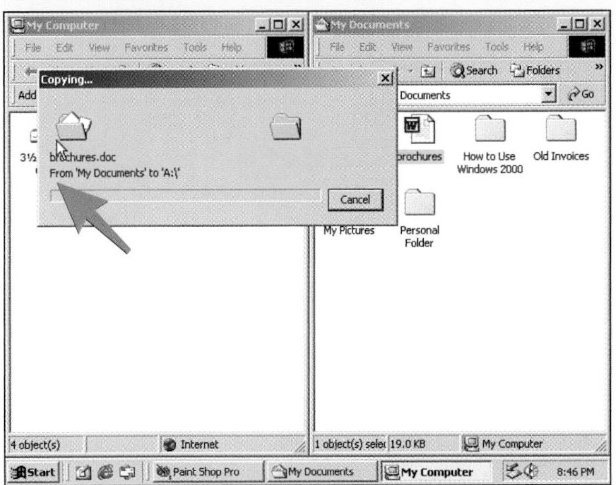

6 Select a File

Another way to send a file to the floppy drive is to first just select the file by clicking it once.

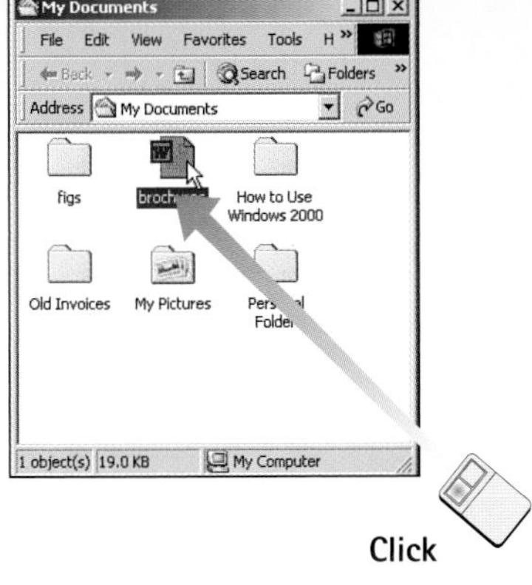

Click

7 Choose Send to Floppy Drive

Right-click the selected file, point to **Send To** on the shortcut menu, and then choose the floppy drive. Windows copies the file.

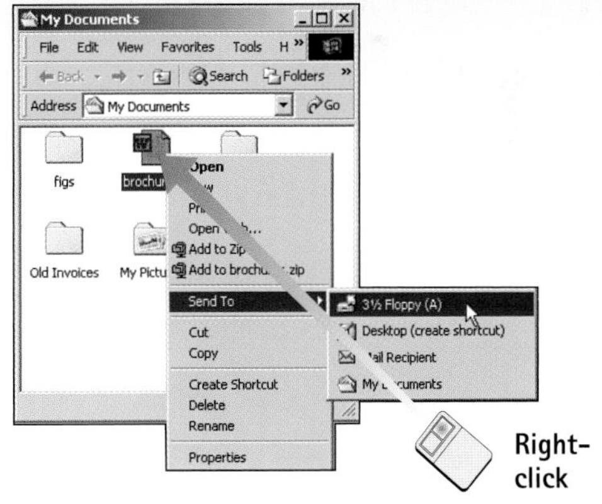

Right-click

End

TASK 13

How to Open a File with a Different Program

Files usually have a certain program associated with them, normally the program that created them. A text file, for example, is associated with Notepad. Windows knows what program to open a file with because of the three-character extension after a file's name. For example, a text file might be named Groceries.txt. Windows knows that files with the .txt extension should be opened in Notepad. Sometimes, however, you might want to open a file with a different program or even change the associated program altogether.

Begin

1 Right-Click the File

Right-click the file you want to open with a special program and choose **Open With** from the shortcut menu.

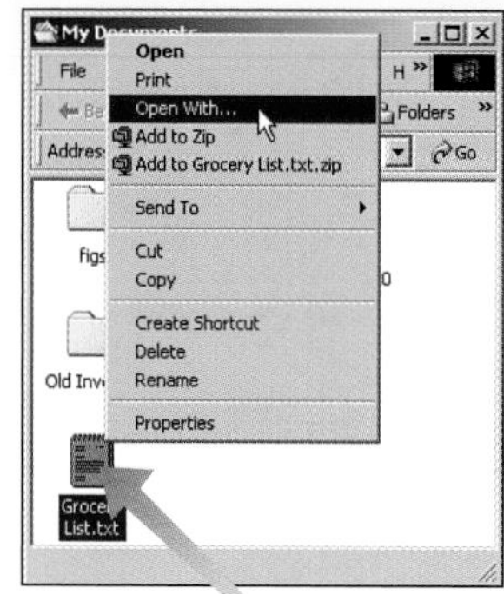

Right-click

2 Choose the Program

In the dialog box that opens, select the program you want to use to open the file.

Click

3 Find Another Program

If the program you want to use does not appear on the list, click **Other** to find the program file on your computer yourself.

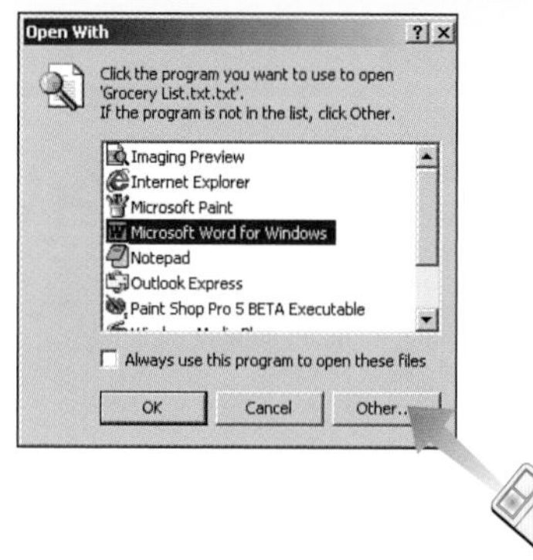

Click

4 Make It the Default Choice

If you want to change an extension's association (make files of that type open with the new program you've selected from now on), check the **Always use this program to open these files** option.

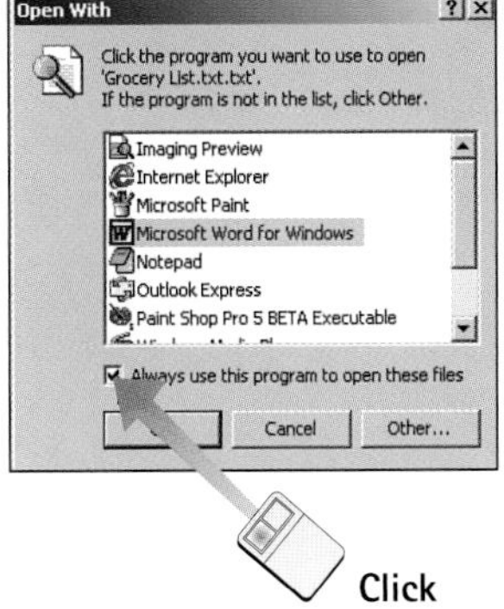

5 Open the File

Click **OK** to open the file in the selected program.

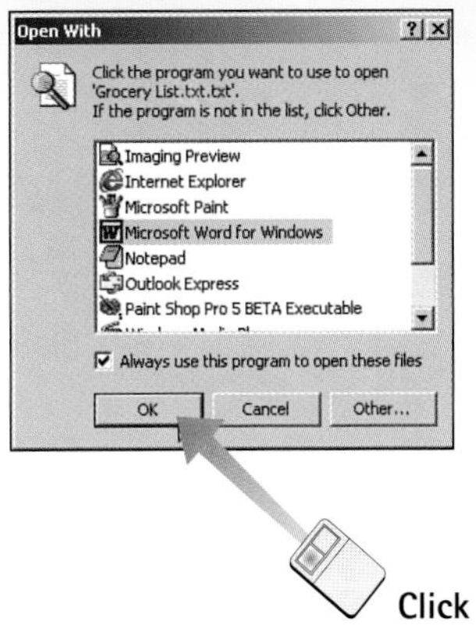

End

How-To Hints

Viewing File Associations

You can view a complete list of file associations in Windows. Open the **My Computer** window and then double-click **Control Panel**. Next, double-click **Folder Options**. On the dialog box that appears, click the **File Types** tab. All associations are listed here. You can create new ones and change existing ones, if you want.

Task

PART 3

Printing

Printing is one the basic functions you will perform with your computer. Windows 2000 makes printing as easy as it has ever been, coordinating all the mechanics in the background so that you can focus on your work.

In this part, you learn how to print a document from within the program that created it and also from the Windows 2000 Desktop. You also learn how to manage various printer settings, such as how to set your default printer, paper source, and paper size. You learn how to install a printer attached to your own computer and how to set up a network printer. Finally, you learn how to share your own printer with others on the network.

TASK 1

How to Print a Document from a Program

Most of the time, you print documents directly from the program you used to create them, whether that program is a word processor such as Microsoft Word or a drawing program such as Paint. Because most programs designed for Windows follow similar guidelines, you will find that the process of printing from them is very similar to the following steps.

Begin

1 Open the File

Open the file you want to print using the **File, Open** command of the program used to create the file. In the program's **Open** dialog box, navigate to the folder where the file is stored, select the file, and click **Open**.

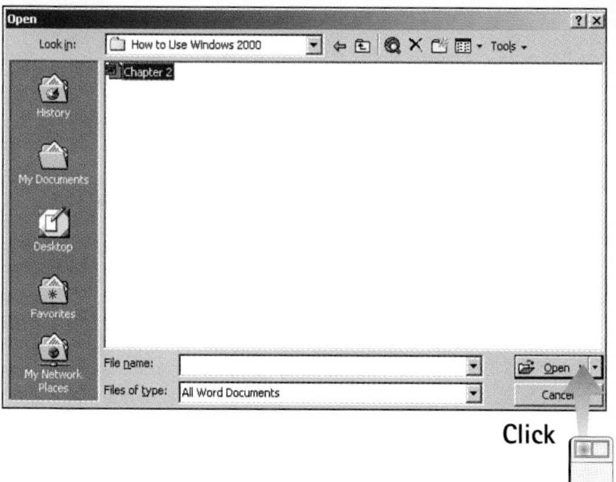

2 Choose the Print Command

When you are ready to print the open document, open the **File** menu and choose the **Print** command. The **Print** dialog box opens, which allows you to specify which pages of the document you want to print as well as how many copies.

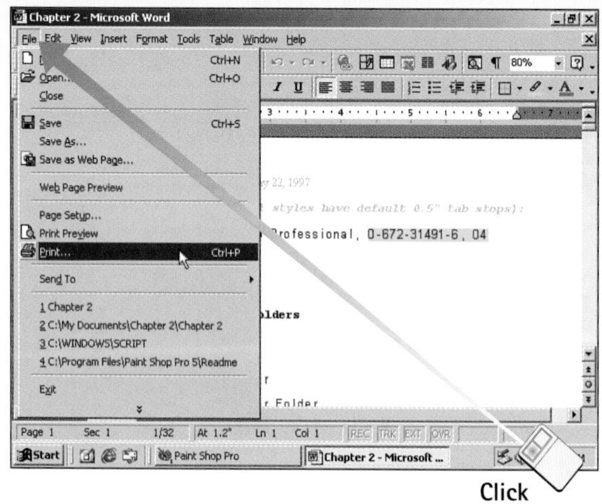

3 Choose the Printer to Use

If you have access to more than one printer, use the **Printer** drop-down menu to select the printer you want to use.

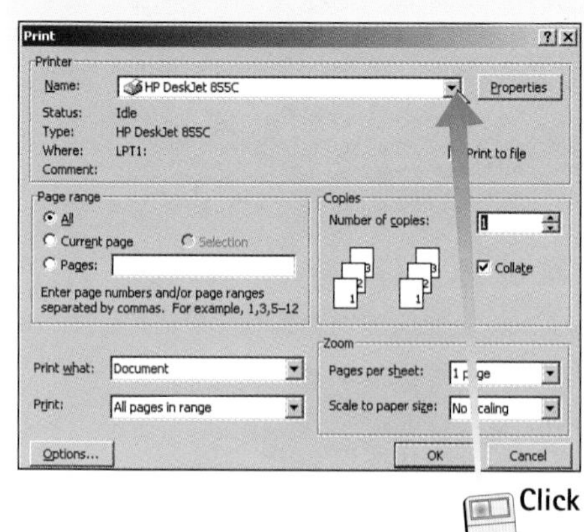

4 Choose Printing Options

Some programs let you set special printing options that are specific to the program you are using. This is usually done by clicking an Options button on the **Print** dialog box. Some programs, for example, allow you to print a document in draft mode, which can save a lot of time and printer ink.

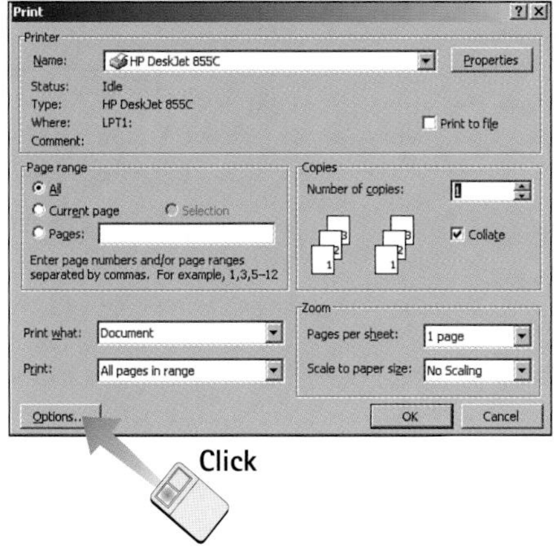

5 Print the Document

After you have selected your printer, specified the pages you want to print and how many copies, and set any extra options, click **OK** to print. Most programs allow you to continue working while your document is being printed.

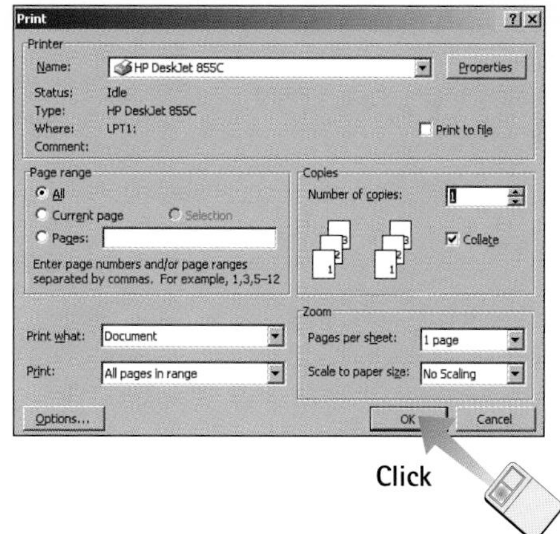

End

How-To Hints

Setting Printer Properties

The **Print** dialog boxes for most programs include a **Properties** button. This button gives you quick access to system-wide properties for your printer—the same properties you can set from within Windows.

Printing Without the Dialog Box

Many programs, like those in Microsoft Office, offer a **Print** button on the **Standard** toolbar. This button usually prints one copy of the document using all the default printer settings. If you print this way, you bypass the **Print** dialog box altogether.

Previewing Before You Print

Some programs offer a feature named **Print Preview**, usually available from the **File** menu, that lets you see your document onscreen as it will look when it is printed. This can be a handy way of making sure that your document looks the way you think it does before using up paper to print it.

TASK 2

How to Print a Document from Windows

Most of the time, you print documents from within programs. However, Windows also offers a few ways to print documents straight from the desktop without opening the document's program. This is a great way to dash off quick copies of documents, or even print multiple documents at once.

Begin

1 Find the Document You Want to

The first step to printing a document in Windows is to find the document. You can use the **My Computer** folder, the **My Documents** folder, or **Windows Explorer**—whichever you prefer. Here, a document is selected in a folder named **Personal Folders**. You learn more about navigating in Windows in Part 2, "Working with Files and Folders."

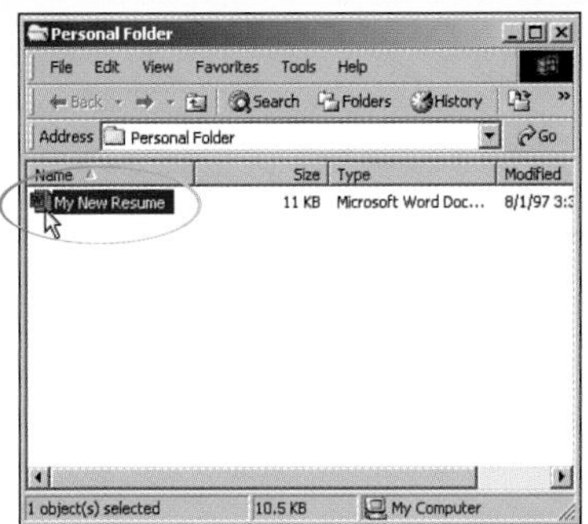

2 Right-Click the Document and

To quickly print the document using your default printer and the default settings of the document's program, right-click the document (or select multiple documents and right-click any one of them) and choose **Print** from the context menu. Windows prints one copy of the document without opening the program at all.

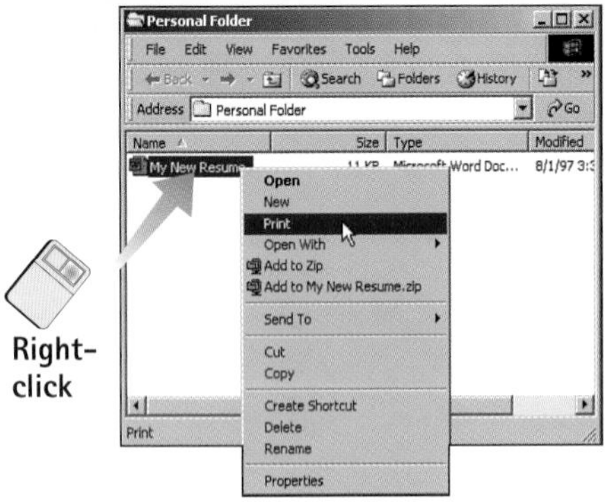

3 Open Your Printers Folder

Another way to print a document in Windows is to drag the document onto a printer icon. To perform this action, both the folder that holds the document and your **Printers** folder must be open. To open the **Printers** folder, select **Start, Settings,** and **Printers**.

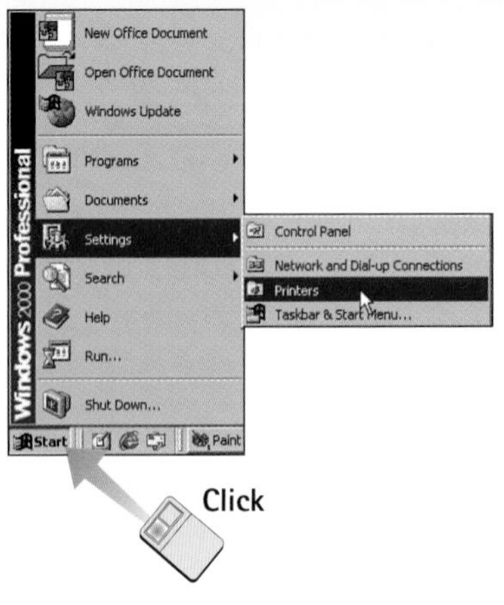

4 Select Documents to Print

Using **My Computer** or **Windows Explorer**, find the folder with the document or documents you want to print and select those document icons.

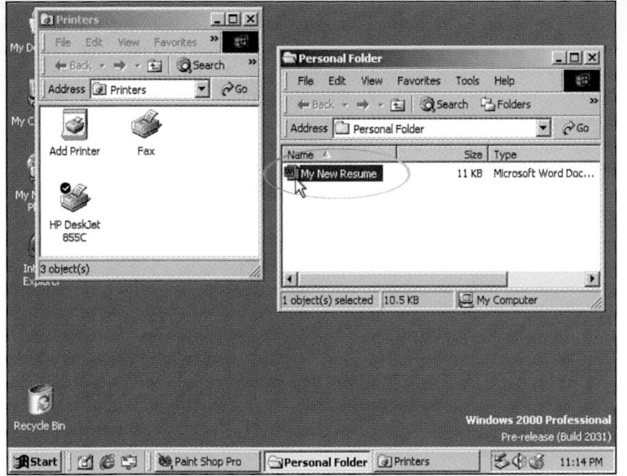

5 Drag a Document to a Printer

Drag any document (or group of documents) from the folder and release it on the icon for the printer you want to use. Windows prints the documents using the default settings for the program that created the documents. This method is the same as using the **Print** command in Task 1, but lets you choose the printer you want to use.

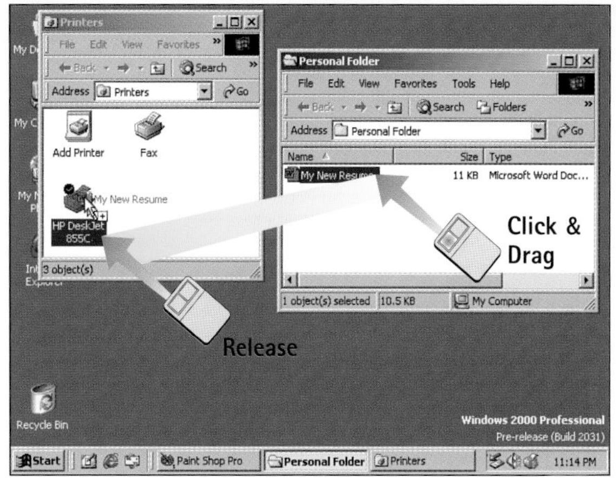

End

How-To Hints

Dragging Multiple Files

You can drag multiple documents to a **Printer** icon in one step: Hold down the **Ctrl** key while you left-click documents in the **My Computer** window. Each document you click while holding down the **Ctrl** key is added to your selection.

Create a Printer Shortcut on Your Desktop

If you frequently drag files to a printer icon and don't want to keep your **Printers** folder open all the time, you can create a shortcut to the printer on your desktop: Drag the desired printer icon to your desktop and release it. Windows offers to create a shortcut for you; click **OK**.

Add a Printer to the Send To Menu

An even better solution than adding a shortcut icon to your desktop is to add the shortcut to the **Send To** menu that you can access whenever you right-click a file. This way, you can send a document to any printer just by using the document's context menu. For information on how to add items to the **Send To** menu, see Part 9, "Changing Windows 2000 Settings."

TASK 3

How to Manage Documents Waiting to Print

Whenever you print a document, that document enters a print queue, which is essentially a line of documents waiting for their turn at the printer. A printer icon appears in your system tray next to the clock to let you know the queue is active. You can open the print queue and do some document management. Some of the things you can do in the print queue depend on whether you are using a printer hooked up to your computer or a network printer. Network printers are usually shared by many users; you can manage only the documents that belong to *you*. You cannot affect other user's documents or the print queue itself.

Begin

1 Open the Print Queue

To open the print queue, double-click the printer icon in the system tray when it appears. Right-clicking the printer icon opens a shortcut menu that lets you open the print queue for any printer on your system, not just the actively printing one.

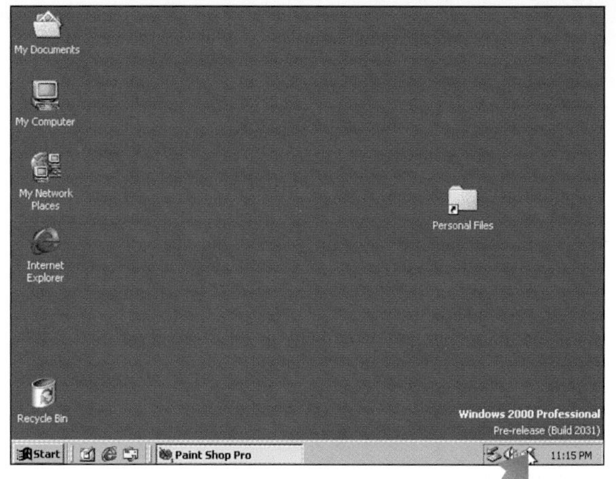

2 View Documents Waiting to Print

The print queue shows a list of documents waiting to print in the order in which they are to be printed. For each document, details such as owner, number of pages, document size, and time of submission are also shown.

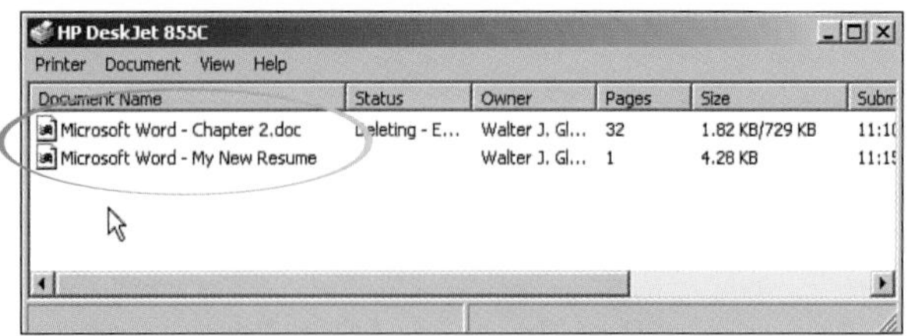

3 Cancel the Printing of a Document

To remove a document from the print queue—that is, to stop it from being printed—right-click the document and choose **Cancel** from the pop-up context menu. Be sure that you choose the correct document, because Windows does not ask you whether you are sure you want to remove the document.

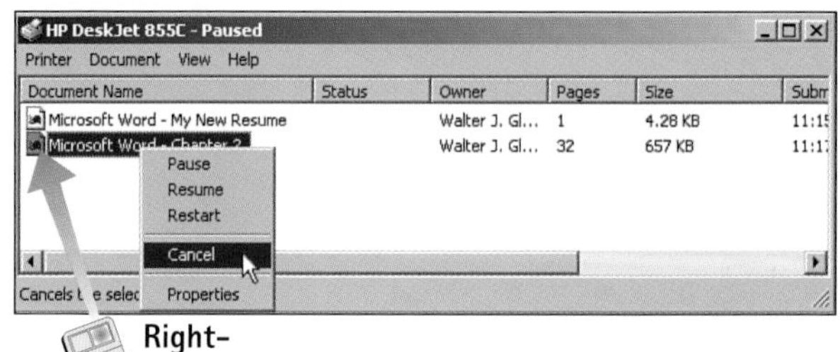

4 Pause the Printing of a Document

If you *pause* a document, it remains in the print queue but does not print until you choose to resume printing. Other documents waiting in the queue print. To pause a document, right-click the document and choose **Pause** from the context menu; the status of the document in the print queue window changes to Paused. Choose **Resume** from the document's context menu when you are ready for the document to continue printing.

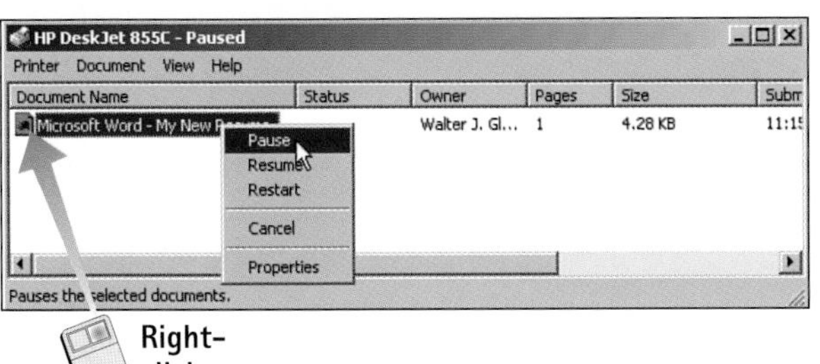

5 Restart the Printing of a Document

When you *restart* a paused document, it begins printing again from the beginning. This can be useful if, for example, you start to print a document and then realize the wrong paper is loaded in the printer. You can pause the document, change the paper, and then restart the document. To restart a document, right-click the document and choose **Restart** from the context menu.

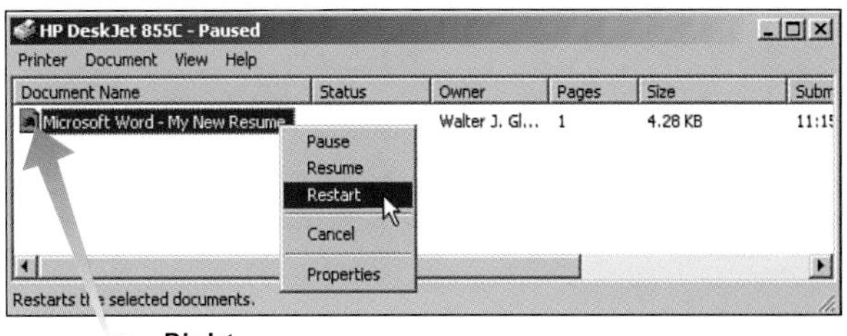

6 Change a Document's Priority

A document's *priority* governs when it prints related to other documents in the print queue. By default, all documents are given a priority of 1, the lowest priority available. The highest priority is 99. Increasing a document's priority causes it to print before other waiting documents. Double-click the document to open its property sheets. Then drag the **Priority** slider to set a higher priority.

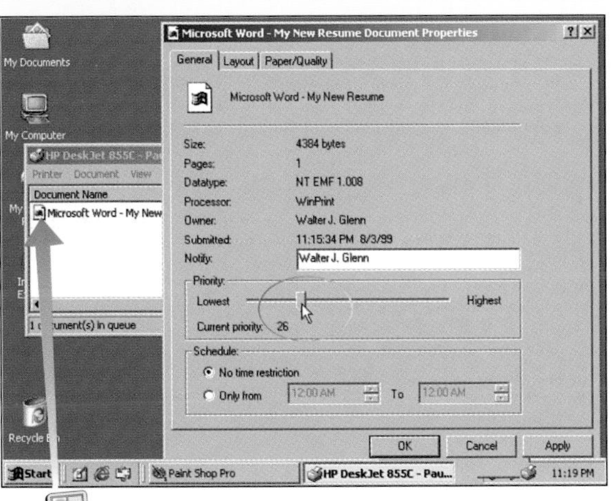

Double-click

7 Pause the Whole Print Queue

Pausing the entire print queue keeps *all* documents from printing. To pause the queue, open the **Printer** menu and choose **Pause Printing**. The title bar for the print queue window changes to indicate that the printer is paused. To resume printing, choose the **Pause Printing** command again.

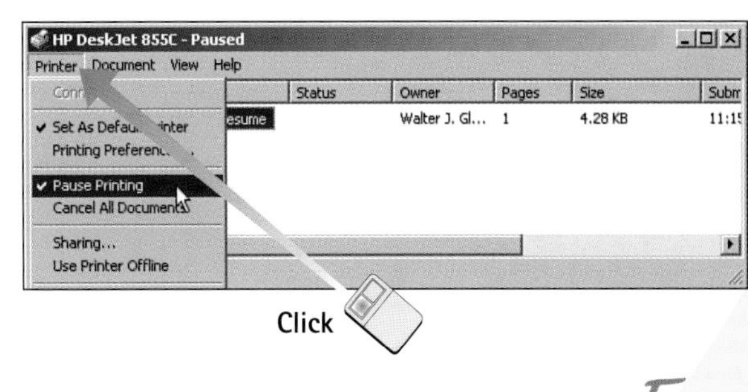

End

TASK 4

How to Change Printer Settings

When you first install a printer in Windows 2000, common settings are configured for you. After you use your printer for a while, however, you might find you need to change those printer settings once in a while.

Begin

1 Open the Printers Folder

Click the **Start** button, select **Settings, Printers**.

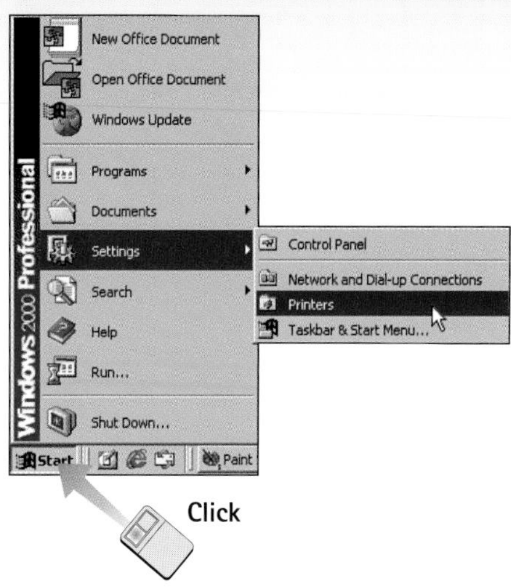

2 Set the Default Printer

The default printer is the printer that programs try to print to unless you specify a different printer when you print a document. In the **Printers** window, the default printer has a small check by it. To make a printer the default, right-click it and choose **Set as Default Printer** from the shortcut menu.

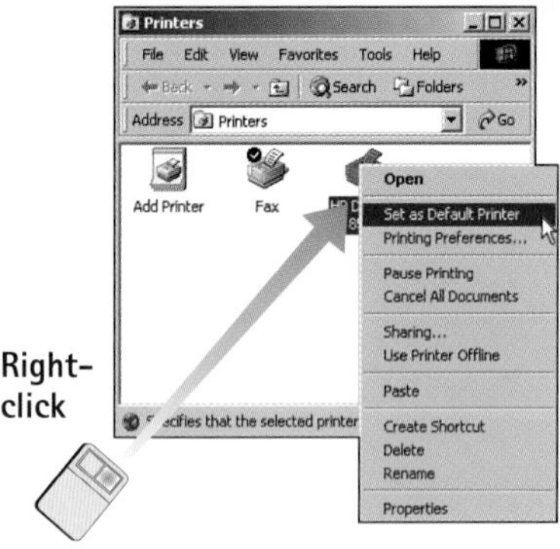

3 Open Printer Preferences

Right-click on a printer and choose **Printing Preferences** from the shortcut menu.

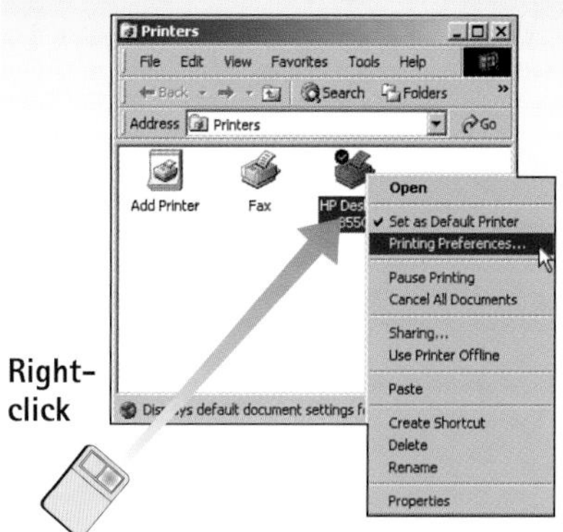

4 Change the Page Layout

Choose to print the page in **Portrait** format (normal vertical orientation) or **Landscape** (horizontal orientation).

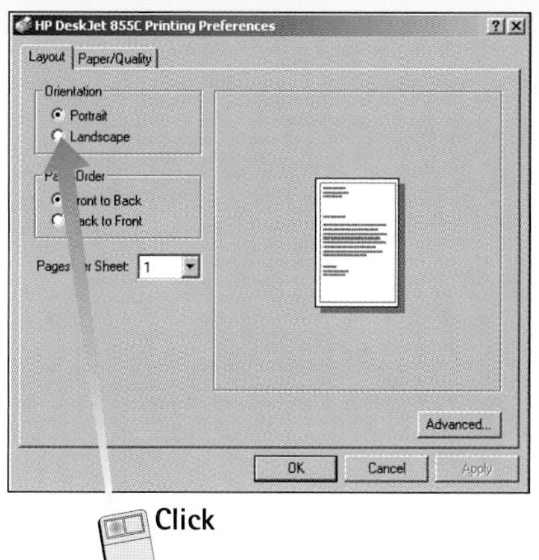

5 Change the Paper Source

Click the **Paper/Quality** tab to see more preferences. Click the **Paper Source** drop-down list to choose a different tray on your printer.

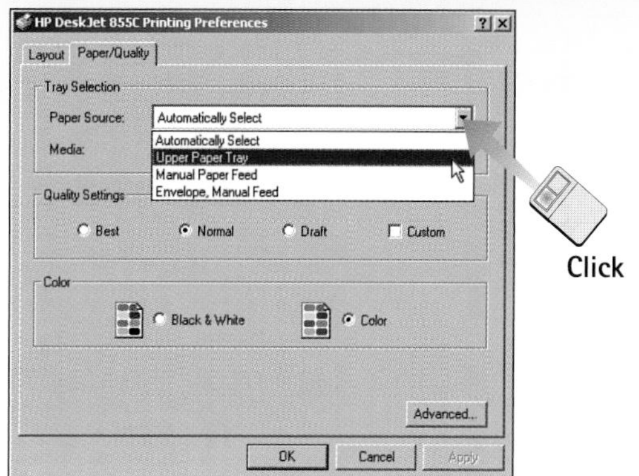

6 Change the Media Type

Click the **Media** drop-down list to choose the type of paper you want to print to.

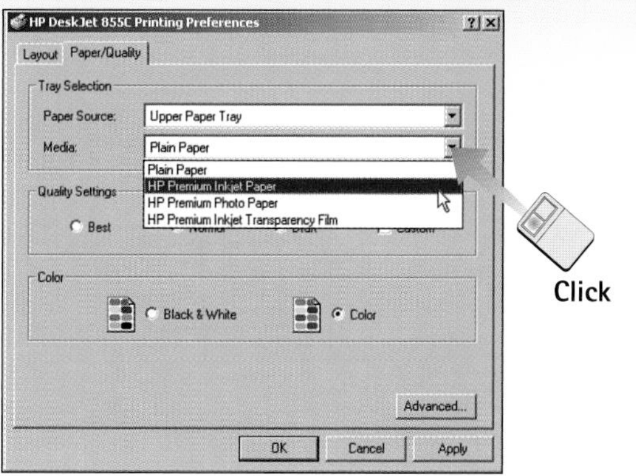

7 Change the Print Quality

Choose the quality of print you want. Better quality uses up more ink and takes more time. Draft quality prints quickly and uses less ink.

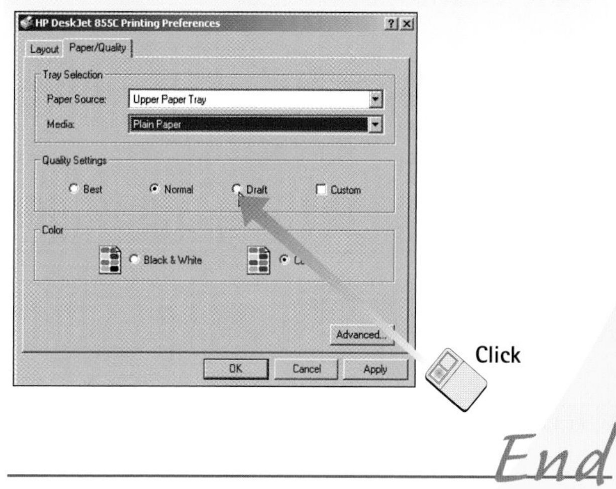

End

TASK 5

How to Share a Printer with Others

When you share a printer, it becomes accessible to other users on your network. By default, all users on the network can see and print to your printer. You can change this so that only particular users or groups of users can use your printer. To share your printer, your computer must be on a network and your network administrator must have already set your computer up so that you can share items with others.

Begin

1 Open the Sharing Dialog Box

Right-click the printer you want to share and choose **Sharing** from the shortcut menu.

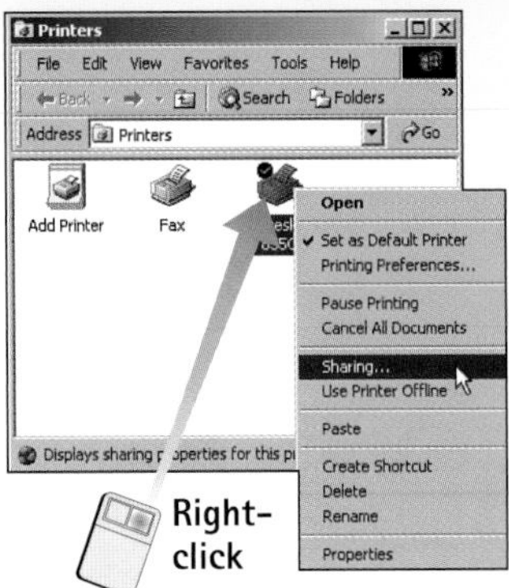

2 Share the Printer

Click the **Shared As** option and enter a name for the shared printer. This is the name others on the network will see.

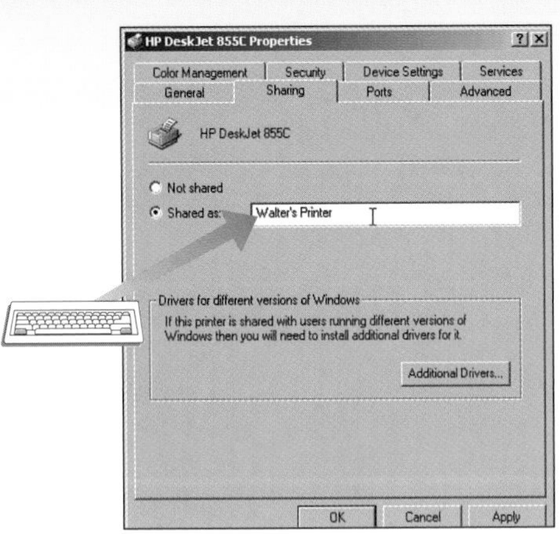

3 Click the Security Tab

If you want to limit the users that can access your printer, click the **Security** tab.

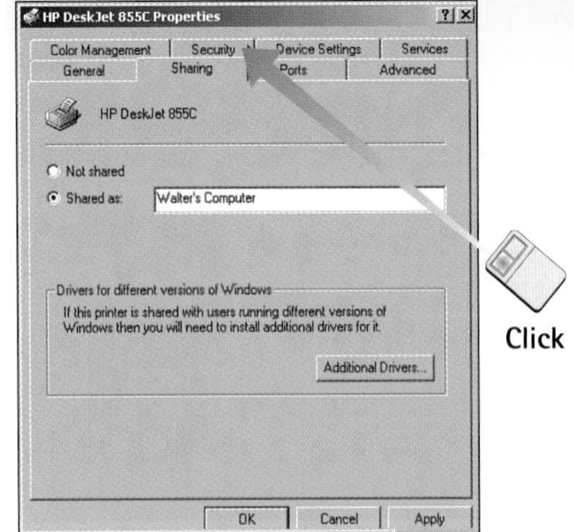

4 Remove the Everyone Group

Select the group named **Everyone** and click **Remove**. This removes the permissions for all users to access the printer.

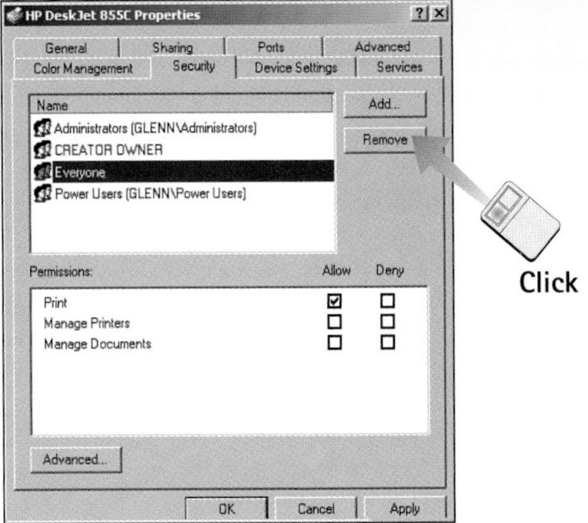

5 Add New Users

Click **Add** to give a new user or group permission to access the printer.

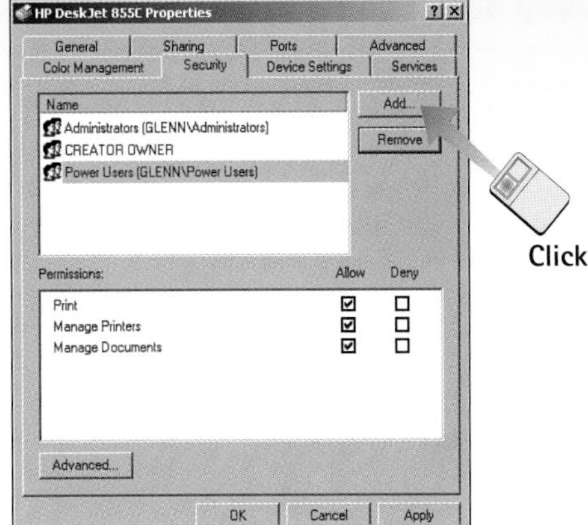

6 Select a User to Add

Select a user from the list and click **Add** to add them to the list of users to grant access. When you are done adding users, click **OK**.

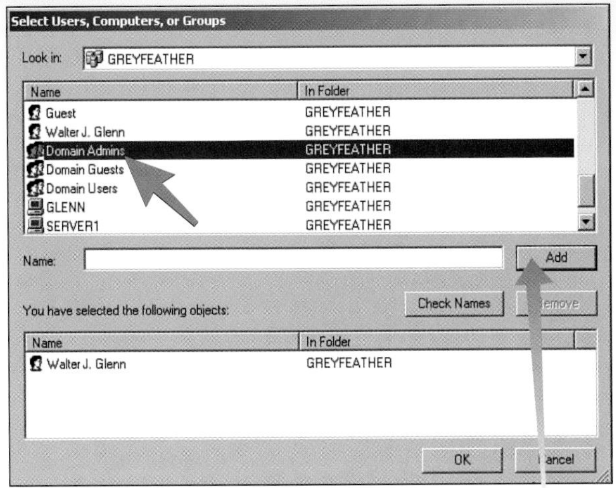

7 Apply the New Permissions

Select the exact permissions each user should have using the checkboxes. **Print** allows the user to print to the printer. **Manage Printers** allows the user to change printer settings. **Manage Documents** allows the user to move, pause, and delete documents waiting to print. Click **OK** to grant the new users you have added access to your printer.

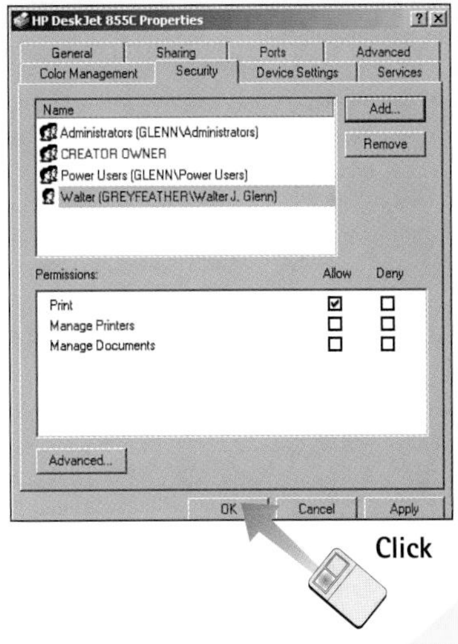

End

TASK 6

How to Install a Local Printer

In Windows lingo, the actual piece of hardware you usually think of as the printer is called the *print device*. The printer is the icon you install in the **Printers** folder that represents a print device. Once you have attached the print device to a computer, it is relatively easy to install the printer to the printers folder. In fact, Windows will normally find the printer automatically and configure it for you. If Windows doesn't find it, use this procedure for adding the printer yourself.

Begin

1 Run the Add Printer Wizard

In the **Printers** folder, double-click the **Add Printer** icon to launch the Add Printer Wizard. When you see the Welcome screen, click **Next**.

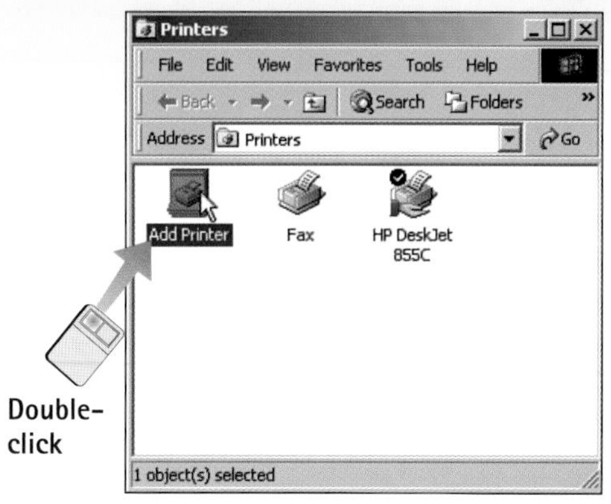

2 Choose Local Printer

Click the **Local Printer** option. A local printer is attached directly to your computer.

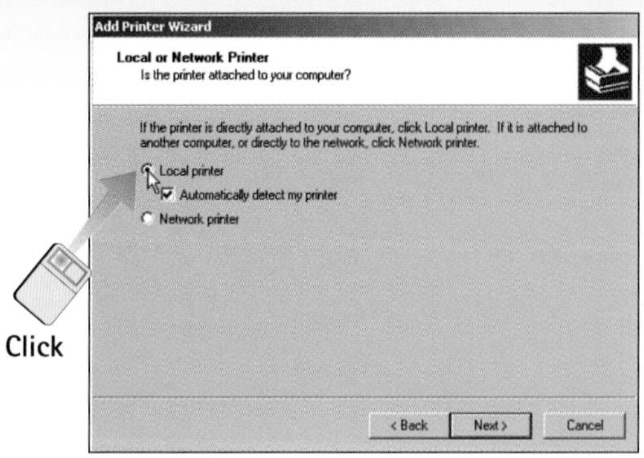

3 Don't Detect the Printer

Uncheck the option to automatically detect the printer. If Windows didn't find it automatically already, it probably won't now.

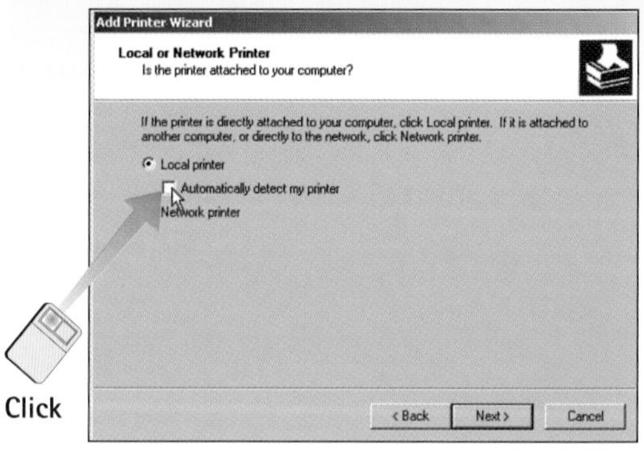

4 Go to the Next Page

Whenever you finish with the options on one wizard page, just click **Next** to go to the next page.

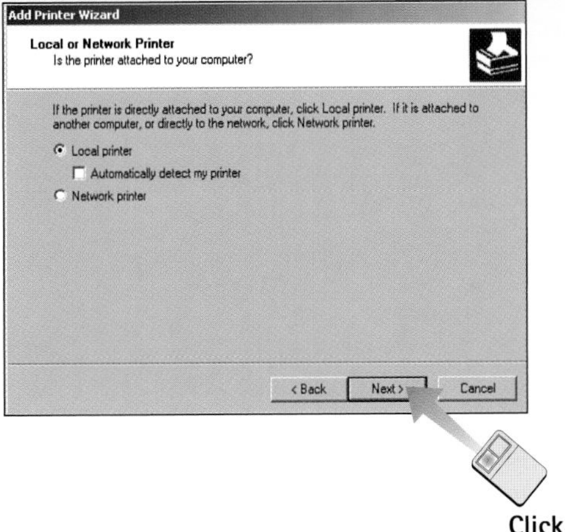

5 Choose a Port

Choose the Port on your computer to which the print device is attached. The first printer on a computer is usually on the LPT1 port (the first parallel port). The second is usually on the LPT2 port (the second parallel port). When you've selected the Port, click **Next** to go on.

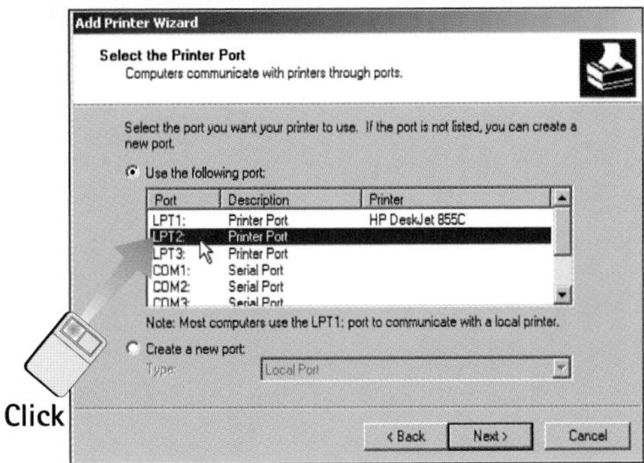

6 Choose a Manufacturer

On the left side of this page is a list of common manufacturers of printers. Choose the manufacturer for the printer you are installing.

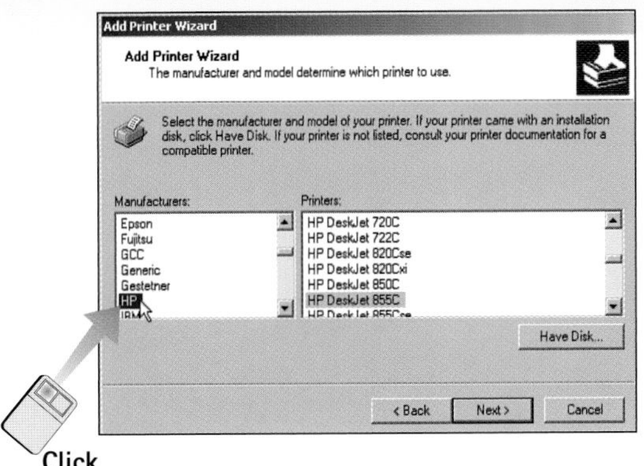

7 Choose a Model

After you choose a manufacturer on the left, the list on the right changes to display printer models made by the selected manufacturer. Choose the model printer you are installing. Click **Next** to go on.

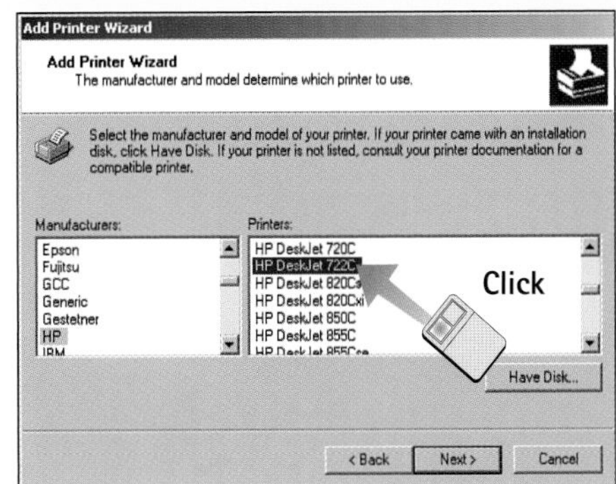

Continues

8 Name the Printer

By default, your printer is named by the manufacturer and model number. Enter a new name, if you want.

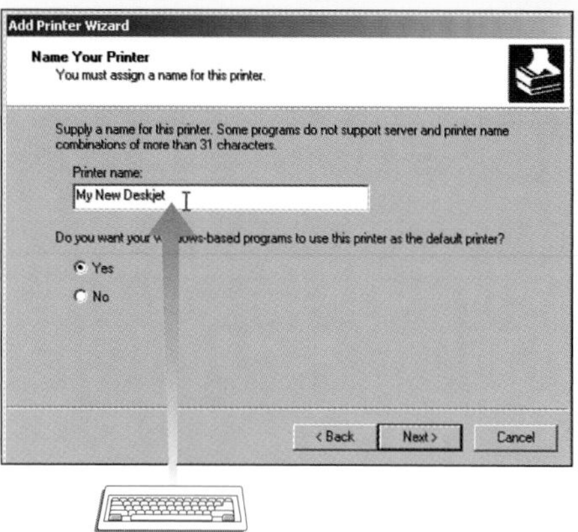

9 Make It the Default Printer

If you want your new printer to be the default printer used by programs, click **Yes.** If you prefer to preserve an existing default printer, click **No.** Click **Next** to go on.

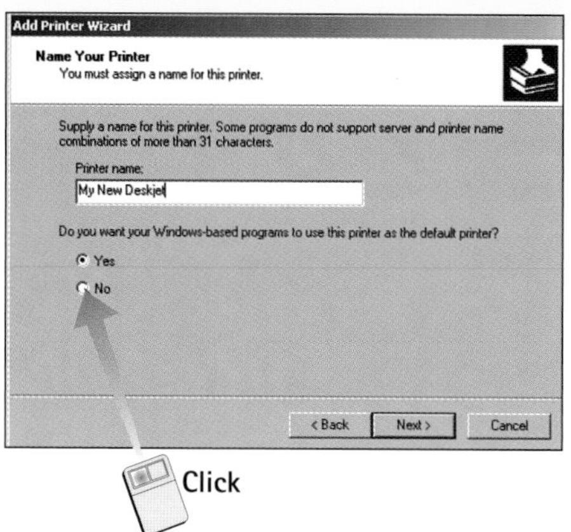

10 Share the Printer

If you want to share the new printer, click the **Share as** option and enter a share name. For more on sharing a printer, see the earlier task, "How to Share a Printer with Others." Click **Next** to go on.

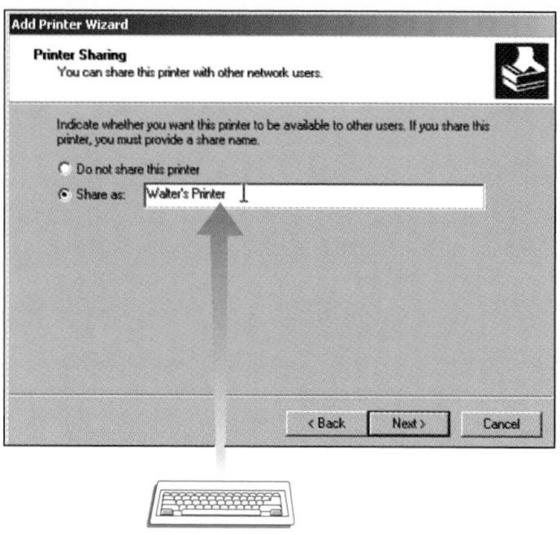

11 Print a Test Page

Click **Yes** if you want Windows to print a test page to ensure that your new printer is working properly. If the test doesn't work, you are shown how to troubleshoot the installation. Click **Next** to go on.

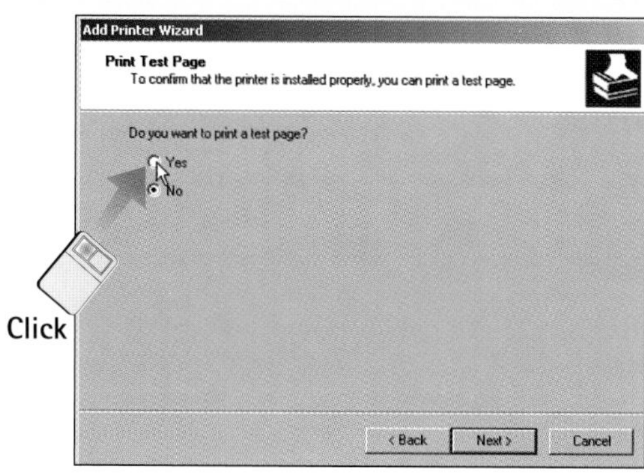

12 Finish the Installation

Review the configuration of your new printer. If you discover any problems, you can click **Back** to go back through the steps of the installation. If you are satisfied, click **Finish**.

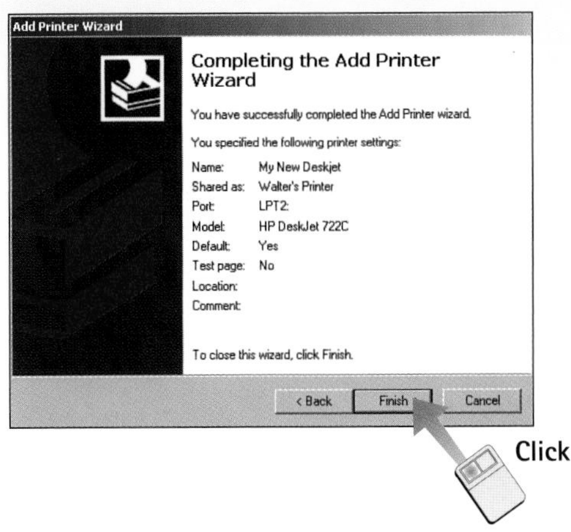

End

TASK 7

How to Install a Network Printer

A network printer is often one that is attached to another computer on the network. That computer's user has shared the computer with other users on the network. Some network printers are attached directly to the network and are not on a computer at all. Installing a network printer requires that you know basically where on your network the printer is located. This means knowing the name of the computer the printer is attached to and maybe the workgroup that computer is part of.

Begin

1 Run the Add Printer Wizard

Double-click the **Add Printer** icon to launch the Add Printer Wizard. Click **Next** to skip the Welcome page.

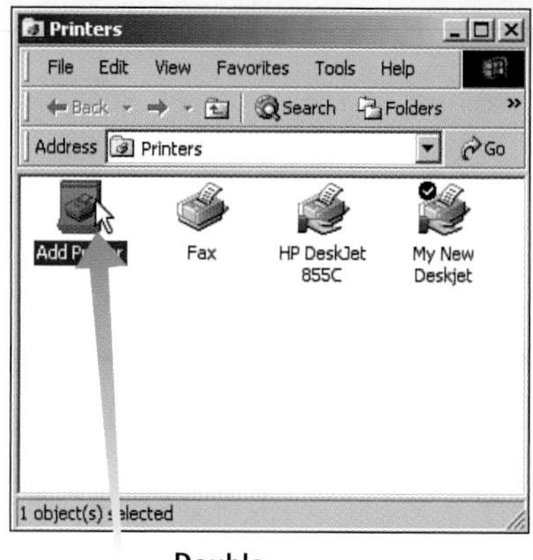

Double-click

2 Choose Network Printer

Click the **Network Printer** option.

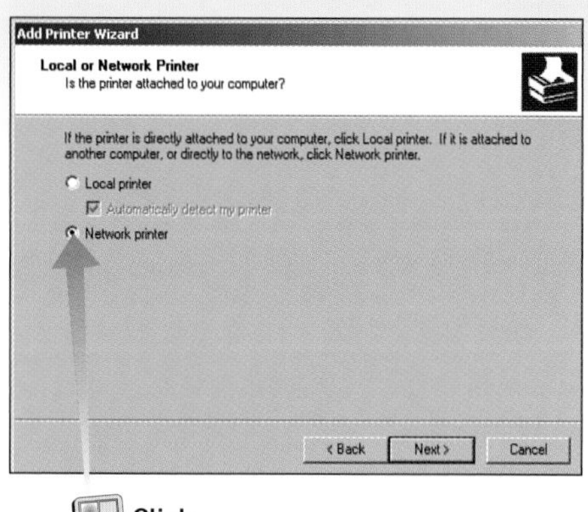

Click

3 Go to the Next Page

Whenever you finish with the options on one wizard page, just click **Next** to go to the next page.

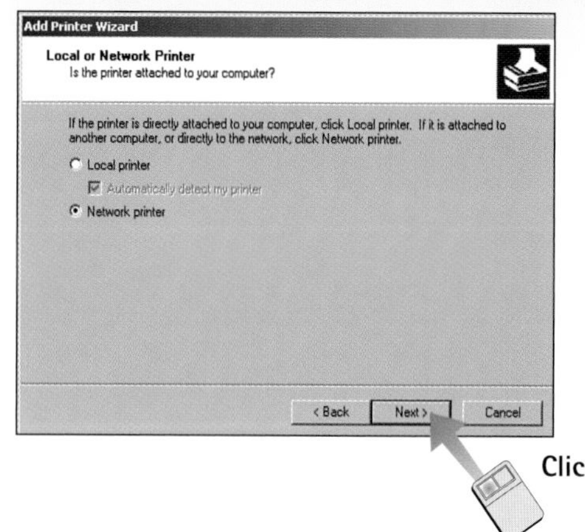

Click

4 Click Next

If you know the exact name of the printer you want to connect to, you can enter it in the **Name** text box. If you don't know the name (which is usually the case), just click **Next** to browse the network for the computer.

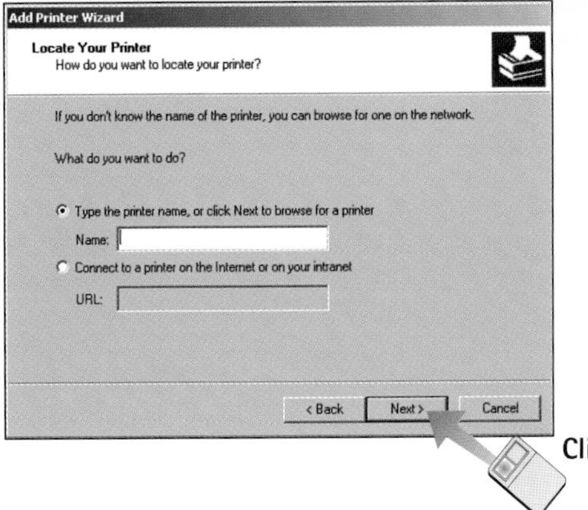

5 Choose the Printer

This page shows a hierarchical view of the workgroups and computers on your network. All shared printers are listed at the top. Choose the printer you want to install and click **Next**.

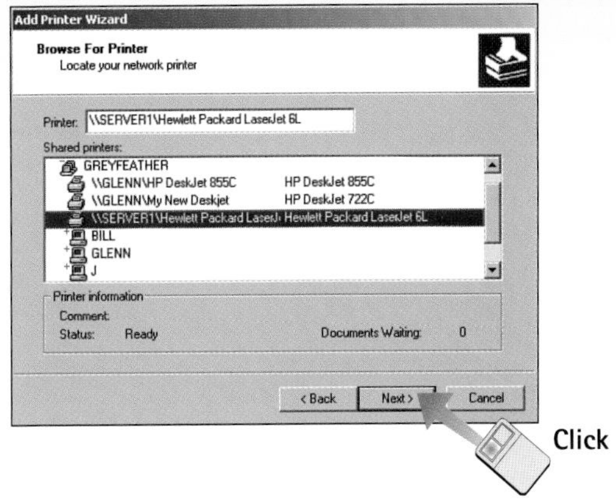

6 Make It the Default Printer

If you want your new printer to be the default printer used by programs, click **Yes.** If you prefer to preserve an existing default printer, click **No.** Click **Next** to go on.

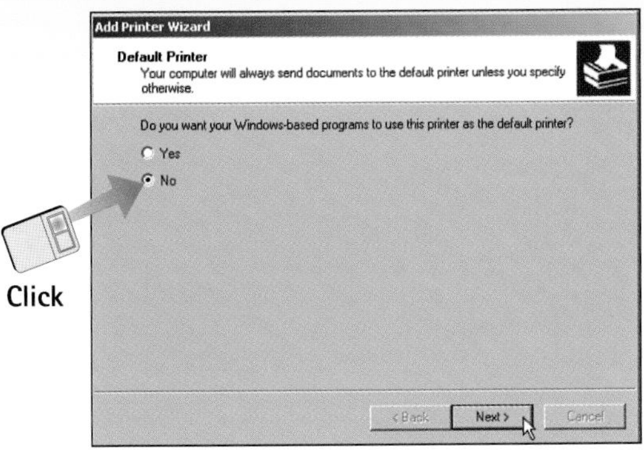

7 Finish the Installation

Review the configuration of your new printer. If you discover any problems, you can click **Back** to go back through the steps of the installation. If you are satisfied, click **Finish**.

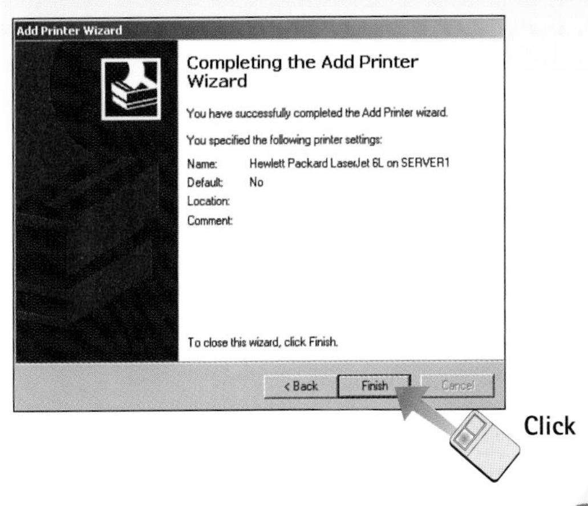

End

Task

PART 4

Working on a Network

If you're using Windows 2000 Professional at work, the chances are that your computer is on a network. A network is a bunch of computers (and sometimes other devices) all connected together with wires—a setup you often hear called a local area network, or LAN. Sometimes these LANs are connected together over different types of telephone lines to form one large network—often called a wide area network, or WAN.

When your computer is part of a network, you can share files, folders, and printers on your computer with other users on the network. You can also access resources that other users have shared from their computers. On a Windows network, computers and users are grouped together into large units named *domains*. You can think of a domain as a big group of users that can all share resources with one another. Domains are often divided up into smaller units named *workgroups*. Workgroups are small groups of users who share work frequently.

When you allow other users to access resources on your computer, you must think about security. There might be some resources that you want everyone on the network to be able to get to. There are others that you want only certain people to be able to use. Windows 2000 lets you do this with permissions. For each resource you share with the network, you can specify who can access that resource and exactly what he or she can do with it.

Don't worry if all of this sounds complicated. Windows 2000 does a pretty good job of hiding the complexities of networking from users. Most of the gory details are handled by the people who set up the network.

TASK 1

How to Use My Network Places

Most of what you do on the network is done using the My Network Places icon on your desktop. With it, you can access all of the shared resources your network has to offer, add new network places of your own, and even search for computers and documents on the network.

Begin

1 Open My Network Places

Double-click the **My Network Places** icon on your desktop to open the **My Network Places** window.

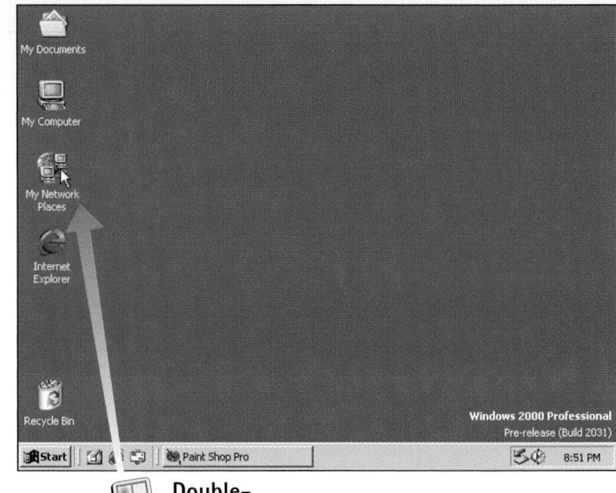

Double-click

2 Open Computers Near Me

Double-click the **Computers Near Me** icon to open the **Computers Near Me** window. Double-clicking the **Entire Network** icon opens a similar window that lets you browse domains on your network and computers in those domains. The steps in this procedure work for both **Computers Near Me** and **Entire Network**.

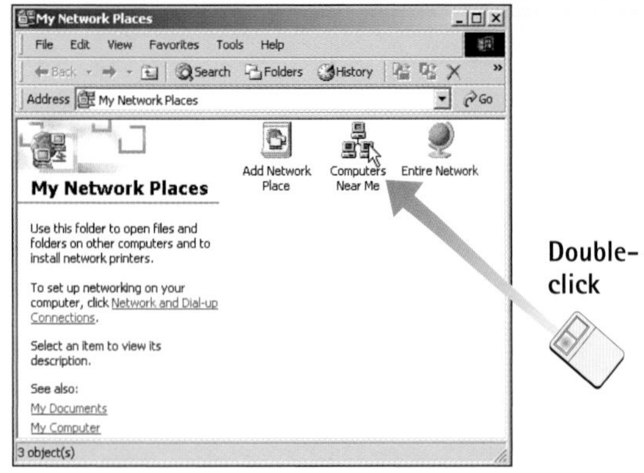

Double-click

3 Open a Computer

The **Computers Near Me** window shows all of the other computers in your workgroup. Double-click a computer to open its window.

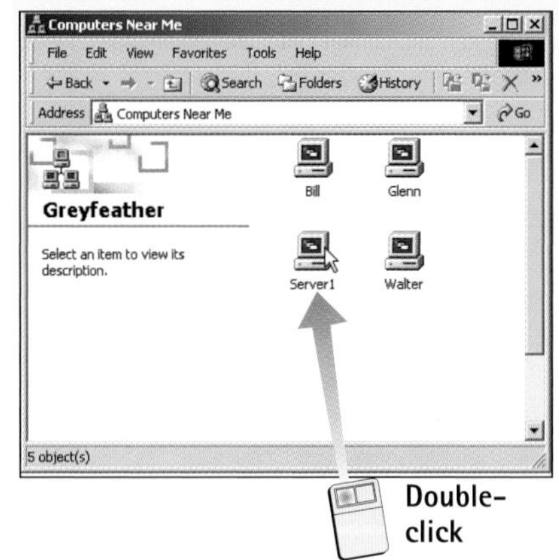

Double-click

4 Open a Shared Folder

After you open a particular computer, all of the resources shared on that computer are shown in this window. This includes shared folders, files, and printers. Double-click any shared object to open it.

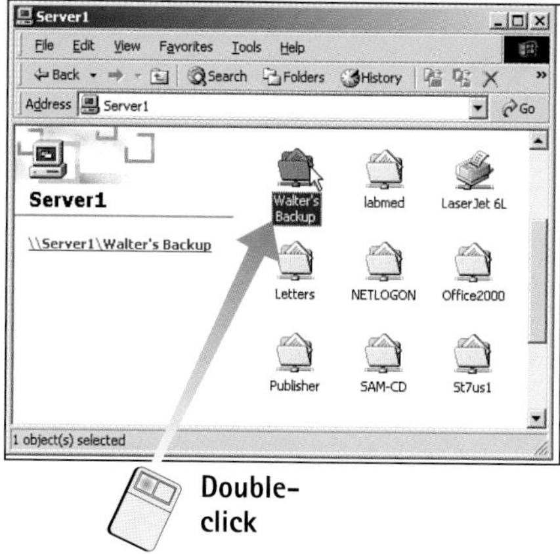

5 Open a File

You can use items in a shared folder just as you use items on your own computer. For example, double-click a file to open it.

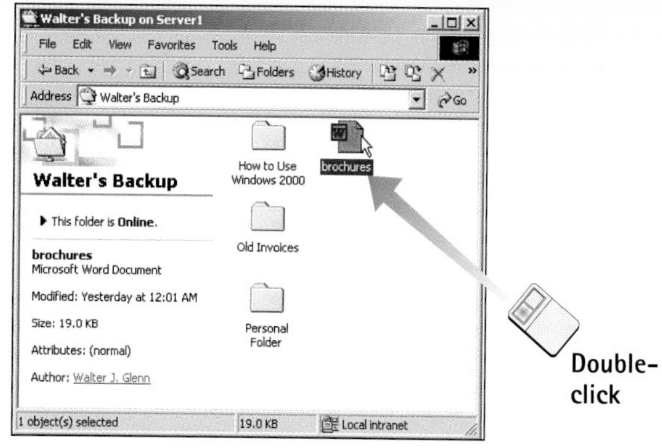

6 Copy a File to Your Computer

Instead of just opening and modifying a file on someone else's computer, you might want to copy it to your computer. To do that, just drag the file directly onto your desktop or into any open folder on your desktop.

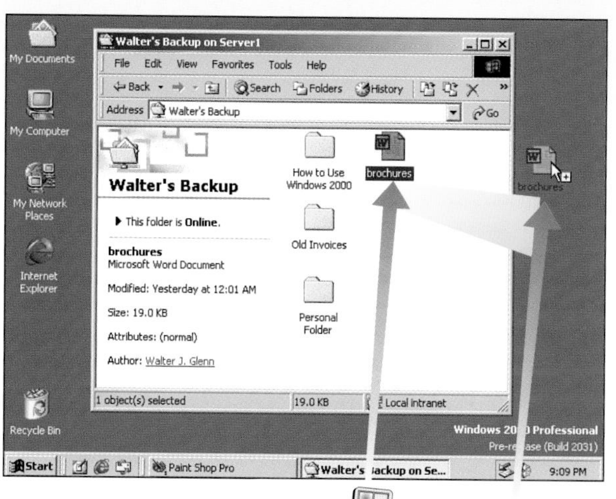

End

How-To Hints

Using Files and Folders

For more information on using files and folders, see Part 2, "Working with Files and Folders."

TASK 2

How to Add a Network Place

Although you can use **My Network Places** to browse the network looking for the right folder, you might want to add frequently used shared folders on your network, Web sites, or even FTP sites directly to the **My Network Places** window. This lets you quickly get to files you use often.

Begin

1 Add a Network Place

Double-click **Add Network Place** to launch the Add Network Place Wizard.

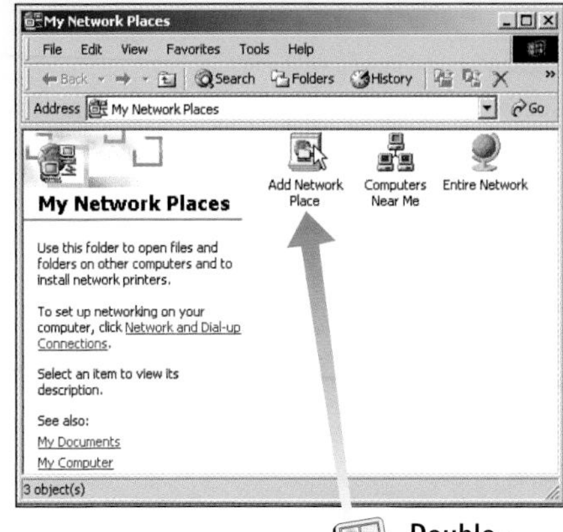

2 Browse for a Computer

If you know the exact path to the network resource you want, you can enter it in the text box. Otherwise, just click the **Browse** button.

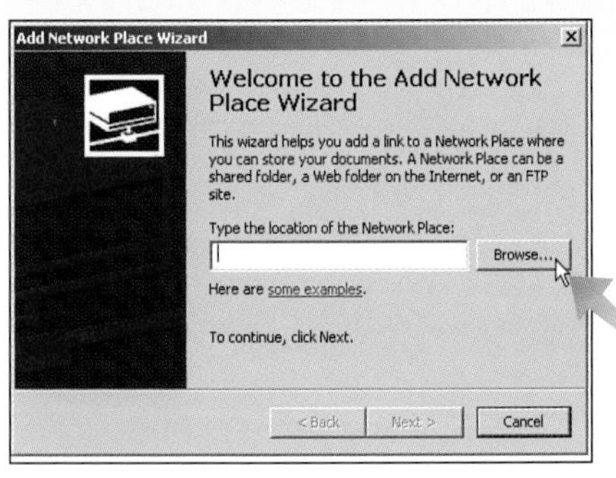

3 Select the Computer You Want

This window lists all the computers in your domain or workgroup. Select the computer that contains the shared resource you want from the list and click **OK**.

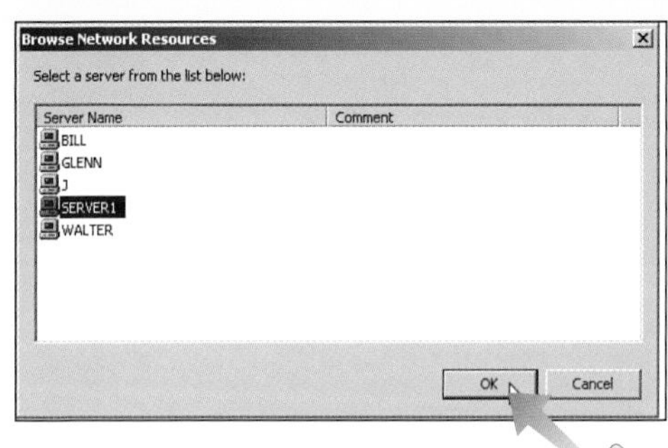

4 Click Next

The path for the server you've chosen appears in the text box. Click **Next** to go on.

5 Select a Shared Folder on the Computer

From the list of shared folders on the chosen computer, select the folder you want to make a new network place from and click **Next**.

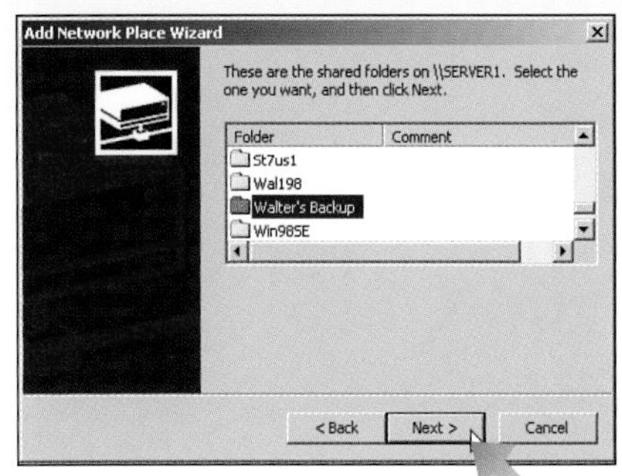

6 Finish

Change the name of the new network place if you want to and then click **Finish**.

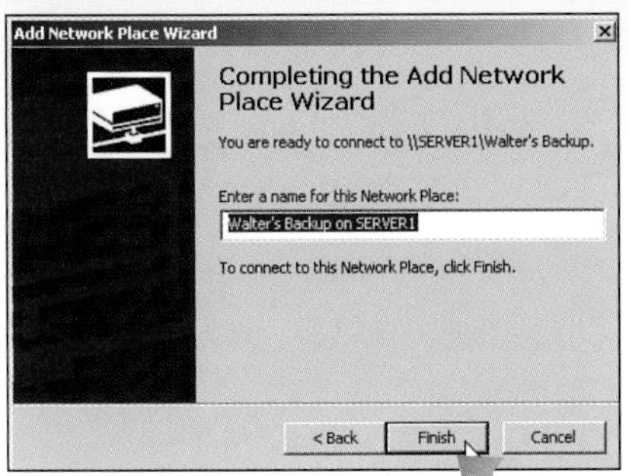

7 Open the New Network Place

The new network place appears in the **My Network Places** window for easy access. To open it, just double-click the **My Network Places** icon.

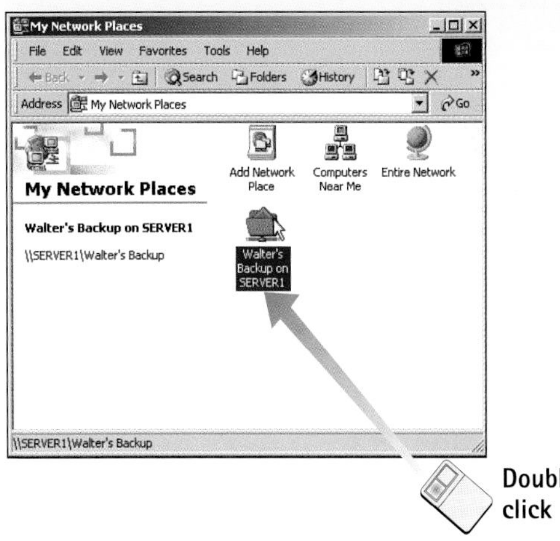

End

TASK 3

How to Find a Computer on the Network

Using the **My Network Places** window to browse your network and look for a computer works fine if there are not a lot of computers on your network. Sometimes, however, the list of computers can be so long that scrolling through looking for a particular computer can be quite time consuming. Fortunately, Windows lets you quickly find a computer on the network, even if you know only part of its name.

Begin

1 Open My Network Places

Double-click the **My Network Places** icon on your desktop to open the **My Network Places** window.

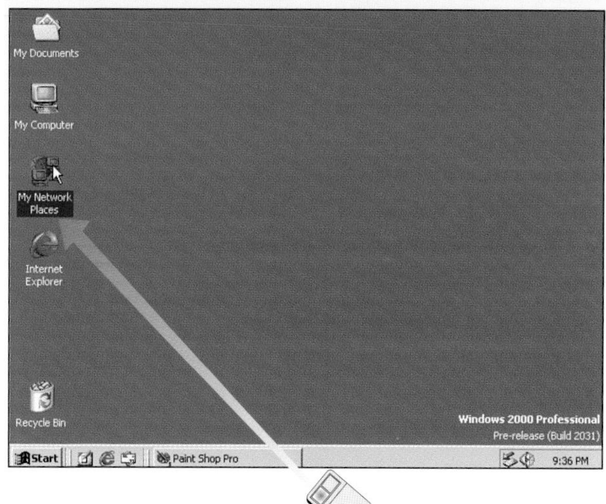

2 Open the Search Pane

Click the **Search** button on the toolbar to open a search pane in the left part of the **My Network Places** window.

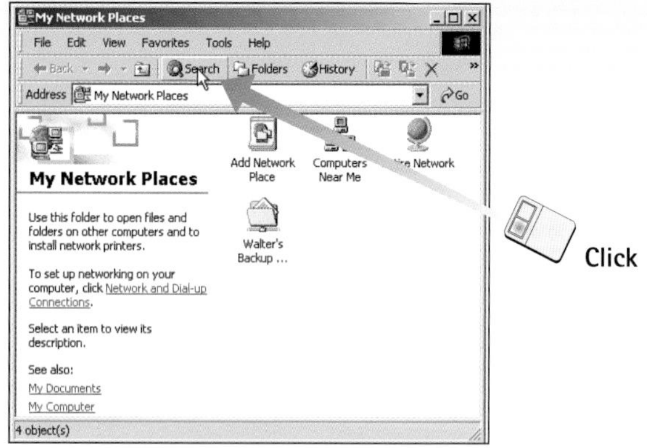

3 Enter a Computer Name

Enter the name of the computer you are looking for in the **Computer Name** text box. You can even enter part of a name if you don't remember the whole thing.

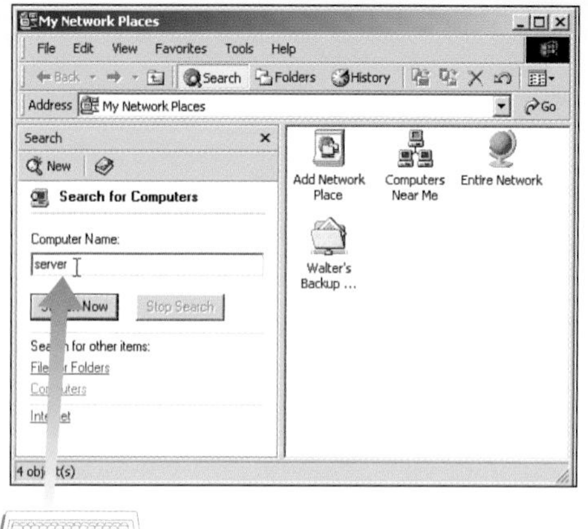

4 Search for the Computer

Click the **Search Now** button to begin the search. Search results are displayed in the right-hand pane of the window.

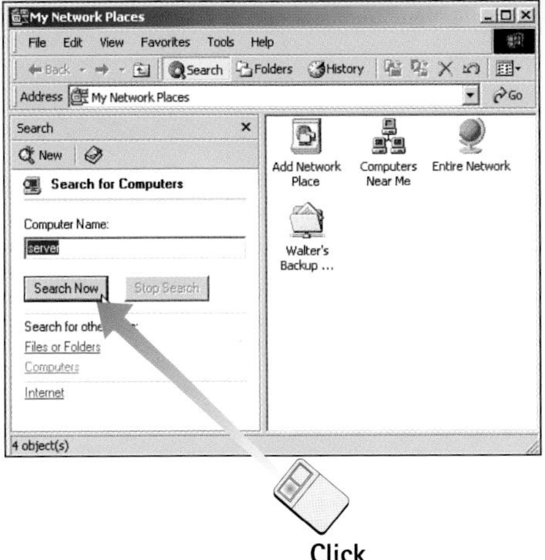

5 Open the Computer

You can open any computer displayed in the search results simply by double-clicking it.

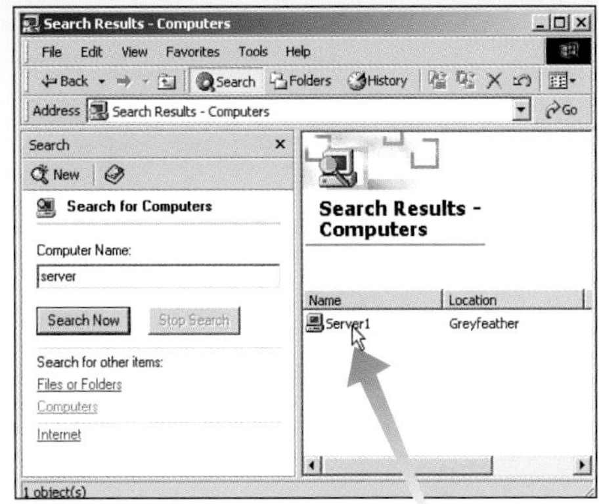

6 Close the Search Pane

Click the **Search** button on the toolbar again to close the search pane and get back to work.

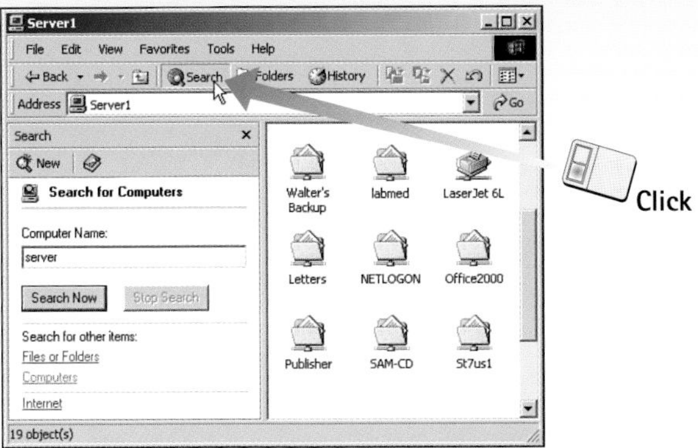

End

How-To Hints

Start a New Search

To clear the current search results and the Computer Name text box so that you can begin a new search, click the **New** button at the top of the Search pane.

TASK 4

How to Find a File on the Network

Windows does not really have the built-in capability to search an entire network full of computers for a particular file. However, it is easy enough to perform a regular search on a shared folder. This, at least, saves you from having to rummage through the shared folder and its subfolders yourself. The trick is to at least know the computer and shared folder that hold the document you are looking for.

Begin

1 Open Computers Near Me

Double-click the **Computers Near Me** icon to open the **Computers Near Me** window.

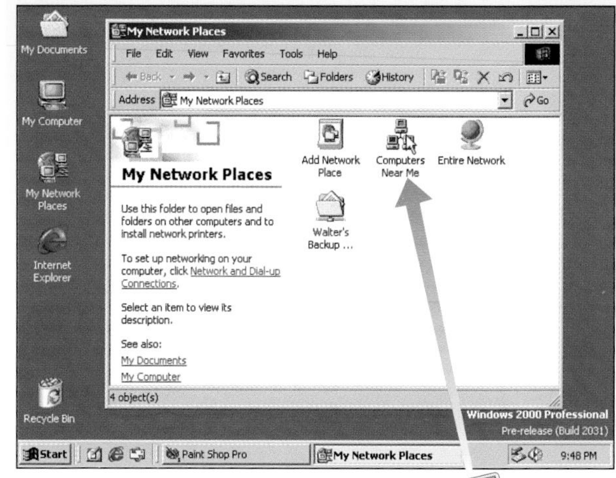

2 Open a Computer

Double-click the computer on which you want to search for a file.

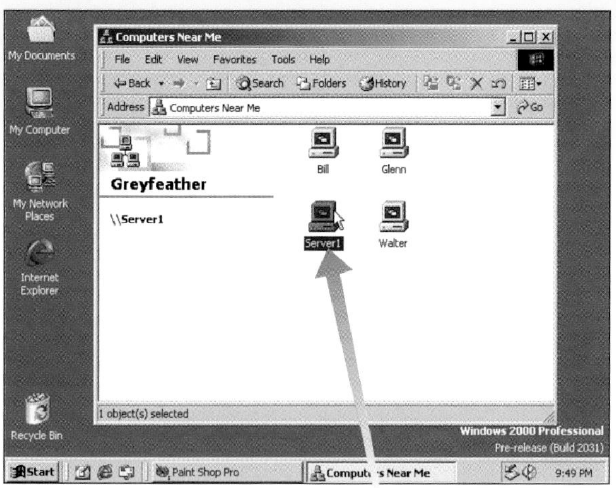

3 Search a Shared Folder

Find the shared folder in which you want to search for a file. Right-click the folder and choose **Search** from the shortcut menu that appears.

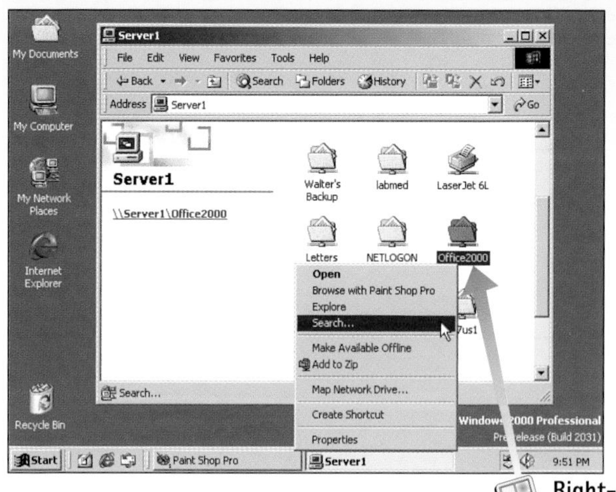

4 Enter the Name of a File

Enter the name of a file you want to search for in the text box. You can also enter part of a name if you don't remember the whole thing.

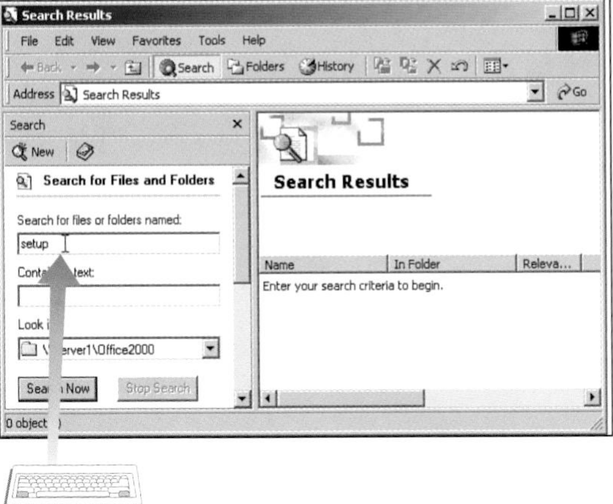

5 Search for the File

Click the **Search Now** button to begin the search. Results are displayed in the right-hand pane.

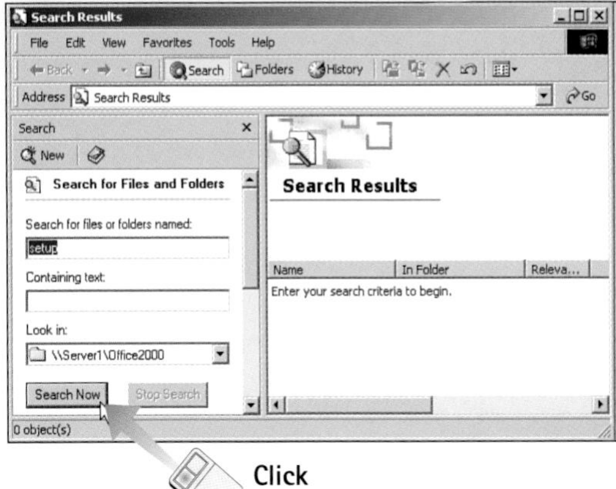

6 Open the File

After you find the file you are looking for, double-click to open it, or drag it to your desktop to copy it to your computer.

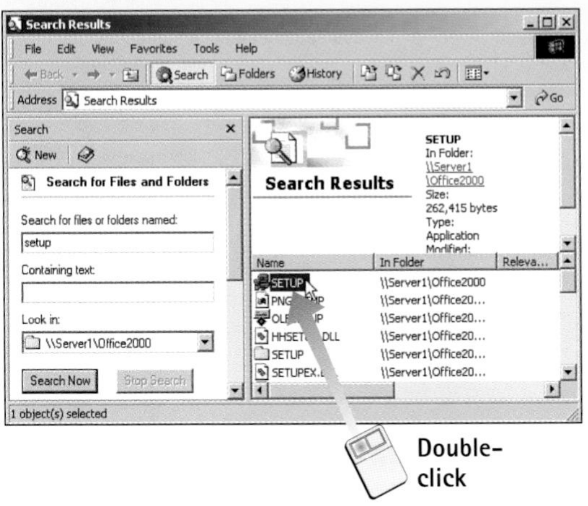

End

How-To Hints

Search from the Start Menu

You can also get to the **Search** window by choosing **Search for Files and Folders** from the **Start** menu. When the **Search** window appears, enter the filename and use the **Look In** drop-down list to browse to the shared folder you want to search.

TASK 5

How to Share a File or Folder with Others

In addition to giving you access to other user's files, folders, and printers, networks allow you to share your resources with other users. To share resources, your computer must be on a network and your network administrator must have already set your computer up so that you can share items with others.

Begin

1 Open the Sharing Dialog Box

Using the **My Computer** or **My Documents** window, find the object you want to share. Right-click it and choose **Sharing** from the shortcut menu to open the **Sharing** tab of the folder's **Properties** window.

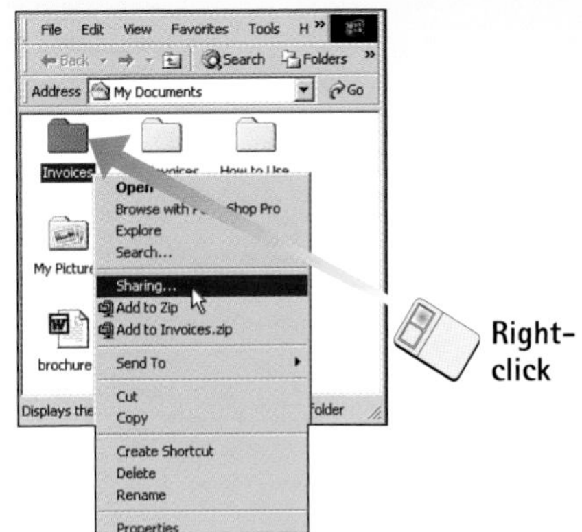

2 Share the Folder

Click the **Share This Folder** option to enable sharing of the folder.

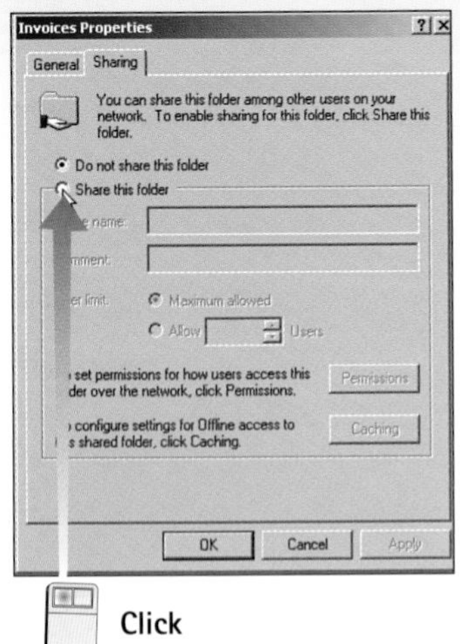

3 Change the Share Name

If you want, enter a new share name for the folder you are sharing in the text box.

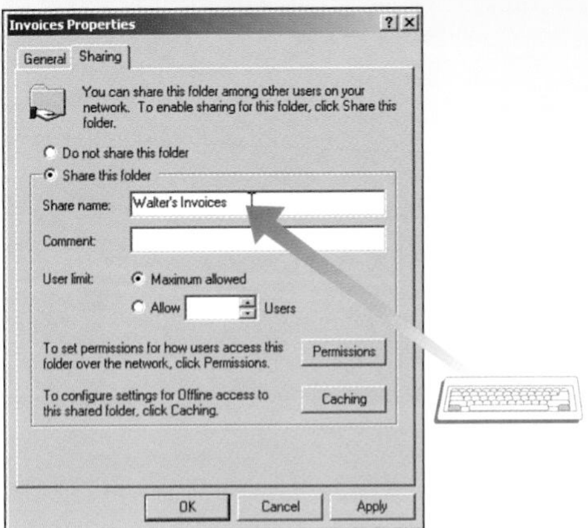

4 Add a Comment

Optionally, you can add a comment to the shared folder to give other users a better idea of what the folder contains. Just click the text box and type your comment.

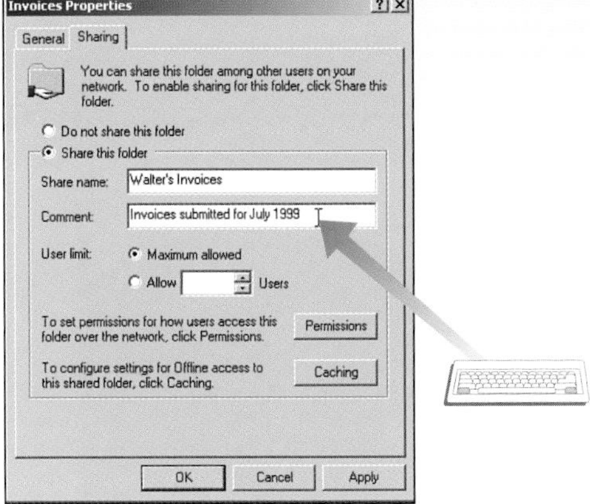

5 Limit Users

The maximum number of users that can connect to a single computer running Windows 2000 Professional at one time is ten. If you want to lower this limit, click the **Allow** option and then click the down arrow to lower the number in the box. Too many users at once can slow your computer down.

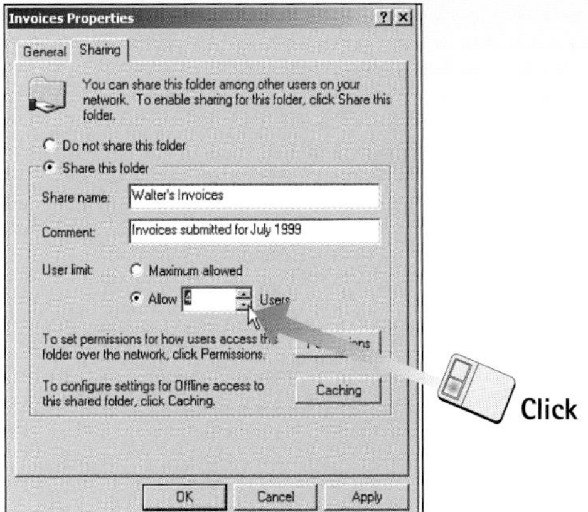

6 Close the Properties Window

Click **OK** to close the **Properties** window. Users can now access the folder you just shared.

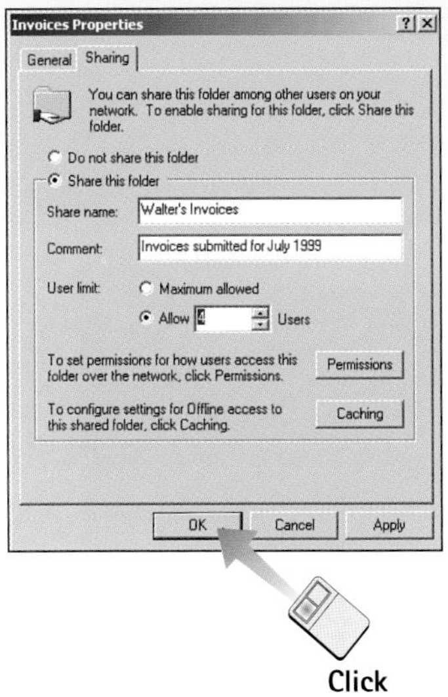

End

How-To Hints

How Do You Know It's Shared?

A shared file or folder shows up on your computer as a standard icon with a hand underneath the icon.

Setting Permissions

By using the procedure outlined in this task, you are sharing a resource with everyone on a network. See Part 8, "Protecting Your Files," for more on sharing with only some users.

TASK 6

How to Map a Network Drive

Earlier in this part, you learned how to add a new Network Place so that you could access frequently used shared folders more easily. Before there was such a thing as Network Places, this was done by mapping a network drive. When you map a network drive, you essentially tell your computer to treat a shared resource as a drive on your computer—it even gets its own drive letter and shows up in the **My Computer** window. Older programs sometimes don't know how to use **Network Places** and can only open files on real disk drives. By mapping a network drive, you can fool these programs into thinking that a shared folder is a real disk drive.

Begin

1 Open Computers Near Me

In the **My Network Places** window, double-click the **Computers Near Me** icon.

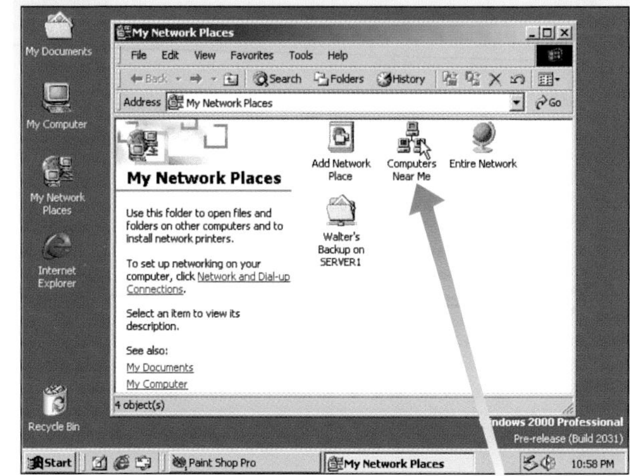

2 Open A Computer

Find the computer that contains the shared folder you want to map as a network drive and double-click it.

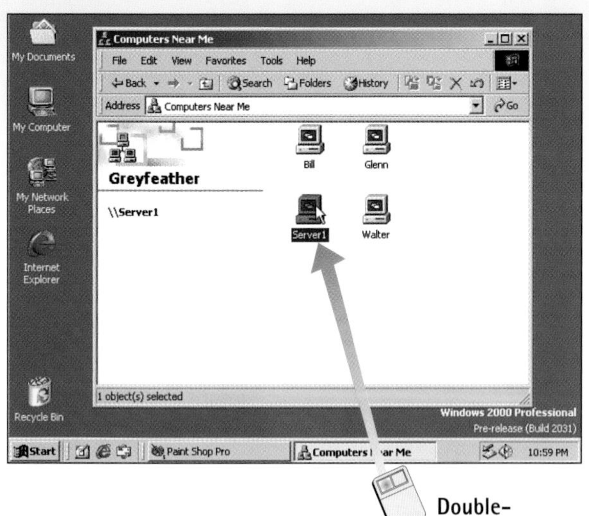

3 Select a Shared Folder

Find the shared folder you want to map and select it by clicking it once.

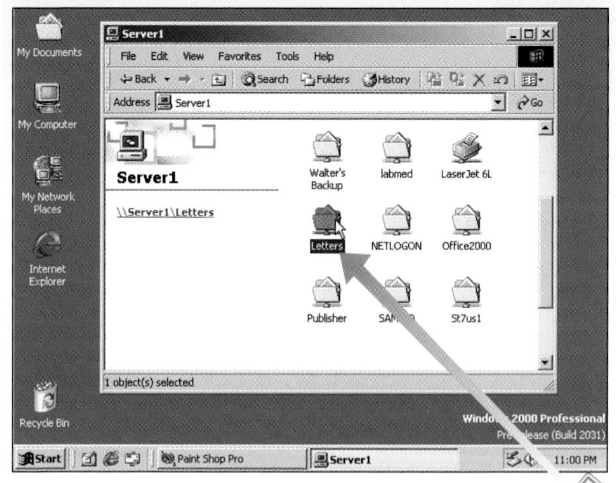

4 Choose Map Network Drive

From the **File** menu, choose the **Map Network Drive** command.

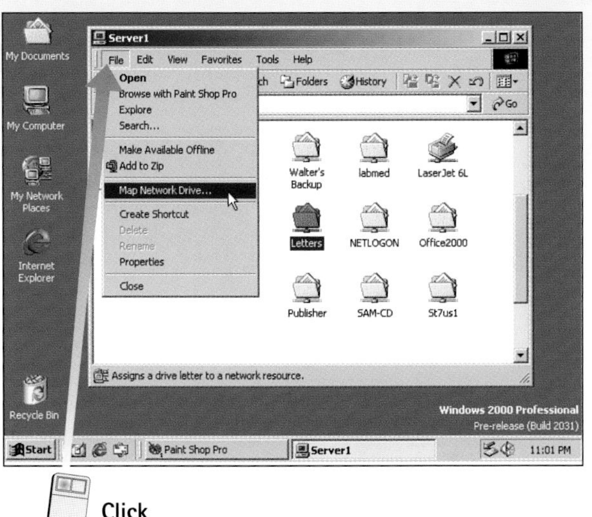

Click

5 Select a Drive Letter

Select a drive letter using the drop-down menu. Only letters that are not already used are listed, so don't worry about conflicts.

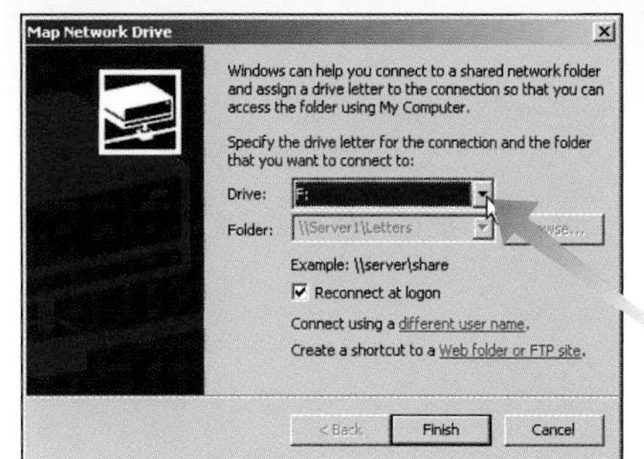

Click

6 Reconnect at Logon

If you want the network drive to be remapped to the same drive letter each time you log on to your computer, click the **Reconnect at Logon** option. When you're done, click **Finish**.

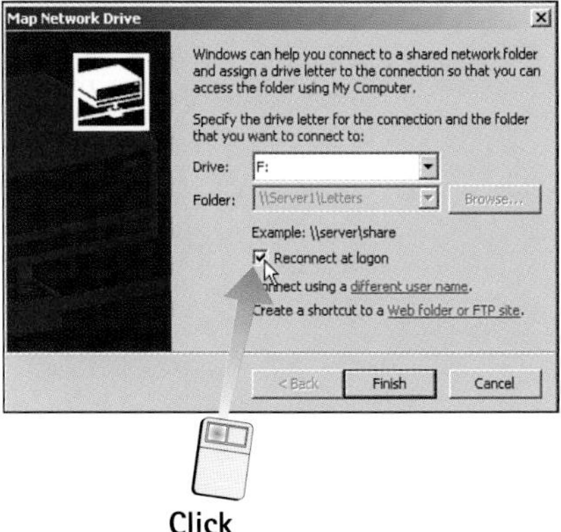

Click

7 View the New Drive

In the **My Computer** window, the new network drive appears using the drive letter you assigned it. Network drives look like a regular disk drive with a network cable attached.

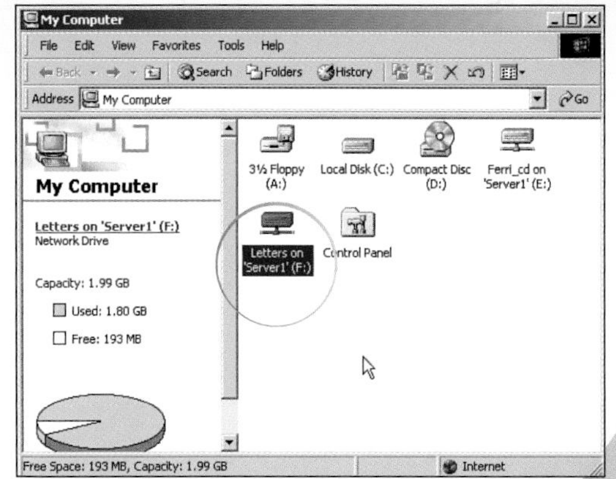

End

Task

PART 5

Working When Away from the Network

Many people work when away from the network. Some connect to the network over a modem, some take work home with them on disk, and some actually take their computers off the network and on the road with them. Windows 2000 Professional offers two distinct ways to work when you are away from the network. The first is a utility named the Windows Briefcase. The second way is to use offline folders.

The briefcase is a specialized folder that is designed primarily for users who want to take work home with them using a floppy or other type of removable disk. All you have to do is copy files from your work computer into the briefcase, move the briefcase to a floppy disk, and carry the disk home with you. At home, you can work on and save the files right in the briefcase. In the morning, carry the disk back to work, move the briefcase back onto that computer, and synchronize the updated files in the briefcase with the originals on your hard disk. Offline folders are a technology designed for those who actually take their computer away from the network, as with a notebook computer, or who dial into the network periodically with a modem. You can mark any shared folder available on the network to be available offline. The contents of these folders are actually copied to the hard drive on your computer. When you are disconnected from the network, you can work on any of these files. When you reconnect to the network, the files are synchronized with the originals. Some people also use offline folders while they are still connected to the network. This allows them to work on copies of the original files instead of on the originals themselves.

TASK 1

How to Create and Fill a Briefcase

Creating a briefcase in Windows is pretty easy, and after it is created, you can move files into and out of it the same way you move other folders on your computer. You can create a briefcase directly on the desktop or in any folder using the same method.

Begin

1 Create the New Briefcase

Right-click any empty space on your desktop, point to **New** on the shortcut menu, and then choose **Briefcase**.

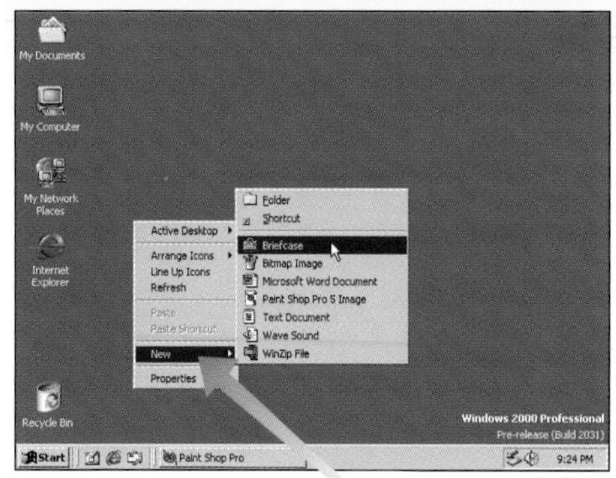

Right-click

2 Open the New Briefcase

Double-click the **New Briefcase** icon to open it. You are shown a welcome screen the first time you open any new briefcase that gives you a brief introduction to using it.

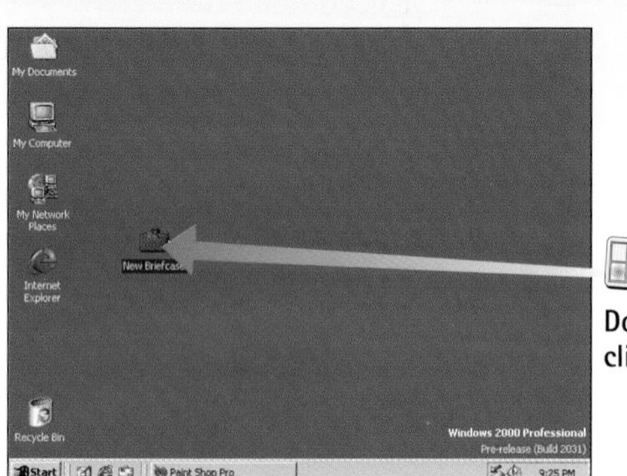

Double-click

3 Open My Documents

Double-click the **My Documents** icon on the desktop to open the **My Documents** window.

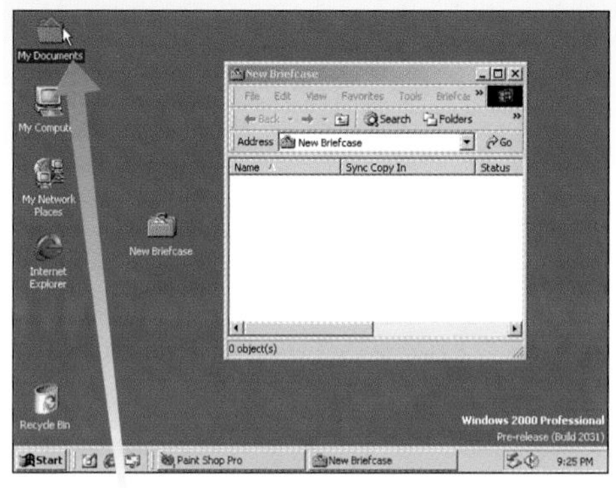

Double-click

4 Tile Windows Vertically

Right-click a blank space on the taskbar and choose **Tile Windows Vertically** so that you can see both the **My Documents** and the **New Briefcase** windows side by side.

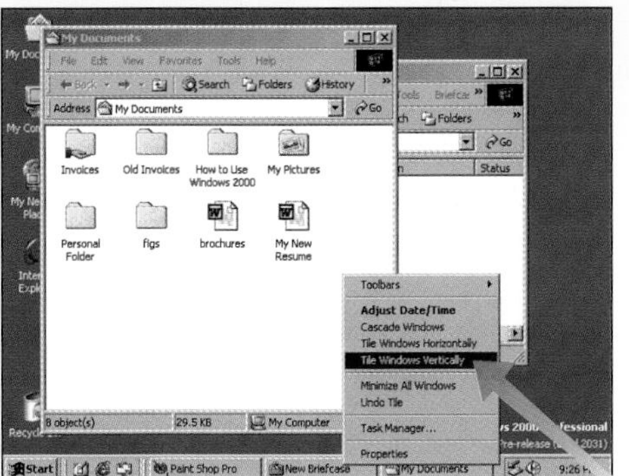

5 Drag a File or Folder to the Briefcase

Copy any file or folder to your briefcase by simply dragging it to the **New Briefcase** window. You can copy as many files and folders as you want.

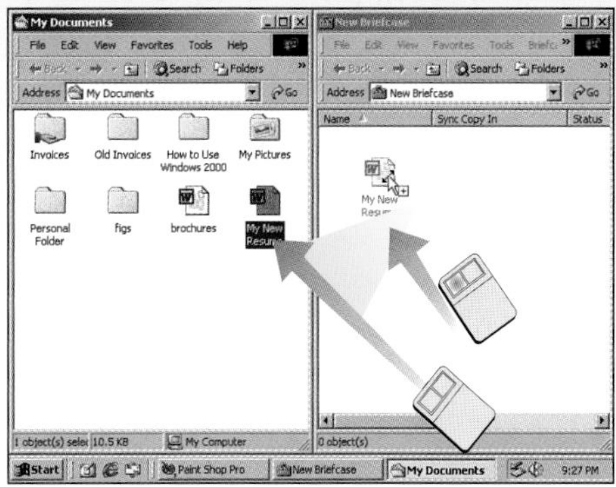

End

How-To Hints

Watch Your Disk Space

If you are using a floppy disk to take your work home, remember not to copy more files to your briefcase than the disk can hold. Find out how big a briefcase is by right-clicking it and choosing **Properties** from the shortcut menu.

Rename Your Briefcase

Rename your briefcase the same way you do any folder. Just right-click it and choose **Rename** from the shortcut menu. See Part 2, "Working with Files and Folders," for more on renaming folders.

TASK 2

How to Take a Briefcase Home

Taking a briefcase home is really as simple as copying it to a floppy disk (or other removable disk). Any computer running Windows 95/98, Windows NT 4.0, or Windows 2000 will recognize the briefcase for what it is.

Begin

1 Open My Computer

Double-click the **My Computer** icon on your desktop to open **the My Computer** window.

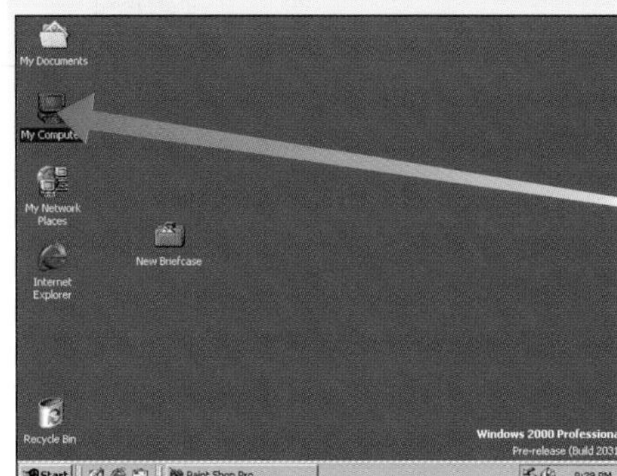

Double-click

2 Move the Briefcase to Your Floppy Drive

Move your cursor over the briefcase, click and hold the left mouse button, and drag the briefcase over the floppy drive in the **My Computer** window. Release the mouse button to move the briefcase. You can also right-click the briefcase and choose the **Send To > 3$^1/_2$" floppy A:** command from the shortcut menu.

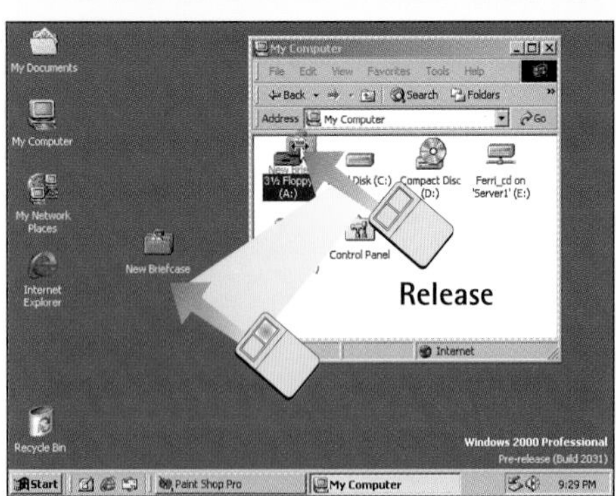

Click & Drag

3 Open the Briefcase on Your Home Computer

At home, pop the floppy disk into your computer. Open the **My Computer** window, open the floppy drive, and then double-click the **New Briefcase** icon to open the briefcase.

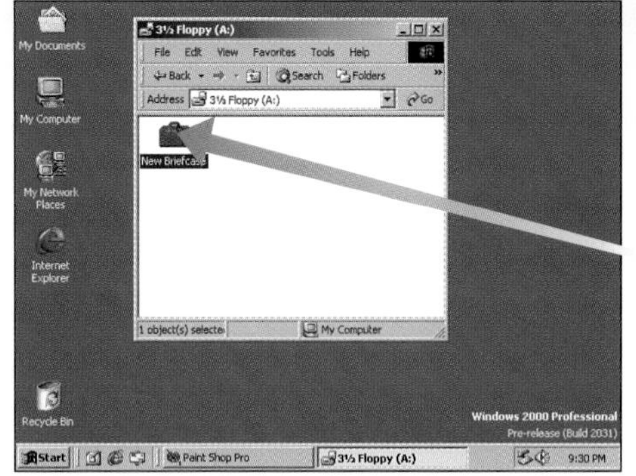

Double-click

4

In the briefcase, find the file you want to work on and double-click to open it.

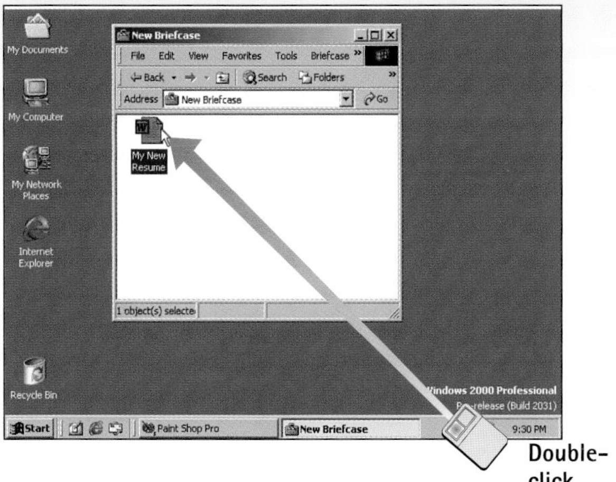

5 Save Your File

Your file opens in whatever application was used to create it. So, for example, you need to have Microsoft Word installed on your home computer to open a Word file. When you're done working, save the file in the normal manner. The file is updated in the briefcase.

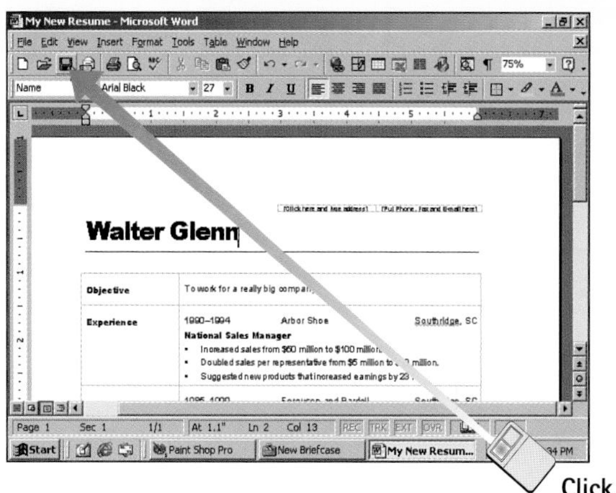

6 Move the Briefcase to Your Work Computer

When you get back to work, put the floppy disk in your computer, open the **My Computer** window, open the floppy drive, and drag the briefcase onto your desktop. In Task 3, you'll see how to update your files with the originals.

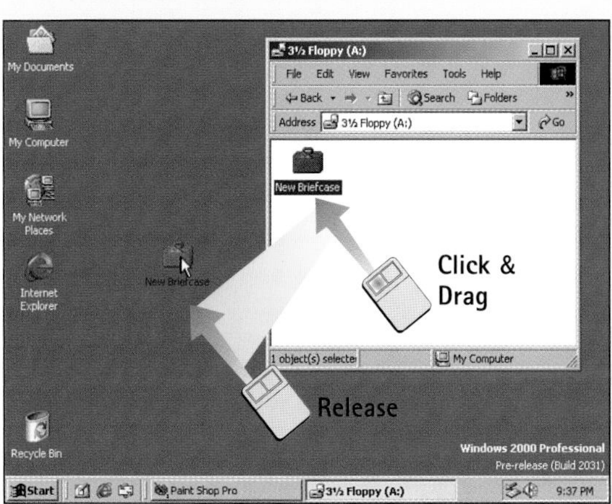

End

How-To Hints

Speed Up Access

Working from a floppy disk can significantly increase the time required to open and save files. You can move the briefcase to your home computer to speed things up and then back to floppy when you're done.

TASK 3

How to Update Files in a Briefcase

Now that you are back at work, you have files in your briefcase that have changed from the originals that are still on your computer. The next step is to update the original files. You do this from within your briefcase.

Begin

1 Open Your Briefcase

Double-click the **New Briefcase** icon to open the **New Briefcase** window.

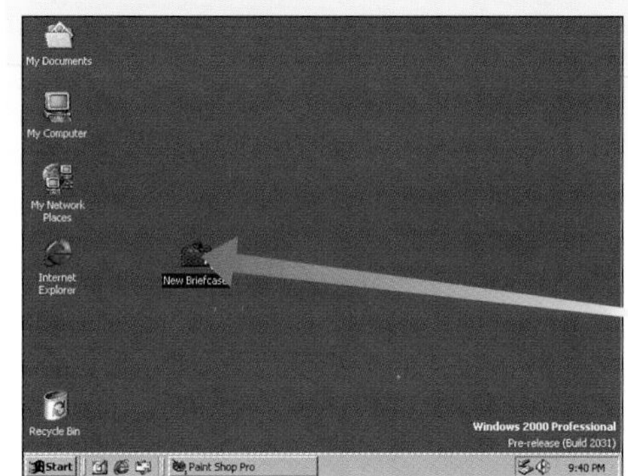

Double-click

2 Note the Status of Files

In the **Briefcase** window, switch to **Details** view on the **View** menu. The status column tells you which files need to be updated.

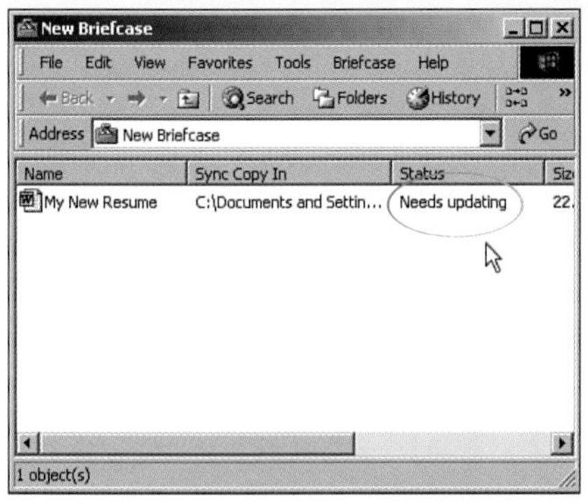

3 Select a File That Needs Updating

Select any file you want to update by clicking it once. You can select additional files by holding down the **CTRL** key while you click other files.

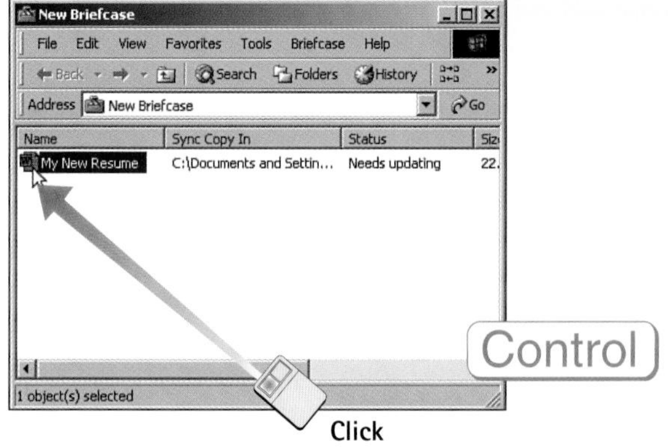

4 Update Selection

From the **File** menu, choose the **Update** command to update the selected files.

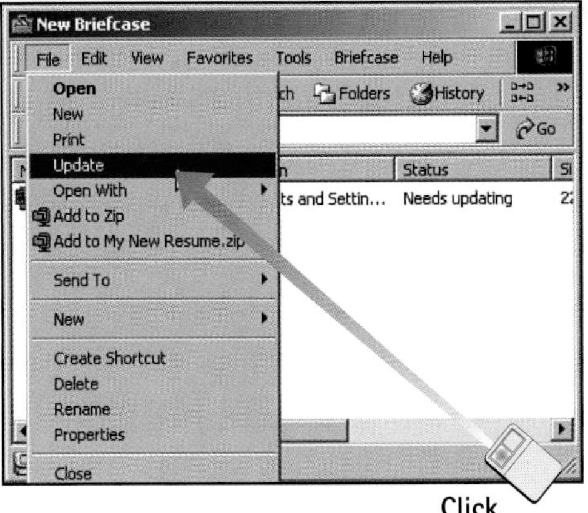

5 Review the Update

After you choose the **Update** command, you are given the chance to review the updates in the **Update** window. The version in the briefcase is shown on the left. The original is shown on the right. The arrow in between indicates which version needs to be updated.

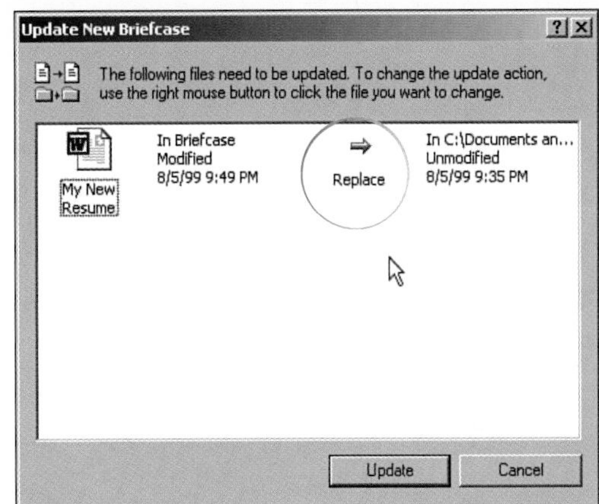

6 Update the File

When you are ready to begin the update, just click the **Update** button.

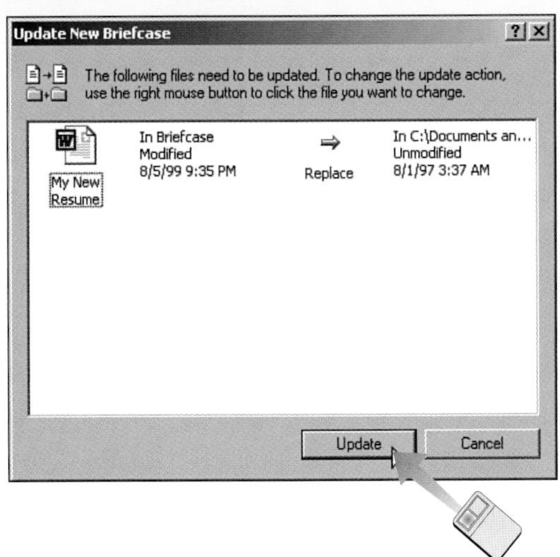

End

How-To Hints

Update All

Use the **Update All** button on the toolbar to update all the files in the briefcase that need to be updated.

Resolving Conflicts

If the **Update** window shows a red arrow pointing down between the two versions of a file, it means that each version has been updated since the original was copied to the briefcase. When this happens, you need to open both versions and figure out for yourself which is the most recent.

TASK 4

How to Make Items Available Offline

If you connect to a network over a modem or take your whole computer away from the network, you'll find offline folders very helpful. You can make any shared folder on the network available as an offline folder so that you can use the files inside when you disconnect from the network. The first time you set up offline access for an item, a wizard walks you through the process. After that, you'll do it man-ually. The following steps take you through the man-ual process.

Begin

1 Open My Network Places

Double-click the **My Network Places** icon to open the **My Network Places** window.

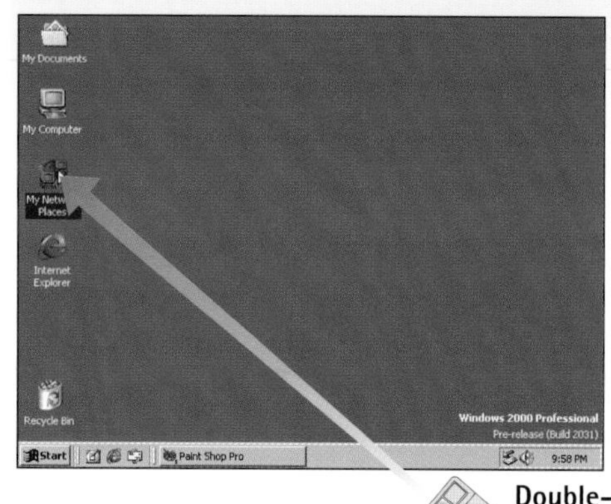

Double-click

2 Open Computers Near Me

Double-click the **Computers Near Me** icon to open the **Computers Near Me** window.

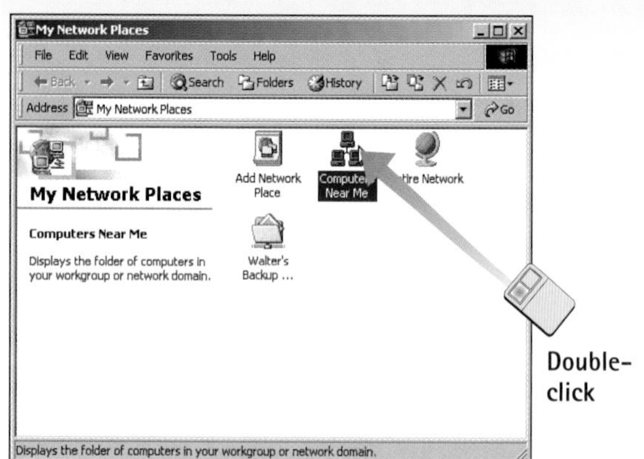

Double-click

3 Open a Computer

Double-click any computer to open its window.

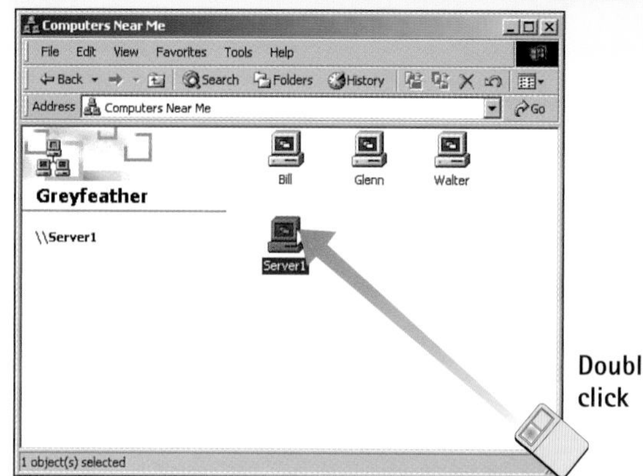

Double-click

4 Locate a Shared Folder

Scroll through the computer window to find a shared folder you want to make available offline.

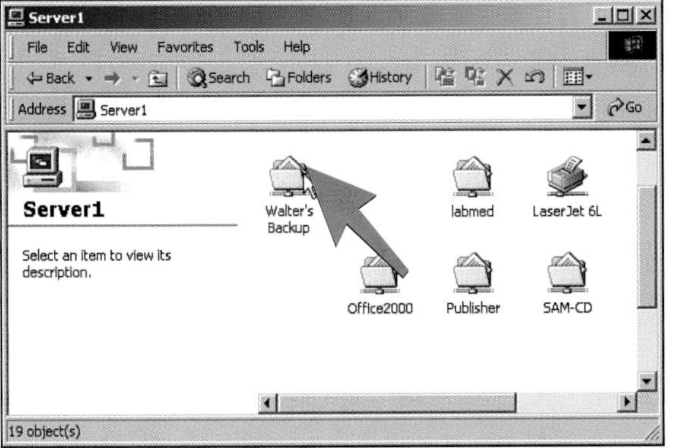

5 Make It Available Offline

Right-click the folder you want to make available offline and choose **Make Available Offline** from the shortcut menu.

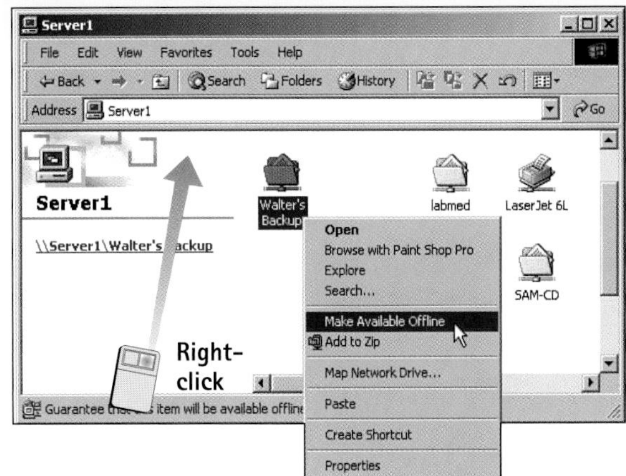

6 Make Subfolders Available

You can decide whether to make just the folder you selected available offline or all of its subfolders available, as well.

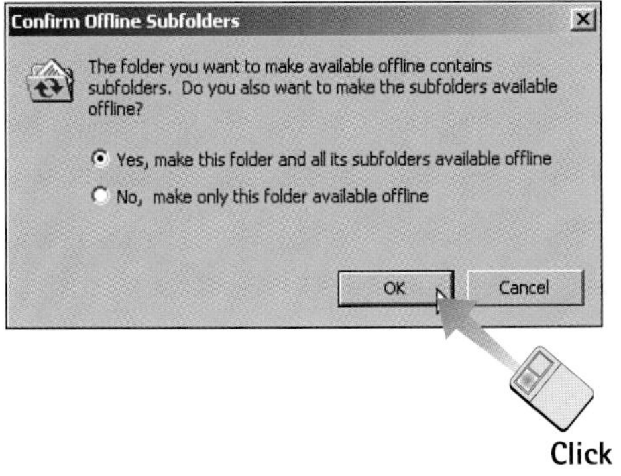

End

How-To Hints

Make an Item Unavailable

After you make a folder available offline, you can make it unavailable again by right-clicking the folder and choosing the **Make Available Offline** command from the shortcut menu again. The temporary files are removed from your hard drive.

Task 5

How to Use Offline Items

After you set up a folder to be available offline, it is surprisingly easy to use. All you have to do is open **My Network Places** and browse to the folder the same way you do when you are connected to the network. When you are offline, only the folders configured for offline use are visible.

Begin

1 Open My Network Places

Double-click the **My Network Places** icon to open the **My Network Places** window.

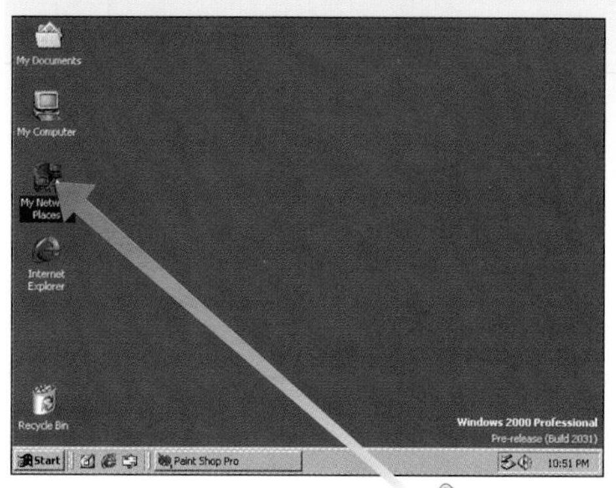

Double-click

2 Open Computers Near Me

Double-click the **Computers Near Me** icon to open the **Computers Near Me** window.

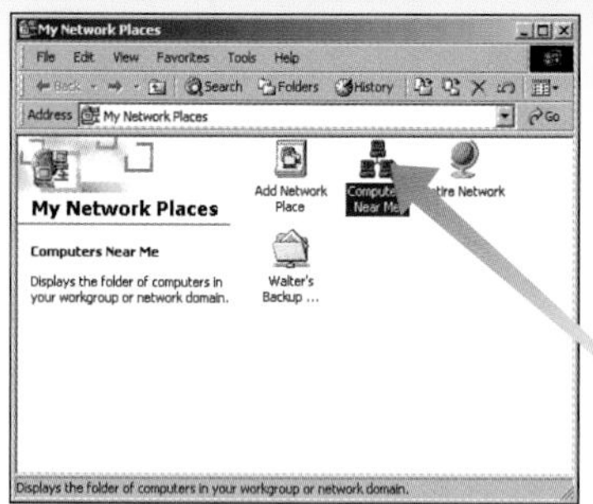

Double-click

3 Open a Computer

When you are disconnected from the network, only computers that have shared folders configured for offline use are visible in the **Computers Near Me** window. Double-click the computer's icon to open it.

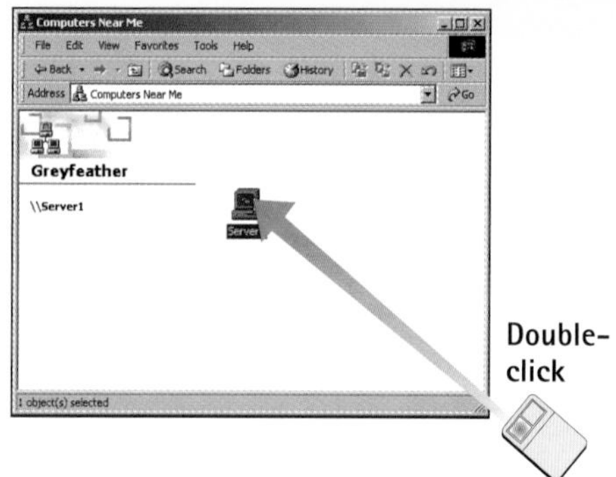

Double-click

4 Open an Offline Folder

When you open a computer, only the shared folders configured for offline use show up in the computer's window—these are called offline folders. Double-click any offline folder to open it.

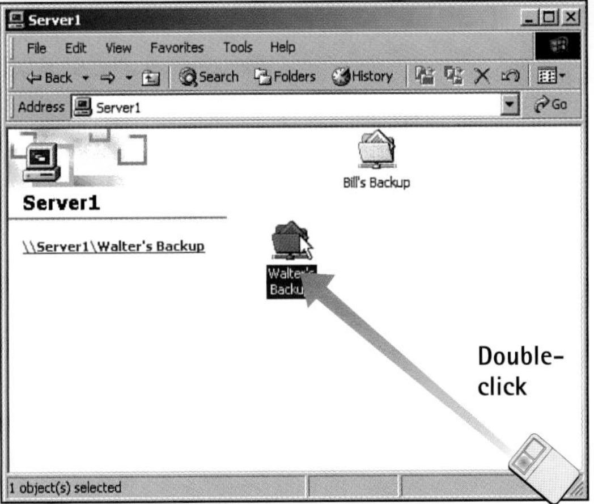

5 Open a File

Folders and files in an offline folder have two small arrows at the bottom left of their icons to show that they are offline copies of original files on the network. Double-click any file or folder to open it, just as you would with any regular file or folder.

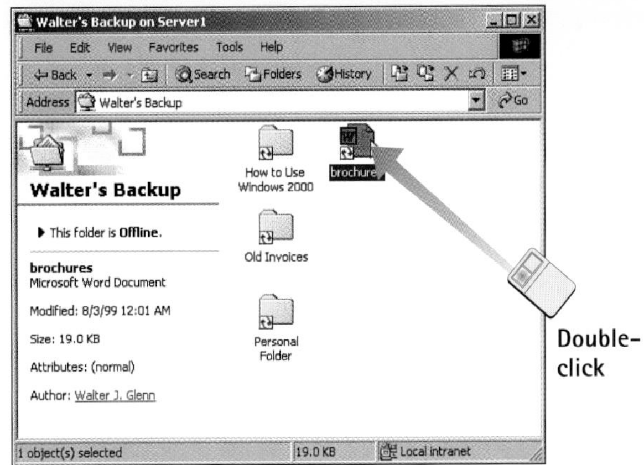

End

How-To Hints

Offline Permissions

When you are using offline folders and files, the same permissions apply to you that would apply if you were using the actual shared folders or files on the network. So don't think that you can bypass security just by using offline folders.

Your Network Places

If you have added any of your own network places that point to a shared folder (see Part 4, "Working on a Network," for more on this), you might notice there's no Make Available Offline command available on the network places shortcut menu. To make it available offline, you actually have to browse to the real shared folder the network place represents.

TASK 6

How to Synchronize Offline Items

By default, all you have to do is log back on to the network to automatically synchronize all of the files that you worked on while you were disconnected. For notebook users, this means hooking your computer back up to the network and logging on. For remote users, this means dialing in and logging on. If you are working with offline folders while you are still connected to the network, you have to synchronize files manually.

Begin

1 Synchronize a Specific Folder

To synchronize a specific offline folder or file, just right-click it and choose **Synchronize** from the shortcut menu. The item is synchronized with the original shared item on the network.

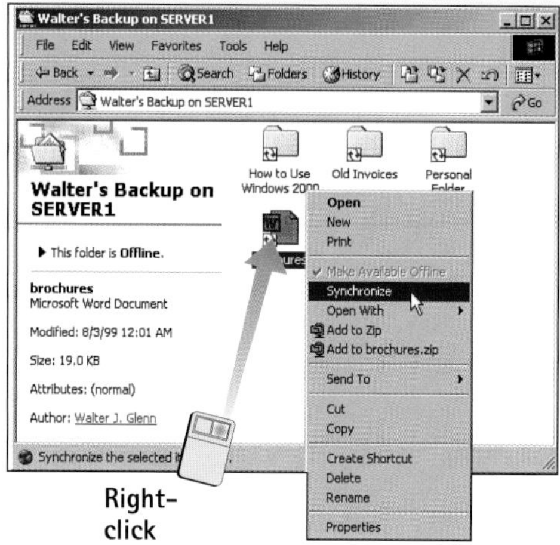

2 Synchronize Multiple Folders

You can also synchronize multiple folders and files at once. To do this, just click the **Tools** menu of any open folder on your computer and choose **Synchronize**.

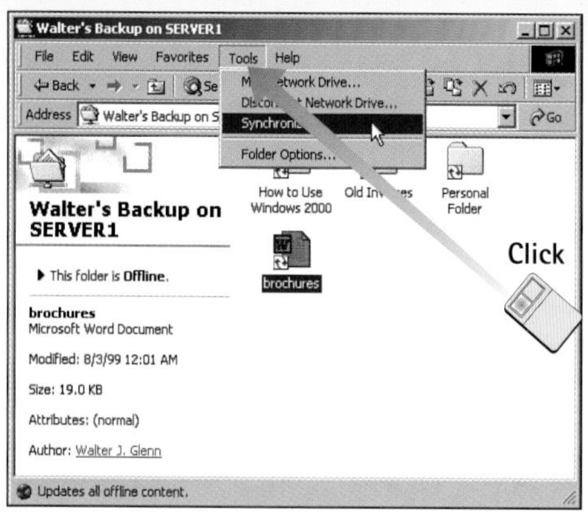

3 Choose Folders to Synchronize

On the **Items to Synchronize** dialog box, select the items you want to synchronize on the list and click **Synchronize** to begin.

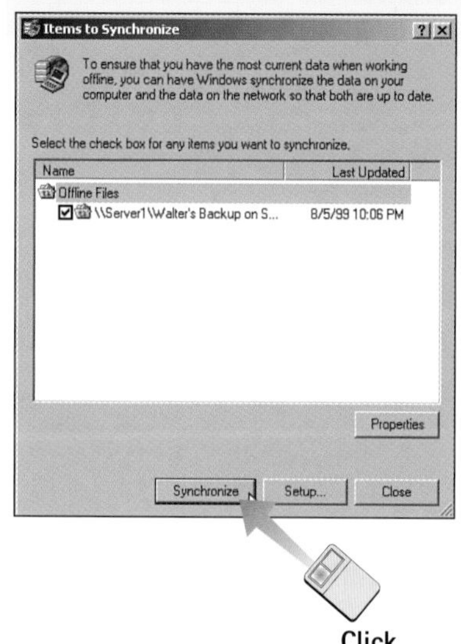

4 Set Up Automatic Synchronization

There are a few ways that you can configure the automatic synchronization of your files. Click the **Setup** button to open the **Synchronization Settings** dialog box.

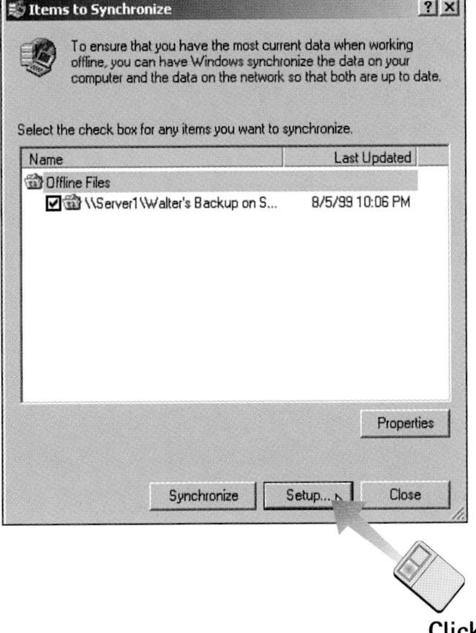

5 Set Up Logon/Logoff Synchronization

From the list, select the items that you want to be automatically synchronized when you log on and/or log off the network. Then choose whether you want the selected items to synchronize during logon, logoff, or both. You can also have Windows ask you before synchronizing any items.

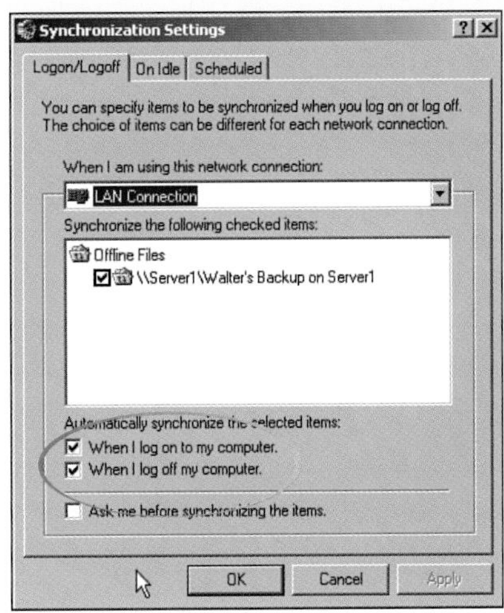

6 Switch to On Idle Tab

Click the **On Idle** tab to configure your computer to synchronize offline files during idle time, when your computer is not being used.

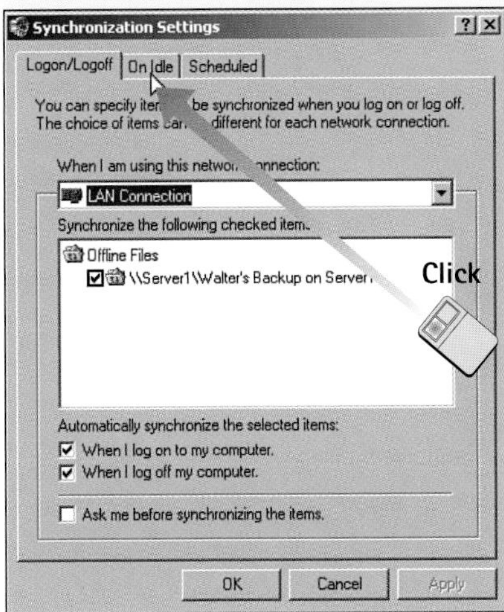

7 Set Up Idle Synchronization

Choose the folders you want to be synchronized during idle time from the list and click the synchronize while idle option. You can also click the **Advanced** button to specify how many minutes should pass before your computer is considered idle.

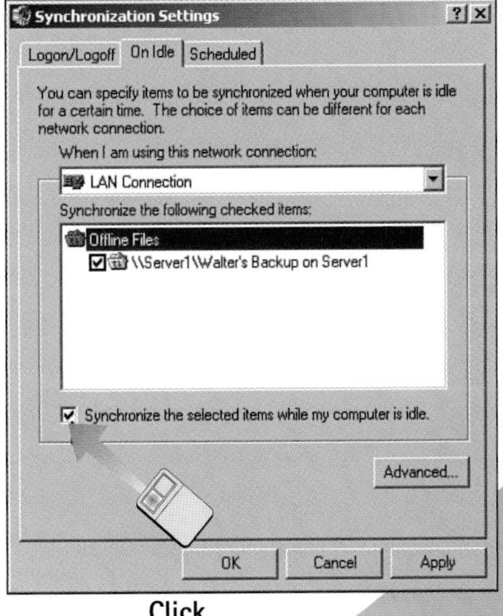

End

Task 7

How to Change Offline Settings

For the most part, the standard settings for offline folders should work pretty well. However, there are a few settings that might be useful to you.

Begin

1 Open Control Panel

Click the **Start** button, point to **Settings**, and then click **Control Panel**.

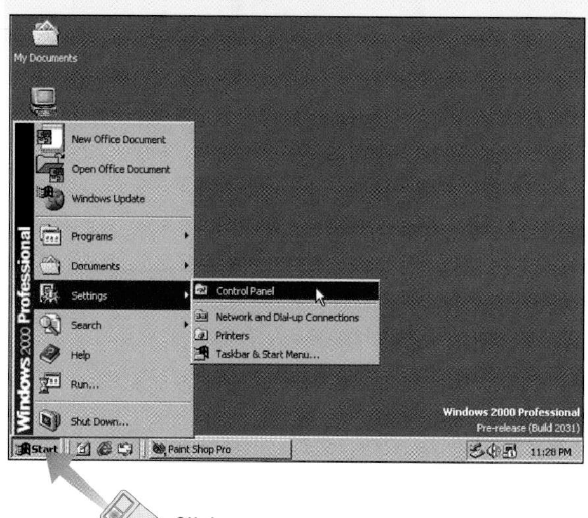

2 Open Folder Options

Double-click the **Folder Options** icon to open the **Folder Options Control Panel** applet. For more on using the Control Panel, see Part 9, "Changing Windows 2000 Settings." You can also open the **Folder Options** applet from the **View** menu of any open folder.

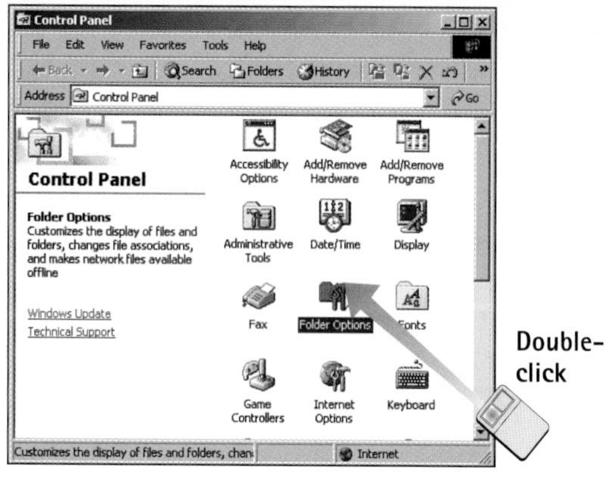

3 Open Offline Files Tab

Click the **Offline Files** tab.

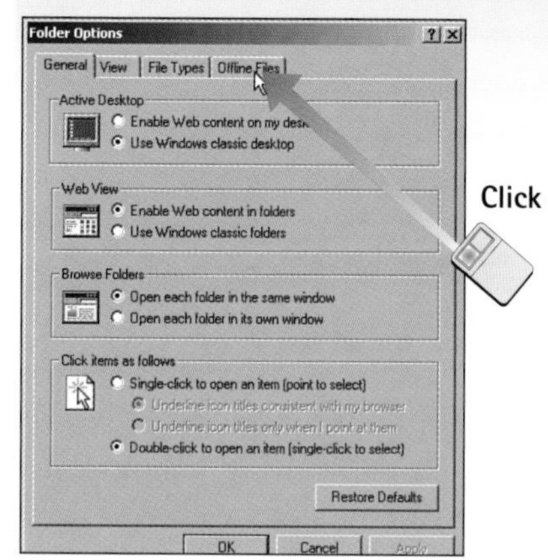

4 Synchronize at Log Off

By default, the **Synchronize All Offline Files Before Logging Off** option is turned on. If you prefer not to wait through this process each time you log off, turn this option on. Remember to synchronize your files before disconnecting from the network, though.

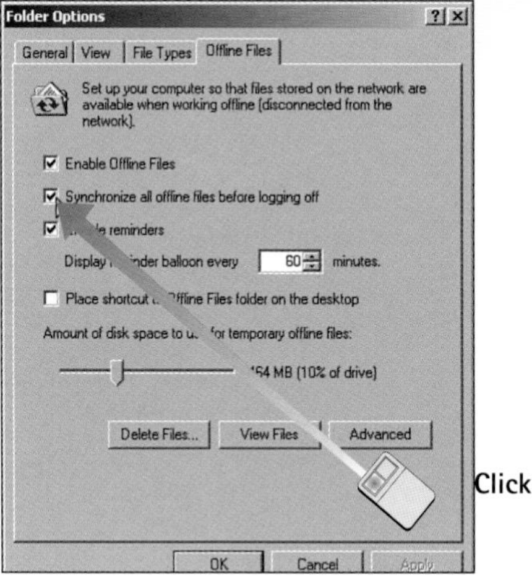

5 Enable Reminders

When the **Enable Reminders** option is turned on, a small icon appears in the system tray next to your clock to indicate that offline files are being used. In addition, a text bubble appears once in a while as yet another reminder. You can specify the interval at which this reminder appears.

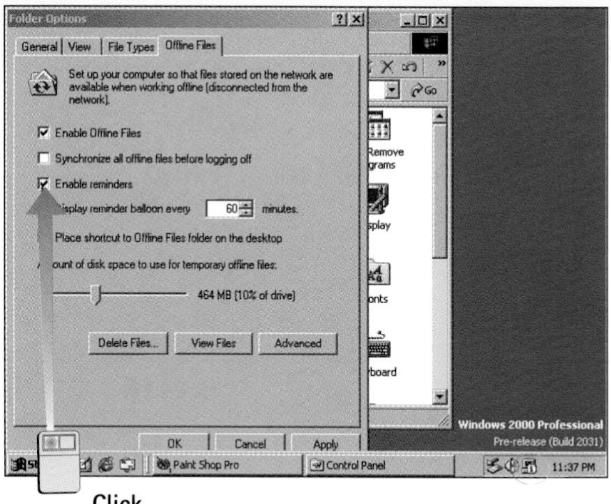

6 Place a Shortcut on the Desktop

When you turn on the **Place Shortcut to Offline Files Folder on the Desktop** option, a shortcut named Shortcut to Offline Files appears on the desktop. Double-clicking this shortcut opens a window that displays all of the files you have configured for offline use.

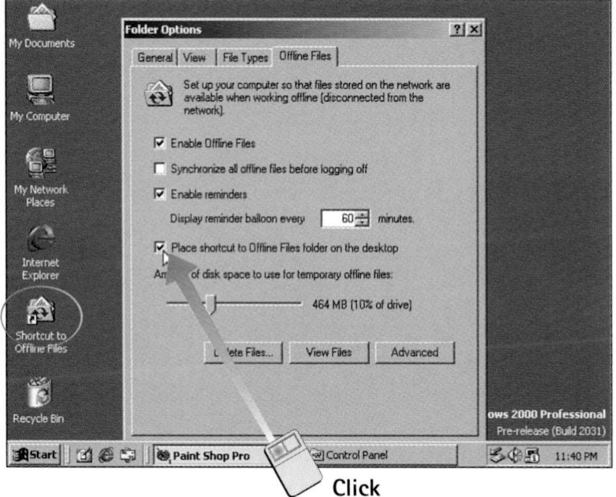

7 Choose Amount of Disk Space to Use

By default, offline folders are allowed to use 10% of your hard drive. You can change this to any amount you like by simply dragging the slider to adjust the percentage.

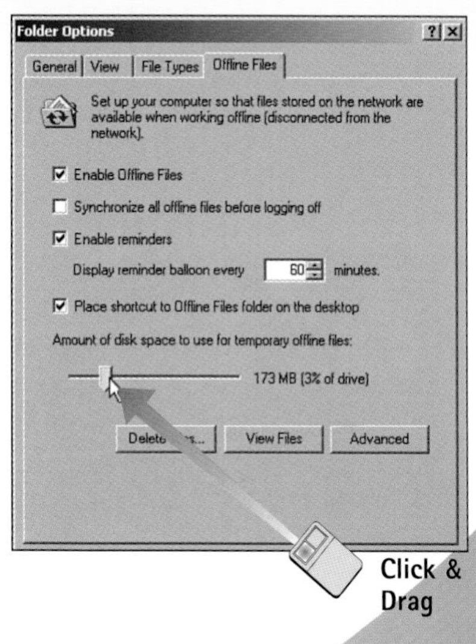

End

Task

PART 6

Working on the Internet

The Internet is made up of lots of networks all connected together into one giant network. The most popular part of the Internet today is the World Wide Web, which provides pages that contain text, graphics, and multimedia to programs named Web browsers. Over the past few years, the Internet (and especially the Web) has become an important business tool, allowing you to find information on just about anything—businesses, investments, travel, weather, news, healthcare, technology, and more. Microsoft provides a Web browser, named Internet Explorer, as an integral part of Windows 2000.

When you visit a Web site, the main page of that site is called the home page. On the home page, there are usually links that you can click to visit other pages in the site. Sometimes, links on one site take you to pages in other Web sites. It is this complex manner of linking pages together that gives the Web its name.

Each page on the Web has a specific address, sometimes called a URL (uniform resource locator), that tells your Web browser how to find it. The URL contains such information as the name of the computer and the name of the folder on that computer that the page can be found, as well as the name of the page itself. For example, the URL **www.microsoft.com/windows/default.asp** tells a browser to find a file named **default.asp** in a folder named **windows** on a computer named **www.microsoft.com**.

TASK 1

How to Start Internet Explorer

If you are on a network, your administrator has probably already configured your computer to use the company's connection to the Internet. If you are not on a network (or if your company does not have a Internet connection), you need a modem and to sign up for an account with an Internet service provider (ISP). The ISP provides software and instructions to get you connected. When connected, your first task is to get to know your Web browser, Internet Explorer.

Begin

1 Open Internet Explorer

Double-click the **Internet Explorer** icon on your desktop to open Internet Explorer. You can also click the **Internet Explorer** icon on the Quick Launch bar.

2 Connect to the Internet

If you connect to the Internet using your company's network, you should connect to a Web page immediately. If you connect using a modem, an extra dialog box might pop up asking you to dial your ISP. If it does, just click **Connect**. Your ISP should provide you with instructions on how to set up the dial-up networking connection

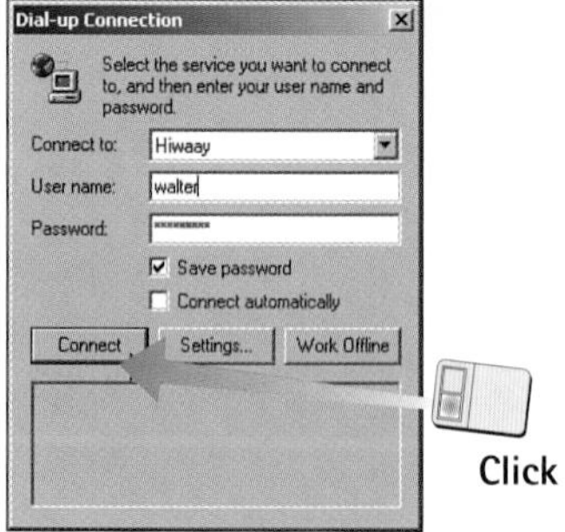

3 View a Web Page

A Web browser works like any other program you use in Windows. Along the top of the window, you find a menu bar and a couple of toolbars. The Address bar lets you enter the address of a page to visit. Use the scrollbar to move through and view the page.

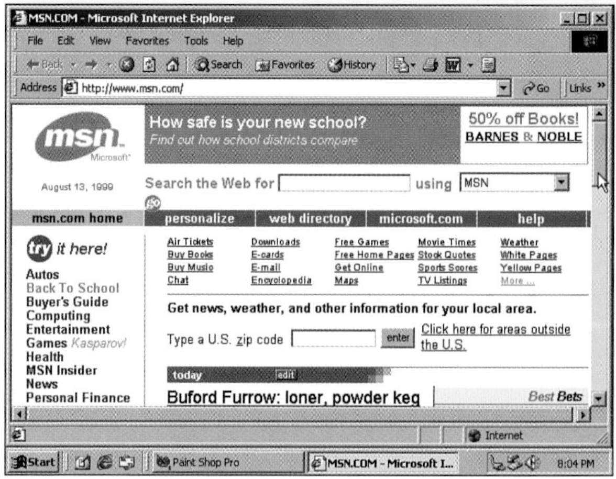

4 Select a Link

On a Web page, links to other pages are typically underlined and in blue text. Links to pages you have visited recently often appear underlined and in red text. When you move your pointer over a link, it turns into a hand pointing its index finger. Just click once to jump to that page. Normally, the page opens in the same window, replacing the page you linked from. Sometimes, pages open in a window of their own.

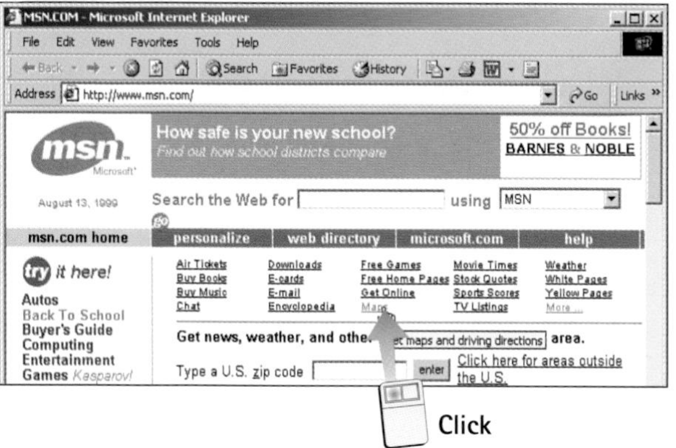

5 Refresh a Page

Some pages change frequently, especially if they contain images that are updated regularly, such as a site that has weather radar images. You can load a page in your browser again by clicking the **Refresh** button on the toolbar.

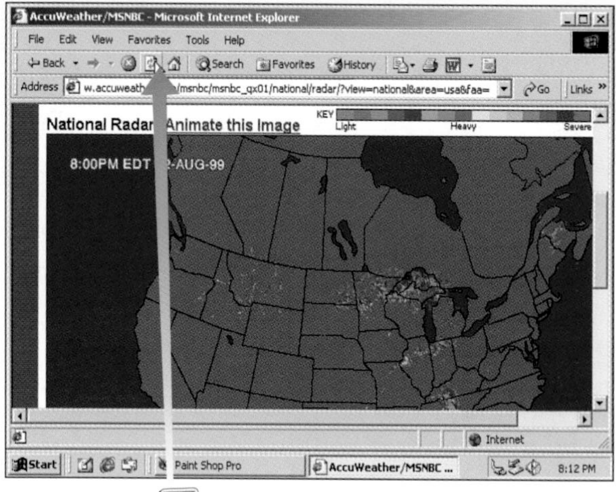

6 Stop a Page from Loading

If a page is taking too long to load, or is having problems loading, you can stop it from loading by clicking the **Stop** button on the toolbar. Your browser displays whatever part of the page has already loaded.

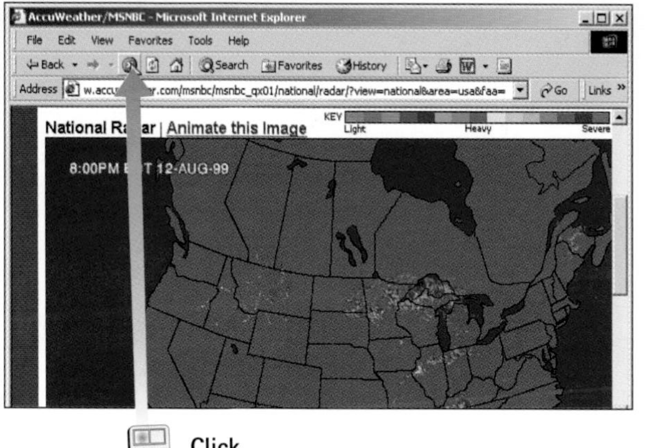

End

How-To Hints

View a Web Tutorial

Microsoft has a tutorial for using the Web on its Web site. You can access it quickly by choosing the **Tour** command from the **Help** menu.

Viewing a Page Fullscreen

You can see more of a page at once by viewing it fullscreen. Just select the **Fullscreen** command from the **View** menu. To get back to the regular view, just press **F11**.

TASK 2

How to Get to a Web Site

If you know the address for a Web page, you can enter it into Internet Explorer's Address bar. But there are often easier ways to get to a page. You can keep favorite pages on a special Favorites menu or on a Link toolbar. You can also use your browser to quickly browse backward and forward through pages you've already visited.

Begin

1 Enter the Address

If you know the URL of the site you want to visit, just enter it into the Internet Explorer Address bar and then press **Enter**. As you type, Internet Explorer tries to complete the address for you based on addresses you've entered before. Internet Explorer loads the page if it can find the address.

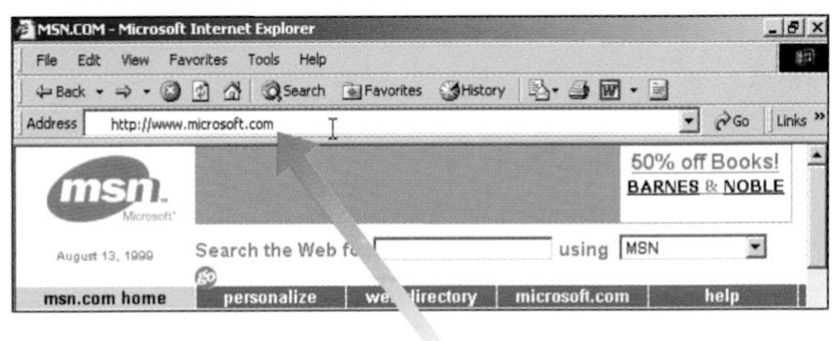

2 Open the Address List

To view a list of recently-visited sites, click the down arrow beside the Address box. Click one of the addresses on the list to go to that page.

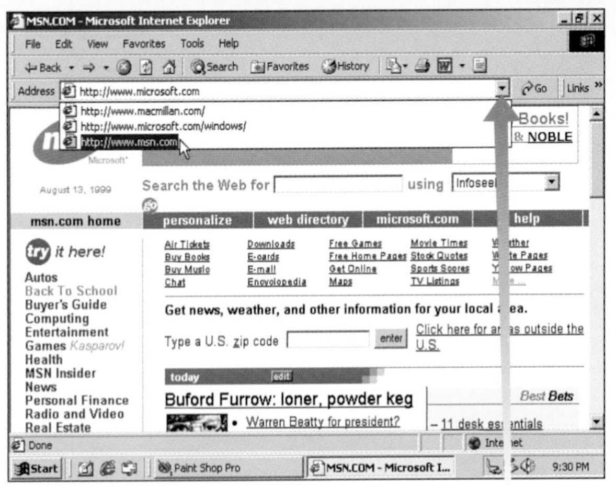

3 Choose a Link Button

Double-click the **Links** title to slide the Links bar open. Then click any button on the Links bar to jump to that Web page.

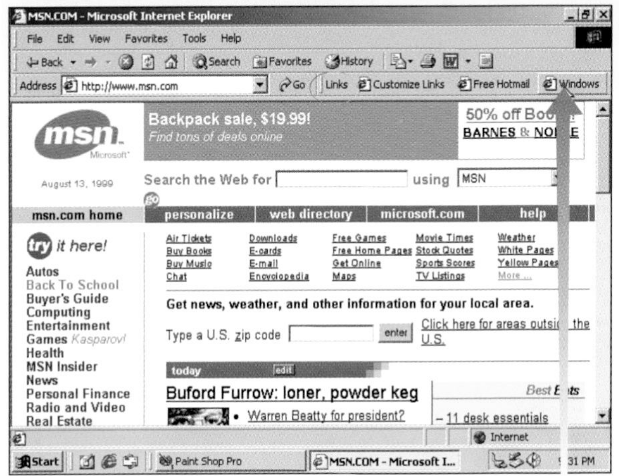

4 Choose a Favorite Site

Internet Explorer lets you keep a list of your favorite Web sites (see Task 4 later in this part to learn how to add favorites). Click the Favorites menu to open it, then click any page on the list to jump to that page.

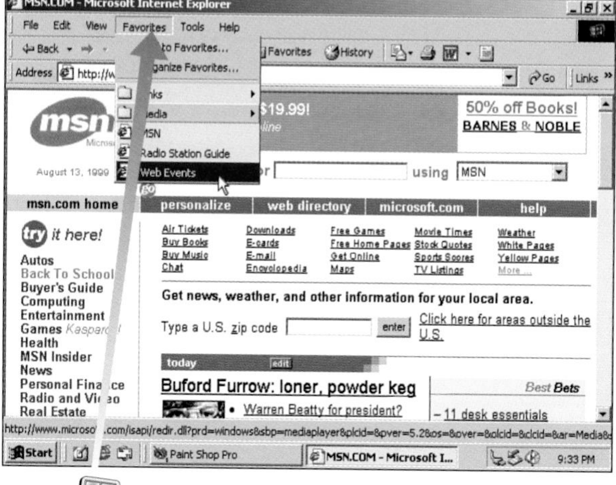

Click

5 Go to Your Home Page

The top page of a Web site is called its home page. The default Web page that loads whenever you open Internet Explorer is also called a home page (it's often called *your* home page). Return to it at any time by clicking the **Home** button.

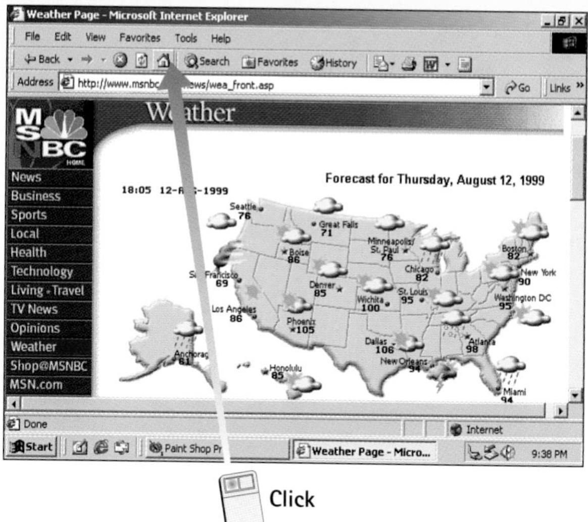

Click

6 Go Backward and Forward

As you use Internet Explorer, you can go backward and forward to the last pages you visited by clicking the **Back** or **Forward** buttons on the toolbar. Click the down arrows next to these buttons to open a history of sites you've visited in this session.

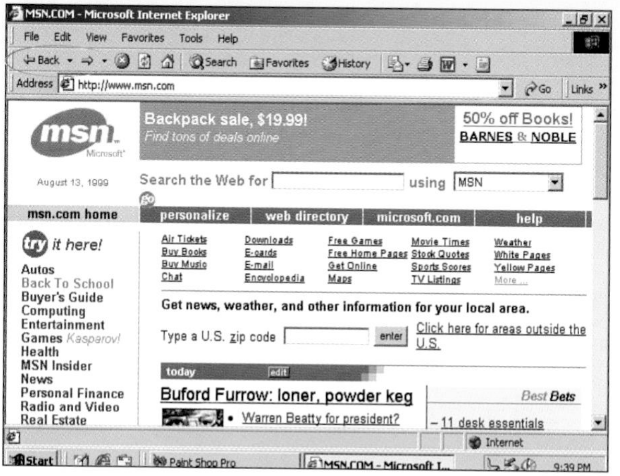

End

How-To Hints

Adding a Link Button

You can add a button for the page you are viewing to your Links bar by simply dragging the icon for the page from the Address bar to the Links bar.

Making a New Home Page

You can make the page you are viewing your home page by dragging its icon from the Address bar to the Home button on the toolbar.

TASK 3

How to Search for a Web Site

If you don't know the address for a Web site you want to visit, you can often find it just by guessing. Try entering the name of the company (or whatever) you're looking for followed by a three-letter domain suffix. For example, if you want to find Microsoft's Web site, you can just type **`microsoft.com`** into the Address bar. Internet Explorer does the rest. Sometimes, however, you need to search for the information you need.

Begin

1 Open the Search Window

In Internet Explorer, click the **Search** button on the toolbar to open the Search window.

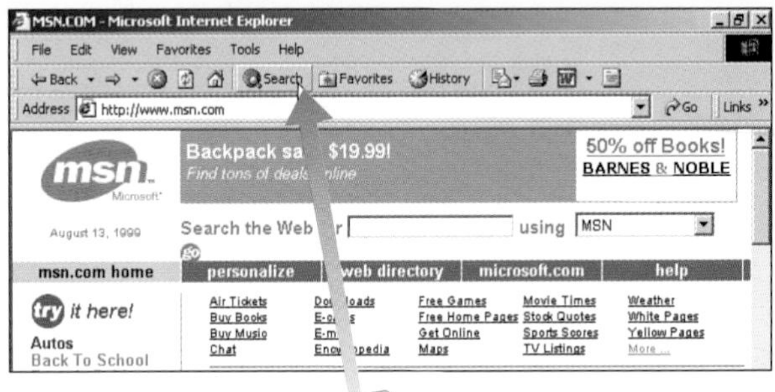

2 Find a Web Page

Internet Explorer lets you search for addresses, businesses, and maps in addition to Web pages. Click **Find a Web Page** to search for Web pages.

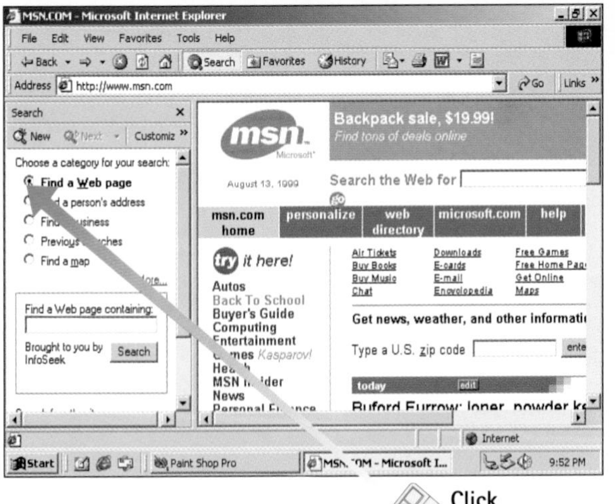

3 Enter Some Keywords

Enter some keywords to define what you are looking for. If, for example, you want to find Web pages that have to do with tigers in India, enter **`tiger india`**. After you enter the criteria, click **Search** to begin.

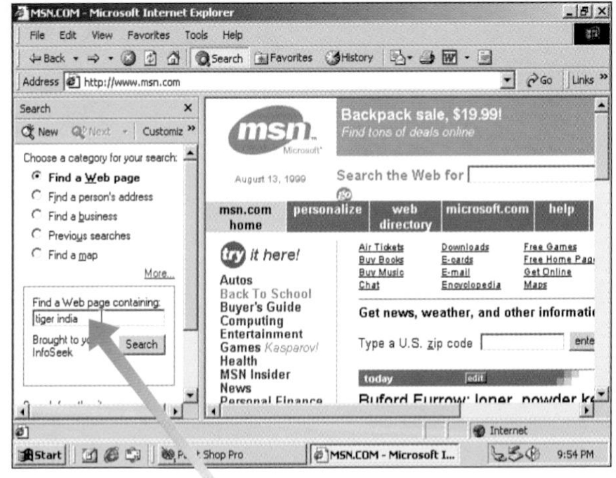

4 Scroll to View Results

Internet Explorer uses one of many popular Internet search engines to perform your search and then displays the results in the Search window. Scroll down to view them.

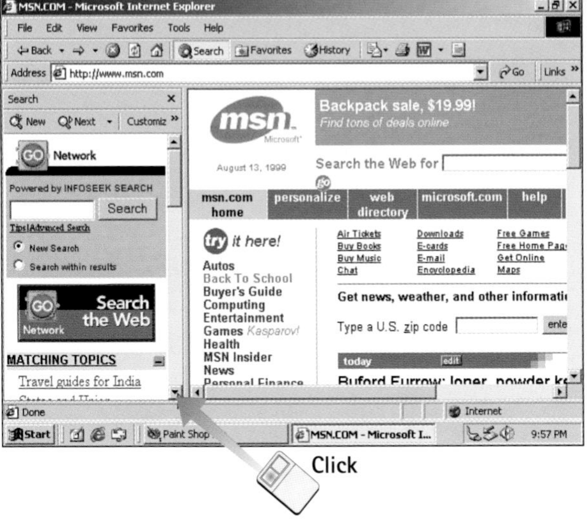

5 Select a Link

Hold your pointer over a link for a moment to view a pop-up window that shows the first several lines of text from the Web page the link represents. When you find a link you want to explore further, click it to jump to that Web page.

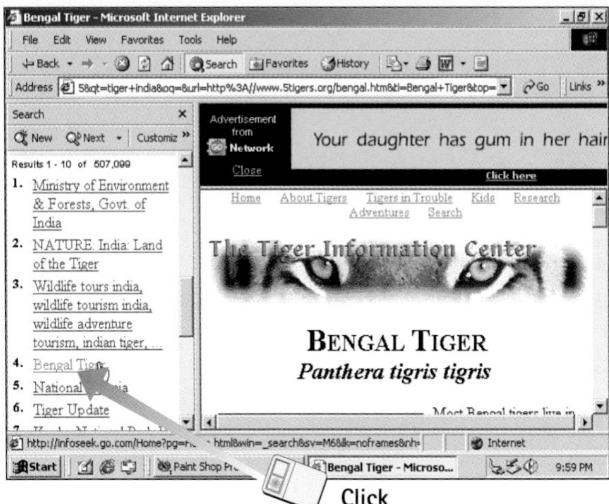

6 Select the Next Search Service

If you want to perform the same search using another search engine, click the **Next** button. Each time you click **Next**, Internet Explorer cycles to the next of its configured search engines. Use the same procedure shown in the preceding step to view the results of the search.

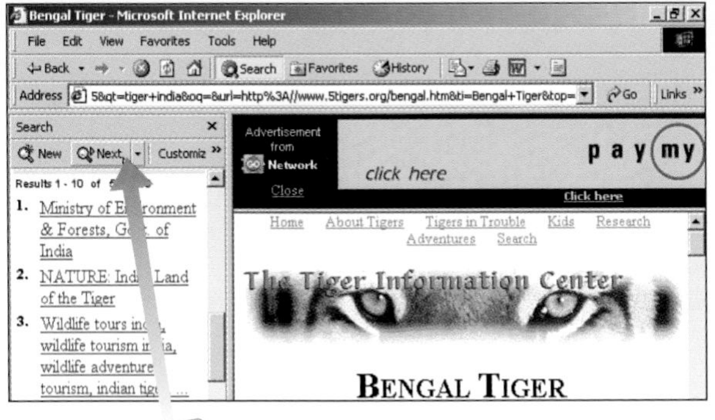

End

How-To Hints

Use Previous Searches

Internet Explorer remembers searches you've already performed. From the main search window, click **Previous Searches** to display a list from which to choose.

Customize the Search Procedure

From the main Search window, click the **Customize** button to open a window that lets you configure which search engines Internet Explorer should use when performing searches.

TASK 4

How to Use the Favorites Menu

To jump to a page on your list of favorites, all you have to do is open the **Favorites** menu and choose the page from the list. Adding a page to the list is easy. The first step is to open the page you want to add in Internet Explorer.

Begin

1 Add a Page to the Favorites Menu

To add a Web page you are viewing to your **Favorites** menu, open the menu by clicking it once and then click **Add to Favorites**.

Click

2 Make Available Offline

If you want the page to be made available for viewing while you are not connected to the Internet, click the **Make available offline** option. Check out Task 6 in this part for more information on doing this.

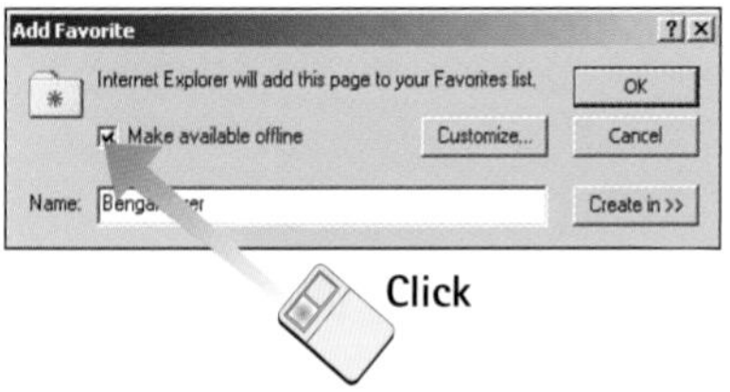

Click

3 Rename the Page

Enter a different name for the page in the **Name** box if you want. This name will appear in your Favorites menu.

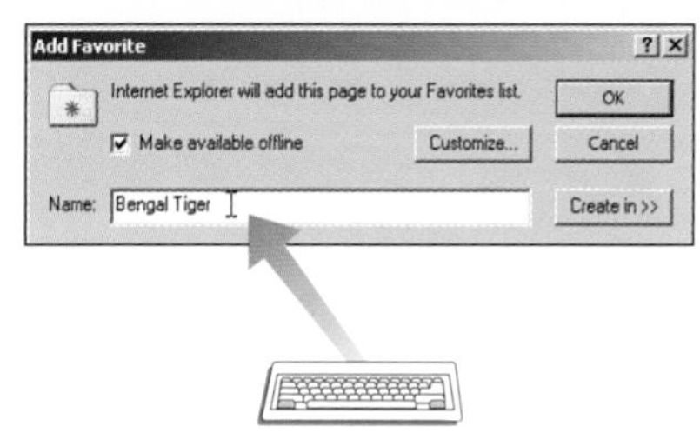

4 Create in a Specific Folder

You can organize your Favorites menu into folders. To add the page to a specific folder, click the **Create in** button. If you do not want to put it in a folder, just click **OK** to add the page to the main Favorites menu.

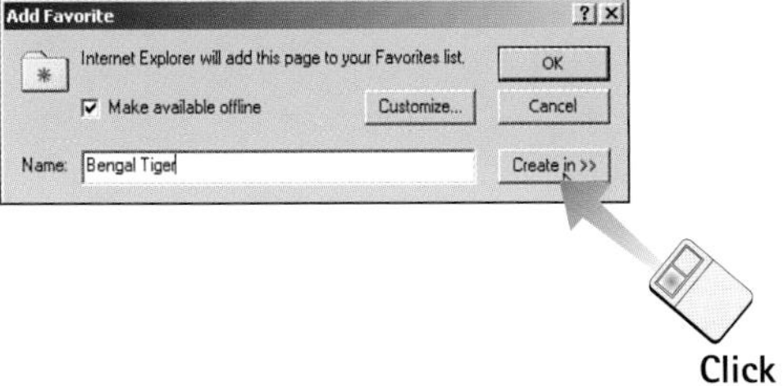

5 Choose a Folder

Click the folder you want to add the page to. You can create a new folder on the menu by clicking the **New Folder** button.

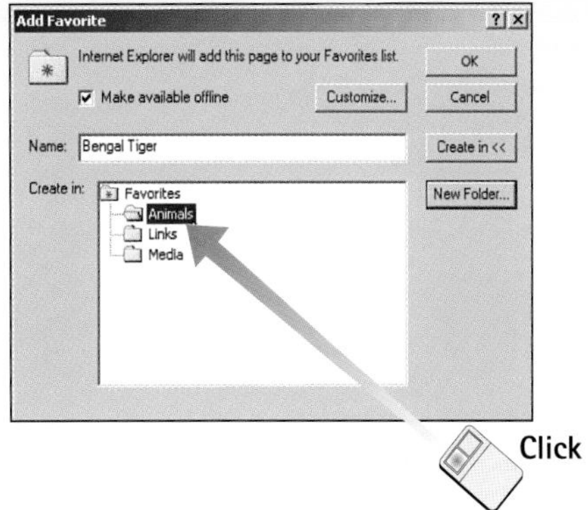

6 Add the Favorite

After you have configured all the previous options you want, click **OK** to add the page to your Favorites menu.

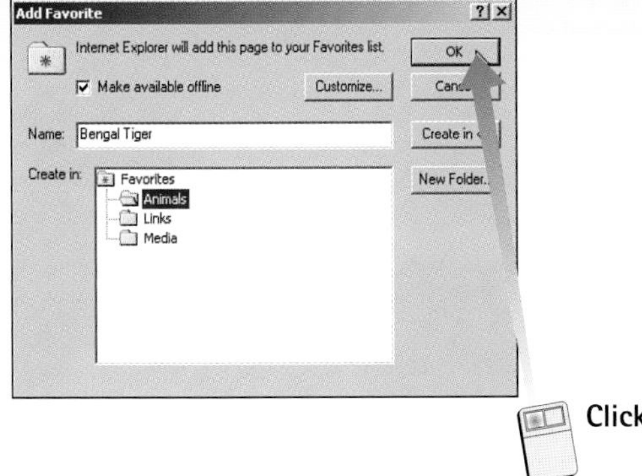

End

How-To Hints

Organize Your Favorites Menu

If you want to move, delete, or remove pages on your Favorites menu, just open the menu and choose the **Organize Favorites** command.

TASK 5

How to Use the History List

Internet Explorer keeps track of all the pages you have visited recently (for the past 20 days, by default). When you can't remember the exact address of a site or page you've visited before, you can use the History list to quickly find it.

Begin

1 Open the History Window

Click the **History** button on the Internet Explorer toolbar to open the **History** window.

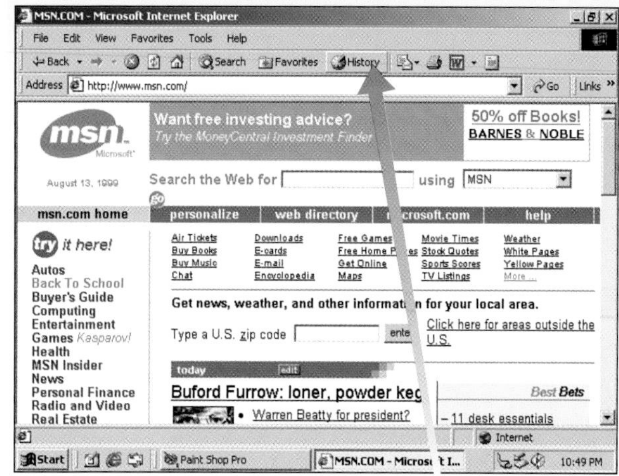

2 Choose a Time Frame

The History window is organized by days and weeks. To look for a site, just click the day when you think you visited it.

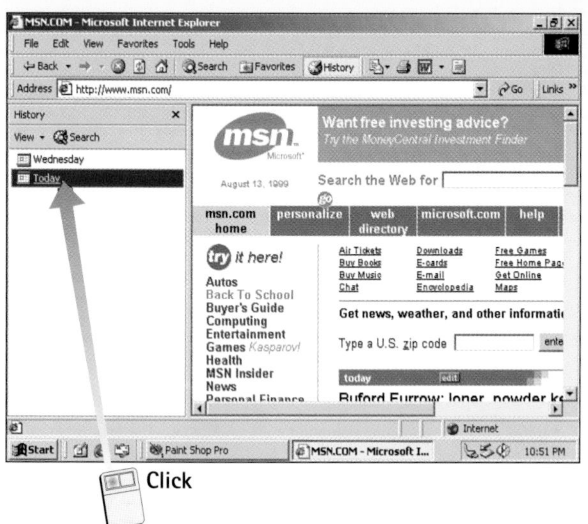

3 Choose a Site

From the list, find the site you want to explore by clicking it once.

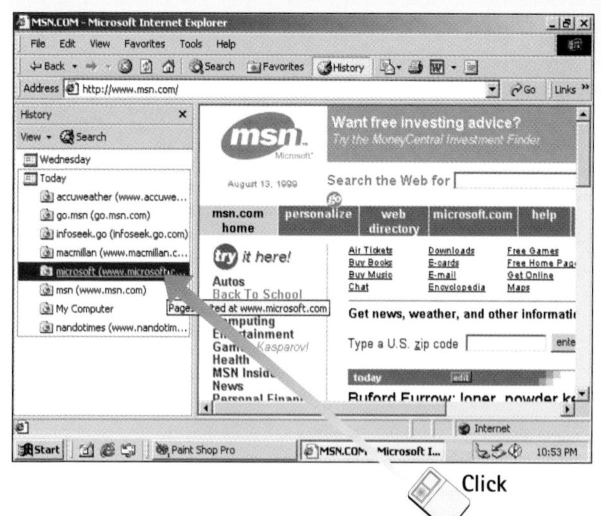

4 Choose a Page

From the list of visited pages on the site, jump to a page by clicking it once.

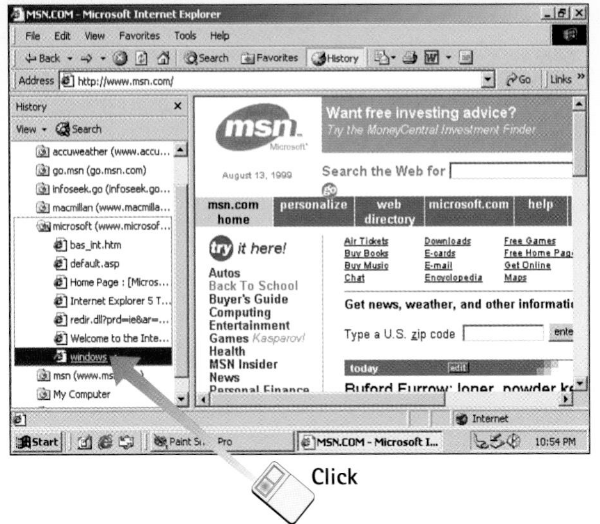

5 Change the View

You can view the History window in different ways. Click the **View** button to organize visited pages By Site, By Most Visited, or By Order Visited Today.

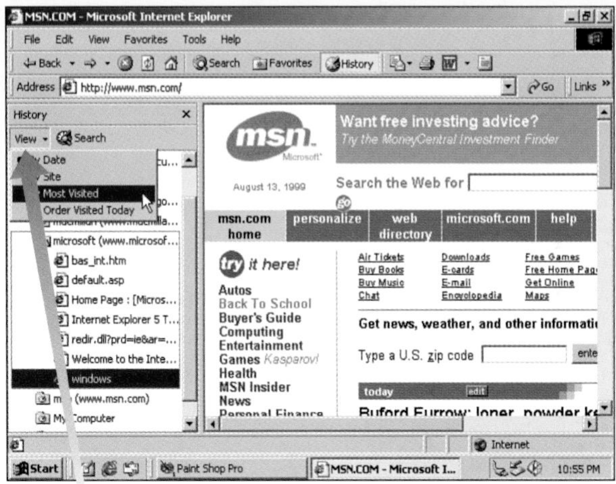

6 Close the History Window

Close the History window by clicking the **X** button in the upper-right corner.

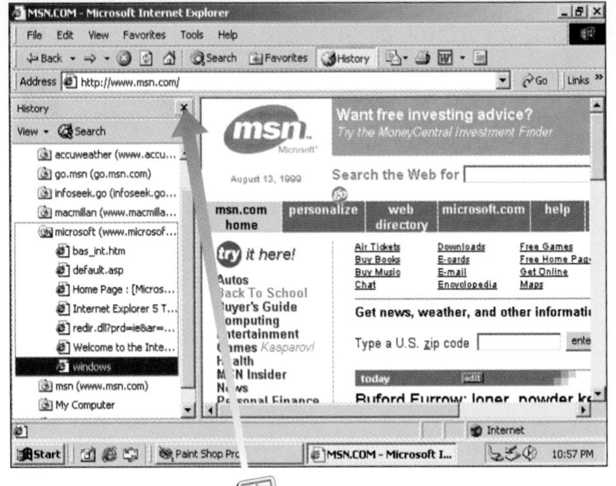

End

How-To Hints

Search Your History

Click the **Search** button at the top of your History window to search the pages in your History list by keyword.

Change History Settings

See Task 7 later in this part for information on how to change your Internet Explorer history settings.

History of Local Files

In addition to keeping track of Web pages, Windows keeps track of the files you've opened on your own computer in its history. These files appear on the History list. Windows and Internet Explorer share the same History list.

TASK 6

How to Make Web Pages Available Offline

Occasionally, you might want to access information on Web pages when you are not connected to the Internet. This can be useful if you are charged for connection time or if you carry your computer around with you. Internet Explorer lets you mark pages for offline viewing, which basically means the pages are copied to your computer so you can view them without being on the Internet. You can also configure when and how the pages are updated.

Begin

1 Make It Available Offline

First, browse to the page you want to make available offline and choose the **Add to Favorites** command from your Favorites menu. Choose the **Make available offline** option and click the **Customize** button. This launches the Offline Favorite Wizard.

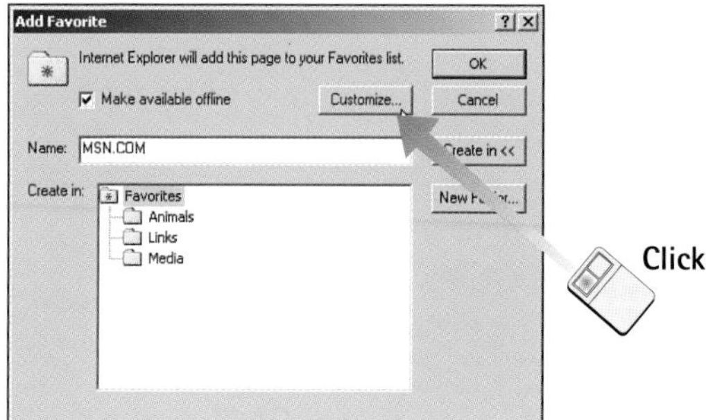

2 Make Links Available Offline

You can choose to make only the current page available or make pages that the current page links to available as well. If you want to make links available, click the **Yes** option.

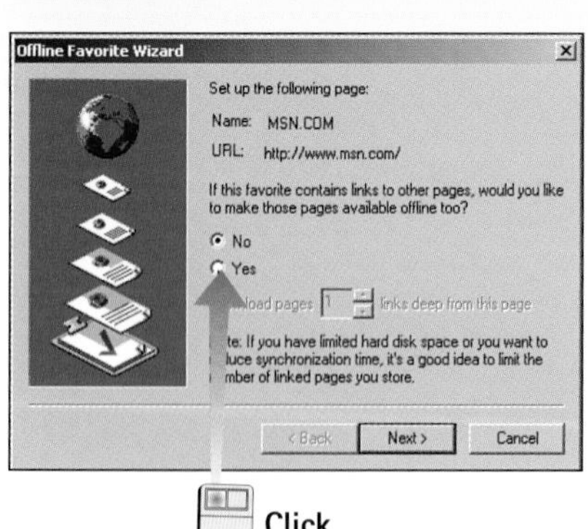

3 Select the Link Depth

Choose how many links deep from the current page you want to make pages available. For example, choosing **2** makes available all pages that the current page links to and all pages that each of those pages links to. Click **Next** to go on.

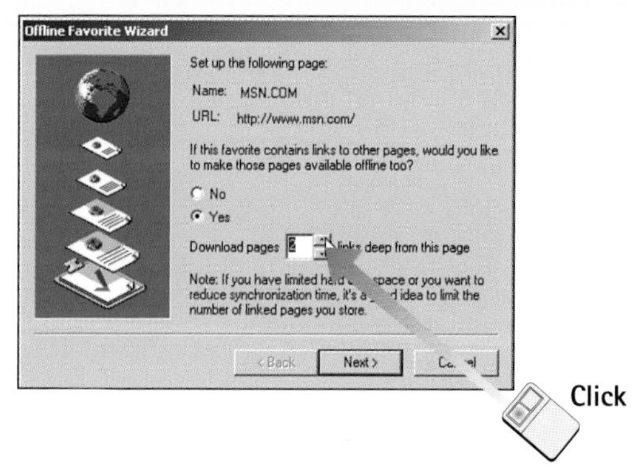

4 Schedule Offline Updates

Synchronizing updates the temporary copies of offline pages on your computer with the most recent copy from the Internet. By default, pages are only synchronized when you choose the **Synchronize** command from the **Tools** menu of Internet Explorer. Create a new schedule by clicking the option once. Click **Next** to go on.

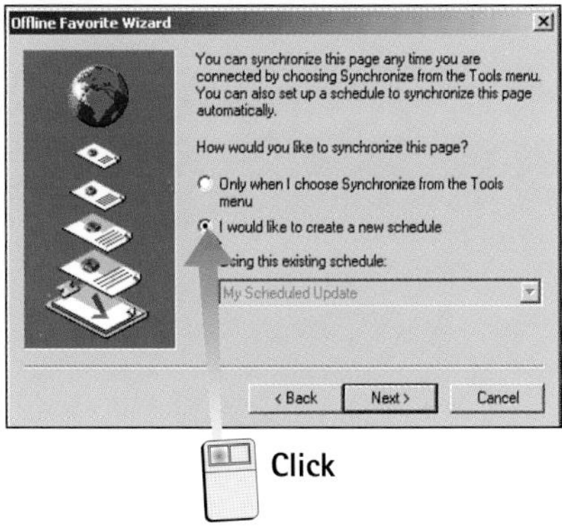

5 Set Up a Schedule

Choose how often (in days) and at what time of the day you want the page to be automatically updated. You can also name your schedule. Click **Next** to go on.

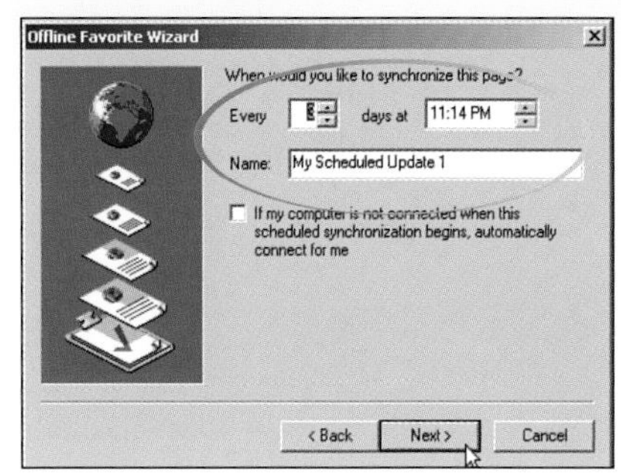

6 Enter a Username and Password

If the page you are making available offline requires that you enter a username and password, click the **Yes** option and supply that information here. When you're done, click **Finish**.

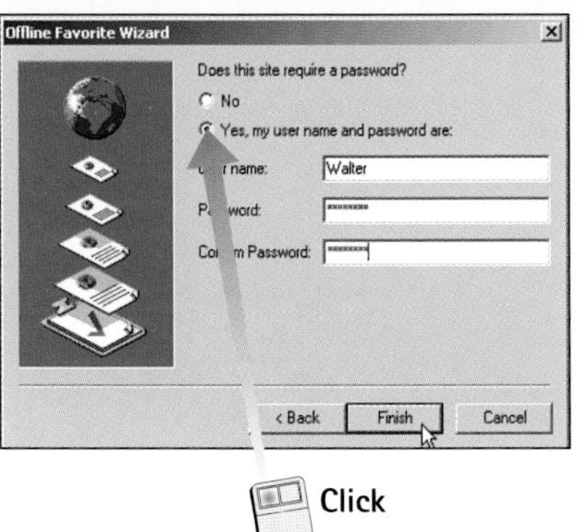

End

How-To Hints

Changing Offline Settings

You can change the offline settings for a page at any time by choosing the **Organize Favorites** from the Favorites menu. Select the page from the list and click the **Properties** button to change the offline settings.

TASK 7

How to Change Settings for Internet Explorer

After you have played with Internet Explorer for a while, you might want to experiment with some of the ways in which you can customize the program using the Internet Options dialog box. The six tabs on this dialog box present a lot of options. Some of the more useful ones are discussed here.

Begin

1 Open Internet Options

Open the **Tools** menu and choose the **Internet Options** command to open the Internet Options dialog box.

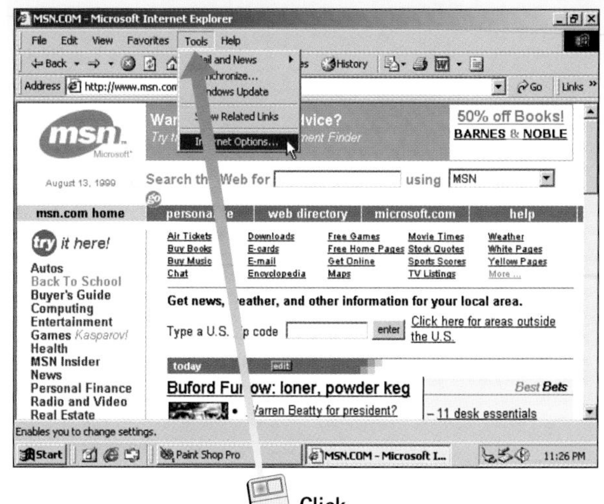

2 Enter a New Home Page

The page that Internet Explorer first opens to is called the home page. You can change the home page by entering a new URL in the **Address** box.

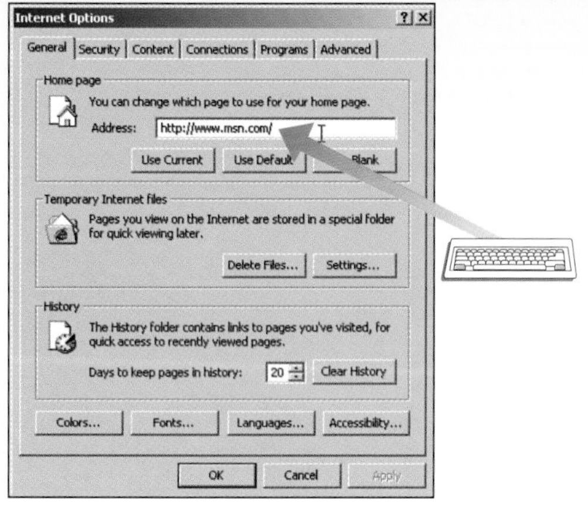

3 Delete Temporary Files

As you browse, Internet Explorer temporarily saves pages and graphics to your hard drive. When you open a previously-visited page, Internet Explorer checks to see if the page has changed. If it hasn't, the temporary files are opened; this way, the page loads faster. You can delete these temporary files by clicking **Delete Files**. This option also lets you delete offline files stored on your drive.

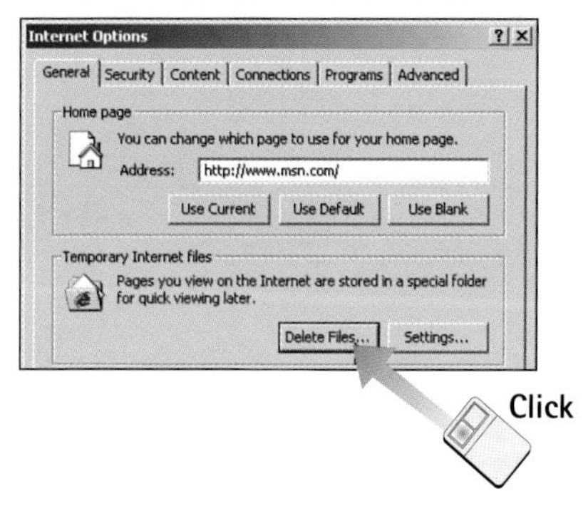

4 Change Temporary Settings

Click the **Settings** button to open the Settings dialog box. Here, you can change how often Internet Explorer checks for new versions of the pages stored as temporary files.

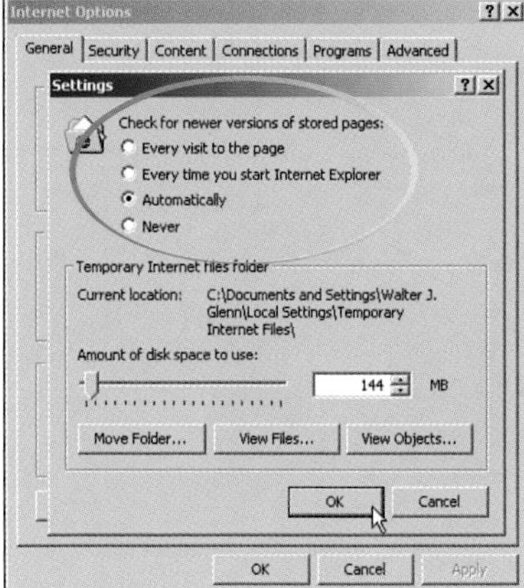

5 Reduce Disk Space Used

Temporary files use up disk space—by default, about 2% of your hard disk. This can be quite a lot of space on larger drives. However, storing more temporary files can mean quicker loading of some Web pages. Change the disk space used by dragging the slider or by entering a specific value in megabytes.

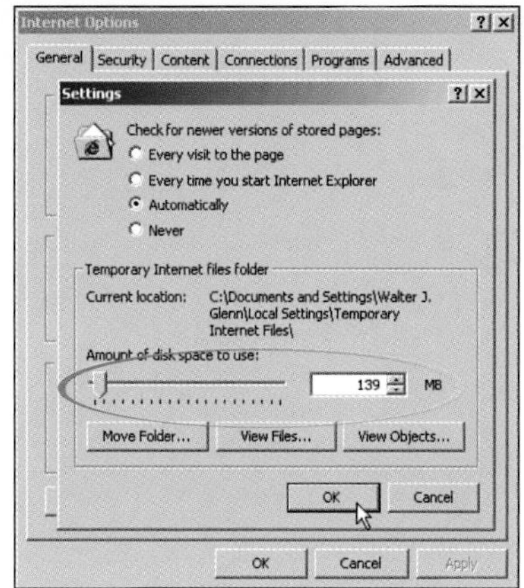

6 Change History Setting

By default, Internet Explorer keeps track of the Web pages and local files that you have opened in the last 20 days. You can change this value using the scroll buttons.

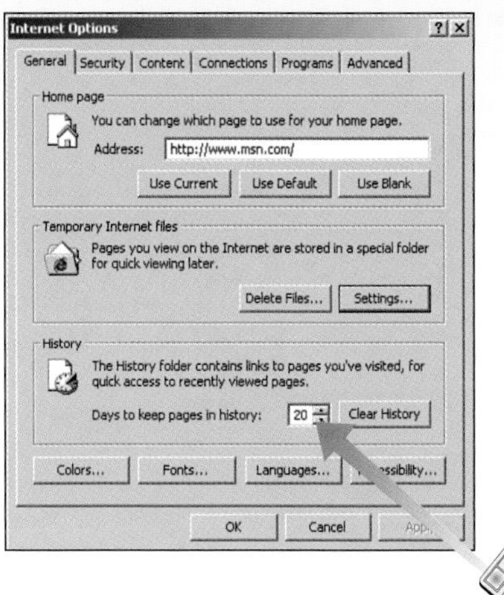

Click

7 Open the Colors Dialog Box

Click the **Colors** button at the bottom of the General tab of the Internet Options dialog box to change the colors of the text and background of Web pages you visit. Click one of the color buttons to open a palette from which you can choose a new color.

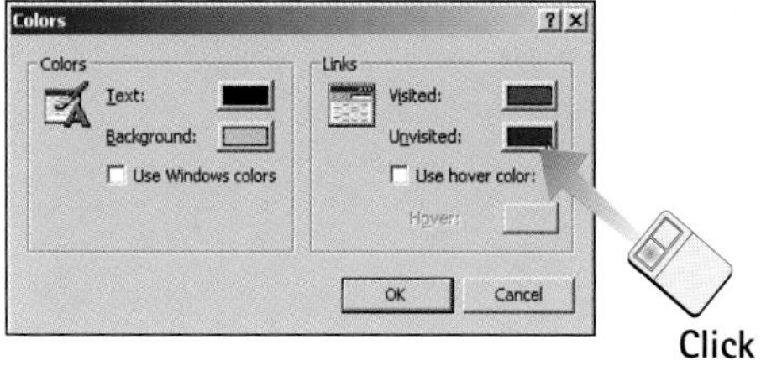

End

Task

PART 7

Using Internet Email and Newsgroups

Over the past few years, email has become so popular that it's difficult to find people who don't use it. If you're on a company network, it's almost a sure bet that you use email to communicate with other employees. If your network is hooked up to the Internet, or if you have a computer at home, the chances are that you can exchange email with other Internet users.

This chapter is about using Outlook Express, a program that comes with Windows 2000 Professional, to send Internet email. If you are on a company network, you might use a program other than Outlook Express to send and receive company email—and maybe Internet email, too. Outlook, which is a part of Microsoft Office, is one such program. Whatever the program you use to send and receive email, you'll find that the steps for performing the basic email operations are pretty similar.

In this chapter, you will learn to send and receive a message, use the built-in address book, and find email addresses for people. You will also learn to send and receive file attachments with an email message. Finally, you will learn how to subscribe to and use Internet newsgroups. Internet newsgroups are message forums open to the public in which many people post and reply to messages. There are literally tens of thousands of newsgroups available on the Internet on just about any topic you can think of. Outlook Express acts as a newsreader, a program that lets you read and reply to articles in these newsgroups.

TASK 1

How to Send Email with Outlook Express

Sending a message with Outlook Express really only requires that you know one thing before you start—the Internet email address of the person you want to send mail to. This address usually takes a form like *username@company.com*. If you don't know a person's address, the easiest way to find it out is to call and ask.

Begin

1 Start Outlook Express

Double-click the **Outlook Express** icon on your desktop to start Outlook Express. If you use a modem to connect to the Internet, Outlook Express launches the connection to sign you on.

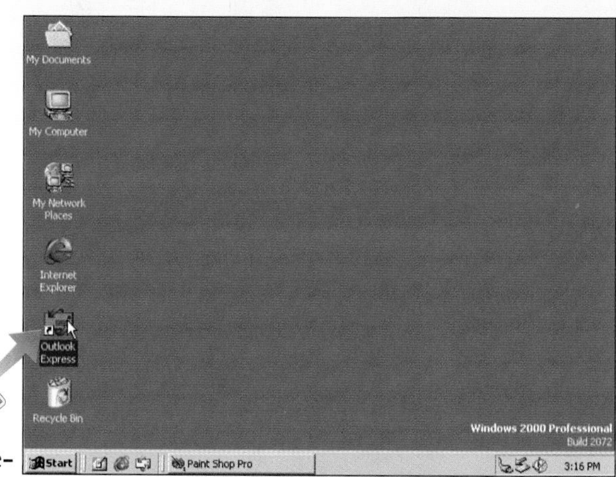

2 Compose a New Message

To start a new message, click the **New Mail** button on the Outlook Express toolbar. This action opens a new window for the message.

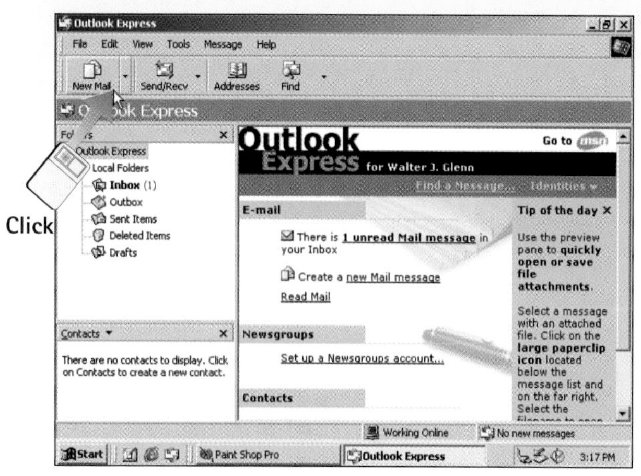

3 Enter an Address

In the **To** box, type an Internet email address for the person you want to send mail to. You can enter multiple addresses by separating them with a comma or semicolon.

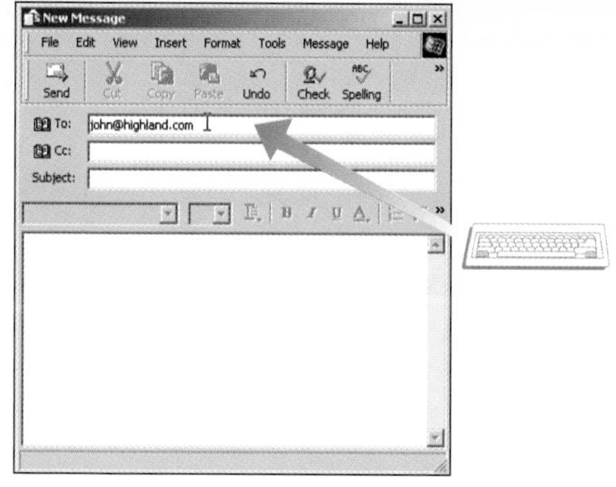

4 Enter a Subject

Enter a subject for your message in the **Subject** box. Although you do not have to enter a subject to send the message, it is considered good form.

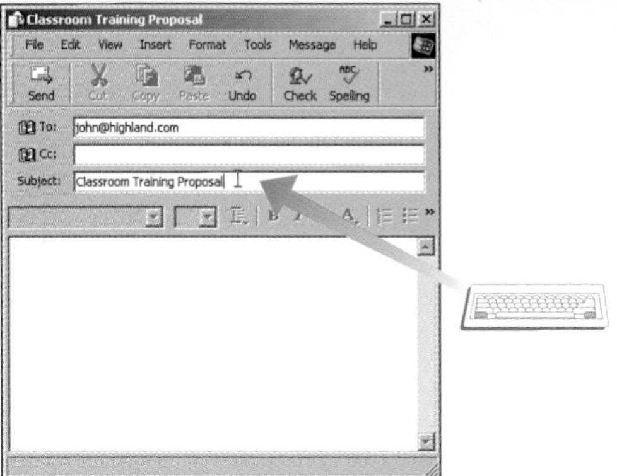

5 Write Your Message

Type the body of your message in the main window. Note that the toolbar above this window has standard tools for formatting your message.

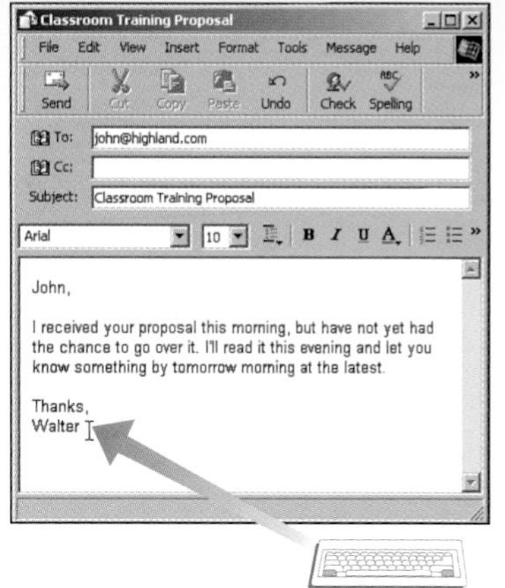

6 Send It

When you are done addressing and typing your message, click the **Send** button on the message window's toolbar to send the message.

End

How-To Hints

Your Outbox

When you send a message, it actually goes into your Outbox first. Depending on your settings, Outlook Express might send the message immediately or the message might sit in the Outbox until you click the Send/Receive button on the main Outlook Express toolbar. You can tell that messages are in your Outbox when the folder name becomes boldfaced.

Check Your Spelling

You can spell-check your message before you send it by clicking the **Spelling** button on the message window's toolbar.

Task 2

How to Receive Email

Whenever you start Outlook Express, it automatically checks to see if you have new mail. If you use a modem to connect to the Internet, Outlook Express starts the connection for you. By default, it also checks for new messages every 30 minutes while the program is open. You can also force it to check for new messages at any time by clicking the **Send/Receive** button on the toolbar.

Begin

1 Switch to Your Inbox

When you start Outlook Express, it opens to the Outlook Express home page, which shows an overview of your email and newsgroups. To see new messages, switch to your **Inbox** by clicking it once.

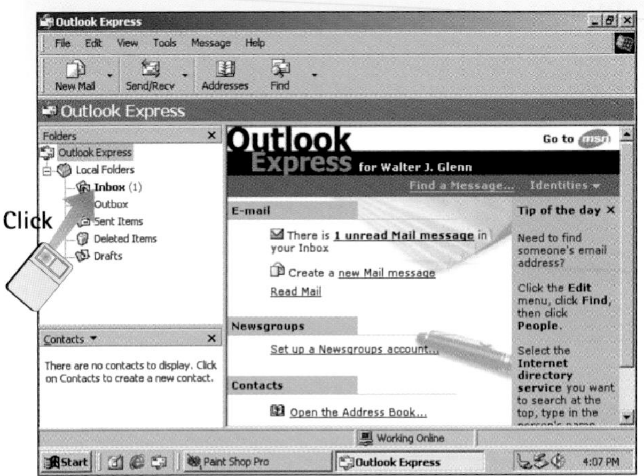

2 Select a Message

All new messages are delivered to your Inbox. Columns indicate who each message is from, the subject of the message, and the date the message was received. To select a message, just click it once. The contents are displayed in the preview pane below the message list.

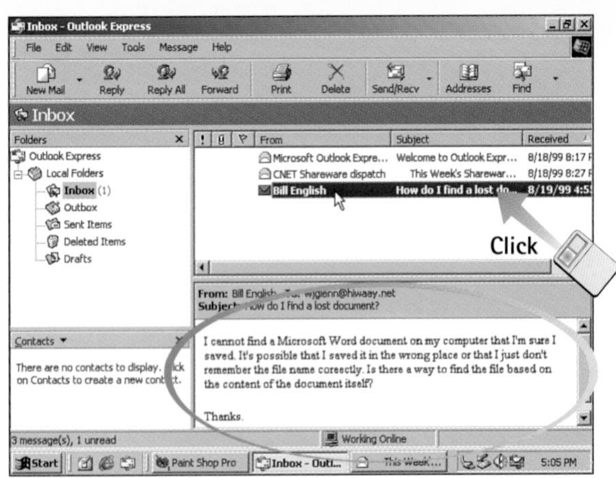

3 Open a Message

You can also open a message in a separate window by double-clicking any message in the list. Use the **Previous** and **Next** buttons on the toolbar to view other messages in the same window.

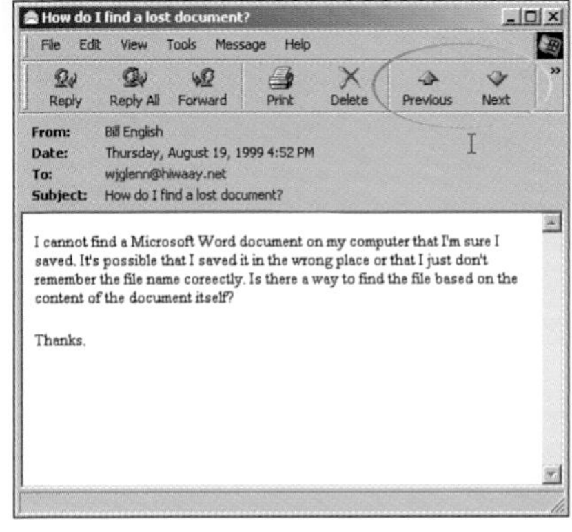

4 Reply to a Message

To reply to the sender of a message, select the message from the list and click the **Reply** button on the toolbar. A new message window appears that includes the email address, subject, and content of the original message. Just type in a reply message and click **Send**.

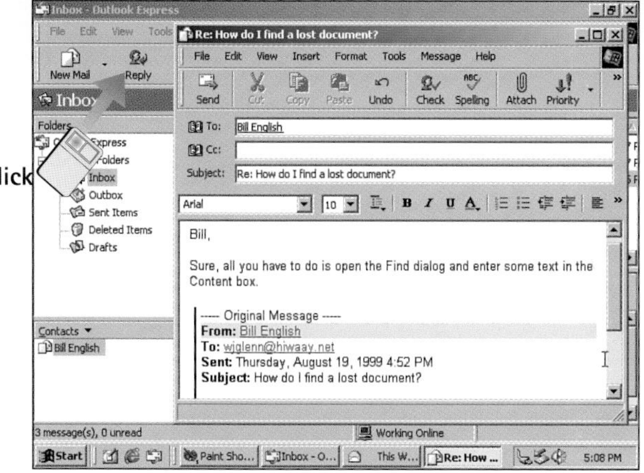

5 Forward a Message

You can also forward a message that you received from one person to one or more other people altogether. Just select the message and click the **Forward** button on the toolbar. A new message window appears that includes a subject and the original message. Enter an email address, type a new message if you want, and click **Send**.

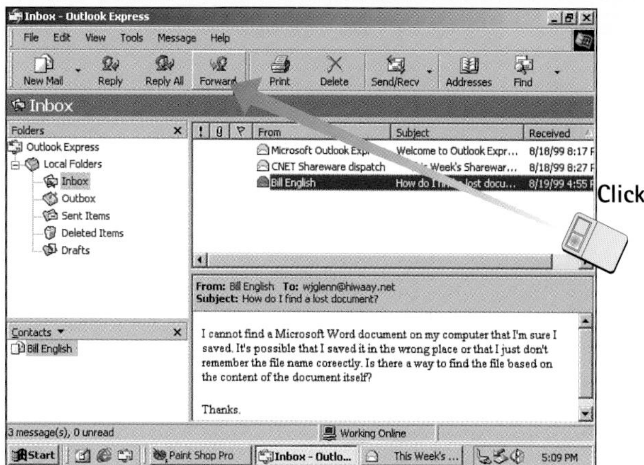

6 Delete a Message

To delete a message from your Inbox, select the message and click the **Delete** button on the toolbar. Deleted messages are placed in the **Deleted Items** folder, where you can retrieve them later if you need. Right-click the **Deleted Items** folder and choose **Empty Deleted Items Folder** from the short-cut menu to permanently delete messages inside.

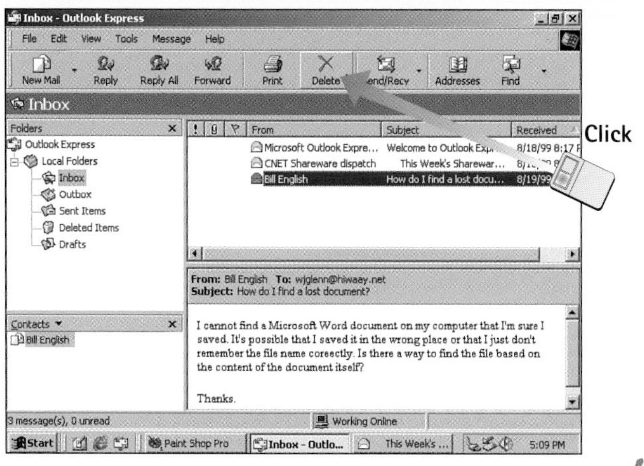

End

How-To Hints

Creating New Folders

If you like to save old messages, you can organize them by creating new folders to store them in. Select the **Local Folders** item by clicking it once, then choose the **New Folder** command from the **File** menu to create and name a new folder. When created, you can simply drag messages from your Inbox to the new folder.

TASK 3

How to Use the Address Book

The Address Book is a handy tool that lets you store the email addresses of people you mail regularly so that you don't have to remember addresses and type them in each time you send a message. You can also use the Address Book to store other personal information for people, such as postal addresses and telephone numbers.

Begin

1 Open the Address Book

To open the Address Book, click the **Addresses** button on the Outlook Express toolbar.

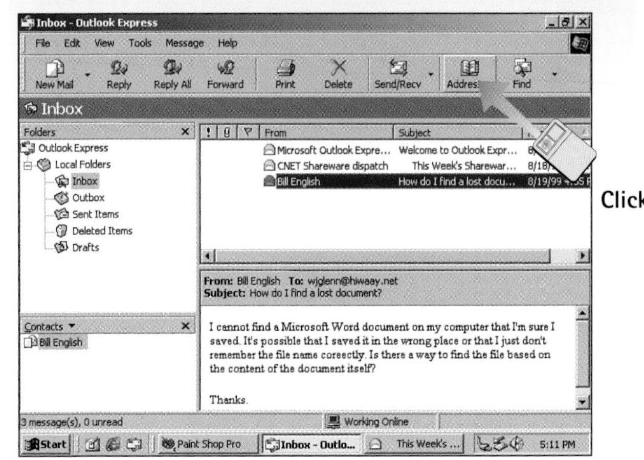

2 Select an Address

The Address Book displays a list of contacts, email addresses, and phone numbers. Select any contact by clicking it once.

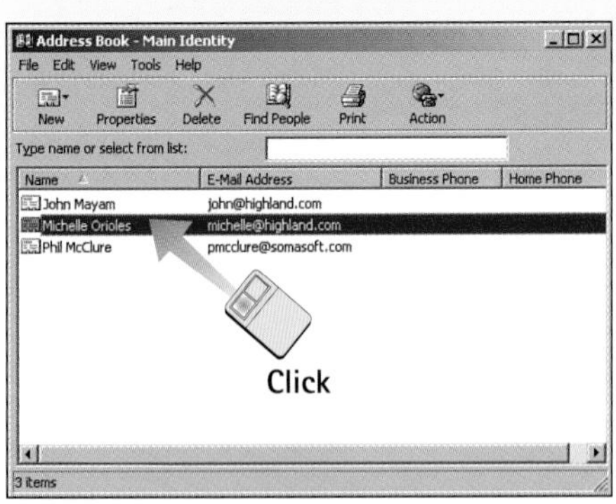

3 Send a Message

You can send an email message to any selected contact by clicking the **Action** button on the toolbar and choosing **Send Mail**. This opens a new message window with the address already filled in.

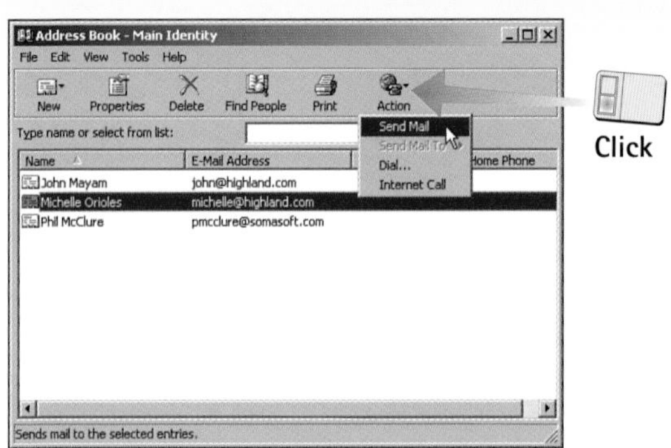

4 Add a New Contact

Whenever you send or reply to a message in Outlook Express, the email address you are sending to is automatically added to your Address Book. You can add a new contact to your Address Book manually by clicking the **New** button on the toolbar and choosing **New Contact**.

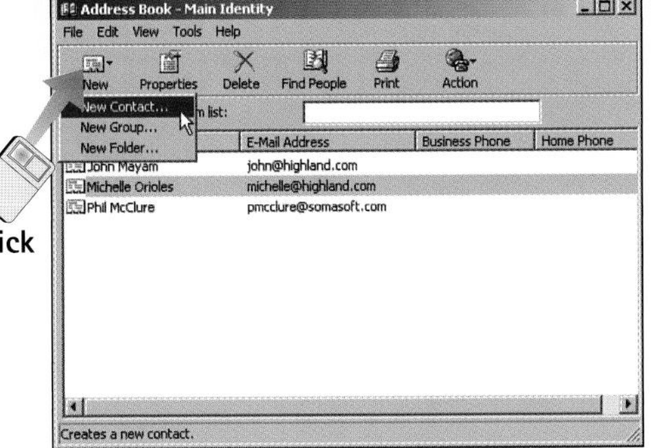

5 Fill in Personal Information

Fill in the first, middle, and last names of your new contact. You can also enter a nickname, if you want, which you can enter into the **To** box of a new message to quickly address new messages.

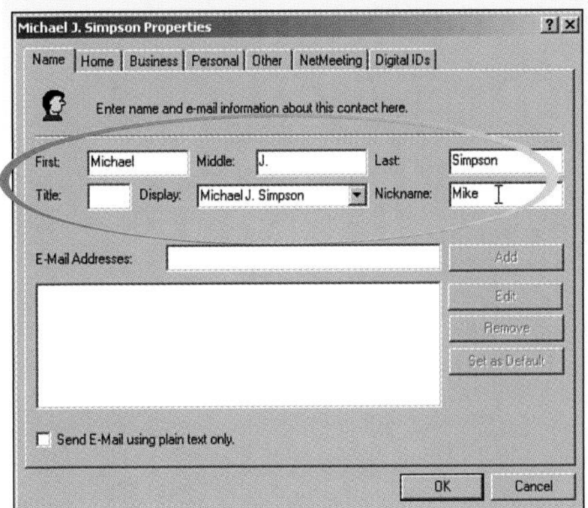

6 Enter an Address

Type in the email address for your new contact in the **Email Addresses** box, then click the **Add** button to add the address. You can even enter extra email addresses if your contact has more than one. Click the other tabs of this dialog box to enter information such as home and business addresses and phone numbers.

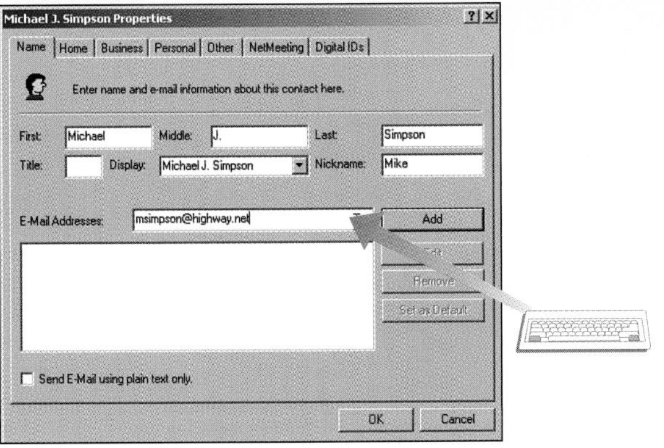

End

How-To Hints

The To Button

In a new message window, move your pointer over the word To, which is next to the **To** box, and a button appears. Click the button to open the Address Book and choose a contact to send the message to.

The Contacts List

Underneath the Folders list in the **Outlook Express** window, you find a list of the same contacts that appear in your Address Book. Double-click any name to start a new message to that contact.

Task 4

How to Change Settings for Outlook Express

There are a lot of things that you can customize in Outlook Express, including the way mail is received and sent, how spelling is checked, and much more. The following steps show you some of the more useful settings you can change in Outlook Express.

Begin

1 Open the Options Dialog Box

In Outlook Express, open the **Tools** menu and choose the **Options** command to open the Options dialog box.

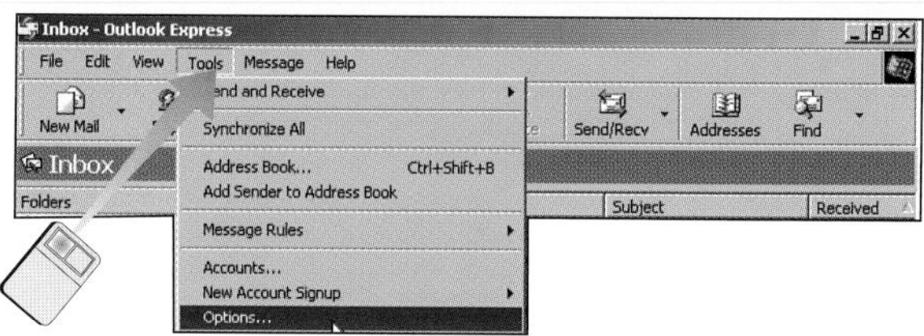

Click

2 Set General Options

Use the **General** tab to set some basic options about how Outlook Express behaves. You can have Outlook Express open the Inbox as soon as you start the program, play a sound when messages arrive, and change the time interval for checking for new messages.

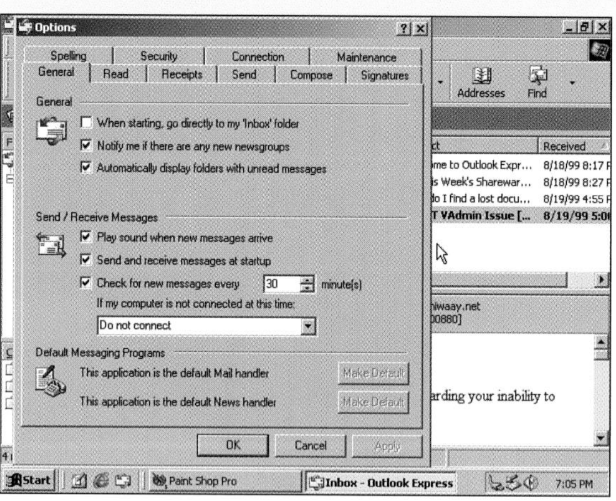

3 Set Read Options

Click the **Read** tab to configure settings pertaining to incoming messages. For example, Outlook Express marks a message as read 5 seconds after you select and view it in the preview pane. You can increase this value or change the option altogether. You can also set how many news articles are downloaded when you update a newsgroup.

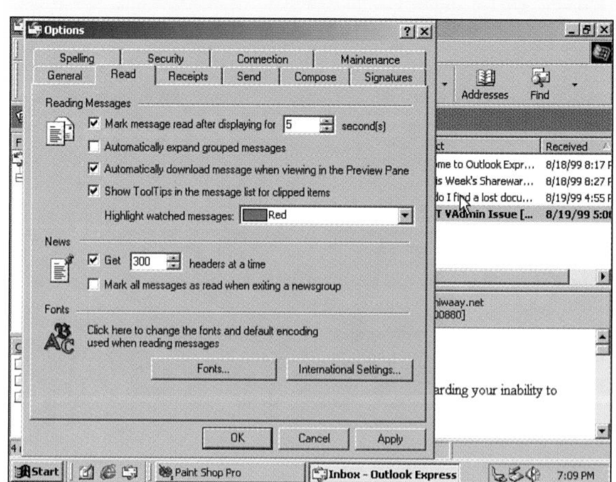

4 Set Send Options

Click the **Send** tab to change settings regarding how Outlook Express sends messages. You can specify such things as whether copies of outgoing messages should be saved in the **Sent Items** folder, whether the contents of original messages should be included in replies, and the format of outgoing messages. HTML formatting lets you apply format to the characters in your text (bold, italic, font size, etc.), but it may not be readable to people using older email programs.

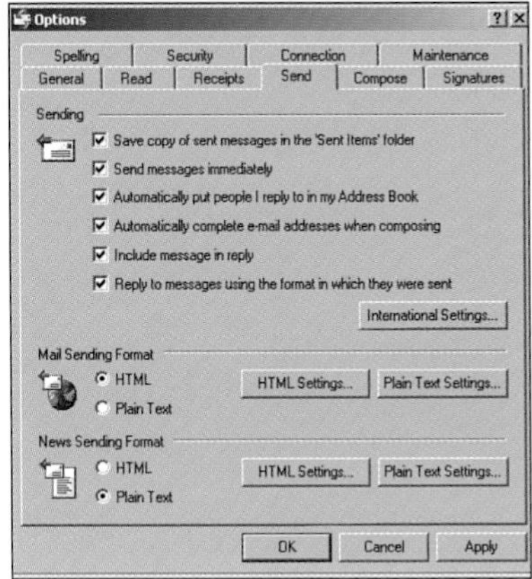

5 Create a Signature

A signature is text that is automatically included at the end of outgoing messages. Click the **Signatures** tab to set up a signature. You can even set up multiple signatures and then select which one to attach to a message.

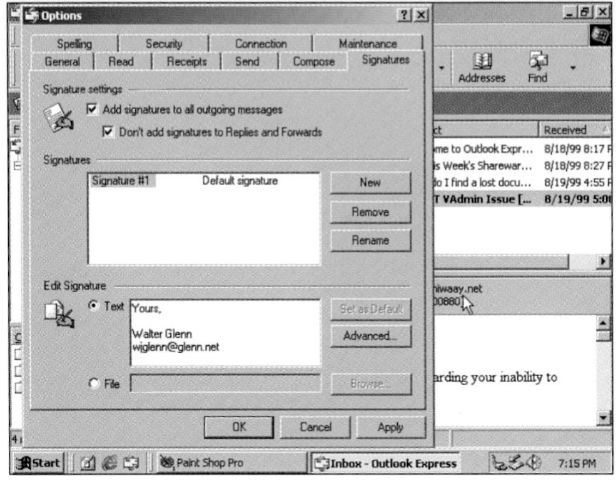

6 Set Spelling Options

Click the **Spelling** tab to change how Outlook Express spell-checks outgoing messages. You can, for example, specify that messages are checked automatically and set several options for what kinds of words are checked.

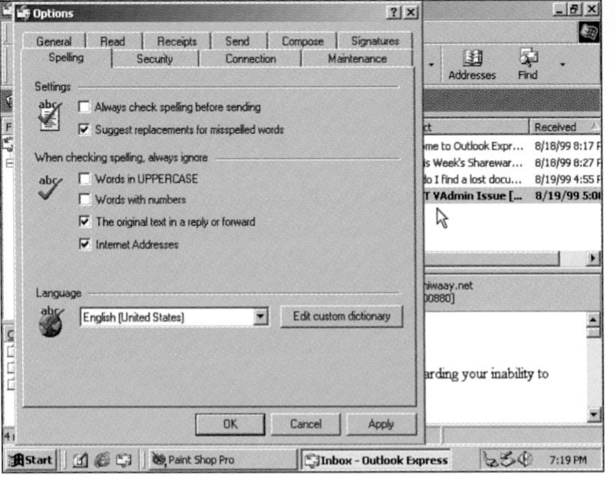

7 Set Connection Options

If you connect to the Internet using a modem, click the **Connection** tab to change how Outlook Express manages the connection. You can have Outlook Express check with you before dialing a connection and have it hang up automatically after sending and receiving messages.

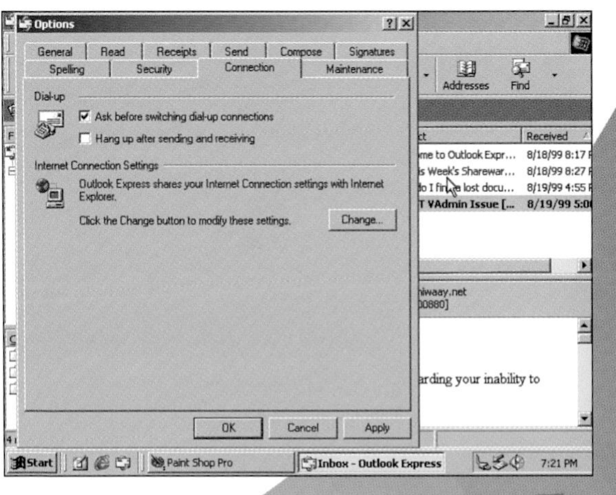

End

TASK 5

How to Receive an Attached File

One of the greatest uses of email is the capability to attach files to a message and send them to others. This sure beats copying the file to a floppy disk and carrying or mailing it. In the steps that follow, you'll see how to open a file that is attached to a message you have received.

Begin

1 Start Outlook Express

Click the **Outlook Express** shortcut on the Quick Launch Bar.

2 Select a Message

A message with an attachment shows up in your message list with a paper clip icon in the attachment column. When you select the message by clicking it once, the paper clip icon also appears in the header of the message in the preview pane.

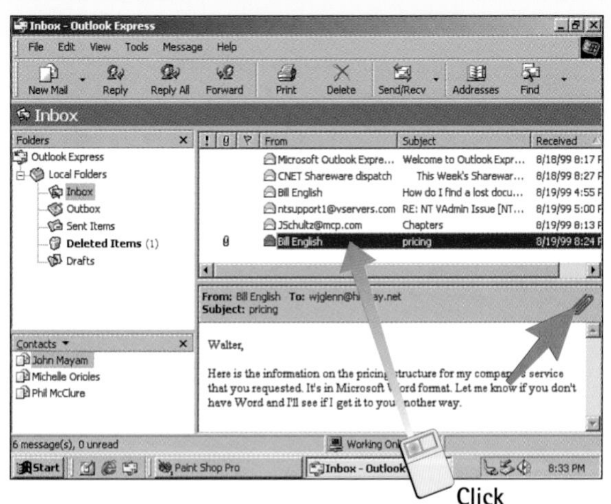

3 Open the Attached File

Click the paper clip icon in the header of the message in the preview pane to open a drop-down list that shows the files attached to the message. Click the attachment on the list that you want to open. If Windows knows what program the file belongs to (Microsoft Word for a .doc file, for example), the file opens. Otherwise, Windows prompts you to save the file.

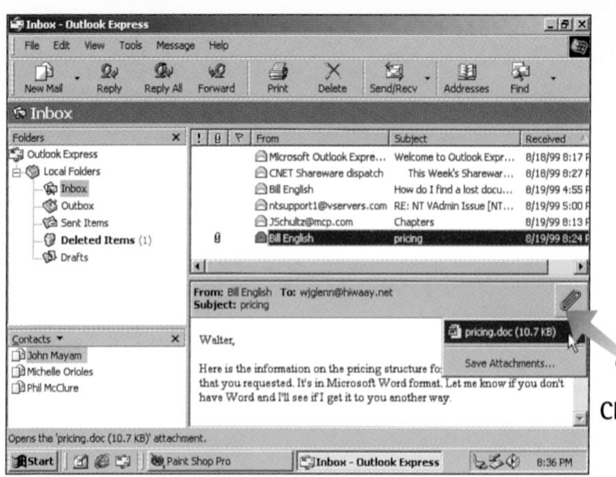

4 Save the Attachments

Choose **Save Attachments** from the drop-down list to save all files attached to the message to a specific location.

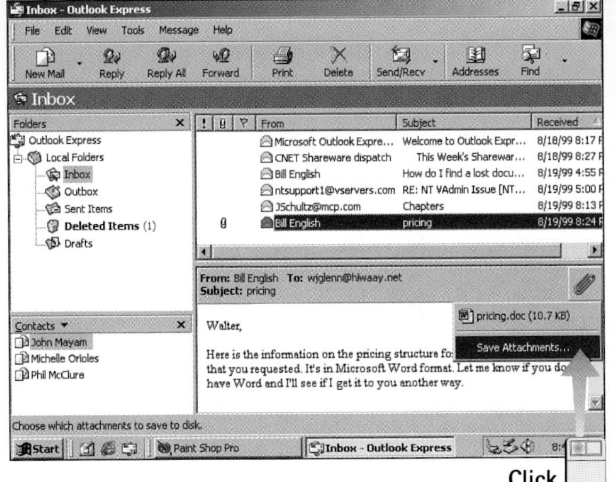

5 Choose a Save Location

In the **Save Attachments** dialog box, select the attachments to be saved and enter a location in the **Save To** box. You can also click the **Browse** button to find a location instead of typing it in. Click the **Save** button to save the selected attachments.

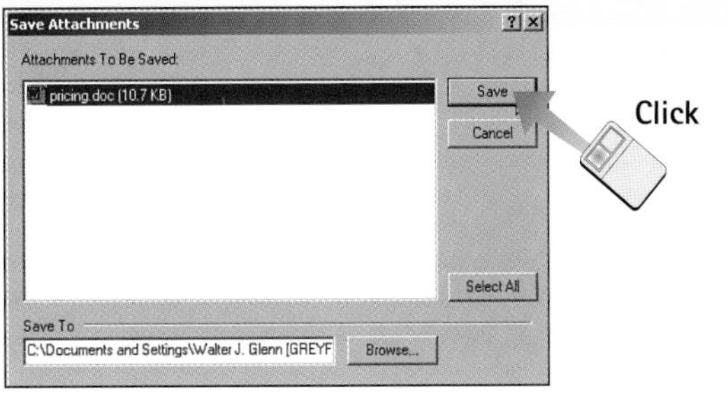

End

How-To Hints

File Associations

Windows knows what files go with what programs because of file associations. All files have a three-letter extension (the three characters after the dot) that tell Windows what program the files should open with. For more on this, see Part 2, "Working with Files and Folders."

TASK 6

How to Send an Attached File

Outlook Express also allows you to send messages with files attached. The first step to sending a file attachment is to create a new message. For specifics on this process, see Task 1.

Begin

1 Start a New Message

Click the **New Mail** button on the Outlook Express toolbar to start a new message.

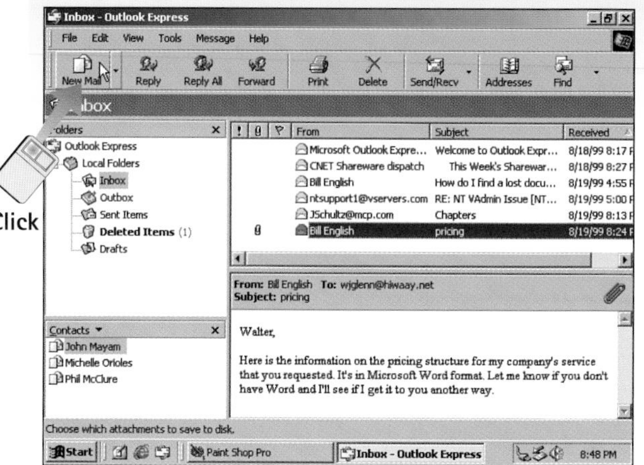

2 Write Your Message

Address and write your message the same way you normally would.

3 Insert a File Attachment

When your message is ready to send, click **File Attachment** from the **Insert** menu. You can also click the **Attach** button on the Outlook Express toolbar.

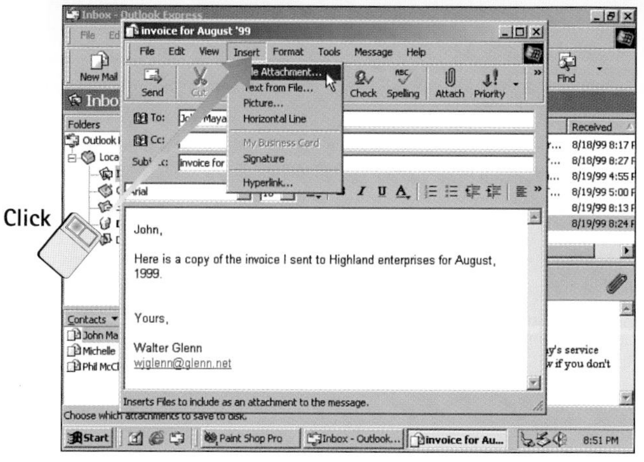

4 Select the File

Locate the file you want to send by browsing through the folders in the normal manner. Select the file by clicking it once and then click the **Attach** button.

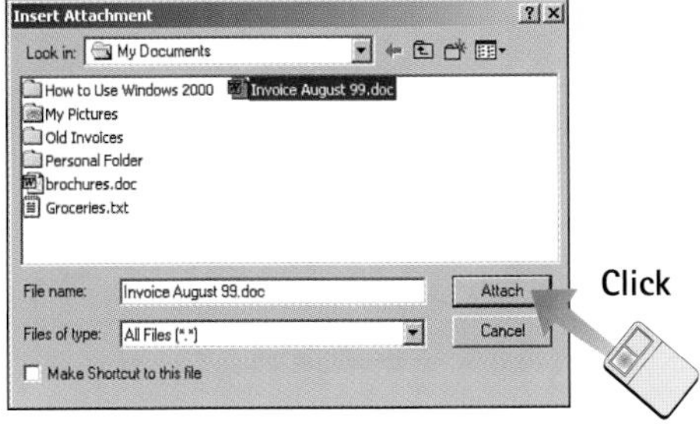

5 Send the Message

Attached files appear in the **Attach** box just underneath the subject. When you're ready to send the message and attachment, just click the **Send** button on the toolbar.

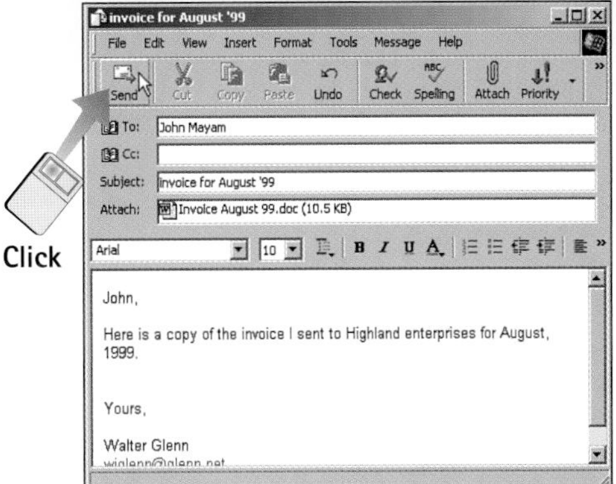

End

How-To Hints

Send a File from Windows

You can actually send a file using email right from Windows. Just right-click on the file and choose **Send To Mail Recipient** from the shortcut menu. This starts a new message with the file already attached.

Attachment Etiquette

Even modest documents today can make for pretty large files. Many people use modems to access the Internet and large files can take some time to download. If you plan to send someone a large file attachment, it is best to send them a brief message ahead of time warning them when you will send the file.

TASK 7

How to Subscribe to a Newsgroup

A news server often hosts as many as thirty or forty thousand newsgroups or more. To make it easier to sift through these newsgroups, most newsreaders, including Outlook Express, let you subscribe to particular groups. Subscribing does not mean you have to pay anybody to use the group. It's just a way of telling Outlook Express which groups to show you in your program window.

Begin

1 Switch to Your News Server

News servers to which you have access show up in your Outlook Express window below your mailbox folders. Clicking a server once selects that server and shows the newsgroups you are subscribed to in the right-hand window.

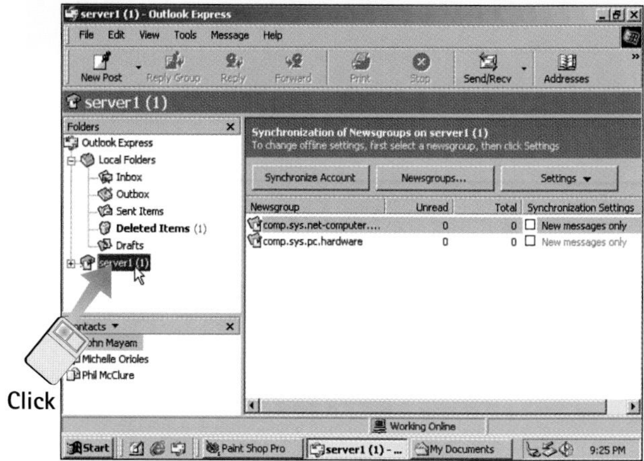

2 Open the Newsgroups List

To see what newsgroups your server carries, open the **Tools** menu and click the **Newsgroups** command.

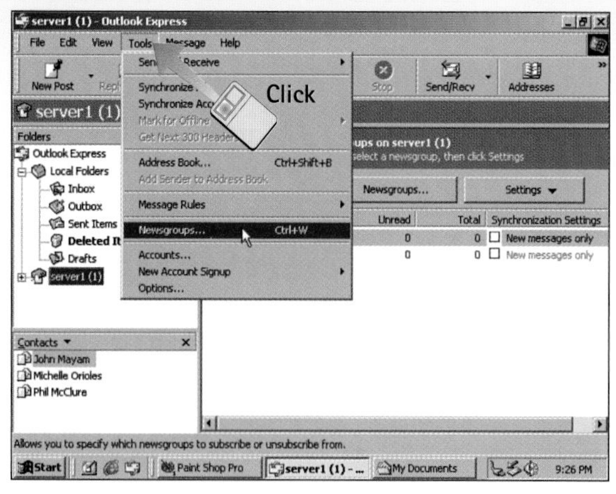

3 Browse for a Newsgroup

All available newsgroups are displayed in this window. You can browse for newsgroups by scrolling through the list. However, with many thousands of groups available, this could take a while.

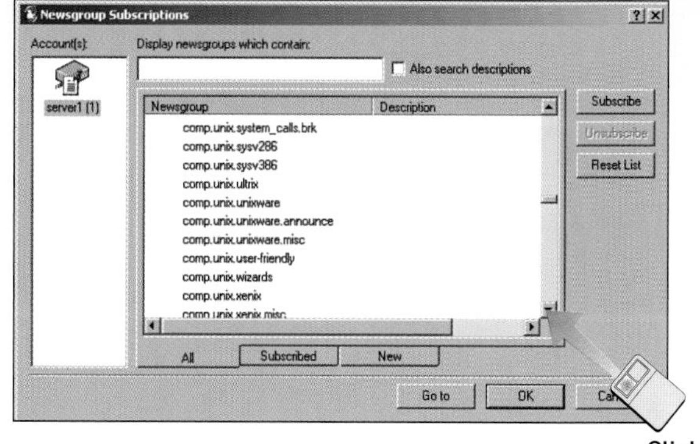

4 Search for a Newsgroup

Fortunately, Outlook Express offers a convenient way to search for newsgroups. Enter any text in the **Display Newsgroups Which Contain** box to show only newsgroups that have that text in their titles. Most newsgroup titles have something to do with their topic.

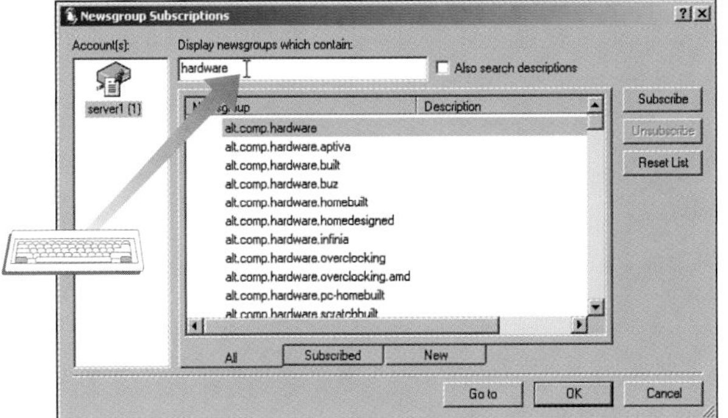

5 Go to a Newsgroup

When you find a newsgroup you like, you can go to it to check it out by clicking the group once to select it and then clicking the **Go to** button.

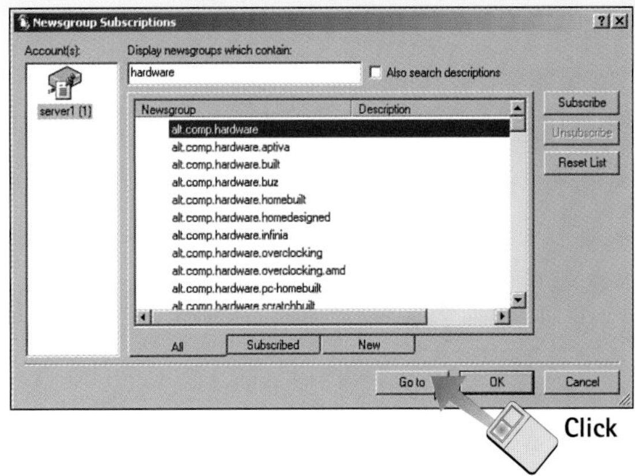

6 Subscribe to a Newsgroup

If you find a newsgroup that you want to go to often, it's easiest to subscribe to it so that it shows up in your **Outlook Express** window. Select the group you want to subscribe to and click the **Subscribe** button.

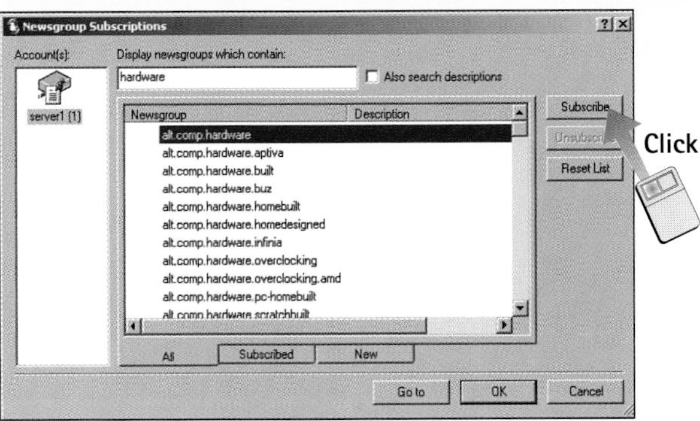

7 View Subscribed Newsgroups

Newsgroups that you have subscribed to show up in the newsgroup list with a subscription icon next to them. You can also view a list of only subscribed newsgroups by clicking the **Subscribed** tab at the bottom of the list.

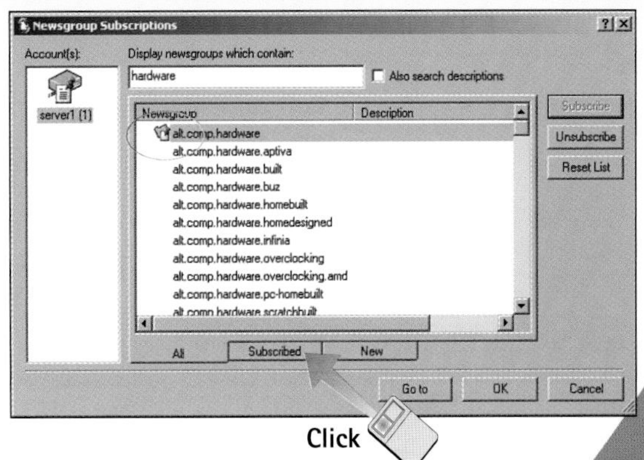

End

TASK 8

How to Read a Newsgroup Posting

Reading newsgroup postings is a lot like reading email messages. Just keep in mind that the postings are available to the general public and that any message can be part of a thread, which is an original message, a reply to that original message, or a reply to those replies.

Begin

1 Open a Newsgroup

First, open a newsgroup by clicking one of the groups beneath your news server. The newsgroup opens and new headers (the part of the message that lets you know the message subject and who the message is from) are downloaded from the server. This sometimes takes a minute or so.

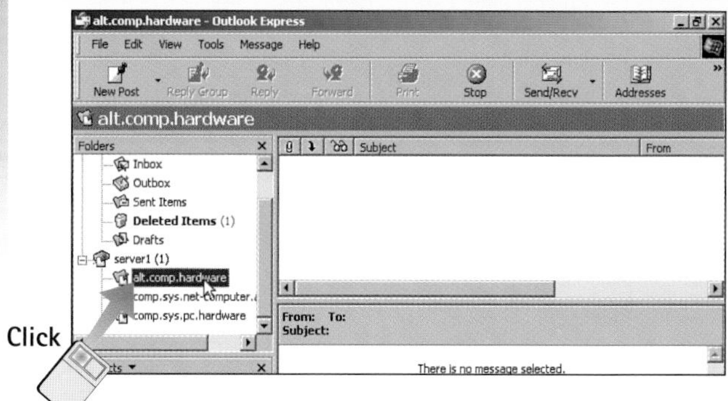

2 Select a Message

After the message headers are downloaded, the messages are displayed to the right, much like email messages. Click any message to download the message body from the server and display it in the preview pane below.

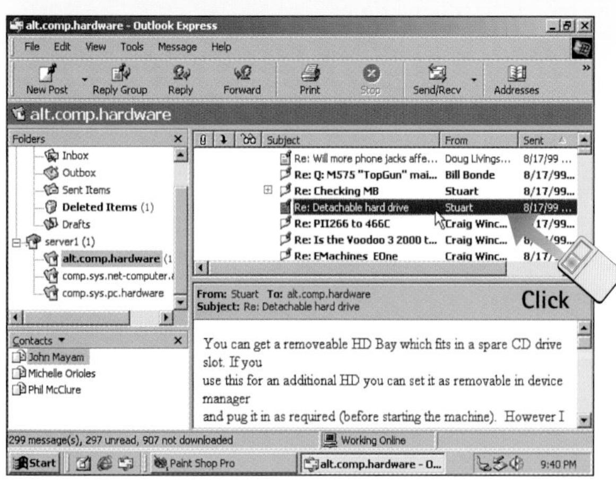

3 Expand a Thread

Messages with a plus sign next to them are part of a thread and have replies. Click the plus to expand the thread and see the other messages. Replies are indented from the original message.

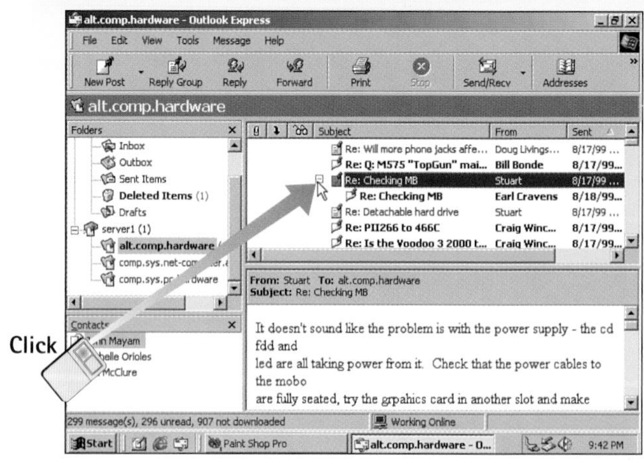

4 Post a Reply to the Group

If you want to post a reply to a message for the whole newsgroup to read, select the message by clicking it once and then click the **Reply Group** button on the toolbar. A window opens that lets you type in and send your reply.

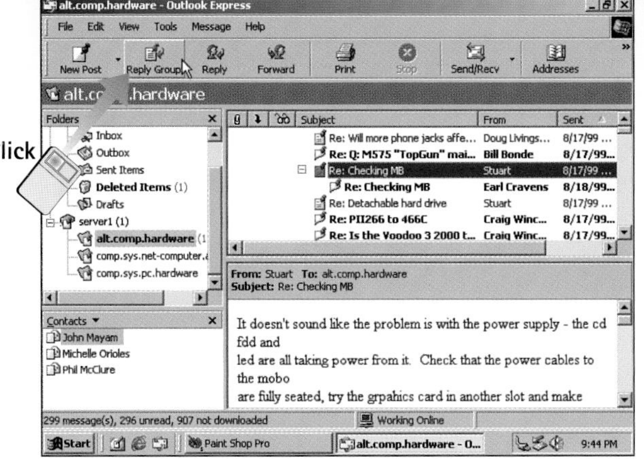

5 Send a Reply to the Poster

You can also reply to the poster of a message privately by email. To do this, select a message and click the **Reply** button on the toolbar. A standard new email message window opens with the address already filled in.

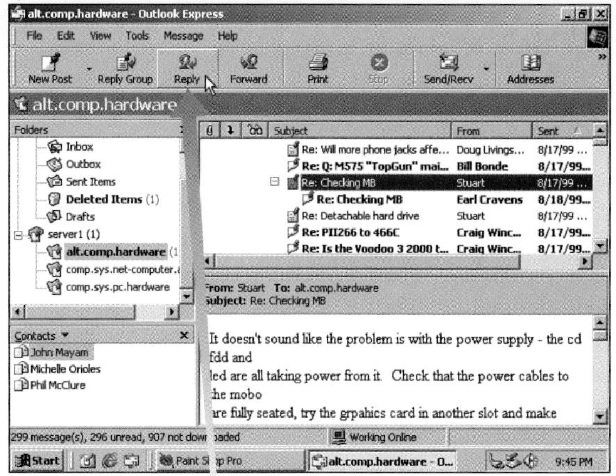

End

How-To Hints

Questionable Content

Many Internet newsgroups host content that you might find very offensive. These groups are usually easily identified by the name of the newsgroup itself and can thus be avoided. Nonetheless, Outlook Express contains no safeguards that you can employ to make these groups off-limits. For this reason, many companies do not permit the use of newsgroups at all. Don't let this scare you away from using them, however. Newsgroups can also be a very valuable resource.

Privacy

When you post a message to a newsgroup, the email address configured in your newsreader program (Outlook Express, for example) is posted along with that message. Many collectors of email addresses (collections are sold to those people who send you all that unsolicited email) collect these names from newsgroup postings. If privacy is a major concern of yours, you may want to avoid posting or change the email address configured in your newsreader program.

TASK 9

How to Post to a Newsgroup

You've seen how to subscribe to a newsgroup and how to browse the messages inside. You've also seen how to reply to messages you find. Posting a message of your own is a very easy task, much like sending an email message.

Begin

1 Open a Newsgroup

Open the newsgroup you want to post a message to by clicking it once.

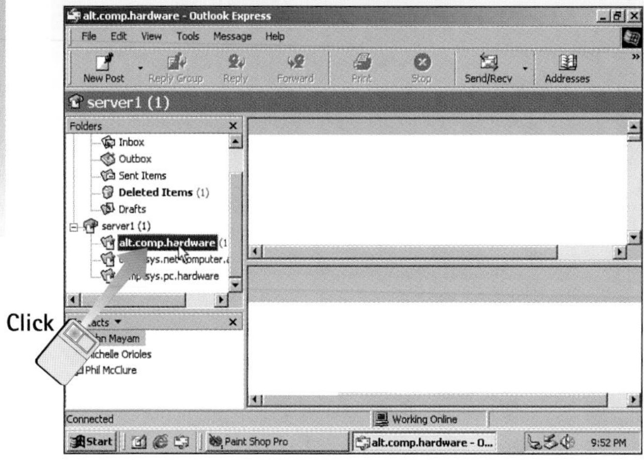

2 Start a Message

After you are connected to a newsgroup, start a new posting by clicking the **New Post** button on the Outlook Express toolbar.

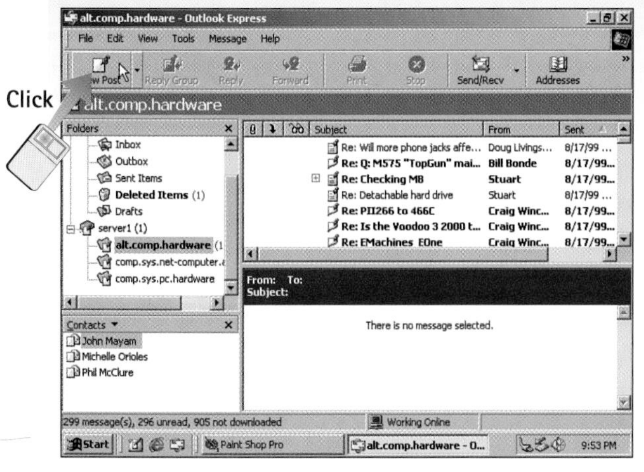

3 Enter a Subject

In the new message window, enter a subject for your message in the **Subject** box. Try to keep it fairly short (so others can see it all in their windows), but also as specific as possible.

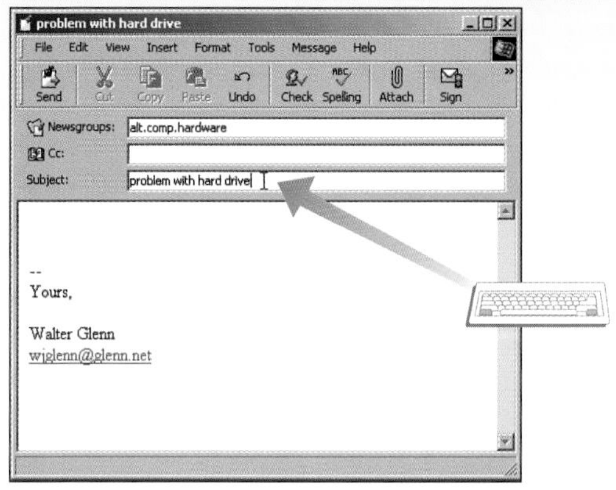

4 Write a Message

Type your message into the main window.

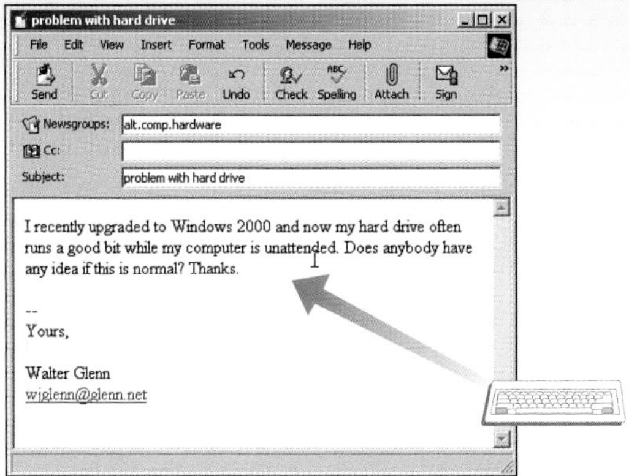

5 Post the Message

After you have typed your message, click the **Send** button on the toolbar to post your message. Check back with the newsgroup occasionally to see if anyone has responded.

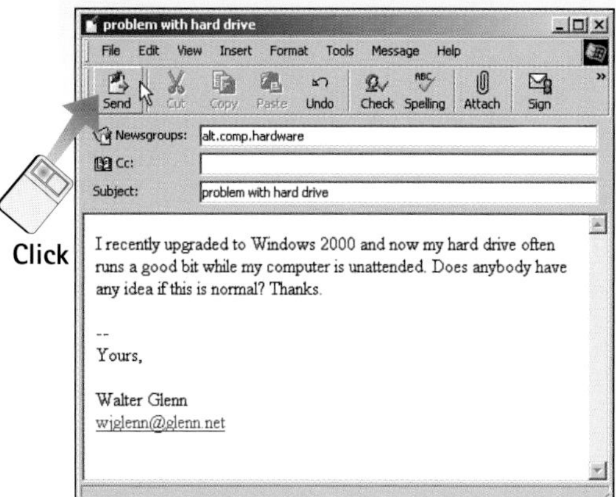

End

How-To Hints

Newsgroup Etiquette

There is a certain etiquette expected of people who post to newsgroups, and other users are very likely to let you know if you ignore that etiquette. First, don't type your message all in capital letters, even if you think it looks more urgent that way. Capitals are used to indicate shouting and anger. If you have a helpful reply to someone's question, post it publicly so that everyone can read it instead of replying privately. When you reply to a message, try not to include the entire original message in the post unless it is very brief. Instead, trim the message so that only the pertinent parts are reposted. Finally, don't post advertisements for products or services in any newsgroups that don't specifically allow it. This is known as spam and is considered poor form.

Task

Part 8

Protecting Your Files

Part of Windows 2000 Professional's claim to fame is that it is built on Windows NT technology, which is a more secure operating system than most. Security is mostly important when your computer is part of a networking environment where it is possible that other users can access your system. Windows 2000 security is a complicated topic. Fortunately, your network administrator takes care of configuring security for you, and there are only a few things you might need to do yourself.

In this part, you will learn about a few basic aspects of Windows 2000 security. First, you will learn to set permissions on your files. Permissions are given to particular users so that they can access files. There are two types of permissions: local and shared. Local permissions apply to the files as they exist on your hard drive. Anyone who logs on to your computer must have the right permissions assigned to his or her username to get to your files. Shared permissions apply to files that you make available to other users on the network (users that don't have to log directly onto your computer). Sharing files is discussed in Part 4, "Working on a Network." Local and shared permissions interact, as well. Think of it this way. All users must have appropriate local permissions. Users accessing your computer from the network must also have shared permissions. A user who is given shared access but denied local access, for example, cannot access the file at all.

In this chapter, you will also learn how to encrypt folders and files, making the files completely unreadable by anyone but yourself. You'll learn how to lock your workstation while you are away from your computer, which saves you from having to log out and back on when you aren't gone for long. You'll also learn to set a password on your screen saver, which helps when you forget to lock your workstation. Finally, you'll learn how to change your logon password.

TASK 1

How to Set Permissions on a Local File or Folder

For each person that might use your computer, you can assign a specific set of permissions to use an object. Permissions that you can assign to files and folders differ slightly, but each allows you to assign a certain level of control to the object. You can choose to give a person full control, permission to modify things but not delete them, permission only to read files and run programs, or permission to create new items.

Begin

1 Open a Folder's Properties

Find the folder for which you want to assign permissions. Right-click it and choose **Properties** from the shortcut menu.

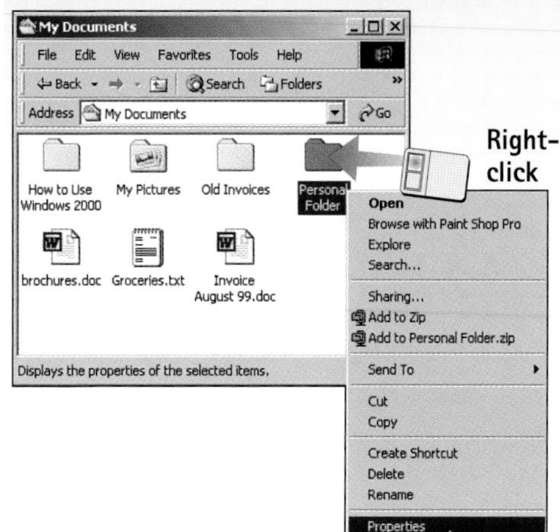

2 Switch to the Security Tab

Switch to the **Security** tab of the **Properties** dialog box by clicking it once.

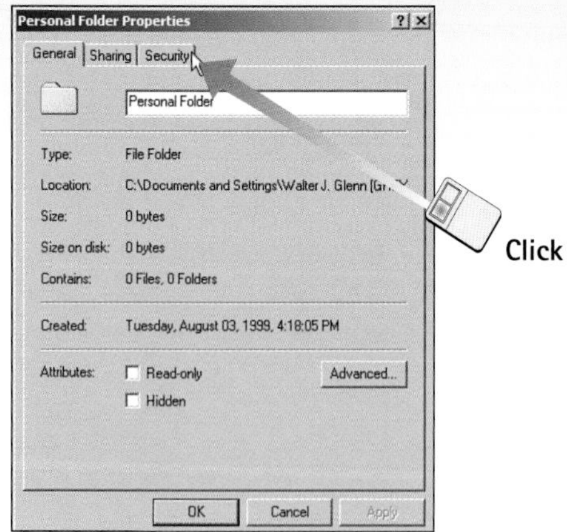

3 Select a User or Group

From the list of users that have access to the folder, select a user or group by clicking the entry once. If you don't see the person on the list, you can add users by clicking the **Add** button and choosing from a list of available users.

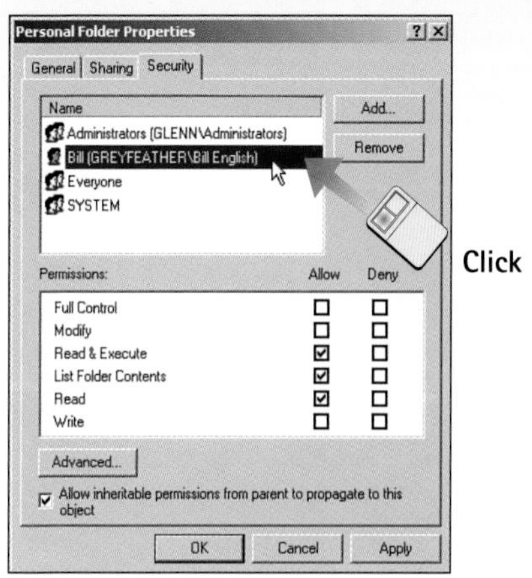

4 Set Permissions

After you have selected a user, set permissions by clicking the check boxes. Sometimes, objects inherit permissions from the folder they are in. In this case, permissions boxes are shaded. Select the opposite permission (Allow or Deny) to override the permission.

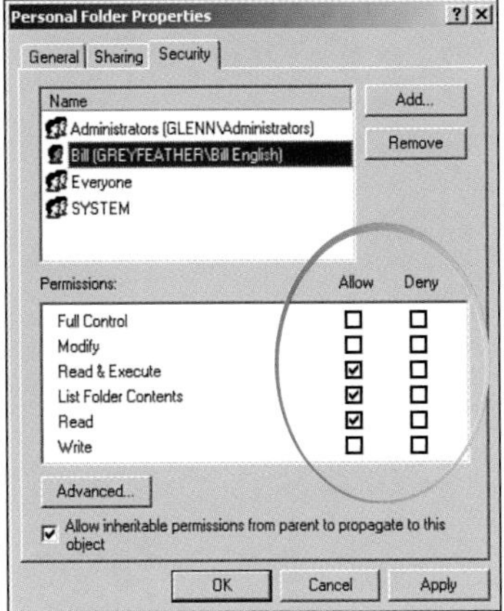

5 Allow Inheritable Permissions

By default, files and folders inherit permissions from the folder they are in. If you want to stop this inheritance, clear the **Allow Inheritable Permissions** check box.

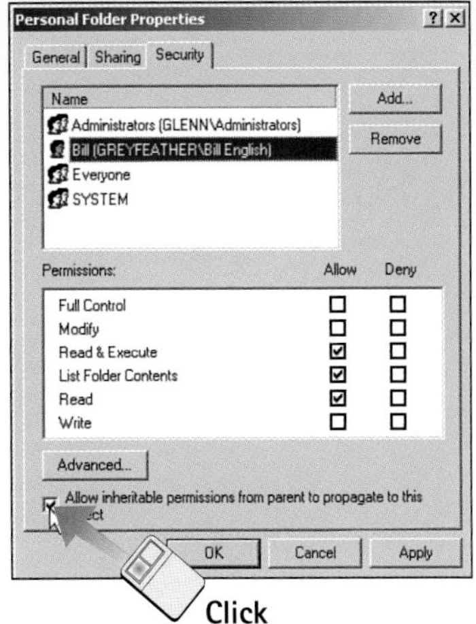

End

How-To Hints

NTFS

The use of local file permissions requires that your disk be formatted using the NTFS file system, which is Windows 2000's file system. If you are on a network, the chances are that your disk uses this file system. If you don't see any of the dialog boxes mentioned in the previous steps on your computer, you probably don't use NTFS. Check with your network administrator.

Windows Help

If you want to know more about Windows security, including what each of the permissions means and how they interact with one another, consult Windows Help (as discussed in Part 1, "Using the Windows 2000 Desktop") or talk to your network administrator.

TASK 2

How to Set Permissions on a Shared Folder

Permissions are also set on folders that you share over the network. The actual process for sharing a folder is discussed in Part 4. The following steps show you how to change permissions on a folder that is already shared. You can assign users permission to have full control of, change but not delete them in, or just read items in shared folders.

Begin

1 Open the Sharing Dialog Box

You can identify shared folders on your computer by the small picture of a hand that looks like it's holding the folder out. Right-click a shared folder and choose the **Sharing** command from the shortcut menu.

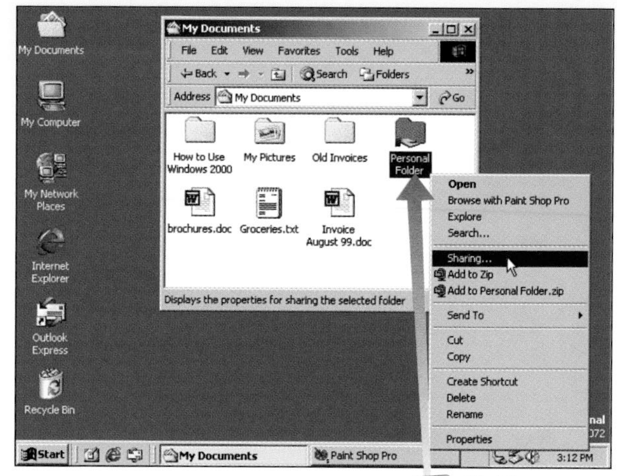

2 Open the Permissions Dialog Box

Click the **Permissions** button to open the **Permissions** dialog box for the folder.

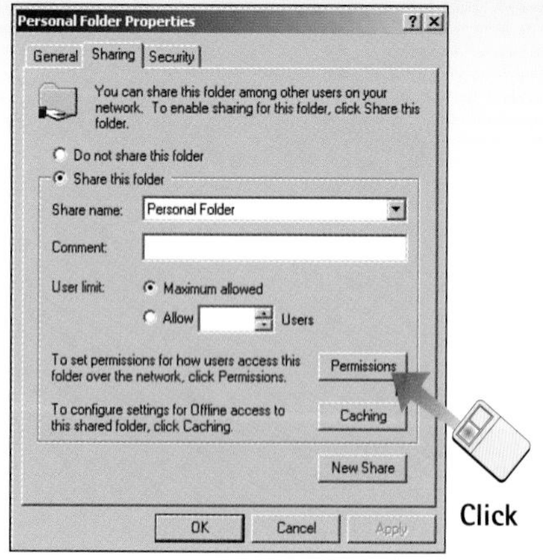

3 Remove the Everyone Group

By default, a special group named **Everyone** is given the full control permission over a shared folder. It is best to remove this group altogether. Just select it and click the **Remove** button.

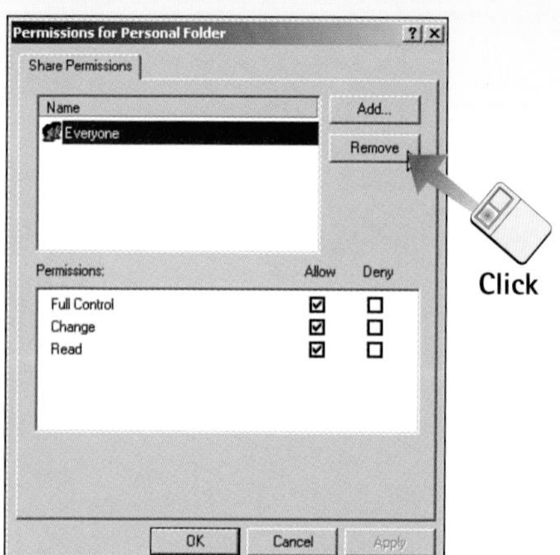

4 Add a New User

Click the **Add** button on the **Permissions** dialog box to open a list of users in the domain. Choose a user or group to which you want to assign permissions. The **Domain Users** group, for example, includes all valid users on the network. Select the group and click the **Add** button to add it to the list. You can select multiple users and groups, if you want. Click **OK** when you're done.

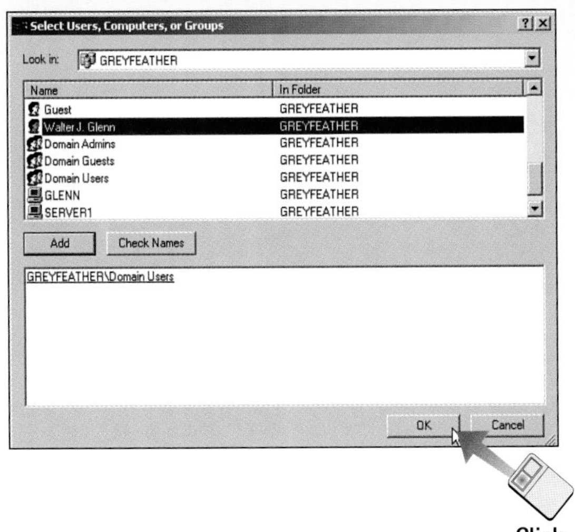

5 Set Permissions

New users and groups you add are given only the **Read** permission by default, meaning that they can open files in the folder, but cannot change or delete them. Allow or deny other actions by clicking the check boxes.

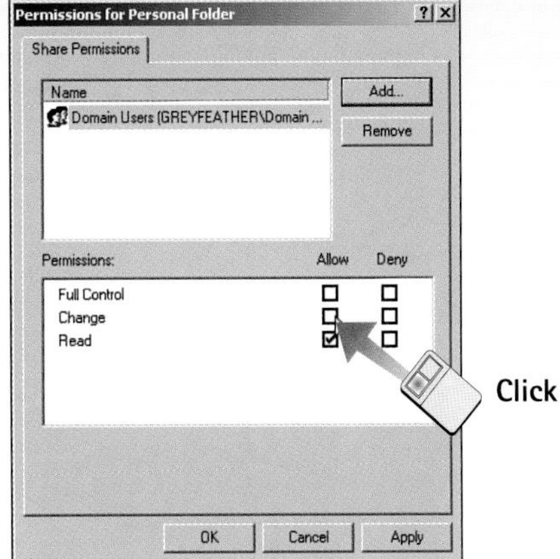

End

How-To Hints

Standalone Computers

If your computer is not on a network and part of a **Windows** domain, you will probably not even see the Sharing command on the shortcut menu, let alone be able to assign shared permissions. Of course, if you're not part of a network, why would you want to?

TASK 3

How to Encrypt a File or Folder

Windows 2000 allows you to encrypt files or folders so that other users cannot make sense of the files even if they manage to bypass permissions and gain access to them. The whole process is pretty transparent. After you encrypt a file or folder, you can continue to use it normally. You only need to decrypt it if you want to share it with others or if you want to take it to another computer to use yourself.

Begin

1 Open a File's Properties

Right-click the file or folder you want to encrypt and choose the **Properties** command from the shortcut menu.

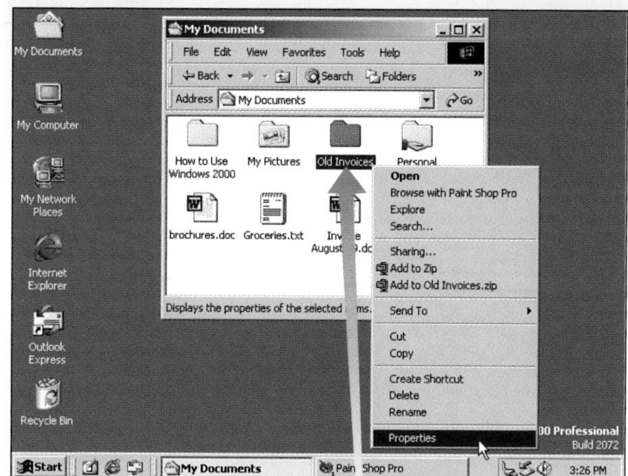

2 Open Advanced Options

On the **General** tab of the **Properties** dialog box, click the **Advanced** button to open the **Advanced Attributes** dialog box.

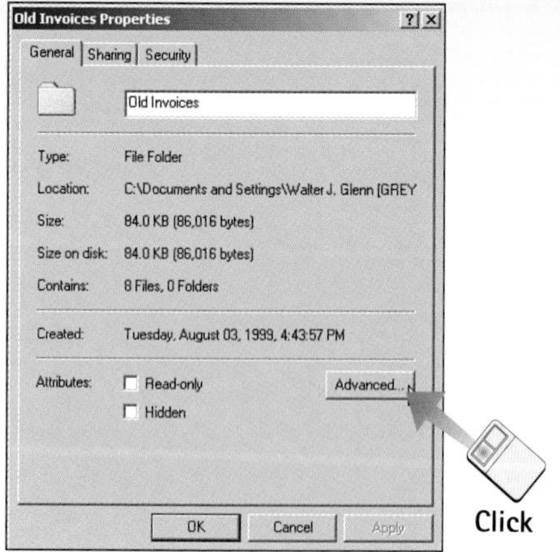

3 Encrypt the Folder

Select the **Encrypt Contents to Secure Data** option. Note that there is also an option here that lets you compress files and folders to save disk space. You cannot use both encryption and compression on an object at the same time.

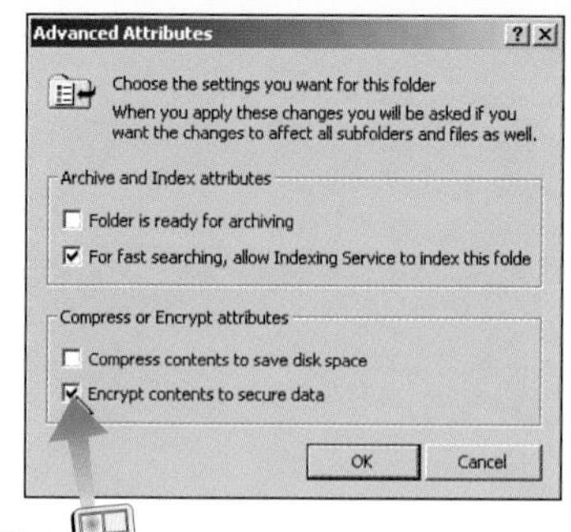

4 Close the Dialog Boxes

Click the **OK** button to close the **Advanced Attributes** dialog box; next, click the **OK** button on the **General** tab of the folder's **Properties** dialog box to close it.

5 Encrypt Files and Subfolders

A dialog box appears that lets you choose whether to encrypt only the selected folder or also to encrypt the subfolders within that folder. Choose the option you want and click the **OK** button.

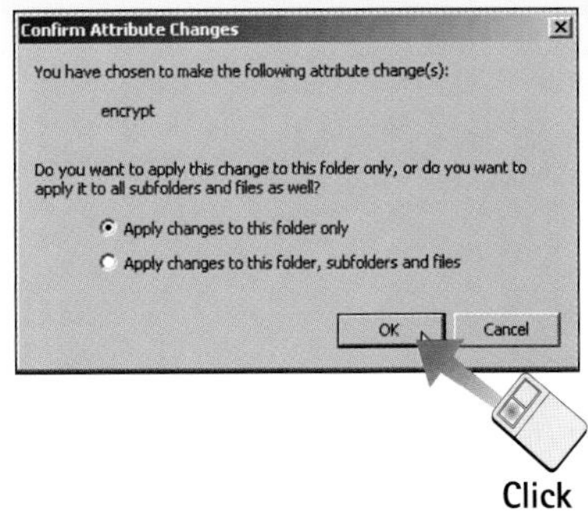

End

How-To Hints

Decrypting a Folder

To decrypt a folder, simply follow the preceding steps and clear the **Encrypt Contents to Secure Data** option on the **Advanced Attributes** dialog box.

When It Doesn't Work

Like local file permissions, encryption is only available if you are using the NTFS file system. Also, Windows 2000 system files cannot be encrypted.

No Visual Indicator

When you encrypt a file or folder, Windows 2000 gives no visual indicator that encryption is present. To see whether an object is encrypted, you actually have to open its properties and see whether the **Encrypt Contents to Secure Data** option is checked.

TASK 4

How to Lock Your Workstation

When you leave your desk for any period of time, it is best to log off of Windows 2000 using the procedure described in Part 1. Sometimes, however, you might even want to prevent other authorized users from gaining access to your computer. Windows 2000 also lets you lock your workstation. When locked, only you or a system administrator can unlock the computer.

Begin

1 Press Ctrl+Alt+Delete

Press the **Ctrl**, **Alt**, and **Delete** keys all at once. This can be done no matter where you are in the system, even if you have programs running.

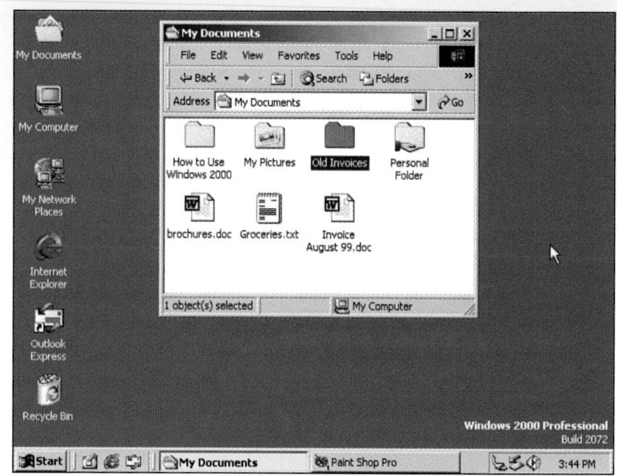

2 Lock Your Computer

From the Windows Security dialog box, click the **Lock Computer** button.

3 Unlock Your Computer

When your computer is locked, you unlock it in much the same way that you log on to Windows. First, press the **Ctrl**, **Alt**, and **Delete** keys all at once.

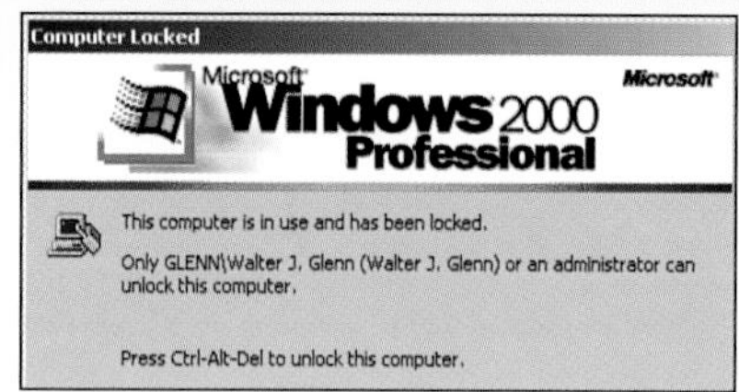

4 Enter Your Password

At this point, only you or a system administrator can unlock the computer. Enter your password in the Password box and then click the **OK** button.

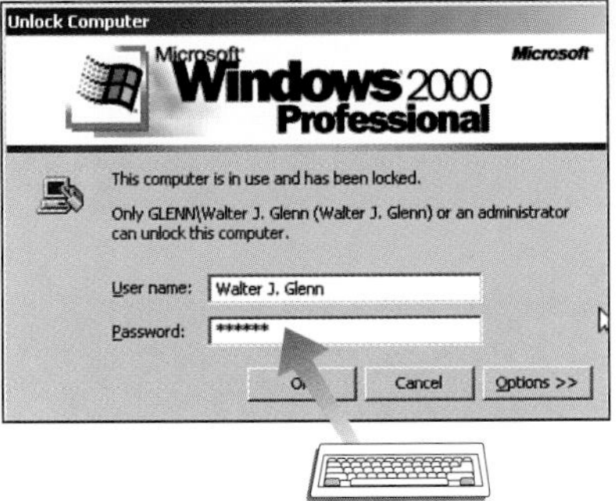

5 Return to Work

After you unlock your workstation, you'll find it in exactly the same state you left it—running programs and all.

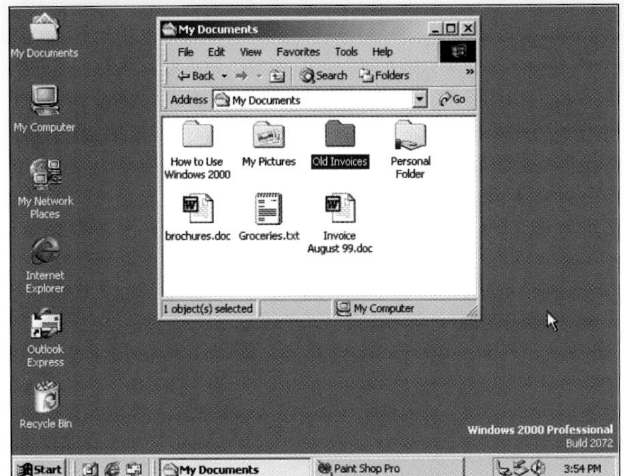

End

How-To Hints

Locking Is Quicker

Many people find that locking their computers when leaving their desks is quicker than logging off, mainly because logging off requires saving work, stopping programs, and running programs again when they get back. This is normally fine, especially if you won't be away for long, but your network administrator might prefer that you log off when you leave for long periods.

TASK 5

How to Assign a Screen Saver Password

Often, people forget to log off or lock their workstations every time they leave their desks, especially if they're late for a meeting or it's 4:57 on a Friday afternoon. One way to create a kind of safety net is use a screen saver that is password protected. This way, when the screen saver comes up, you or an administrator must enter your password to get back into the system.

Begin

1 Open the Control Panel

Select **Start**, **Settings**, **Control Panel** to open the **Windows Control Panel.**

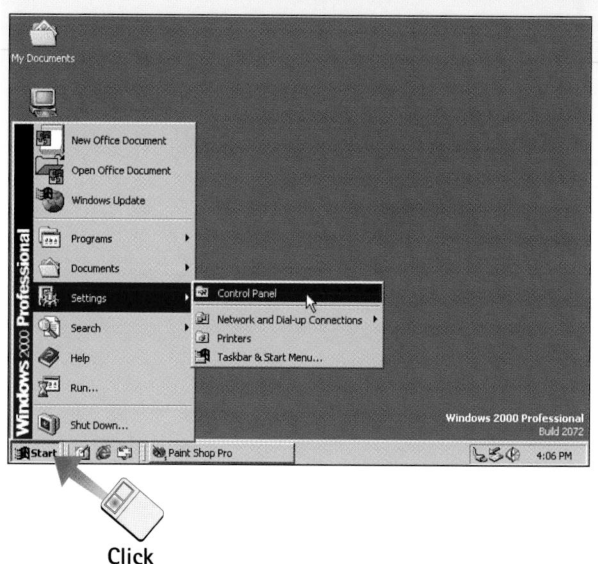

2 Open the Display Applet

The **Control Panel** features a number of applets that let you change various settings for your computer. Double-click the **Display** applet to open the **Display Properties** dialog box.

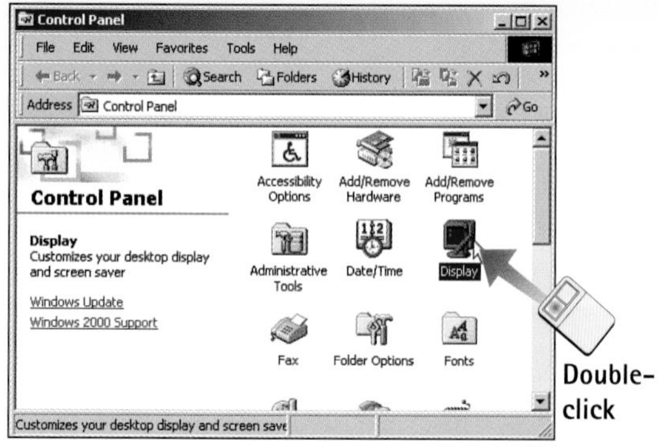

3 Switch to the Screen Saver Tab

Switch to the **Screen Saver** tab by clicking it once.

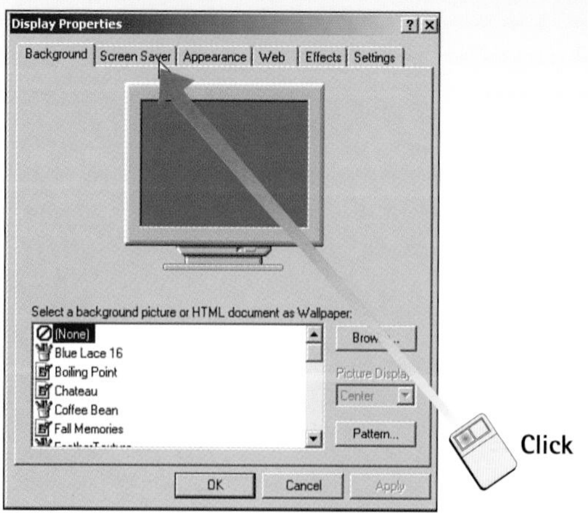

4 Choose Password Protected Option

Click the **Password Protected** option to require that a password be entered when returning to the desktop from a screen saver. If no screen saver is selected, this option is be available. For more on how to set up a screen saver, see Part 9, "Changing Windows 2000 Settings."

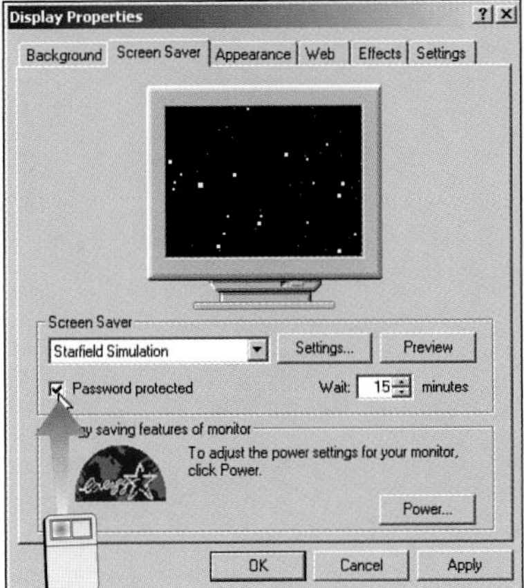

End

How-To Hints

Remember to Log Off

Although a screen saver password can help you protect your system, it is not a good substitute for logging off or locking your workstation. In fact, many network administrators don't allow users to use screen saver passwords at all for fear that they will grow reliant on them.

TASK 6

How to Change Your Logon Password

It is usually a good idea to change your logon password periodically in case someone has gained access to it. On more secure networks, it is often policy that users must change their passwords every month or two. On some even more secure networks, administrators change and distribute new passwords and do not allow users to do it themselves. You should check with your network administrator to find out the policy for your network.

Begin

1 Press Ctrl+Alt+Delete

Press the **Ctrl**, **Alt**, and **Delete** keys all at once to open the **Windows Security** dialog box. On this dialog box, click the **Change Password** button to open the **Change Password** dialog box.

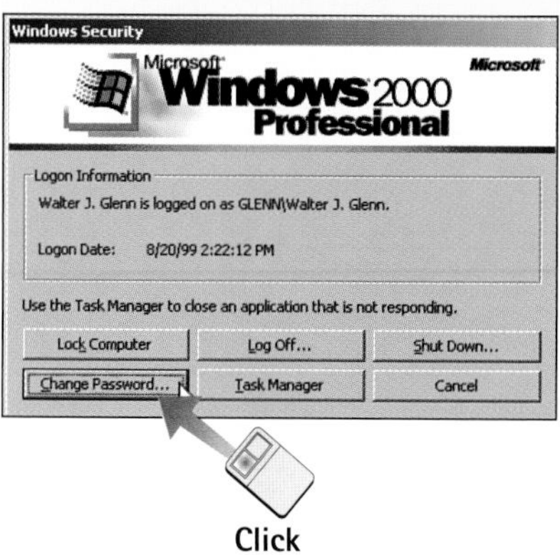

2 Enter Your Old Password

Enter your old password in the **Old Password** box.

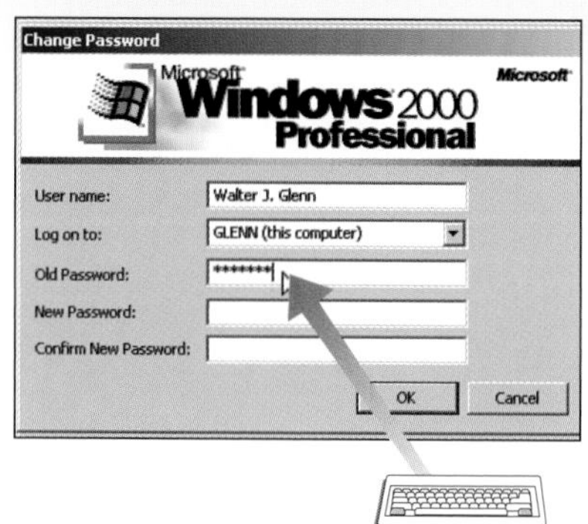

3 Enter a New Password

Enter a new password in the **New Password** box.

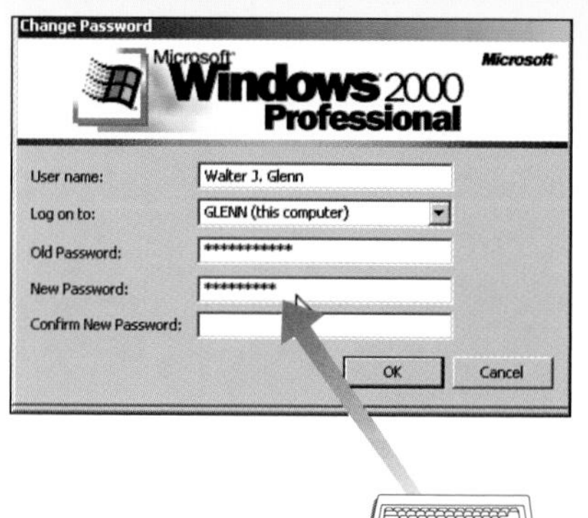

4 Confirm the New Password

Enter your new password again in the **Confirm New Password** box. When you are done, click the **OK** button.

5 Return to Windows

Windows lets you know that the password has been changed. Click the **OK** button to get back to the desktop.

End

How-To Hints

Password Security

For the best possible security, don't write your password down anywhere and never tell it to anyone. You should also change it every so often just in case it has been discovered. If your administrator supplies you with a password, memorize it and destroy the paper it came on.

Password Hints

Never create passwords with words that might appear in the dictionary, names, or dates. If you find it hard to remember cryptic passwords full of upper- and lowercase characters and numbers, you can create a password that is both secure and easy to remember. One way is to think of two four-letter words and join them with a two-digit number. For example, `lion72dunk` is pretty easy to remember and almost impossible to guess. You can also think of an easy-to-remember seven- or eight-letter word. Then, instead of typing in the word itself, type in the characters that are to the upper-left of the real characters on the keyboard. This way, an easy-to-guess word like `astronomy` becomes `qw549h9j6`. Remember to check with your administrator about password policies used on your network.

Task

Part 9

Changing Windows 2000 Settings

After you have worked with Windows 2000 Professional for a while and gotten used to the way things work, you might find that there are changes you would like to make. Windows 2000 is wonderfully customizable and provides many options for changing its interface to suit the way you work.

Most of the changes you will make take place using the **Windows Control Panel**, which is a special folder that contains many small programs called applets. Each applet is designed to let you adjust settings for a particular part of your system. For example, the Display applet lets you change display settings such as background color, window colors, screen saver, and screen size. You can access the **Control Panel** through either the **Start** menu or the **My Computer** window, as you will see in the tasks throughout this part.

You'll also find that many of the **Control Panel** applets are also directly available from the shortcut menu of various desktop items. Right-clicking the desktop itself, for example, and choosing **Properties** from the shortcut menu that opens is exactly the same as opening the **Display** applet from the **Control Panel**. You'll see several such ways for accessing common controls in the following tasks.

TASK 1

How to Change the Volume

If you have speakers hooked up to your computer, you've probably noticed that some programs and certain things that Windows does (called events) make sounds. Many speakers have volume control knobs on them, but there is also a convenient way to change the volume within Windows itself.

Begin

1 Click the Volume Icon

A small volume icon that looks like a speaker appears in the system tray next to your clock to indicate that sound is configured on your computer. Click the icon once with your left mouse button to open a volume control.

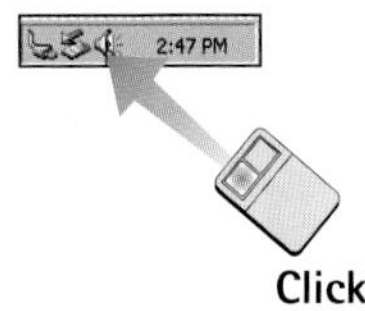

2 Change the Volume Setting

Click and drag the slider with your left mouse button to adjust your volume. Your computer beeps when you release the slider to give you an idea of the volume you've set.

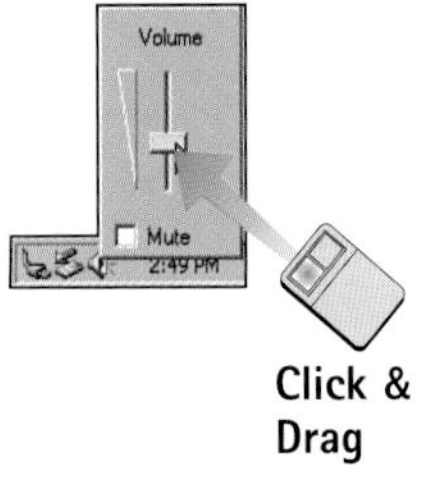

3 Mute Your Speakers

Click the **Mute** option to silence your speakers. While your speakers are muted, the volume icon is overlaid with a red circle and slash. When you want the speakers to play again, open the **Volume** dialog box and deselect the **Mute** option.

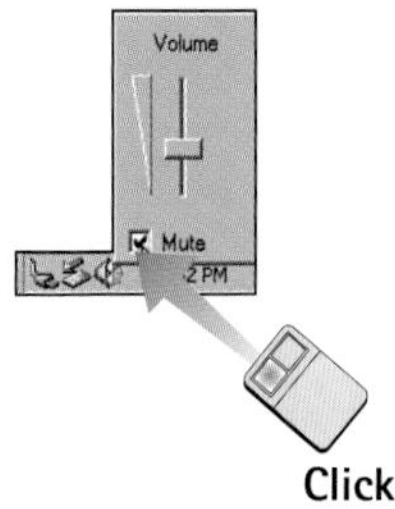

4 Click the Desktop

Click anywhere out on your desktop once to close the **Volume** dialog box.

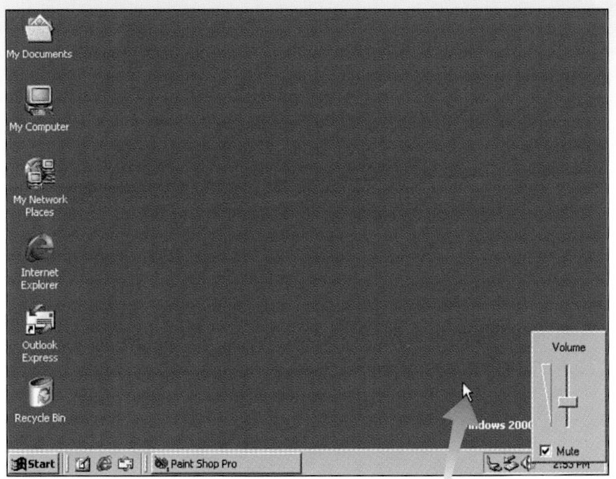

End

How-To Hints

Double-Clicking

The main volume control adjusts the volume for all of the sound on your computer, no matter where that sound comes from. Double-click the **Volume** dialog box to open a more sophisticated volume control that lets you adjust the volume for each audio device configured on your system. For example, you might want to lower the volume for CD-ROMs but leave the volume for **Wave** files (which are used for Windows system events) alone.

TASK 2

How to Set Up a Screen Saver

On older monitors, screen savers help prevent a phenomenon called burn-in, where items on your display can actually be permanently burned in to your monitor if left for a long time. Newer monitors don't really have a problem with this, but screen savers are still kind of fun and do help prevent passers-by from seeing what's on your computer. Windows 2000 provides a number of built-in screen savers.

Begin

1 Open the Display Control Panel

Right-click any open space on your desktop and choose the **Properties** command from the shortcut menu by clicking it once.

2 Switch to the Screen Saver Tab

Switch to the **Screen Saver** tab by clicking it once.

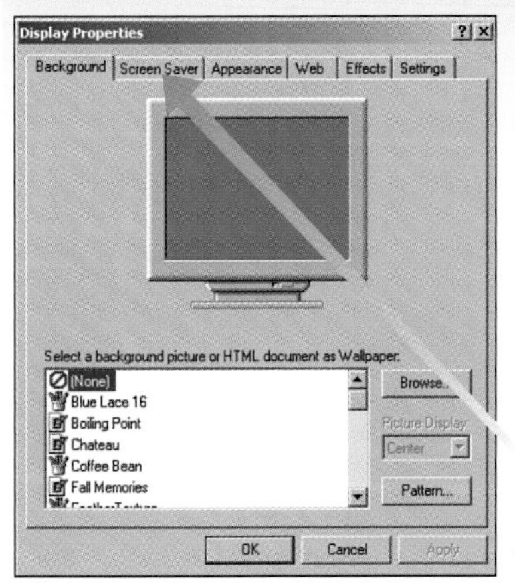

3 Choose a Screen Saver

By default, no screen saver is active. Click the arrow beside the **Screen Saver** drop-down list to choose from a number of available screen savers.

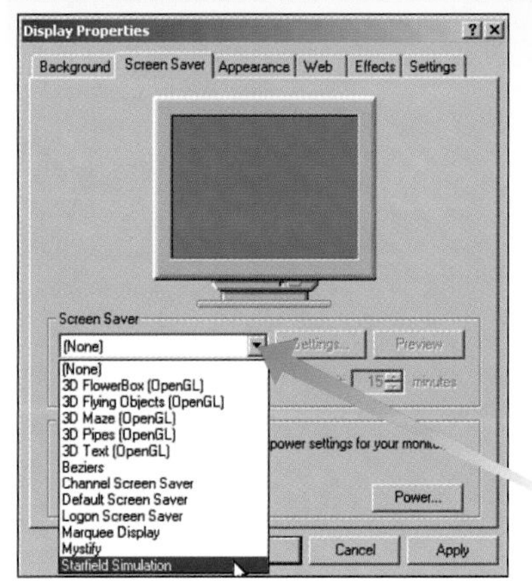

4 Preview the Screen Saver

When you choose a screen saver, Windows displays a small preview of it right on the picture of a monitor in the dialog box. To see how the screen saver will look when it's actually working, click the **Preview** button. Move the mouse or click a key during the preview to get back to the dialog box.

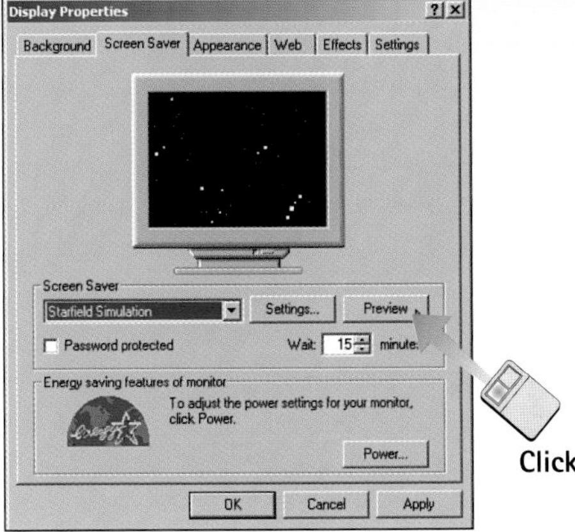

5 Adjust Settings

Each screen saver has its own specific settings so you can change how the screen saver behaves. Settings for Starfield Simulation, for example, let you control how many stars are displayed and how fast they move. Click the **Settings** button to experiment with options for any screen saver.

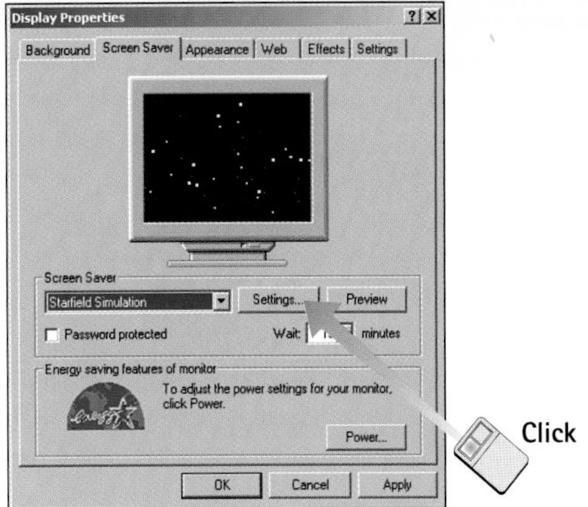

6 Adjust Wait Time

Wait time indicates how long your computer must be idle before the screen saver kicks in. By default, this is 15 minutes, but you can change it to whatever you want by using the scroll buttons.

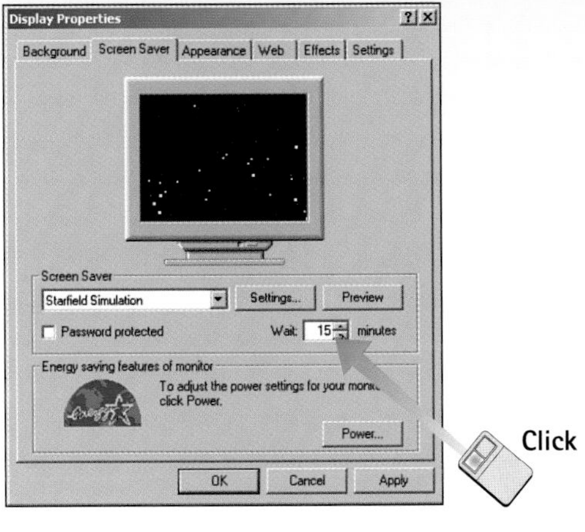

End

How-To Hints

Password Protection

You can make a screen saver password protected by clicking the **Password Protected** option on the **Screen Saver** tab. See Part 8, "Protecting Your Files," for more information.

TASK 3

How to Change Your Wallpaper

Wallpaper is a pattern or picture that is displayed on your desktop just to make things a bit more fun. By default, no wallpaper is used and you only see the standard blue desktop color. Windows 2000 includes a number of interesting wallpapers you can use to spruce up your display.

Begin

1 Open the Display Control Panel

Right-click any open space on your desktop and choose the **Properties** command from the shortcut menu by clicking it once.

Click

2 Choose a Wallpaper from the List

Choose any wallpaper from the list by clicking it once. Some wallpapers listed are pictures, some are patterns that can be tiled to create effects on your desktop. Whatever wallpaper you choose is displayed in the picture of a monitor in the dialog box.

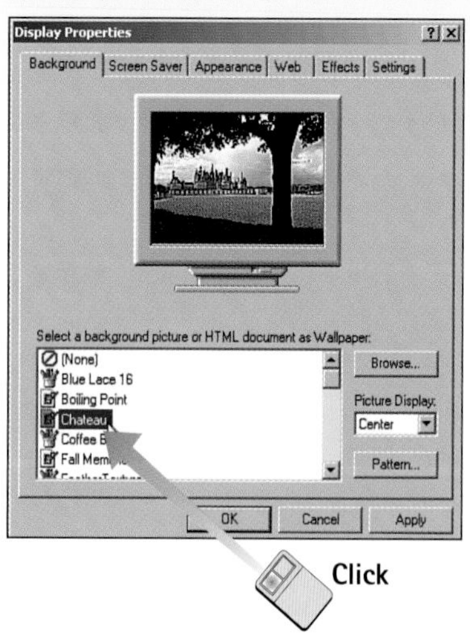

Click

3 Use Your Own Picture

If you have your own picture file that you want to use as wallpaper, click the **Browse** button to open a dialog box that lets you locate it. Background pictures can have the following extensions: **`.bmp`**, **`.gif`**, **`.jpg`**, **`.dib`**, and **`.htm`**.

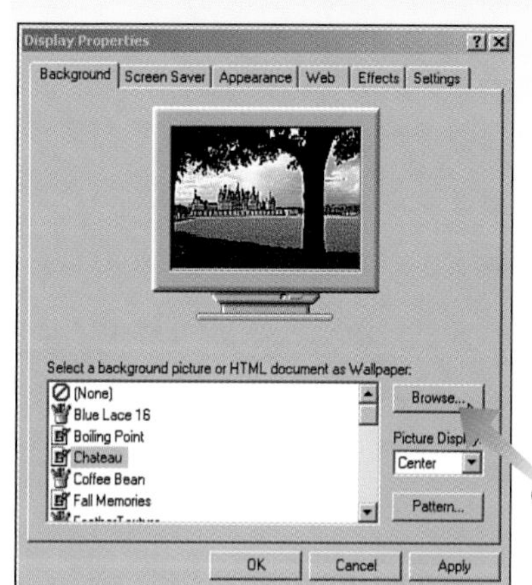

Click

4 Adjust the Picture Display

You can display background pictures in one of three ways. You can center a picture on the screen, stretch a picture so that it fills the screen, or tile a small picture so that it fills the screen. Click the **Picture Display** drop-down list to experiment with these options.

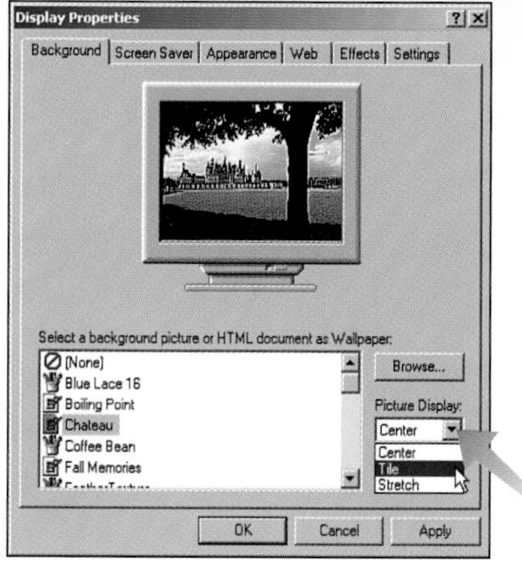

5 Set a Pattern

Patterns are simple designs such as diamonds or paisleys that you can use to fill your desktop. Click the **Pattern** button to choose from a list of patterns to use. If you use a pattern and a wallpaper at the same time, the wallpaper appears on top of the pattern.

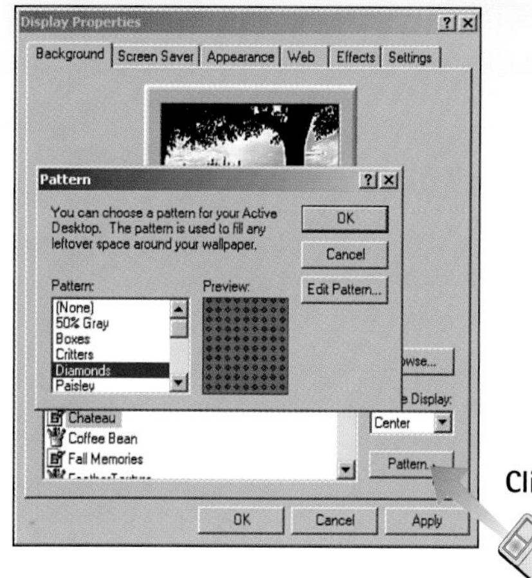

6 Apply the Settings

Click the **Apply** button to apply any new wallpaper to your desktop, but keep the **Display** dialog box open. This lets you more easily experiment with backgrounds. After you find one you like, click the **OK** button to get back to work.

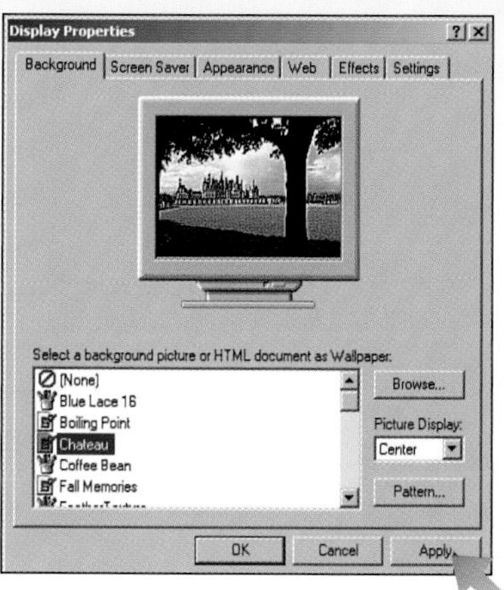

End

TASK 4

How to Change Display Settings

Changing your display settings can really affect how you work. Windows lets you change the colors used on your desktop background, parts of windows, and even menus. Depending on the monitor and video card you use, you might also be able to change your screen size and how many colors are available.

Begin

1 Open the Display Control Panel

Right-click any open space on your desktop and choose the **Properties** command from the shortcut menu by clicking it once.

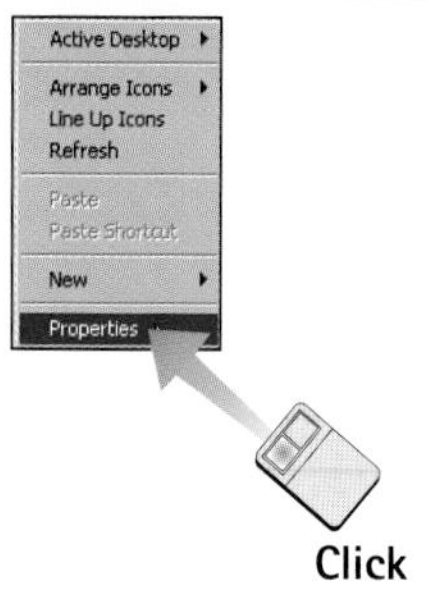

2 Switch to the Appearance Tab

Switch to the **Appearance** tab by clicking it once. The **Appearance** tab is used to change Windows color settings.

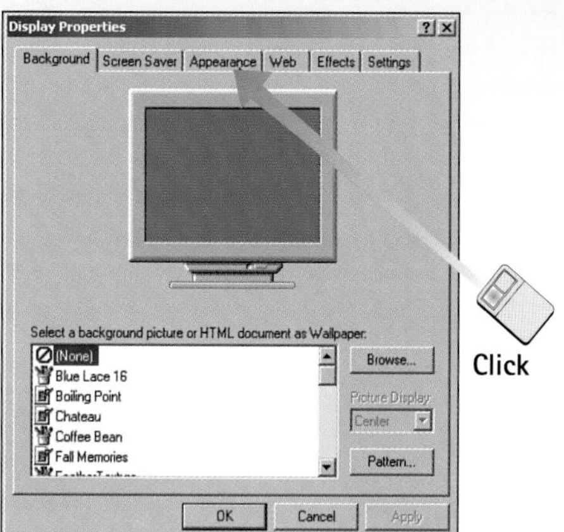

3 Choose a New Color Scheme

Windows comes with many predefined color schemes—sets of colors for individual interface elements that the Windows designers thought would go together. Choose a scheme using the **Scheme** drop-down list. The sample window on the dialog box changes to show you what a scheme would look like.

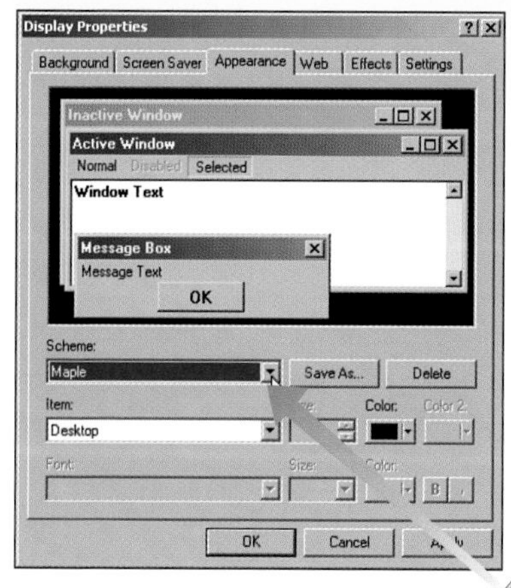

4 Adjust Individual Items

You can also change the colors of individual interface items to create your own scheme. Choose an item from the **Item** drop-down list (or click the element in the sample window) and then use the color palette to choose a color.

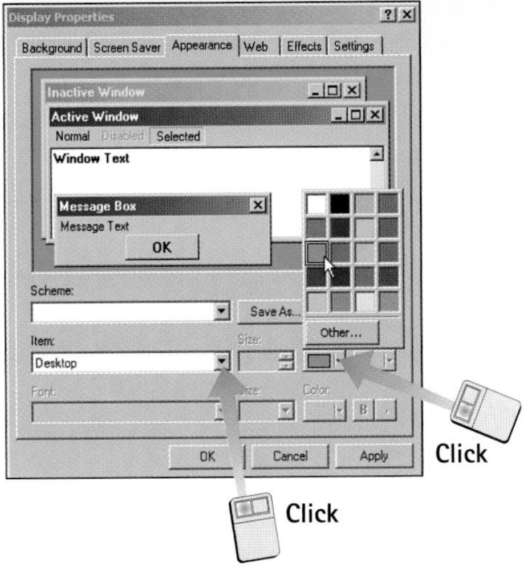

5 Switch to the Settings Tab

Switch to the **Settings** tab by clicking it once. The **Settings** tab is used to change the screen size and number of colors used.

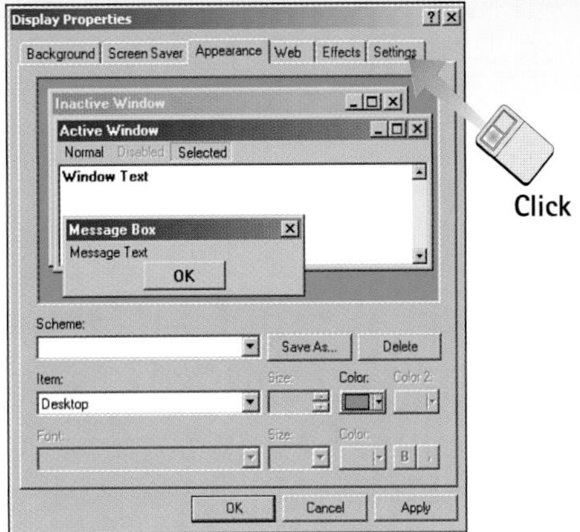

6 Choose a New Color Depth

Color depth refers to the number of colors your screen can display. The default setting depends on the video card and monitor you use. Click the **Colors** drop-down list to choose a new color setting. Keep in mind that the settings available to you depend on the hardware you use.

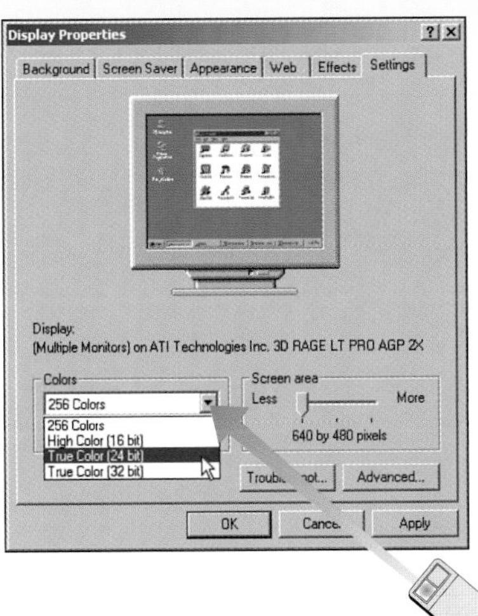

7 Choose a New Screen Area

Screen area refers to the size of items displayed on your screen. Increasing the area means you can see more items on your screen at once, but also means those items will appear smaller. Adjust the screen area by dragging the slider.

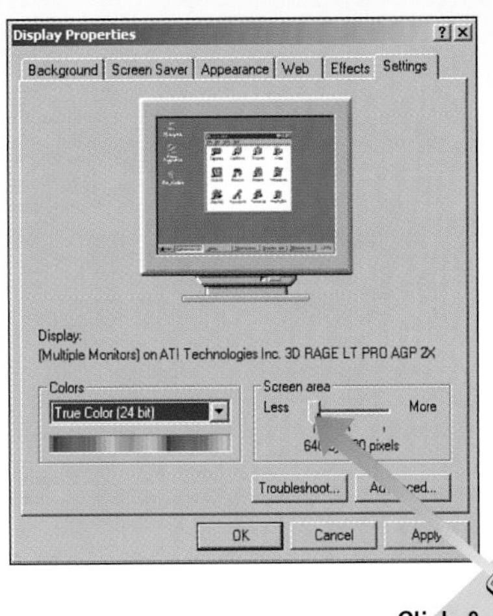

End

TASK 5

How to Change Mouse Settings

Because the mouse will likely be your main tool for getting around in Windows, it should come as no surprise that Windows allows you to change the way your mouse works. Among other things, you can change the clicking speed that makes for a successful double-click and the speed at which the pointer moves across the screen.

Begin

1 Open the Control Panel

Select **Start**, **Settings**, and **Control Panel** to open the **Control Panel** window.

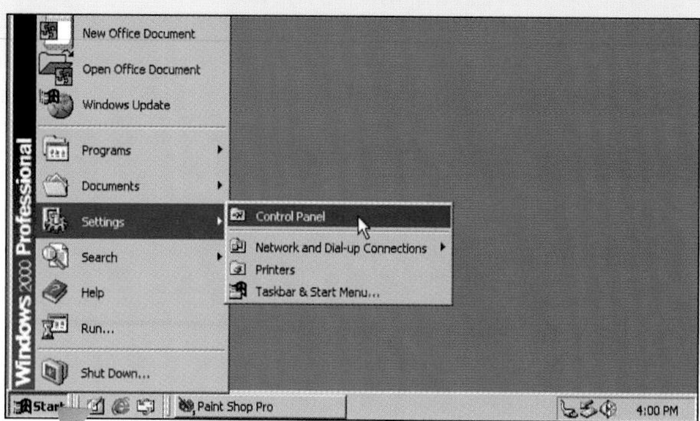

Click

2 Open the Mouse Applet

Double-click the **Mouse** icon to open the **Mouse** applet.

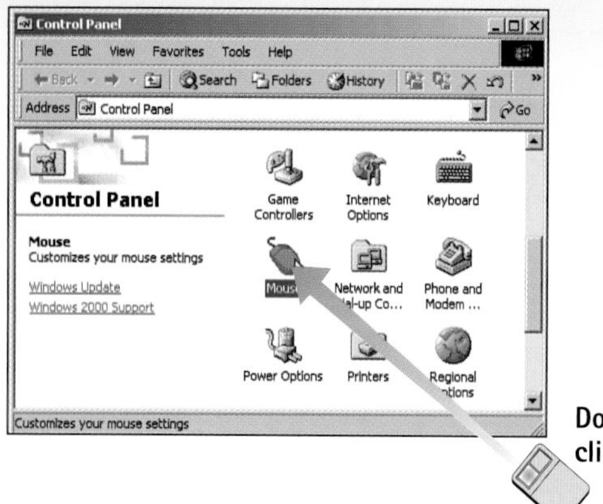

Double-click

3 Choose Single-Click

Windows 2000 lets you use the desktop in two ways. In the conventional way, you single-click items to select them and double-click items to open them. The other way (called single-click or sometimes Web-style) lets you single-click items to open them, just like you do in Internet Explorer. Click the option you want to use.

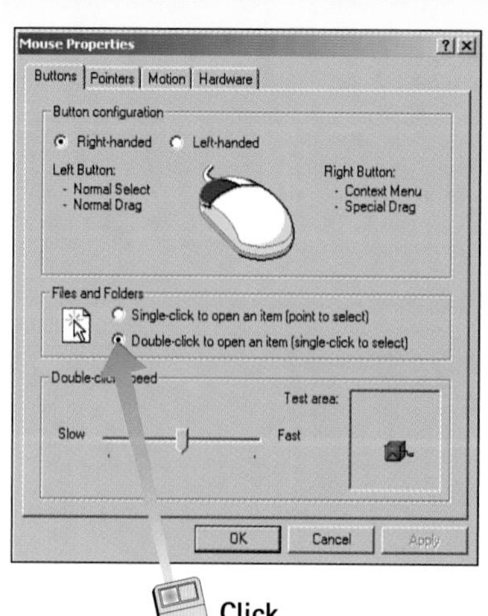

Click

4 Adjust Double-Click Speed

Double-click speed refers to how close together two clicks of the mouse button must be for Windows to consider them a double-click. Drag the slider with your left mouse button to adjust the speed and then test it by double-clicking the **jack-in-the-box** icon in the test area.

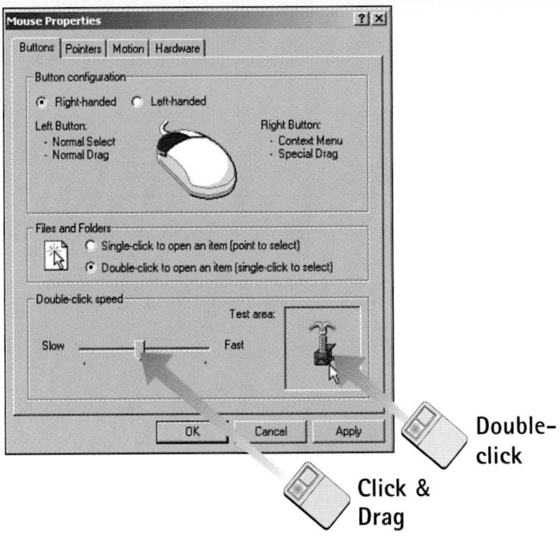

5 Adjust the Pointer Speed

The **Motion** tab (click once to switch to it) lets you set several options relating to how your pointer moves. Drag the **Speed** slider to set how fast the pointer moves across the screen when you move your mouse. Click the **Apply** button to experiment with any settings you make while keeping the **Mouse** applet open.

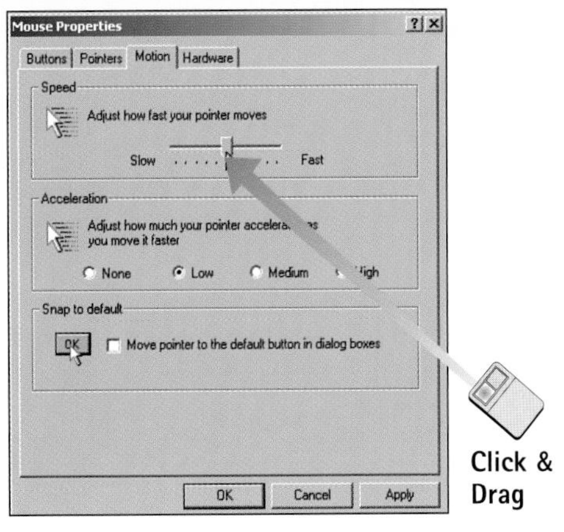

6 Adjust Acceleration

Acceleration refers to how much the movement of your pointer accelerates if you begin moving your mouse more quickly. Selecting **None** keeps the pointer moving at a single speed no matter how quickly you move your mouse.

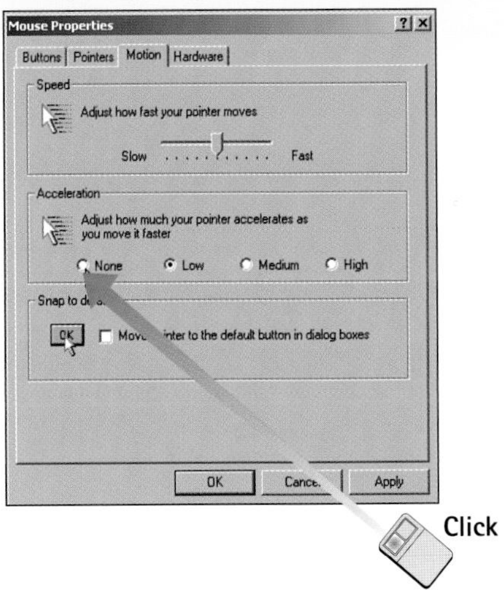

7 Snap to Default

Normally, when a new dialog box opens, your pointer stays right where it is and you must move it to the buttons on the dialog box to do anything. With **Snap to Default** enabled, your pointer automatically jumps to whatever the default button is (usually **Yes**, **No**, **OK**, or **Cancel**).

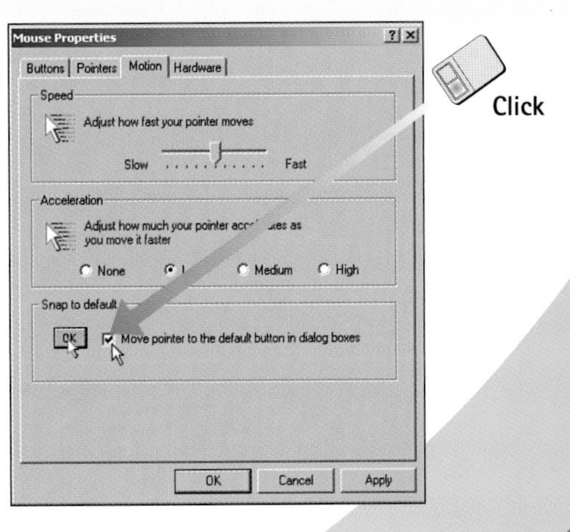

End

TASK 6

How to Change Keyboard Settings

Windows 2000 allows you to change a number of settings related to how your keyboard works. You can change the delay that occurs between when you press a key and when the key starts to repeat from holding it down. You can also change the rate at which the key repeats. Finally, you can change the blink rate for your cursor (the little vertical line that blinks where you are about to type something).

Begin

1 Open the Control Panel

Select **Start**, **Settings**, and **Control Panel** to open the **Control Panel** window.

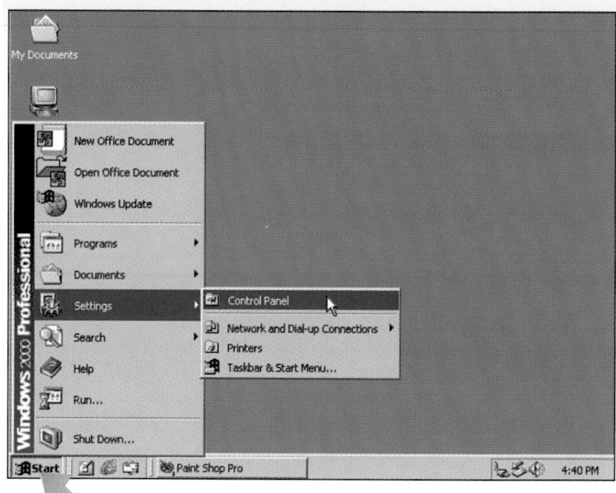

Click

2 Open the Keyboard Applet

Double-click the **Keyboard** icon to open the **Keyboard** applet.

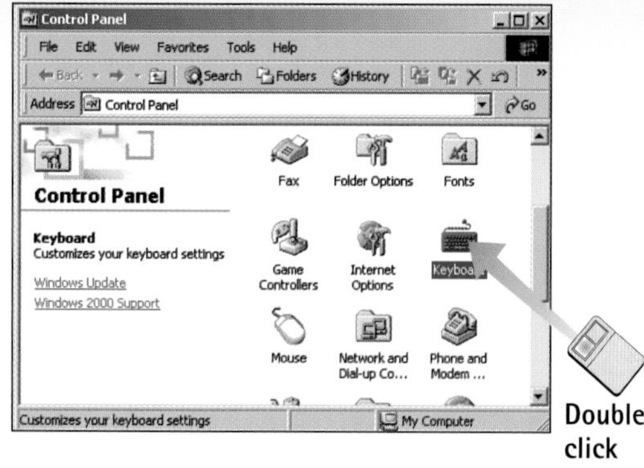

Double-click

3 Change the Repeat Delay

The repeat delay is the delay that occurs between when you press a key and when the key starts to repeat from holding it down. Drag the slider to change the rate.

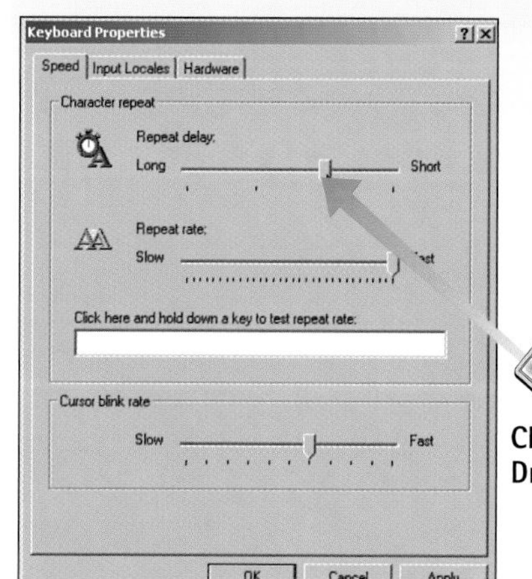

Click & Drag

4 Change the Repeat Rate

When you hold a key down longer than the repeat delay you set in the previous step, the key begins to repeat. Drag the slider to change the repeat rate.

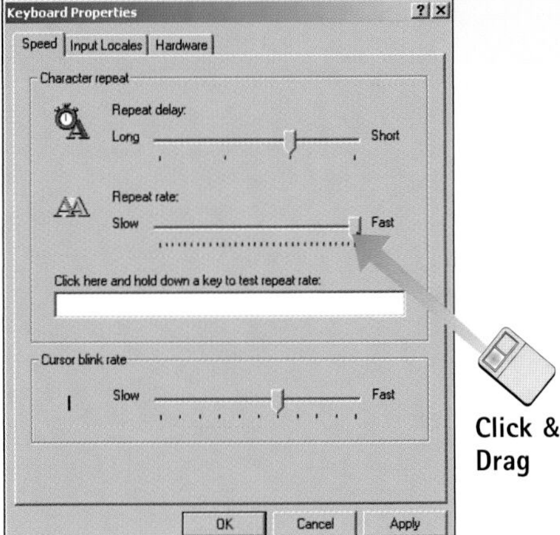

5 Test Your Settings

Click in the test box and then press and hold any key to test your repeat delay and repeat rate settings.

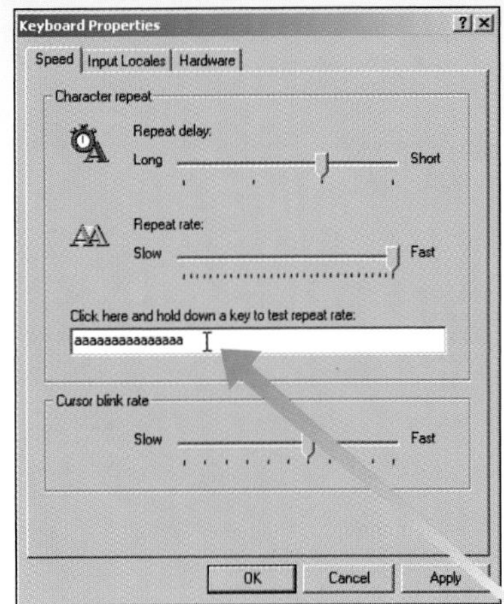

6 Change the Cursor Blink Rate

Whenever you click in a text box to type in a value or type in a document, a little vertical line called a cursor blinks to let you know where the characters you type will appear. It's sometimes called the *insertion point*. Drag the slider to change the rate at which the cursor blinks. A sample cursor to the left of the slider blinks according to your settings.

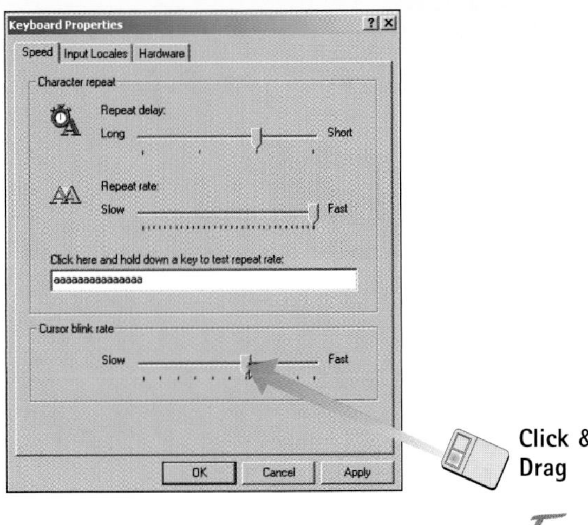

End

TASK 7

How to Change the Date and Time

A small battery inside your computer provides enough power for your computer to keep track of the date and time, even when your computer is turned off. Windows 2000 displays the time in the system tray at the far right of your taskbar. The following steps show you how to change the date and time.

Begin

1 Open the Date and Time Applet

Double-click the clock in the system tray to open the **Date and Time** applet. You can also open it from the **Control Panel** window.

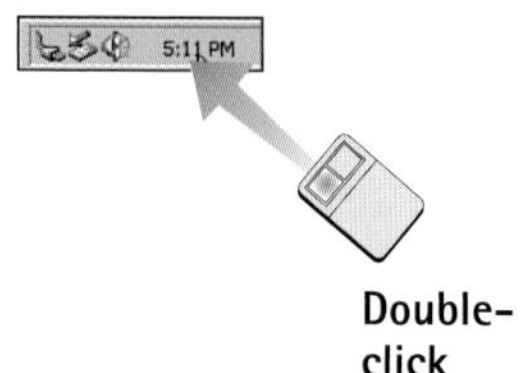

2 Choose a New Date

The calendar at the left displays a month at a time. Click on a date to select it. Use the drop-down menu to select another month. Use the scroll buttons to select a year or type a year in directly.

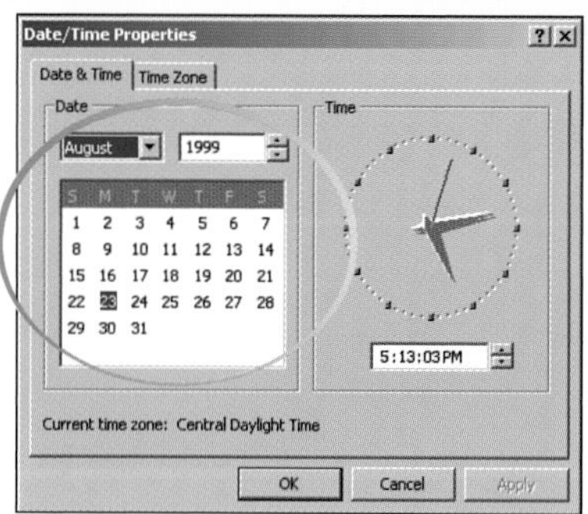

3 Adjust the Time

Select any part of the time (**hour, minute, second, AM/PM**) in the box beneath the clock and use the scroll buttons at the right to adjust the time. You can also just type in a new time.

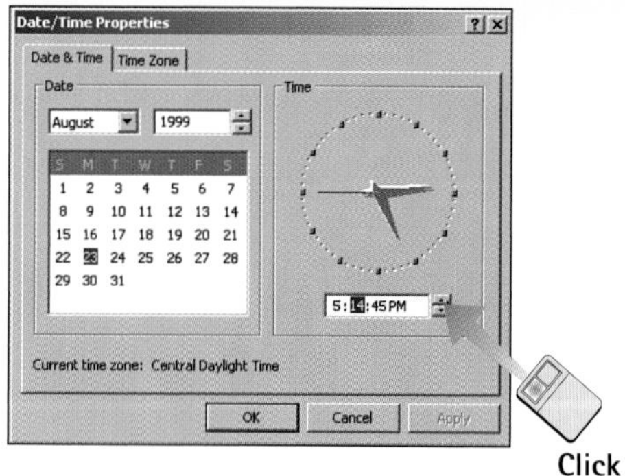

4 Switch to the Time Zone Tab

Switch to the **Time Zone** tab by clicking it once.

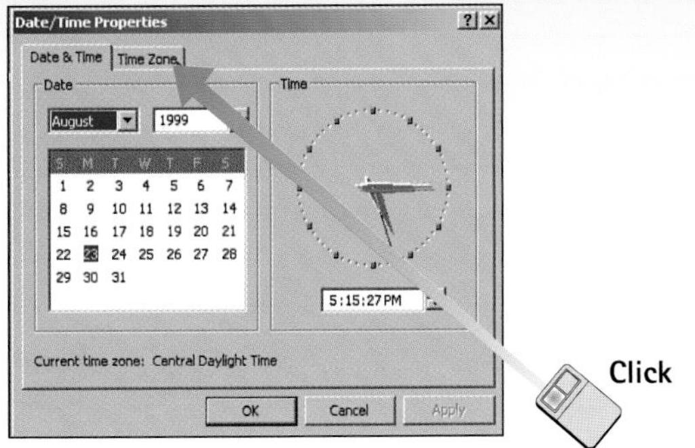

5 Change the Time Zone

Change the Time Zone using the drop-down menu at the top of the tab. The map display changes to center on any time zone you choose. Use the option at the bottom of the tab to have Windows 2000 automatically adjust the time on your computer for Daylight Savings Time.

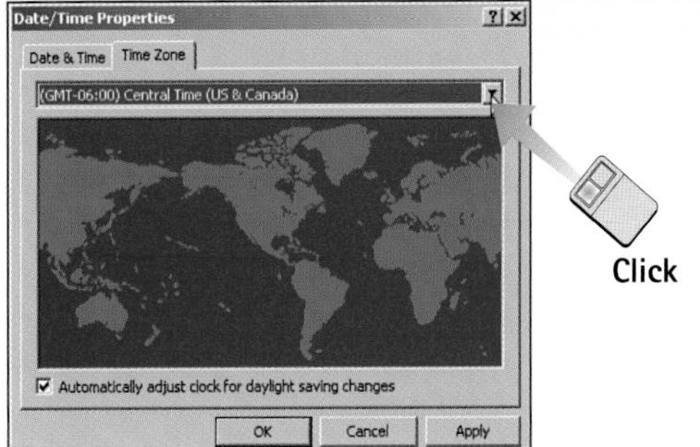

End

How-To Hints

Displaying the Day and Date

Hold your cursor over the clock in the system tray for a moment to open a pop-up window that displays the day and date, as well.

TASK 8

How to Customize the Taskbar

The taskbar is one of the more important tools for working in Windows 2000. There are several ways that you can customize its use, as you will see in the following steps.

Begin

1 Open the Taskbar Properties

Select **Start, Settings, Taskbar and Start Menu.**

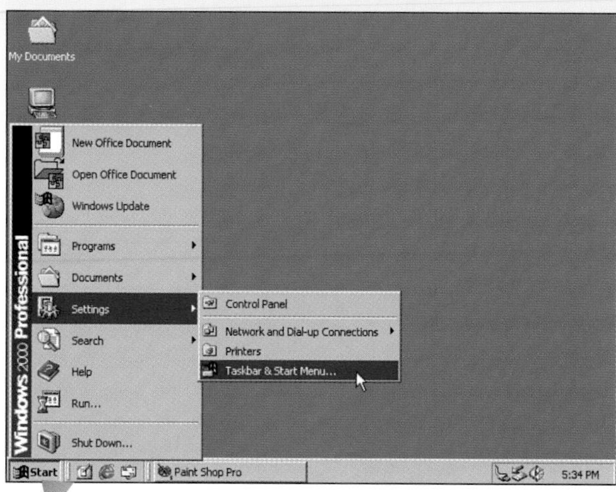

2 Make Always on Top

By default, the taskbar is always on the top of your display. Thus, when you move a window into the same space occupied by the taskbar, the taskbar still appears in front of the window. Click this option so that other items can appear over the taskbar.

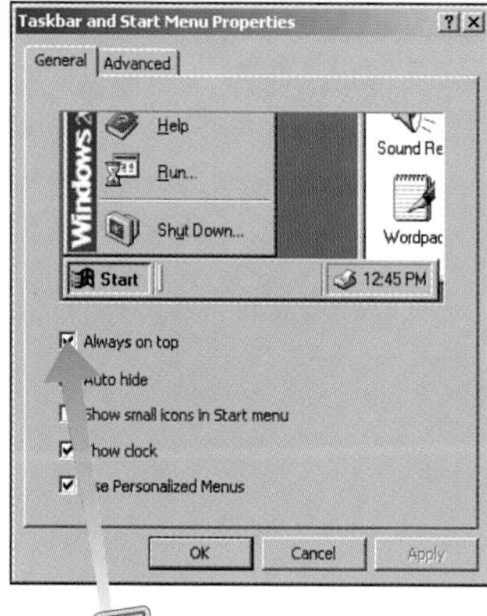

3 Make the Taskbar Autohide

Click the **Auto Hide** option to have the taskbar automatically scroll off the edge of the screen when not in use. Move your pointer to the edge of the screen to make the taskbar scroll back into view.

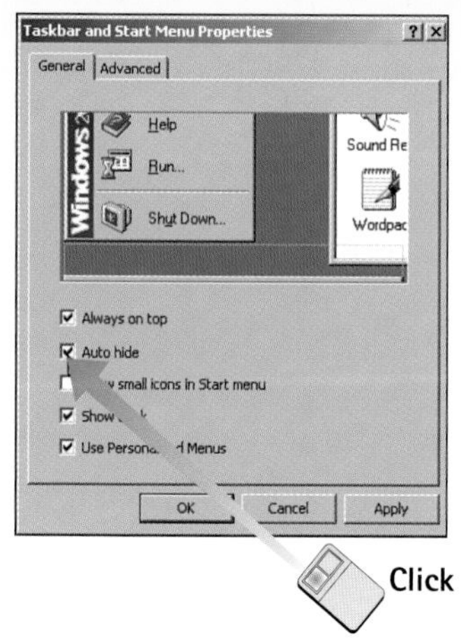

Click

4 Show Small Icons on Start Menu

By default, Windows shows large icons for items listed on the **Start** menu. Click this option to have Windows use small icons instead. This lets more items be shown on the screen at once.

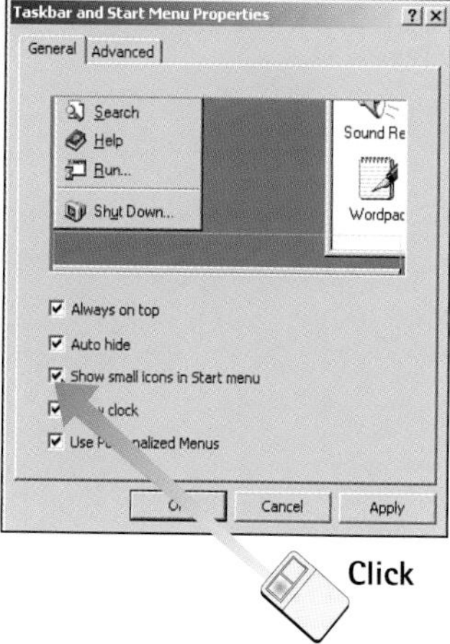

5 Show Clock in System Tray

This option causes Windows to display the clock in the System Tray at the far right of your taskbar. Click once to deselect the option.

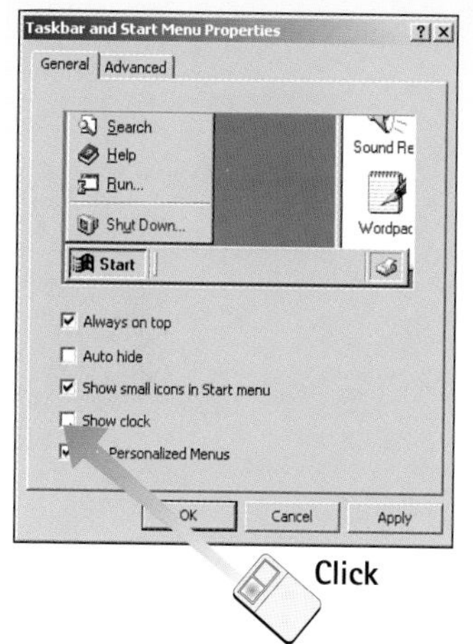

6 Use Personalized Menus

You've probably noticed that when you use the **Start** menu, some items that you know are there are not shown until you expand the menu yourself. Windows 2000 remembers the items you use most and tailors the display to show only the ones you use frequently. Click this option once to turn it off.

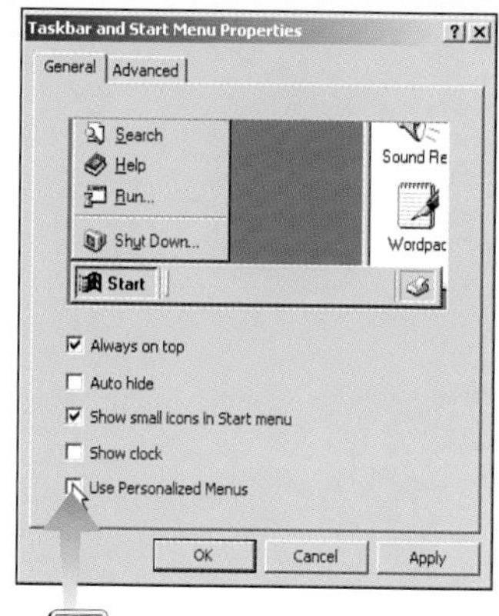

7 Drag the Taskbar

Although most people find that the taskbar works best at the bottom of the screen, you can move it to any of the four edges of the screen. Simply click in any blank space on the taskbar and, while holding down the mouse button, drag the taskbar to another edge.

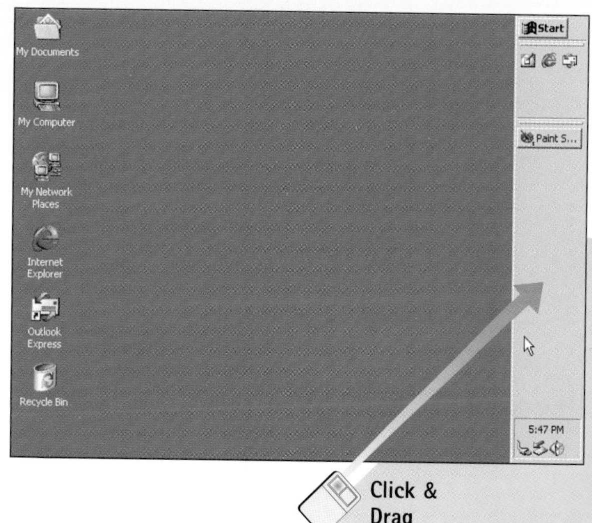

End

TASK 9

How to Change Folder Options

Windows 2000 handles folders in much the same way as Windows 98. You have the option of viewing a folder as a Web page, in which a pane at the left of the folder gives you information on any selected item. You also have the option of having Windows open a new window for each folder you want to open. The following steps illustrate how to access these options using the **Control Panel**. You can also access Folder Options using the View menu of any open folder.

Begin

1 Open the Control Panel

Click the **Start** button, point to **Settings**, and click **Control Panel**.

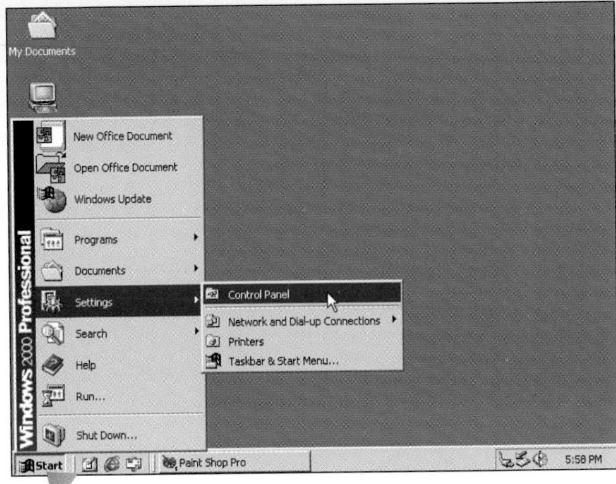

Click

2 Open the Folder Options Applet

Double-click the **Folder Options** applet to open it.

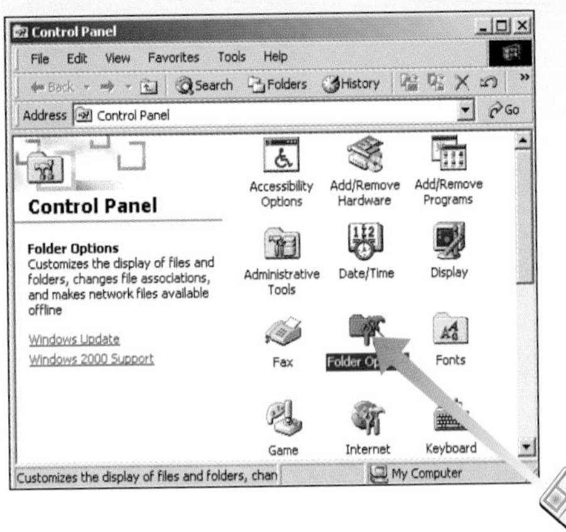

Double-click

3 Enable Active Desktop

Windows 2000 can display Web-based content, such as Web pages and graphics, right on your desktop. This is enabled by default. Click the **Use Windows Classic Desktop** option to disable it.

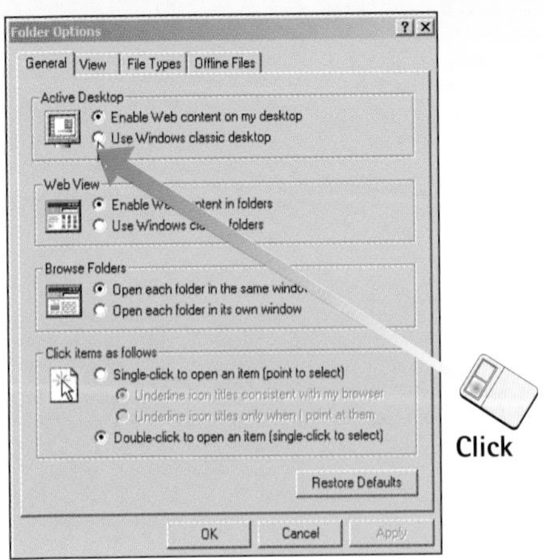

Click

4 Use Web View

Web View is an option that shows Web content in folders. Normally, this just means that a pane at the left of a folder window shows information on selected item(s) in that folder. Some folders, however, might have more specialized content. Click the **Use Windows Classic Folders** option to disable this feature.

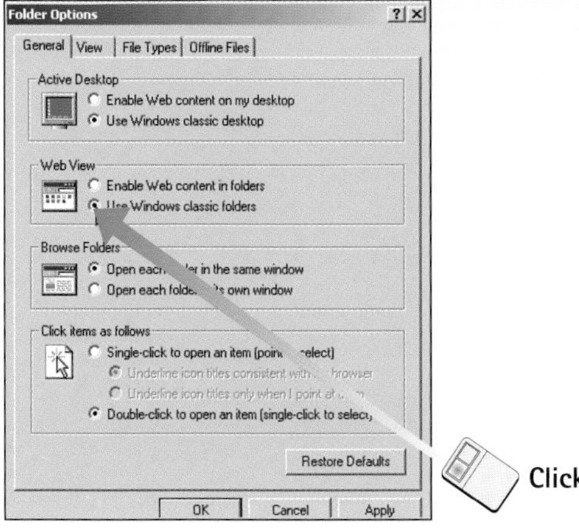

5 Change Folder Browsing

Normally when you open a folder, that folder opens in whatever window you are using at the time. If you would rather Windows open a whole new window for each folder you open, select that option here.

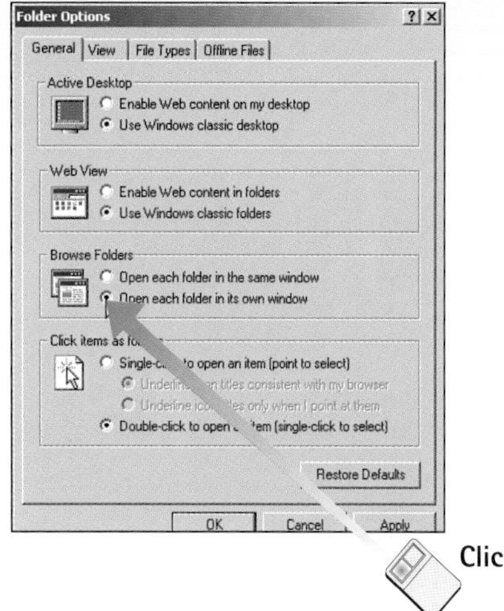

6 Change Click Settings

By default, you single-click items to select them and double-click items to open them. If you prefer, click the single-click option so that you only need to single-click items to open them, much like you do in Internet Explorer. With this option enabled, holding your pointer over an item for a second selects the item.

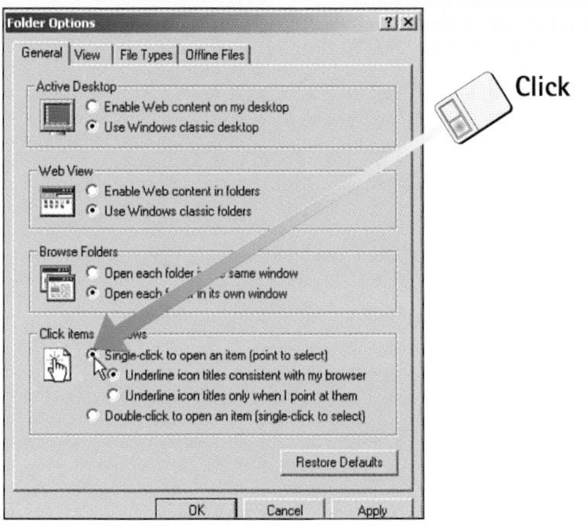

End

How-To Hints

Advanced Options

The **View** tab of the **Folder Options** dialog box features a long list of specific settings relating to how folders work.

TASK 10

How to Change Power Options

You might find it useful to adjust how Windows 2000 handles your power settings. To save energy, Windows 2000 can automatically turn off parts of your computer, such as the hard drive and monitor, after certain amounts of time.

Begin

1 Open Control Panel

Select **Start**, **Settings**, and **Control Panel**.

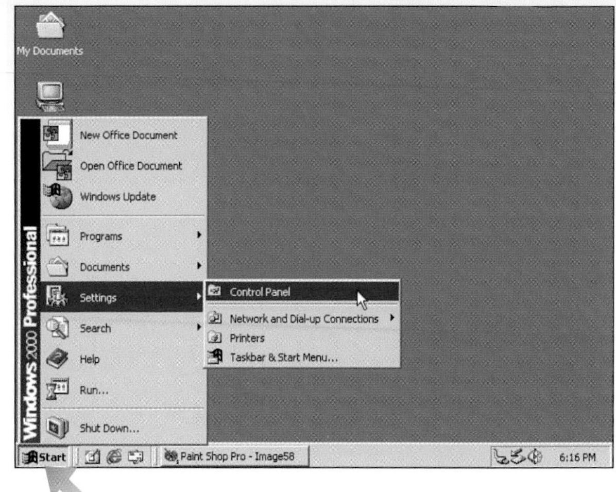

Click

2 Open Power Options Applet

Double-click the **Power Options** applet to open it.

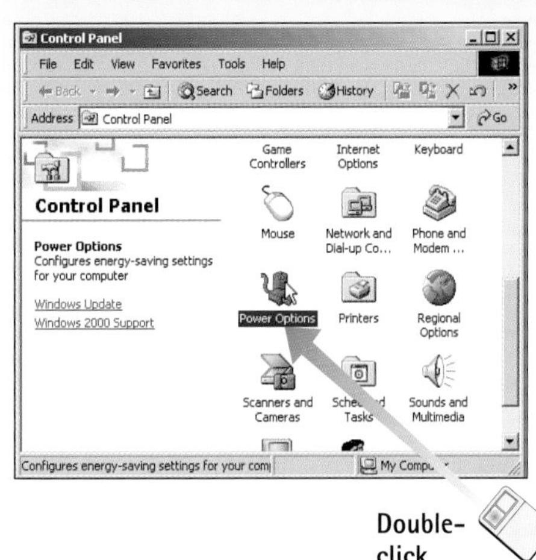

Double-click

3 Choose a Power Scheme

The easiest way to configure power settings is to choose a custom scheme designed to fit the use of your computer. Click the **Power Schemes** drop-down list to choose from a number of schemes.

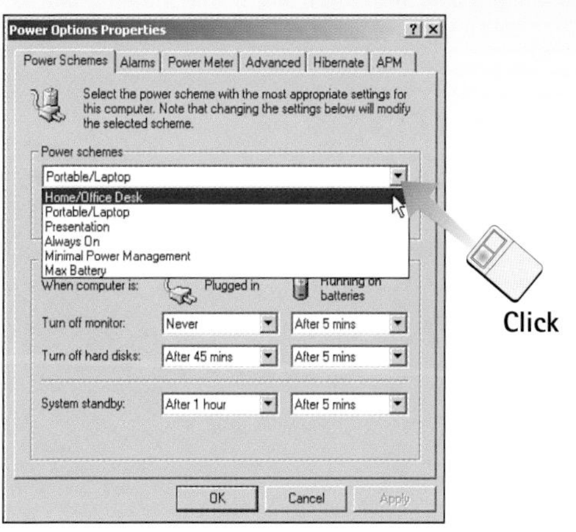

Click

4 Turn Off Monitor

If you want to customize power settings beyond just choosing a scheme, you can choose how long the computer should be idle before certain devices are turned off. Click this drop-down menu to specify how long the computer should be idle before your monitor is turned off.

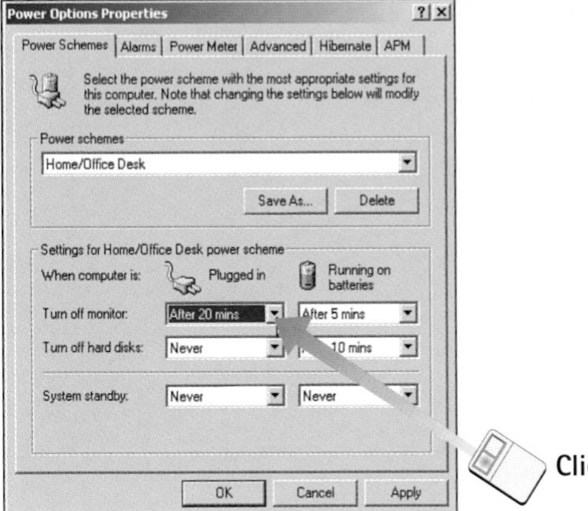

5 Turn Off Hard Disks

Click this drop-down menu to specify how long the computer should be idle before your hard drive is turned off.

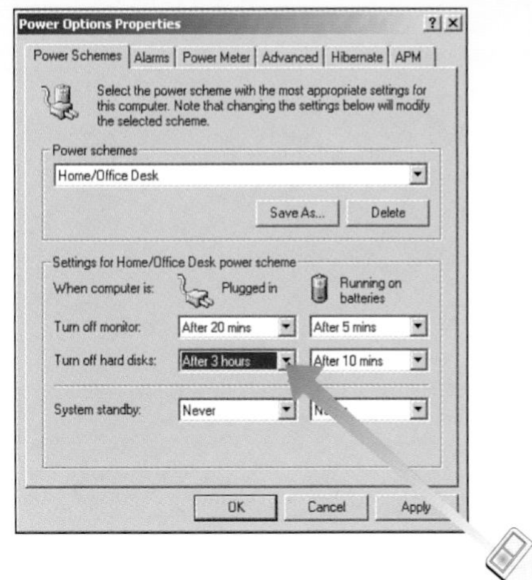

6 Send System to Standby

Some computers have the capability to go into standby, where only a trickle of power is used to keep track of what's in your computer's memory. When you come back from standby, everything should be as you left it. Use the drop-down menu to specify how long the computer should be idle before it goes into standby.

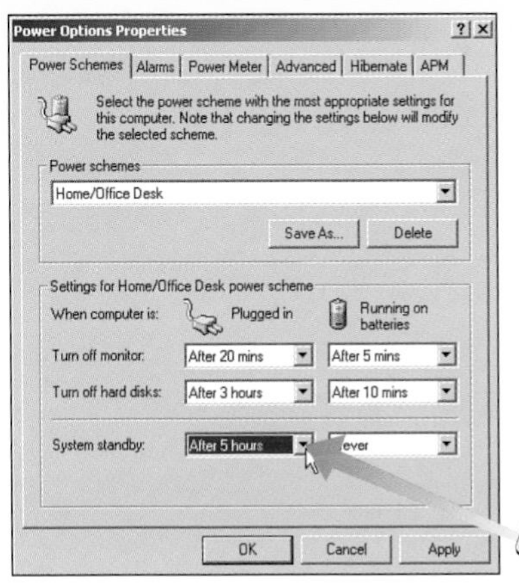

End

How-To Hints

Where Are All Those Options?

Different computers display information on the **Power Options** dialog box depending on the type of computer and type of hardware installed. Notebook computers, for example, have settings both for when the computer is plugged in and when it is running on batteries. Notebooks also boast several more tabs on the dialog box to configure such things as advanced standby and hibernation modes. The best place to find out information about these advanced options is in the documentation for the computer itself.

TASK 11

How to Change System Sounds

If you have speakers on your computer, you might have noticed that certain events make certain sounds. You can easily change the sounds associated with events by using the following steps.

Begin

1 Open the Control Panel

Select **Start**, **Settings**, **Control Panel**.

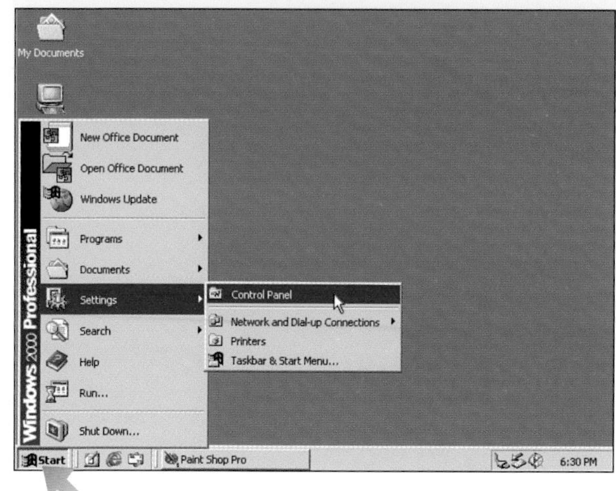

Click

2 Open Sounds/Multimedia Applet

Double-click the **Sounds and Multimedia** applet to open it.

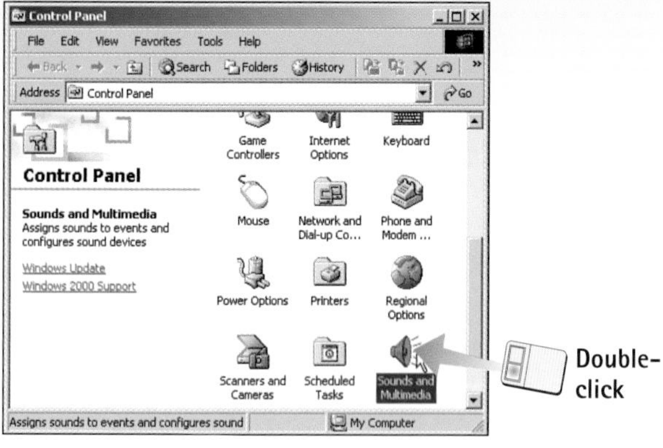

Double-click

3 Choose an Event

From the list, click any system event, such as Exit Windows, to select it.

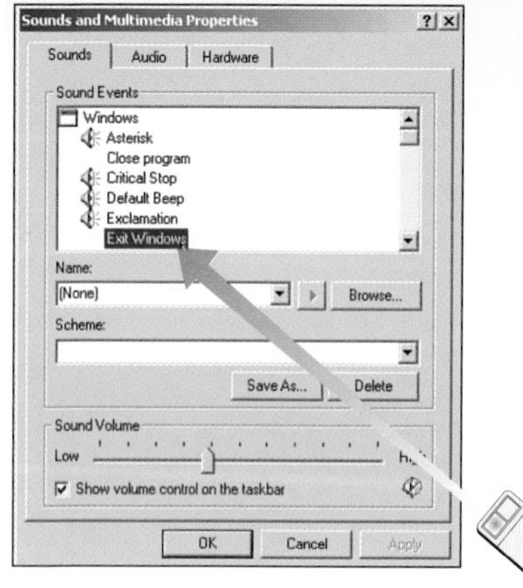

Click

4 Choose a Sound File

Click the arrow beside the **Name** drop-down list to select a sound to associate with the selected event. You can also use your own sound file (a `.wav` file) by clicking the **Browse** button.

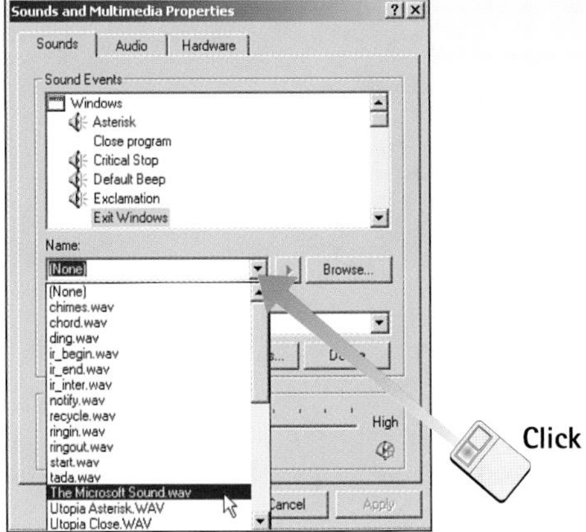

5 Play the Sound

Click the **Play** button to hear the sound.

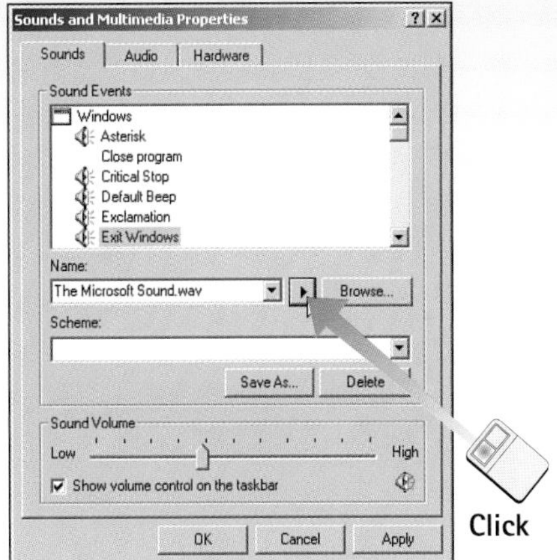

6 Choose a Sound Scheme

Windows comes with a couple of different sound schemes, which are sets of sounds similar in effect that are applied to all the major system events at once. Use the **Scheme** drop-down list to choose a scheme.

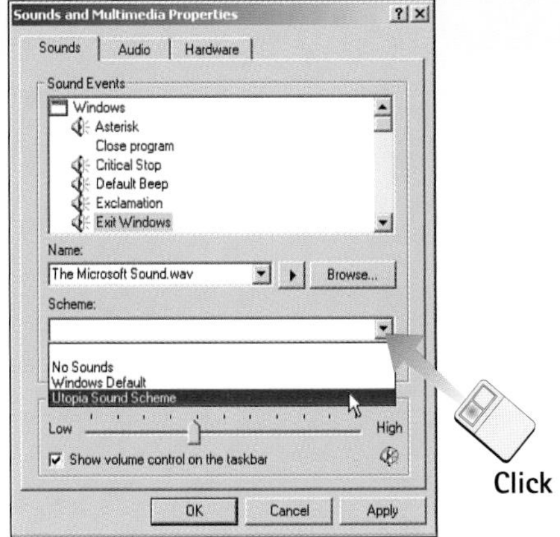

End

TASK 12

How to Add an Item to the Start Menu

The **Start** menu is loaded with shortcuts to various programs and folders on your computer. Whenever you install a new program, that program usually automatically adds a shortcut of its own to the **Start** menu. You can also add items of your own. You can add shortcuts to programs, documents, or even folders.

Begin

1 Open the Taskbar Properties

Right-click any empty space on the **taskbar** and choose **Properties**. This is the same as choosing the **Taskbar & Start Menu** command from the **Start** menu.

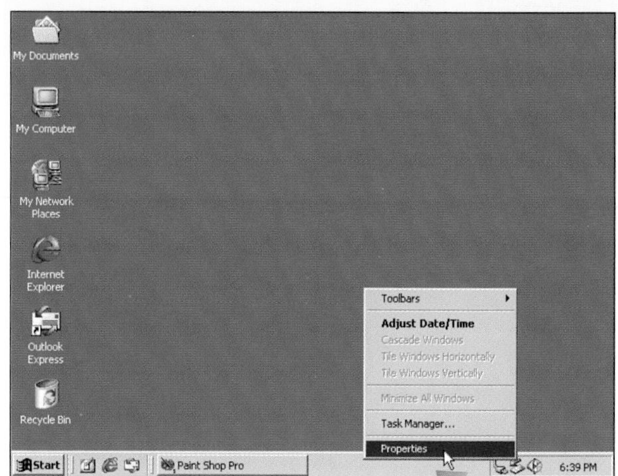

2 Switch to the Advanced Tab

Switch to the **Advanced** tab by clicking it once.

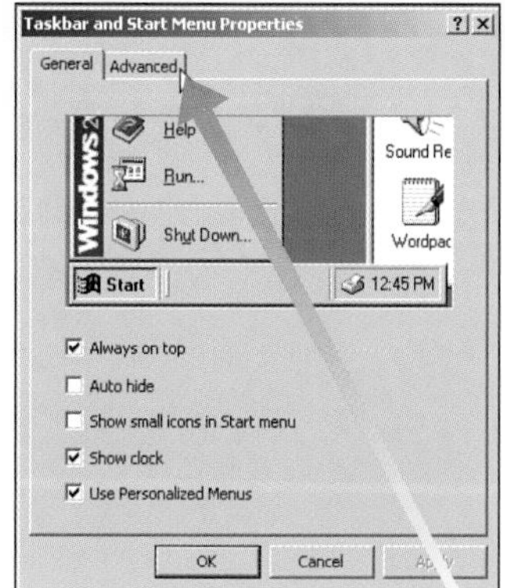

3 Click Add

Click the **Add** button to open the **Create Shortcut** wizard.

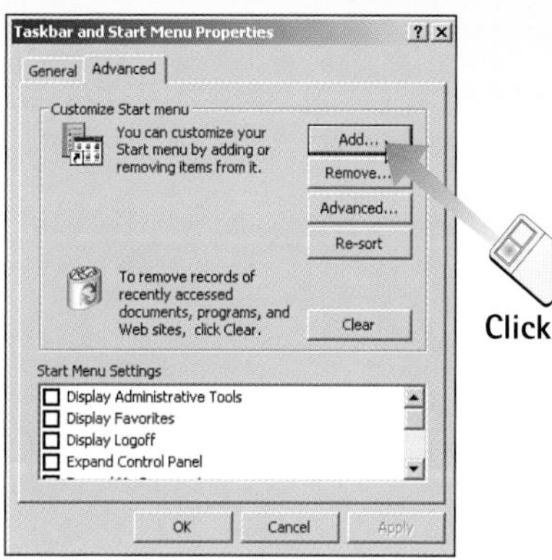

4 Type the Program's Path

Type the path to the program, document, or folder you want to make a shortcut for. You can also click the **Browse** button to locate the file if you don't know the path. When you're done, click the **Next** button.

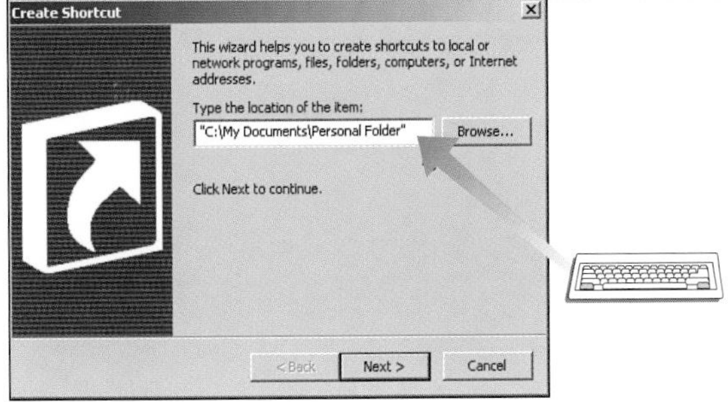

5 Select a Folder for the Program

Select the folder on your **Start** menu into which you want to place the new shortcut. You can create a new folder by clicking the **New Folder** button. When you're done, click the **Next** button.

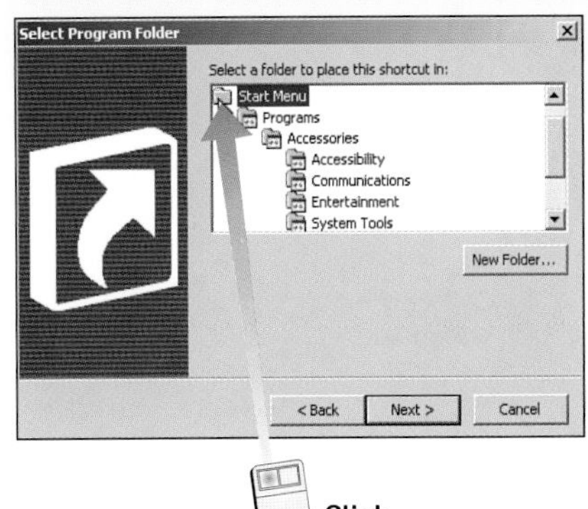

6 Enter a Name for the Program

Enter a name for the shortcut that you want to appear on the **Start** menu. Click the **Finish** button when you are done.

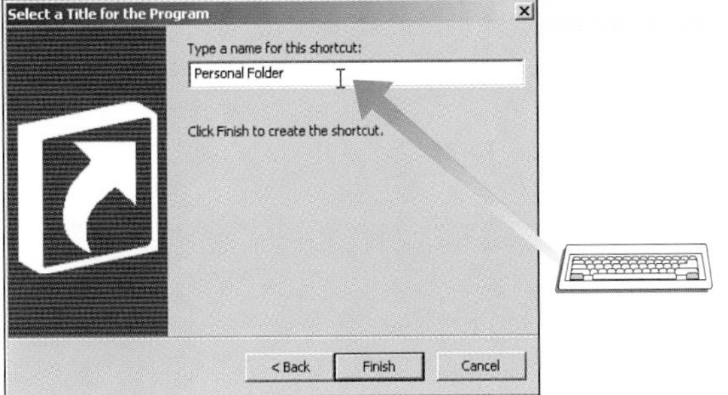

7 Use the New Shortcut

Click the **Start** menu to use your new shortcut.

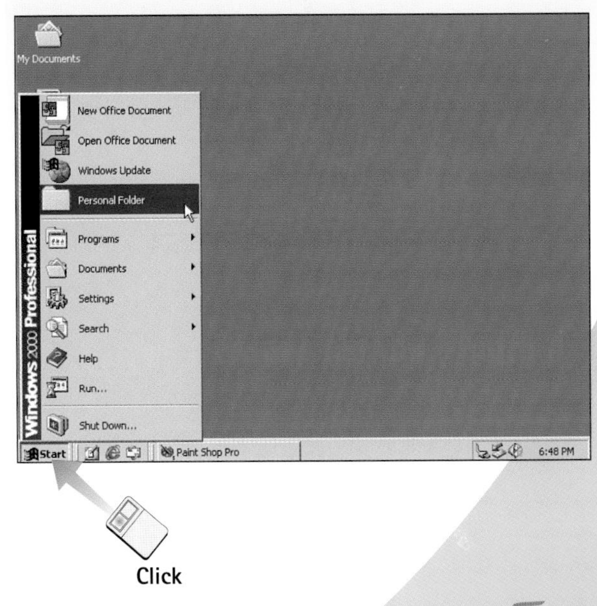

End

TASK 13

How to Add an Item to the Quick Launch Bar

The Quick Launch bar is handy new feature of Windows 2000 that sits next to the taskbar and lets you open certain programs with a single click. Only three shortcuts come standard on the Quick Launch bar: one to launch Internet Explorer, one to launch Outlook Express, and one to show your desktop when there are windows in the way. Fortunately, it's pretty easy to add new shortcuts for programs, documents, and folders.

Begin

1 Find the Item You Want to Add

Use the **My Computer** or **My Documents** window to find the item you want to make a shortcut for.

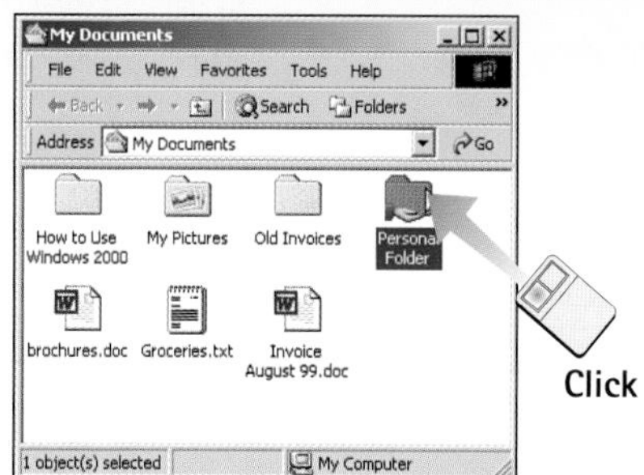

2 Drag Item to Quick Launch

Click the item with your left mouse button and, while holding the button down, drag the item into a blank space on the **Quick Launch** bar. You can even drag the item between two existing shortcuts to put it exactly where you want.

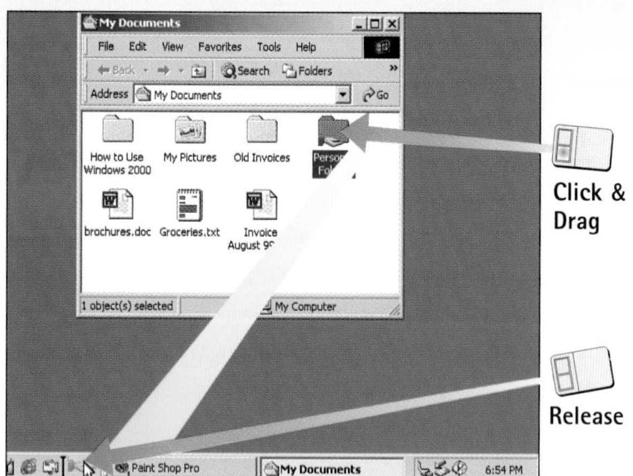

3 Rename the Shortcut

Right-click the new shortcut and choose **Rename** from the shortcut menu to give the shortcut a new name. This name appears in a pop-up window when you hold your pointer over the shortcut for a second.

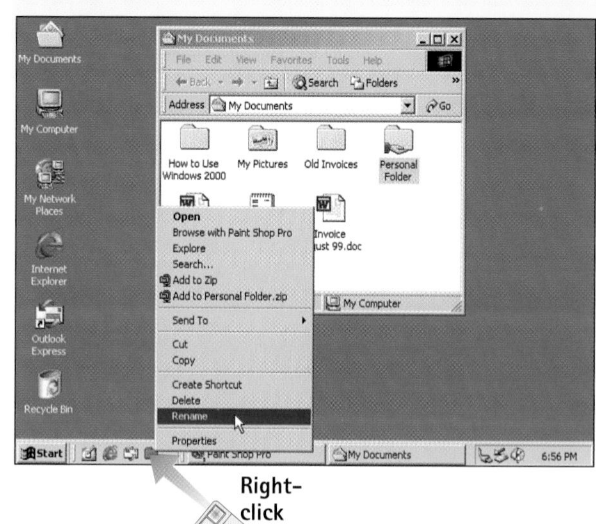

4 Delete the Shortcut

Right-click the shortcut and choose **Delete** from the shortcut menu to remove the shortcut from the **Quick Launch** bar.

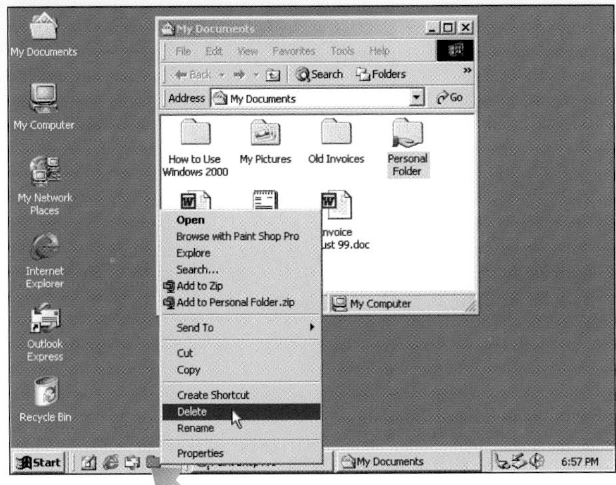

End

How-To Hints

Rearrange Shortcuts

You can rearrange existing shortcuts by simply dragging them to a new location on the **Quick Launch** bar.

Moving the Quick Launch Bar

You can move the **Quick Launch** bar separately from the taskbar by clicking at the leftmost edge of the Quick Launch bar (marked by a small, raised vertical line) and dragging it. You can move to one of the other edges of your display or into the center of your window.

TASK 14

How to Start a Program When Windows Starts

Windows 2000 maintains a special folder named **Startup** that lets you specify programs, folders, and even documents that open every time Windows starts. You can see the **Startup** folder and what's in it by selecting **Start**, **Programs**, and **Startup**. The following steps show you how to add shortcuts to that folder.

Begin

1 Open Taskbar Properties

Select **Start**, **Settings**, and **Taskbar and Start Menu.**

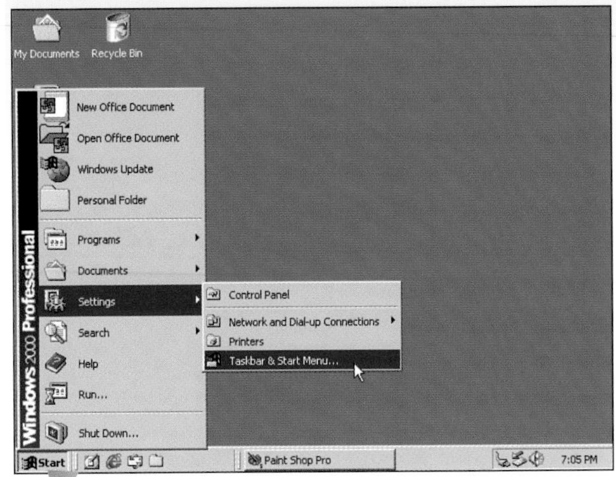

Click

2 Open Advanced Options

On the **Advanced** tab, click the **Advanced** button. This opens the Start Menu folder in Windows Explorer.

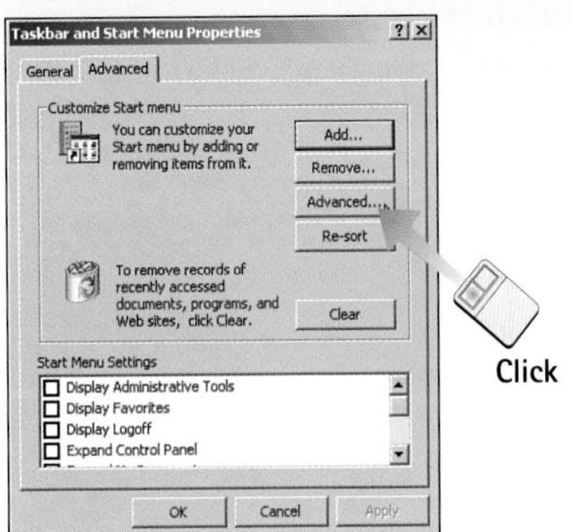

3 Choose the Startup Folder

In the left-hand pane of **Explorer**, click the **Startup** folder once to open it.

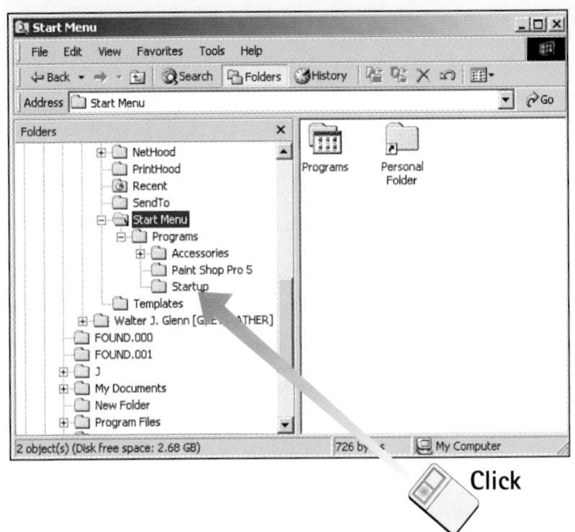

4 Create a New Shortcut

Click the **File** menu, point to **New**, and then click **Shortcut**.

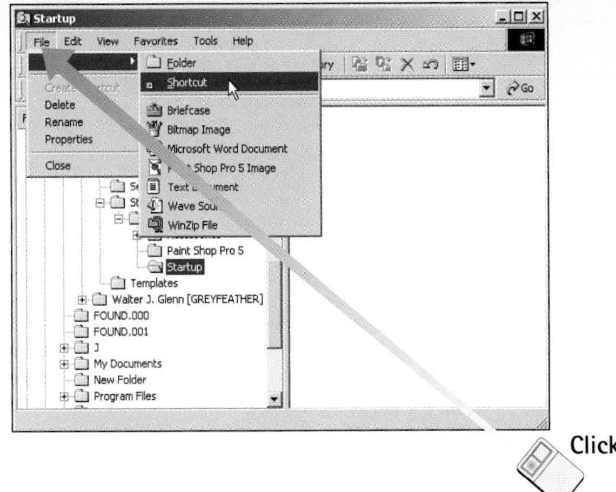

5 Enter Path to Start Item

Type the path to the program, document, or folder you want to start automatically. You can also click the **Browse** button to locate the file if you don't know the path. When you're done, click the **Next** button.

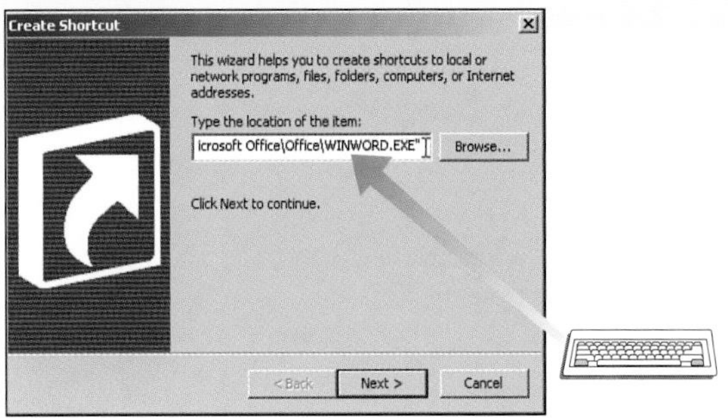

6 Enter a Name for the Shortcut

Type a name for the shortcut in the box. When you're done, click the **Finish** button.

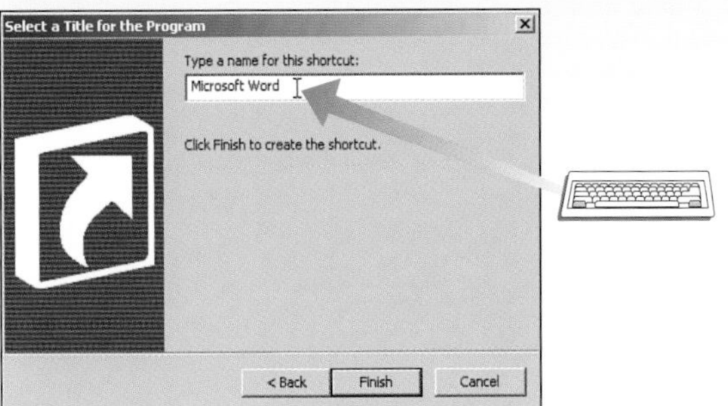

End

Task

PART 10

Using the System Tools

Computers are pretty complicated. There are a lot of things that can happen during the course of normal use that can slow a computer down or keep certain things from working as they should. If you are connected to a network, the chances are that you have a network administrator to rely on for fixing problems when they occur. Nonetheless, there are a few things that you can do to help make sure that your computer is performing well and that your work is not lost if something does go wrong. Windows 2000 provides a number of important system tools to help you protect your files and maintain your computer.

In this part, you learn how to back up your files and how to restore files from a backup. You also learn to create an emergency restore disk, which holds critical information for restoring your system should something go wrong. You learn to use the Disk Cleanup tool to remove unnecessary files from your computer to help free up disk space. You also learn to use the Disk Defragmenter, a tool that helps organize the files on your disk so that everything moves a bit faster. Finally, you learn to use the built-in automatic troubleshooters that Windows provides for determining why a component is not working the way it should and what you can do to fix it.

TASK 1

How to Back Up Your Files

Any experienced computer professional will tell you that the single most important thing you can do to prevent loss of work should your computer fail is to back up your files. Many companies have automated routines for backing up users' files, and you should check with your administrator to see what the policy is at your company. Windows 2000 comes with a program named Backup, that lets you back up files on your computer to floppy disk, a zip drive, a tape drive, or even another computer on your network. Even if your network has backup routines in place, you might also want to use the Backup program on your more important files.

Begin

1 Start Backup

Select **Start**, **Programs**, **Accessories**, **System Tools**, and **Backup**.

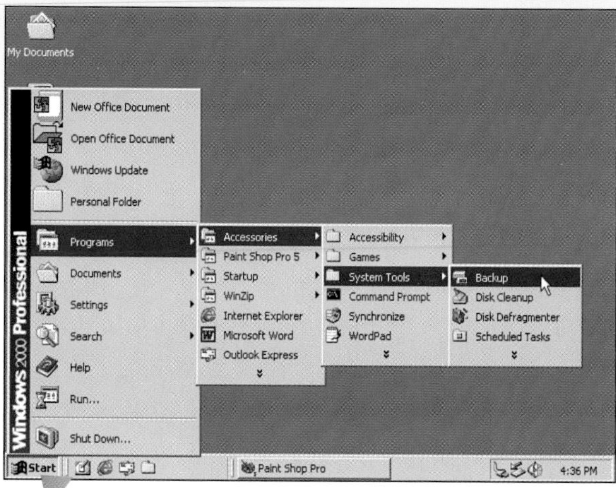

2 Start the Backup Wizard

Click the **Backup Wizard** button to start the Backup Wizard. The first page of the wizard is a welcome page. Just click the **Next** button when you see the Welcome page.

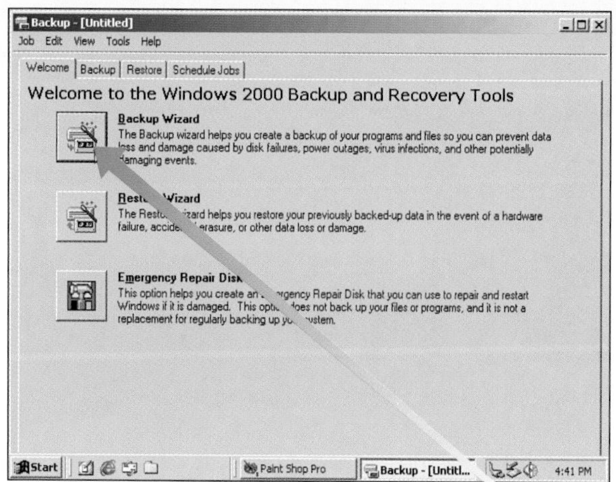

3 Choose What You Want to Back Up

Choose what you want to back up on your computer. Unless your backup media (floppy, tape drive, and so on) is very fast, it is usually best to back up only selected files.

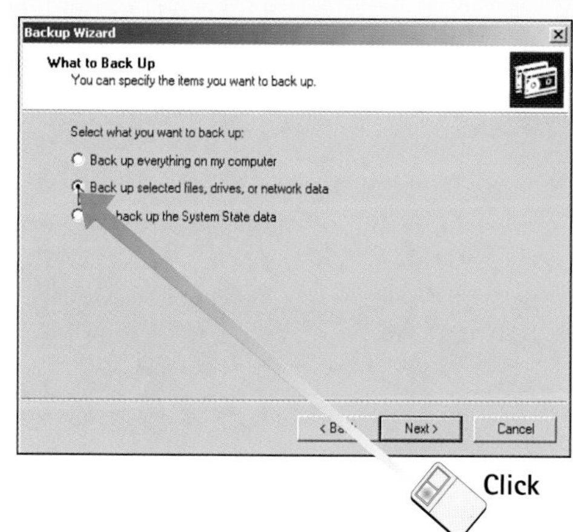

4 Choose What Files to Back Up

This page of the Backup Wizard works just like Windows Explorer. In the left-hand pane, select a folder you want to browse. Files in that folder appear in the right-hand pane. Click the box next to the files to indicate that you want to include those files in the backup. You can also select whole folders. Click the **Next** button to go on.

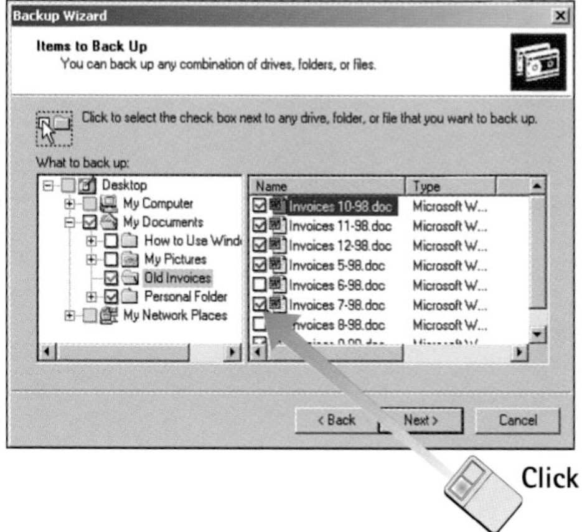

5 Choose Where to Back It Up

No matter how many files you back up, the whole backup is saved as a single file with a **.bkf** extension. Type the path for the drive and folder where you want to save the backup. If you don't know the exact path, click the **Browse** button to locate it. Using the **Browse** button also lets you locate drives on other computers on the network. Click the **Next** button to go on.

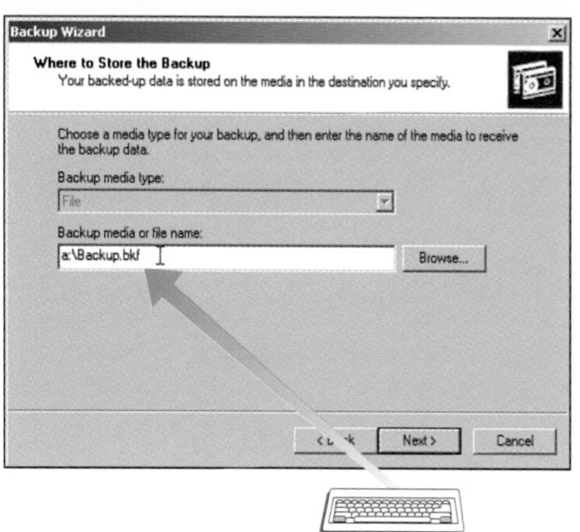

6 Finish

The last page of the Backup Wizard gives you a second look at all of the settings you've made. Click the **Back** button to go back and change settings. Click the **Finish** button to go on with the backup.

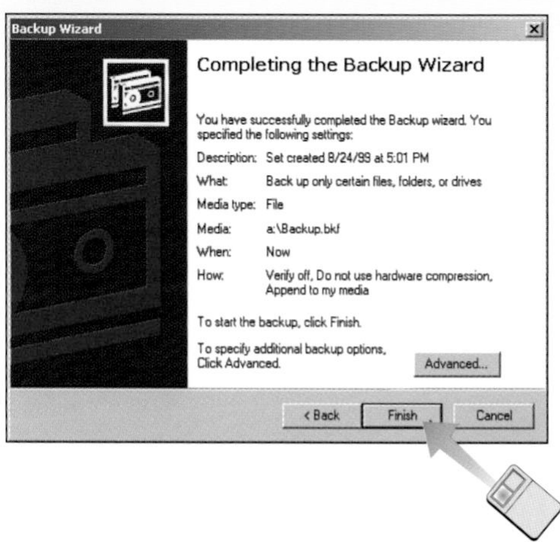

7 View the Report

While the backup is in progress, a dialog box appears that shows you how things are going. When the backup is finished, Windows 2000 lets you know that it was completed successfully. Click the **Report** button to view a detailed report on the backup. Click **Close** to finish up.

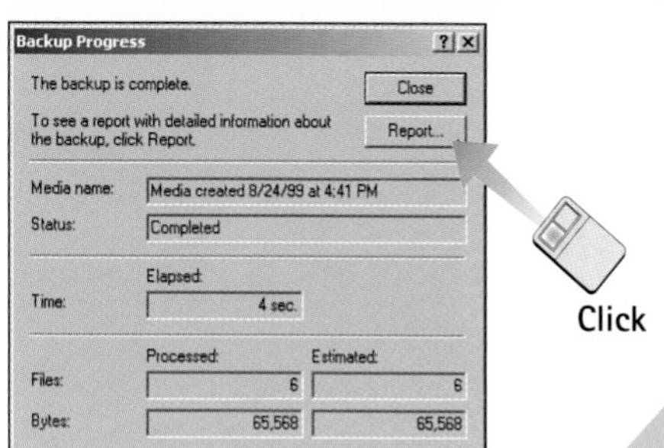

End

TASK 2

How to Restore Files from a Backup

Whether you are restoring files from a backup following a computer failure or you just want to dig up an old file you deleted, Windows 2000 makes the process pretty easy.

Begin

1 Start Backup

Select **Start**, **Programs**, **Accessories**, **System Tools**, and **Backup**.

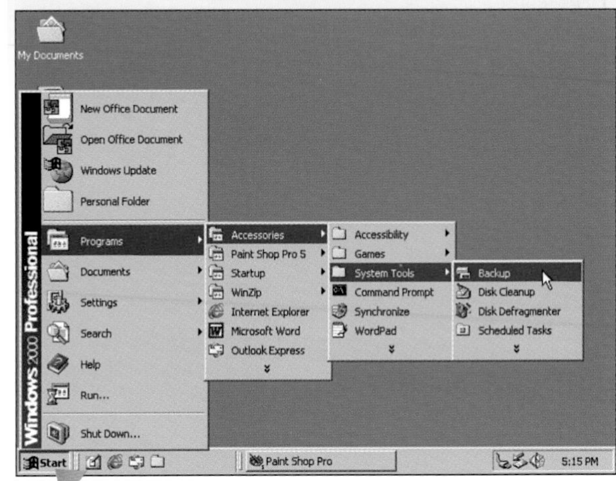

2 Start the Restore Wizard

Click the **Restore Wizard** button to start the Restore Wizard. The first page of the wizard is a welcome page. To continue, just click the **Next** button when you see the welcome page.

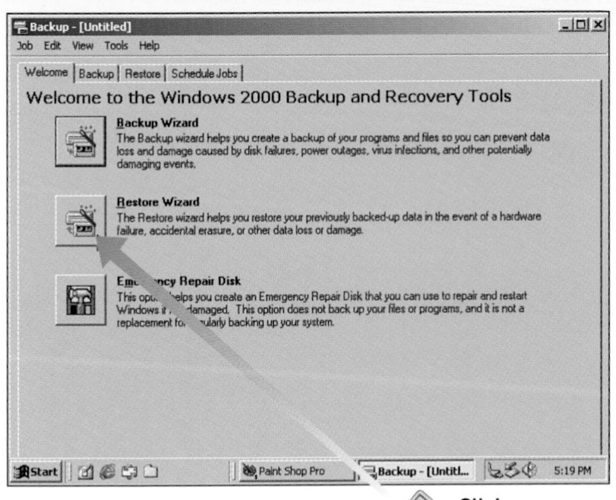

3 Choose What You Want to Restore

Choose the backup session you want to restore by clicking the check box next to it. Sessions are listed by date. If you want to know exactly what is in a session, right-click it and choose **Catalog** from the shortcut menu. When you're done, click the **Next** button.

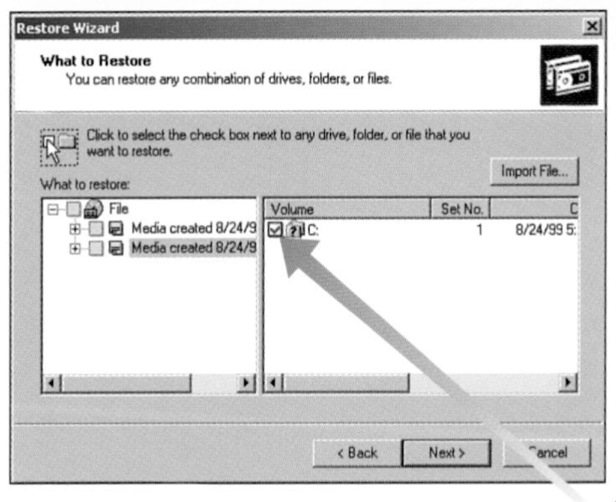

4 Finish

The last page of the Restore Wizard gives you a second look at all of the settings you've made. Click the **Back** button to go back and change settings. Click the **Finish** button to go on with the backup.

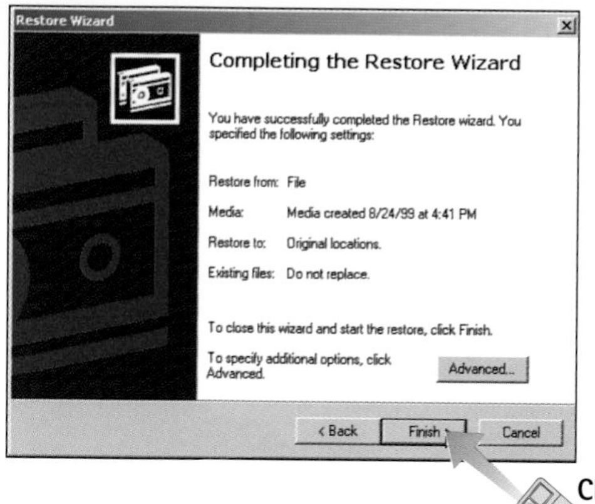

5 Enter the Backup File Name

Type in the path and name of the backup file you want to restore from. If you don't know the exact path or name, click the **Browse** button to locate the file. When you're ready to start, click the **OK** button.

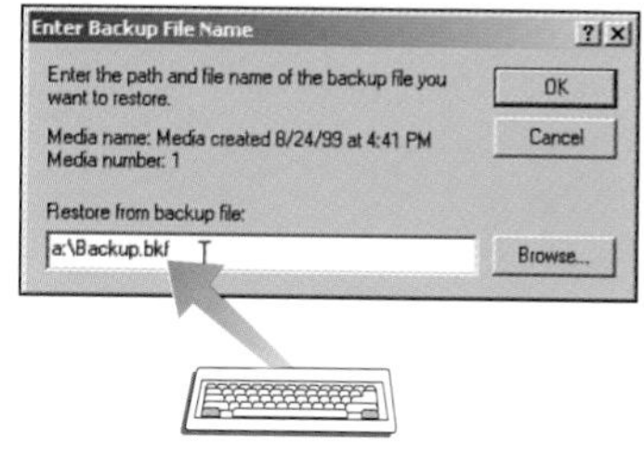

6 View the Report

While the restore is in progress, a dialog box appears that shows you how things are going. When the restore is finished, Windows lets you know that it was completed successfully. Click the **Report** button to view a detailed report on the backup. Click **Close** to finish.

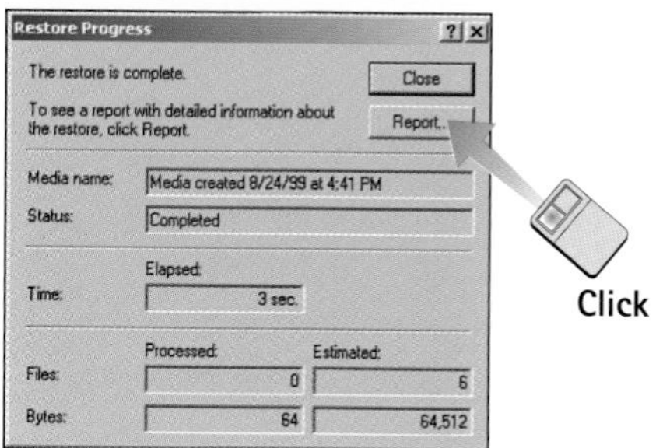

End

TASK 3

How to Create an Emergency Repair Disk

An emergency repair disk, sometimes referred to as an ERD, contains certain important system and settings files. The disk can be used to repair and restart Windows should your system become damaged. You should create a new ERD periodically, whenever you install or remove software or make other changes to your computer.

Begin

1 Start Backup

Click the **Start** button, point to **Programs**, **Accessories**, **System Tools**, and then click **Backup**.

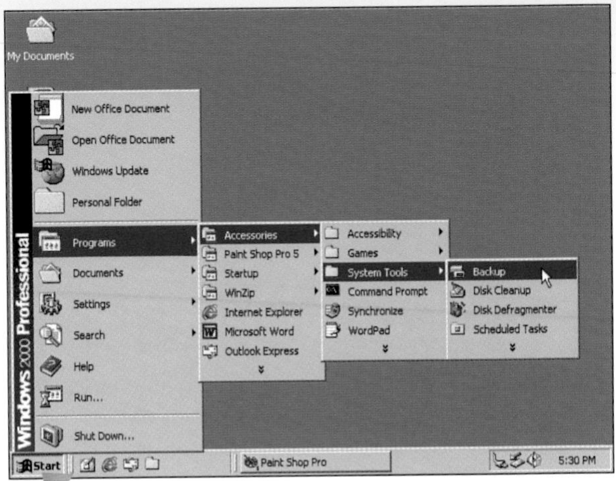

Click

2 Start the Emergency Repair Disk

Click the **Emergency Repair Disk** button to start the **Emergency Repair Disk Wizard**.

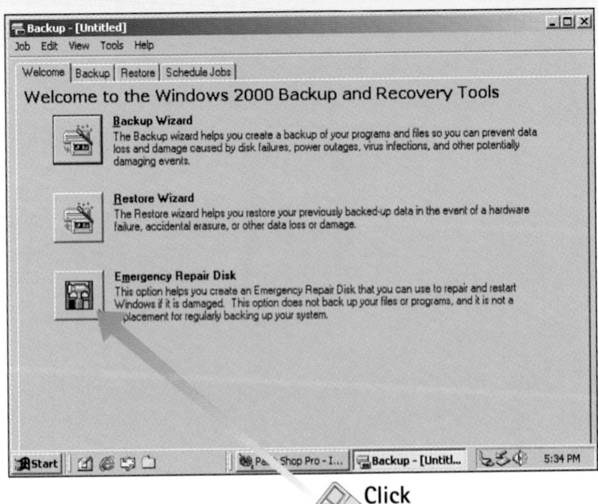

Click

3 Insert a Disk

Insert a blank, formatted floppy disk into your A: drive. If you want to include the Registry (which holds additional Windows settings) on the ERD, click that option. However, be aware that this might require more than one floppy disk. When you're ready, click the **OK** button.

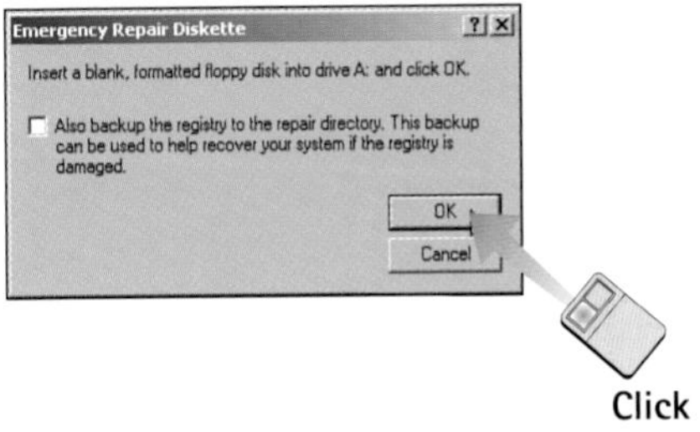

Click

4 Wait While the Disk Is Copied

A dialog box shows you the progress as the ERD is being created.

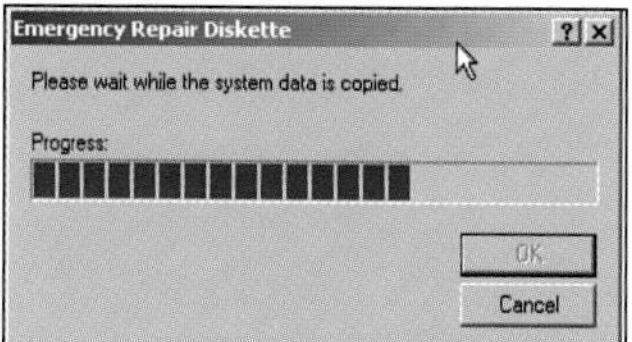

5 Finish and Label the Disk

When the ERD has been created, a dialog box lets you know that the creation was successful. Click the **OK** button to finish. Be sure you label your disk and keep it in a safe place.

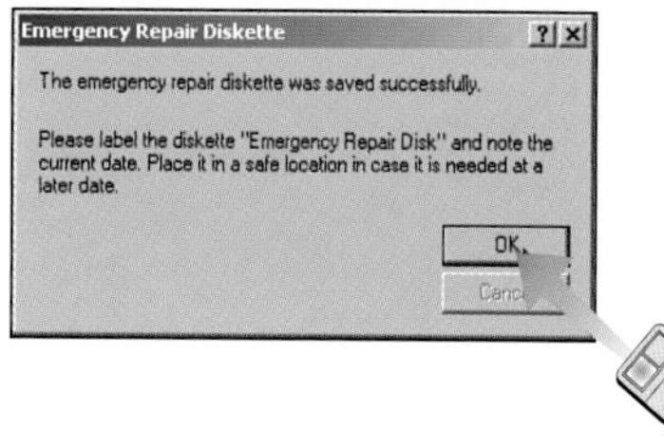

End

How-To Hints

Using the ERD

To start the emergency repair process, you start your computer using the Windows 2000 Professional setup disks or CD. During setup, you are given the option of performing setup or performing a repair. Choose to repair the system and the setup program prompts you when it needs the ERD.

TASK 4

How to Free Up Space on Your Hard Disk

Even with the size of today's large hard drives, you might still find conservation of disk space an issue. During normal operation, Windows 2000 and the programs you run on it create temporary and backup files. Unfortunately, these programs (Windows included) are sometimes not very good at cleaning up after themselves. Windows 2000 includes a tool named Disk Cleanup that you can use to search for and delete unnecessary files.

Begin

1 Run Disk Cleanup

Select **Start**, **Programs**, **Accessories**, **System Tools**, and **Disk Cleanup**.

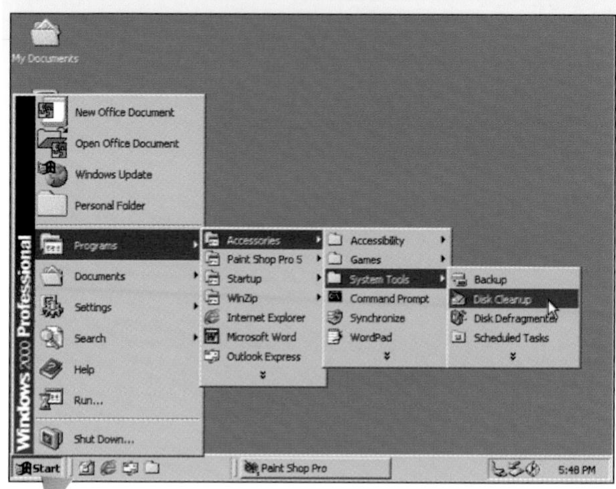

2 Select the Drive to Clean Up

Use the drop-down list to select the hard drive on which you want to free up space. Click the **OK** button after you have chosen your drive. Disk Cleanup scans your drive for files. This process might take a few minutes.

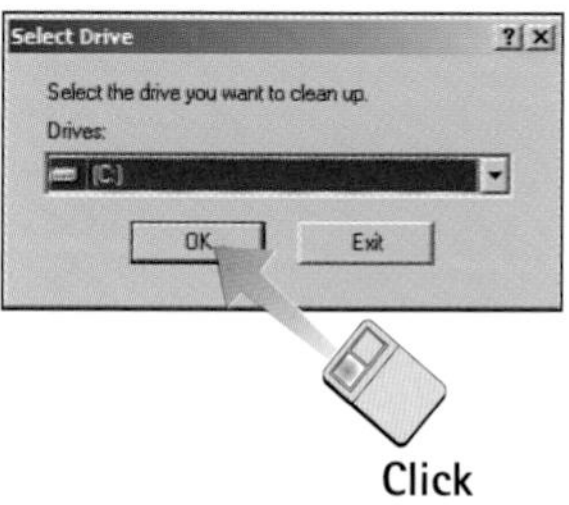

3 Select the Items to Remove

After Disk Cleanup has finished scanning your drive, it presents a list of categories for files it has found. Next to each category, Windows shows how much drive space all of the files in that category take up. You can mark other categories for deletion by clicking the check box next to them.

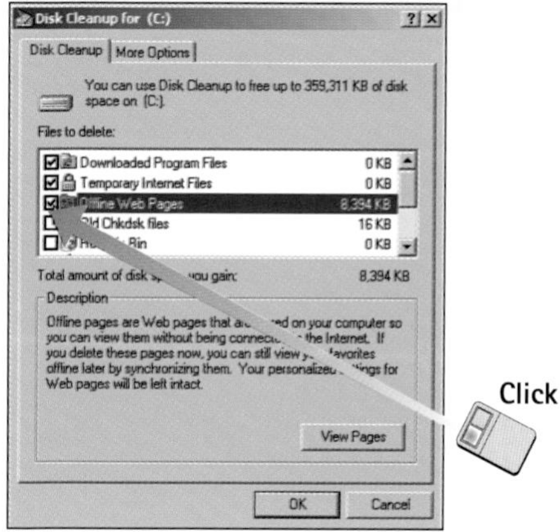

4 View Files

Categories that are already checked, such as Downloaded Program Files, are always safe to delete. Other categories might contain important files, and it is up to you to decide whether they should be deleted. Select a category by clicking its name once and click the **View Pages** button to see what's inside.

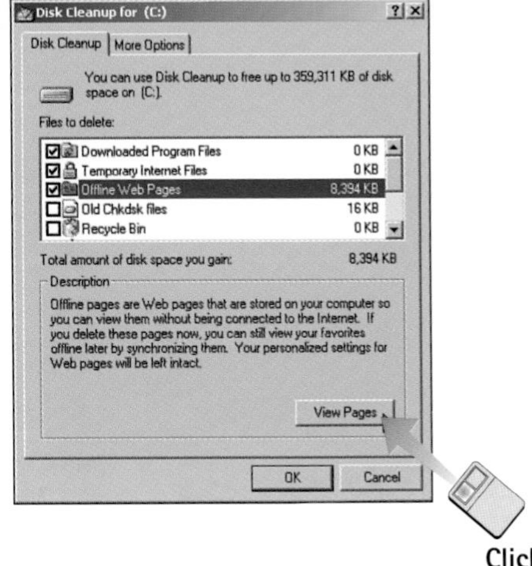

5 Click OK

When you have selected all the categories for files you want to delete, click the **OK** button to proceed. Windows asks you if you are sure you want to delete the files. If you are, click the **Yes** button.

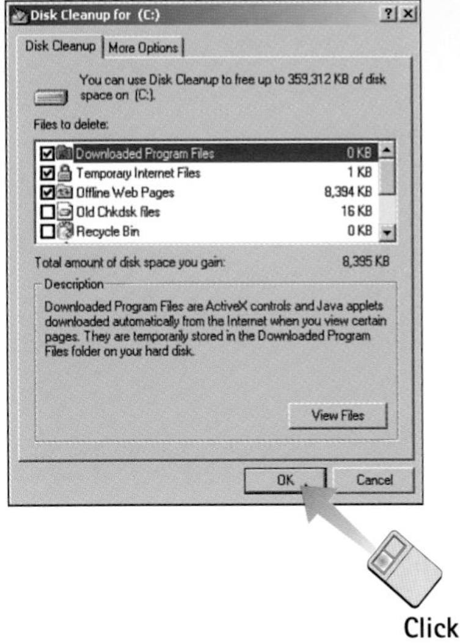

End

How-To Hints

Take Out the Trash

One way to keep space free on your hard drive is to regularly empty your Recycle Bin. Right-click the bin and choose **Empty Recycle Bin** from the shortcut menu to delete all the files it holds. You can also double-click the Recycle Bin to display a list of the files it contains. This lets you delete individual files.

TASK 5

How to Defragment Your Hard Disk

When you delete a file on your computer, Windows doesn't really remove it. It just marks that space as available for new information to be stored. When a new file is written to disk, part of the file might be written to one available section of disk space, part might be written to another, and part to another. This is called fragmentation. It is a normal process and Windows keeps track of files just fine. The problem is that when a drive has a lot of fragmentation, it can take Windows longer to find information it is looking for. You can speed up drive access significantly by periodically defragmenting your drive.

Begin

1 Run Disk Defragmenter

Select **Start**, **Programs**, **Accessories**, **System Tools**, and **Disk Defragmenter**.

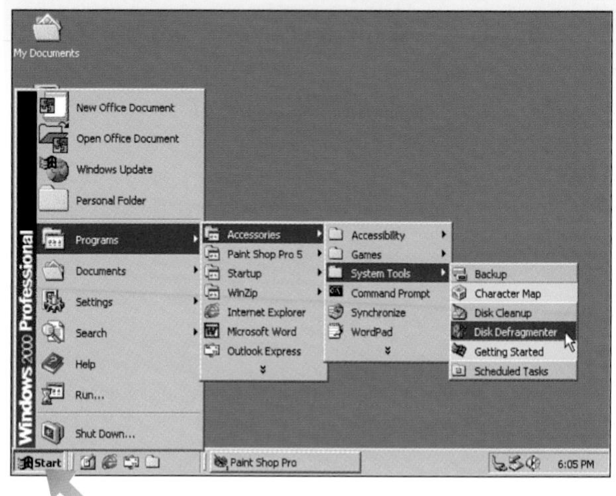

2 Choose a Drive

The window at the top of the program lists all of the drives on your computer. Select the drive you want to defragment by clicking it once.

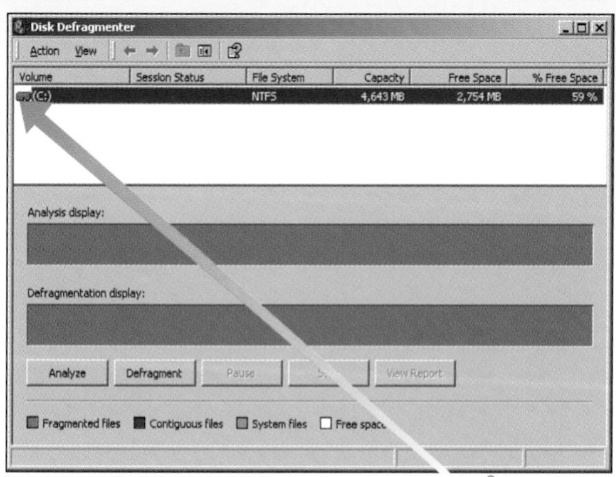

3 Analyze Drive

Click the **Analyze** button to have Disk Defragmenter analyze the selected drive for fragmentation. This process might take a few minutes, and the process is depicted graphically for you while you wait.

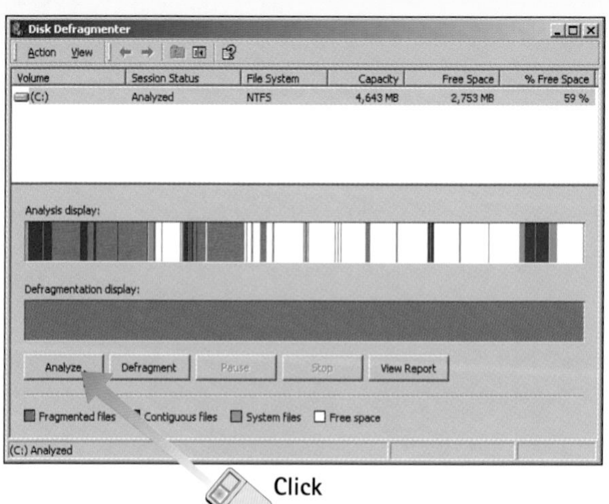

4 View Report

When the analysis is done, a dialog box appears that lets you view a report or go ahead with defragmentation. You can also perform these actions from the main program window itself. Click the **View Report** button to view a detailed report of the fragmented files that the analysis has discovered.

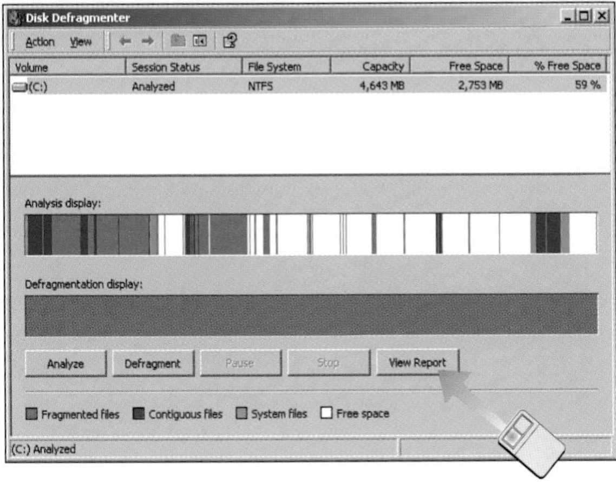

5 Defragment Drive

Should the analysis and report prove that your drive needs to be defragmented, you can start the procedure by clicking the **Defragment** button. This process can take a while, even an hour or so, depending on the size of your hard drive.

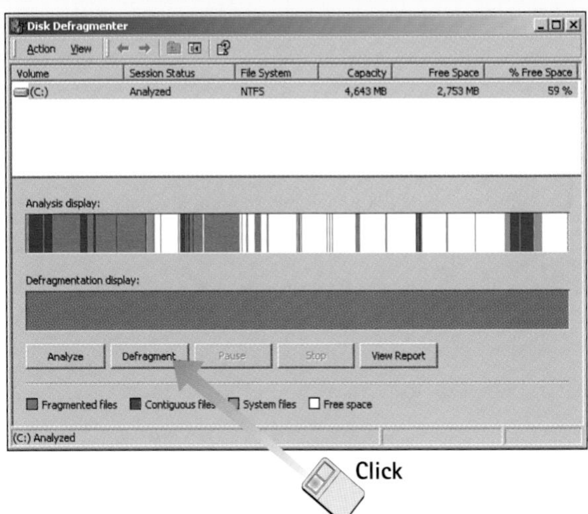

End

TASK 6

How to Schedule a Task to Occur Automatically

Windows 2000 includes a task scheduler that lets you schedule certain programs to run automatically. This can be particularly useful with programs like Disk Cleanup and Disk Defragmenter, although you can schedule virtually any program. You might, for example, schedule Disk Cleanup to run automatically every Friday night after work and Disk Defragmenter to run once a month or so, saving you the time of running these programs when you have better things to do.

Begin

1 Start Scheduled Tasks

Select **Start**, **Programs**, **Accessories**, **System Tools**, and **Scheduled Tasks**.

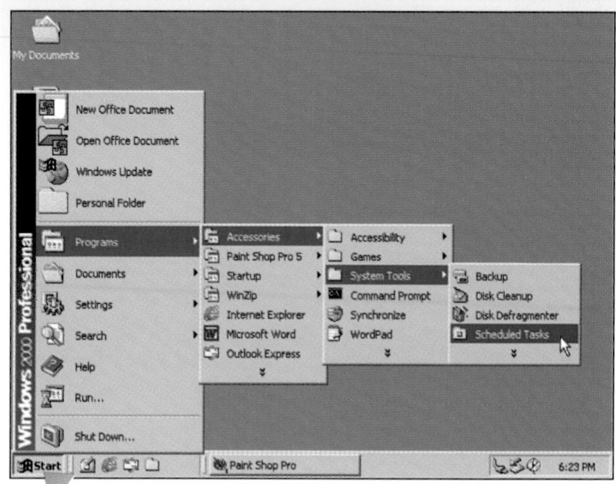

Click

2 Add a Scheduled Task

Double-click the **Add Scheduled Task** icon to start the Scheduled Task Wizard. The first page of the wizard is just a welcome page. Click the **Next** button to go on.

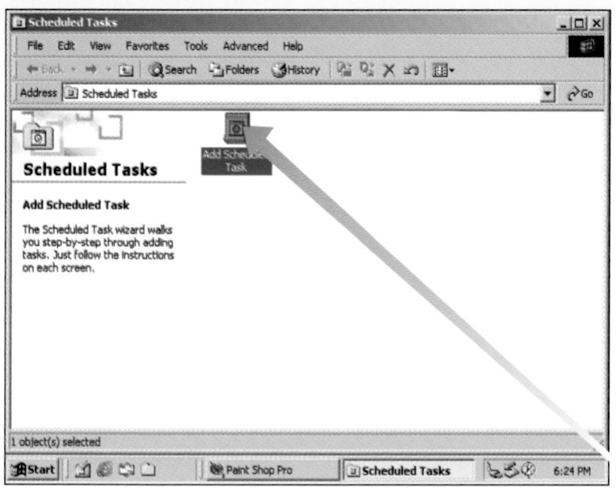

Double-click

3 Choose a Program to Run

Select the program you want to schedule from the list by clicking it once. If you don't see the program on the list, you can try to locate it by clicking the **Browse** button. After you've selected the program, click the **Next** button to go on.

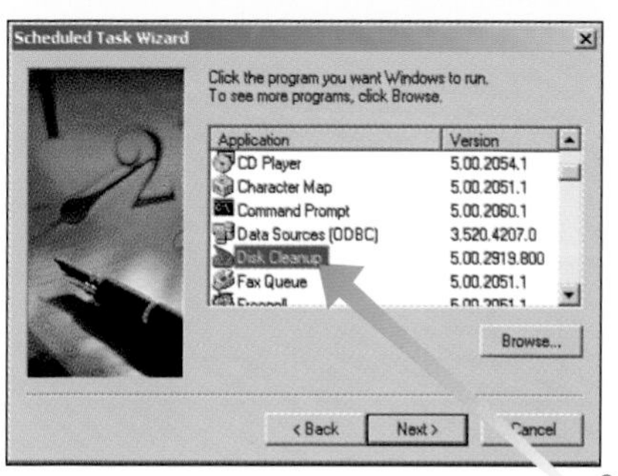

Click

4 Choose When to Run the Program

Type a name for the task in the box, if you want to change the default name. Choose when you want to perform the task by clicking the option once. When you're done, click the **Next** button to go on.

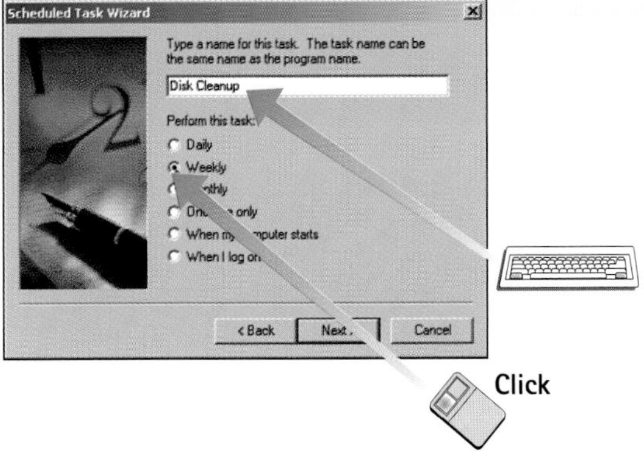

5 Choose a Time and Day

If you chose to run the program daily, weekly, or monthly, you also need to specify the time of day to run the program. Type in a time or use the scroll buttons. You also need to select the day or days you want the program to run by clicking the appropriate check boxes. Click the **Next** button to go on.

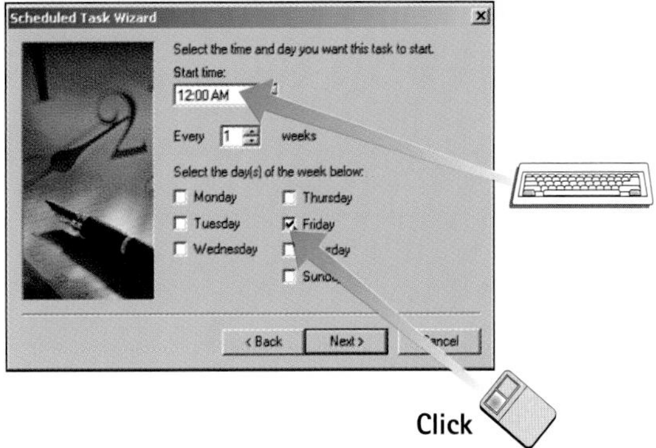

6 Enter a Username and Password

To run a program in Windows 2000, Task Scheduler needs to have your username and password. Type the information into the boxes on this page, then click the **Next** button to go on.

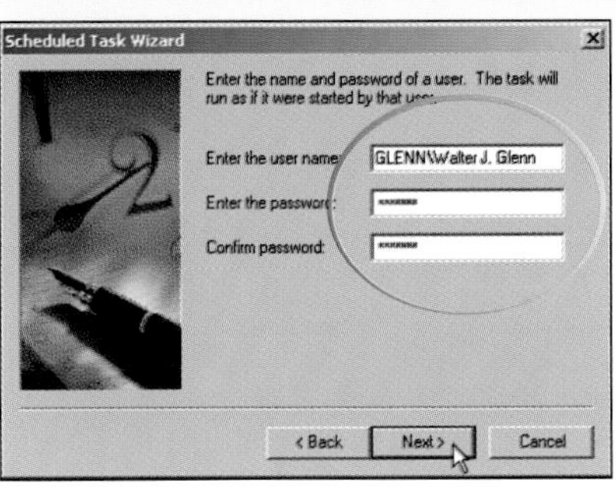

7 Finish

Click the **Finish** button to schedule your new task.

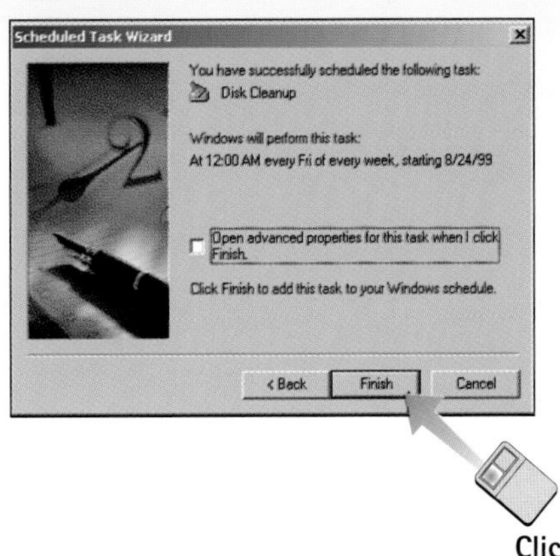

End

TASK 7

How to Use the Windows Troubleshooters

If your computer is on a network, you are probably fortunate enough to have a network administrator to call when your computer has problems. Should you need to fix problems yourself, however, Windows 2000 includes a few useful troubleshooters that can help you diagnose and repair problems.

Begin

1 Start Help

Click the **Start** button, and then click **Help**.

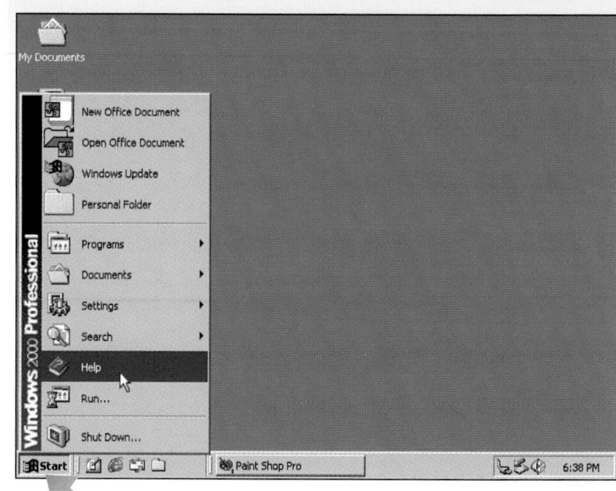

2 Troubleshooting and Maintenance

Click the **Troubleshooting and Maintenance** subject once to expand it.

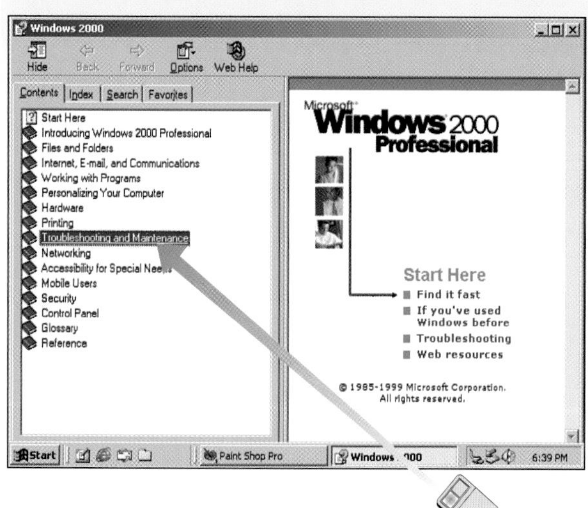

3 Use the Interactive Troubleshooters

Click **Use the Interactive Troubleshooters** to display the document in the right-hand window.

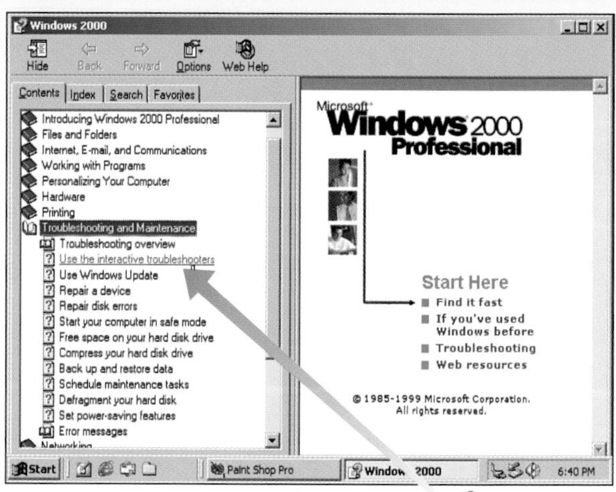

4 Choose a Troubleshooter

Scroll the right-hand window to find the troubleshooter you want to run. After you find the troubleshooter you want, **Hardware** for example, click it once to start it.

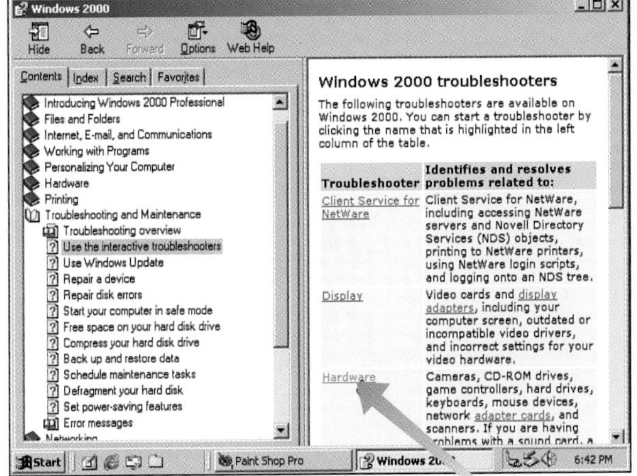

Click

5 Work Through the Steps

Troubleshooters work just like wizards. Each page asks a question. Choose the answer by clicking it once, and then click the **Next** button to go on. Some pages offer steps for you to try to fix your problem. If the steps work, you're done. If they don't, the troubleshooter continues. If the troubleshooter can't fix your problem, it recommends where you should go for more information.

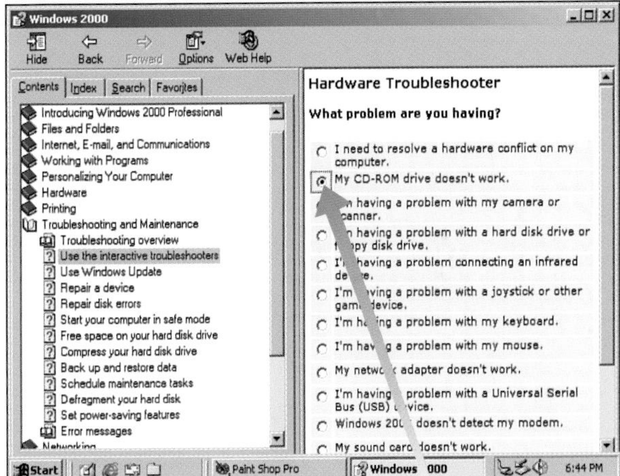

Click

End

How-To Hints

Troubleshooting Overview

In the Troubleshooting and Maintenance help subject, there is also an item named Troubleshooting Overview, which provides a pretty good grounding in various techniques for troubleshooting Windows 2000 problems.

Task

PART 11

Installing New Software on Your Computer

If your computer is connected to your company's network, a network administrator is probably responsible for adding and removing hardware and software on your computer. If so, you should definitely take advantage of his or her expertise. However, with Windows 2000, adding new hardware and software to your system has never been easier.

Most of the hardware and software you get these days literally installs itself. New programs usually come on CD-ROMs. With Windows 2000, you can just insert the CD-ROM and Windows automatically finds and launches the setup routine for the program, which walks you through the installation. Windows 2000 also provides a more hands-on approach to installing software. In this part, you see how to perform a manual installation and how to change settings for already-installed software. You also learn how to add Windows components from the CD and from Microsoft's Windows Update Web site.

Adding new hardware to a Windows 2000 computer is not too difficult. The hardware itself, whether it is a new CD-ROM drive, modem, or video card, comes with instructions on the physical installation of the device. After the device itself is installed and you turn on your computer, Windows 2000 notices that there is new hardware and either configures that hardware for you automatically or asks you for the software that came with the device. Either way, Windows 2000 handles it all for you. In this part, you will learn how to check up on the hardware that is already installed on your system.

TASK 1

How to Add a Program to Your Computer

Programs, whether a word processor, spreadsheet, or game, are the whole reason you use your computer. Almost all new programs today come on CD-ROM. When you insert the CD-ROM into your drive, Windows 2000 should automatically run the setup program for you. If this is the case, you won't need to follow the procedure below. If it does not start automatically, or if your program is on floppy disk, the following steps show you how to start the installation yourself.

Begin

1 Open the Control Panel

Select **Start**, **Settings**, and **Control Panel**.

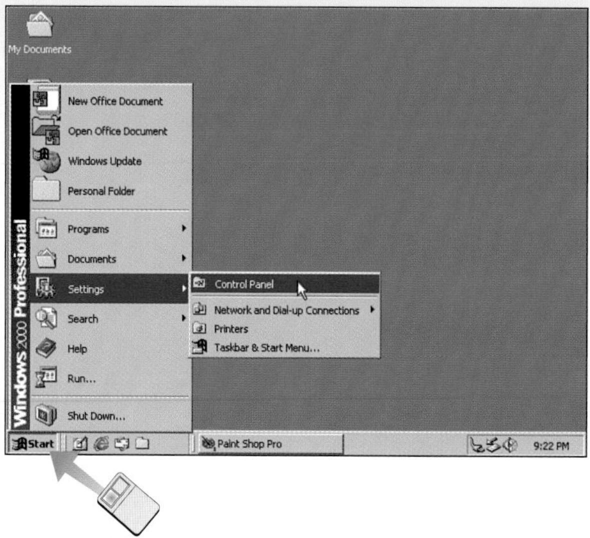

Click

2 Open the Add/Remove Programs Applet

Double-click the **Add/Remove Programs** applet to open it.

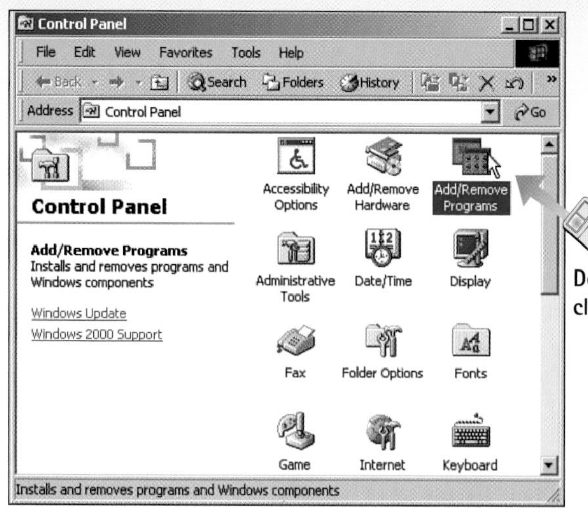

Double-click

3 Add New Programs

The **Add/Remove Programs** applet is used to add, change, and remove programs, as well as install new Windows components. Click the **Add New Programs** button.

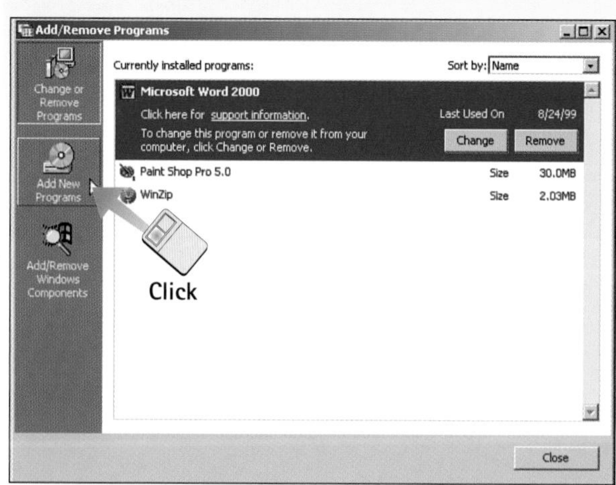

Click

4 CD or Floppy

If programs are available for installation from your network, they will be listed in the window at the bottom of the dialog box. Click the **CD or Floppy** button to indicate that you want to install a program from a disk. This launches a short wizard that helps you start a program's installation routine. The first page is just a welcome screen. Click the **Next** button to go on.

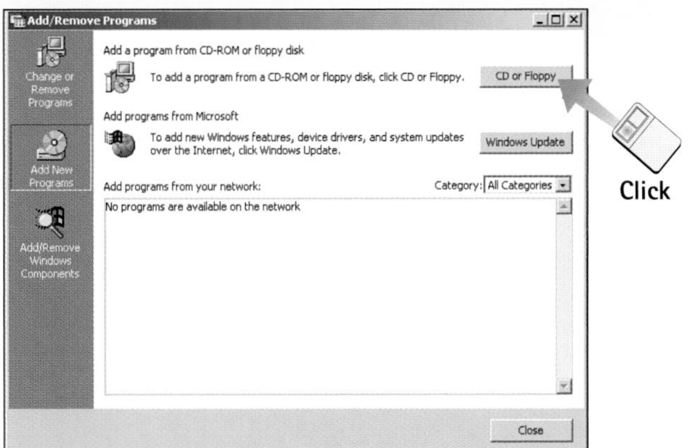

5 Finish

Windows searches both your floppy and CD-ROM drive for a setup program. If it finds one, the path to the program is displayed for your approval. If you think Windows found the right one, click the **Finish** button to launch the setup program. You can also click the **Browse** button to locate the setup program yourself.

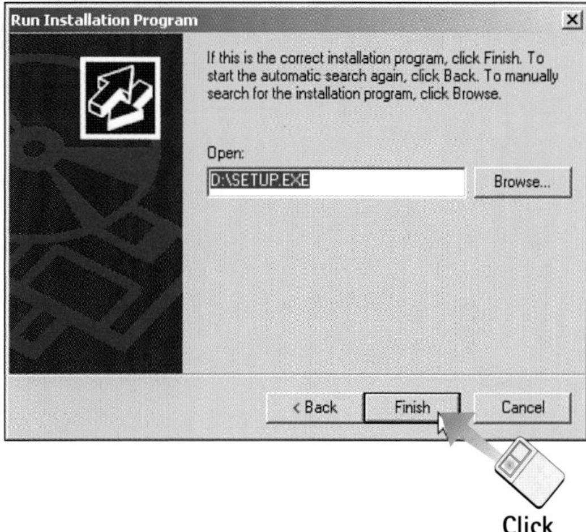

End

How-To Hints

Installing from Explorer

You can also run a setup program manually without using the **Add/Remove Programs** applet. Just open the **My Computer** window and locate the setup program yourself on the floppy or CD-ROM. It is almost always a program named **setup.exe**. Double-click the program to start it.

Restarting

Different programs have different installation routines. Some require that you restart your computer after the program has been installed. This is one reason why it is best to save any work and exit any running programs before you install new software.

The Program Files Folder

Your **C:** drive has a folder on it named **Program Files**. Most new programs that you install create a folder for themselves inside this folder that is used to store the program's files.

TASK 2

How to Change or Remove a Program

Some programs, such as Microsoft Office, let you customize the installation of the program to include only the components that you want in the installation. You can then add new components later if you want. The **Add/Remove Programs** applet lets you change the installation of a program, and it lets you remove the installation altogether (sometimes called uninstalling).

Begin

1 Open the Control Panel

Select **Start**, **Settings**, and **Control Panel**.

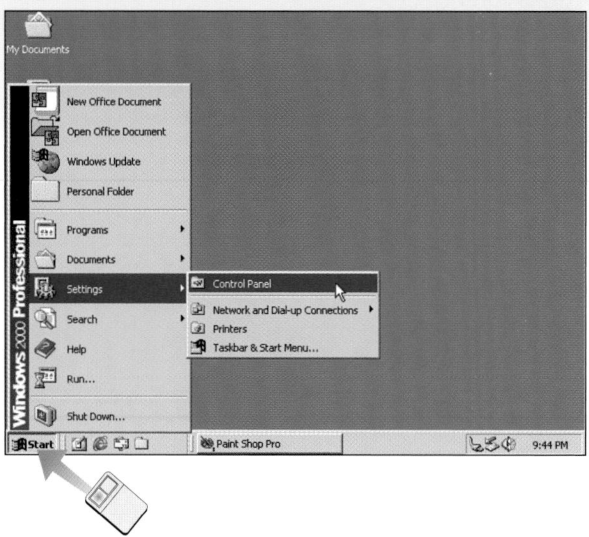

2 Open the Add/Remove Programs Applet

Double-click the **Add/Remove Programs** applet to open it.

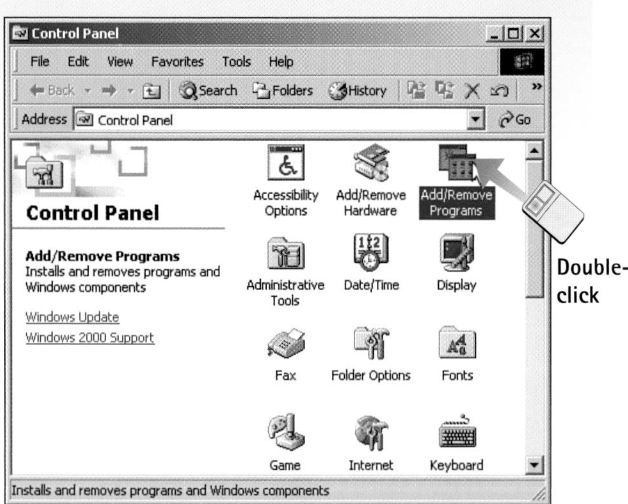

3 Select a Program

Choose a program from the list of currently installed programs by clicking it once. Notice that Windows lets you know how much disk space the program takes up and how often you use the program.

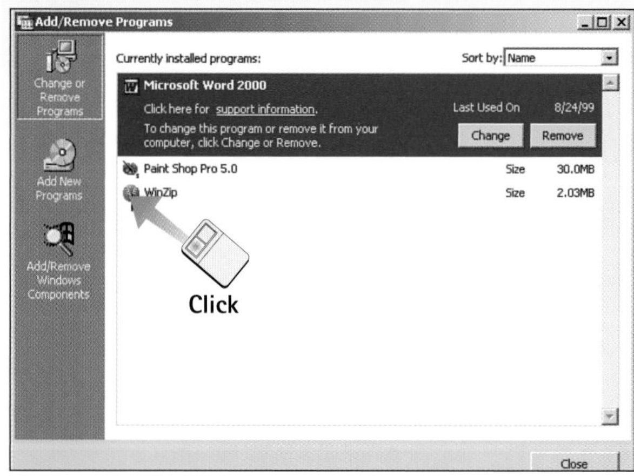

4 Click Change/Remove

Programs that do not let you change the installation show only a **Change/Remove** button. Programs that do let you change the installation show both a **Change** button and a **Remove** button. Click whatever button provides the action you want.

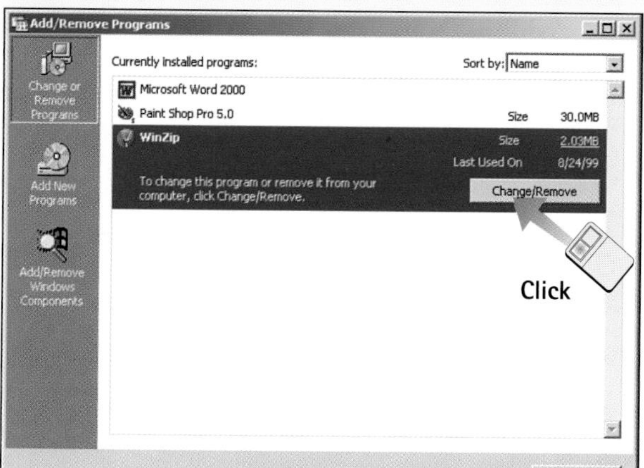

5 Follow the Program's Instructions

Every program has a slightly different routine for changing or removing the installation. Follow the onscreen instructions for the program you are using.

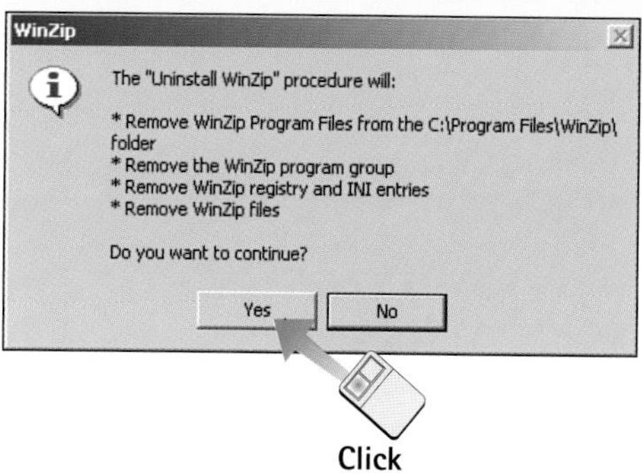

End

How-To Hints

Be Careful

Some programs automatically go forward with a removal as soon as you click the **Change/Remove** or **Remove** buttons, without giving you a chance to confirm. It is best to be sure you want to remove a program before clicking.

TASK 3

How to Add Windows Components from the CD

Windows 2000 Professional literally comes with hundreds of components and not all of them are installed during a normal installation of the operating system. You can add components from the Windows 2000 CD-ROM at any time after installation.

Begin

1 Open the Control Panel

Select **Start**, **Settings**, and **Control Panel**.

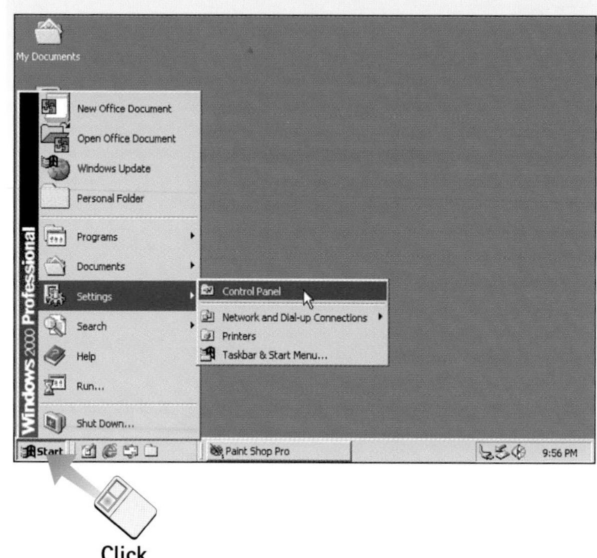

2 Open the Add/Remove Programs Applet

Double-click the **Add/Remove Programs** applet to open it.

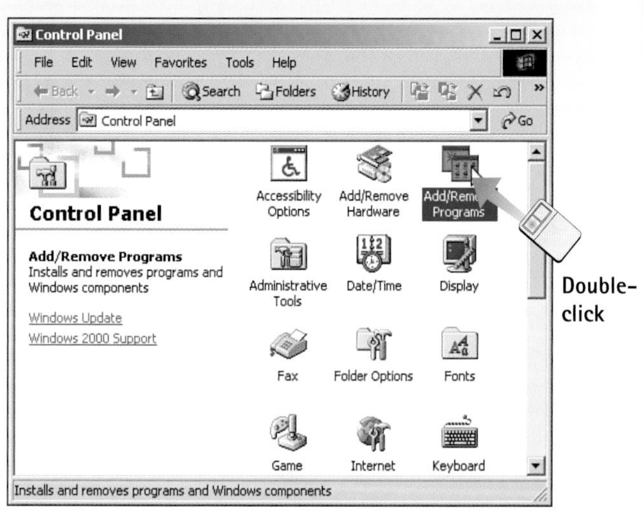

3 Choose Add/Remove Windows Components

Click the **Add/Remove Windows Components** button. Windows searches your computer for installed components and then displays a list of components you can install from the CD-ROM.

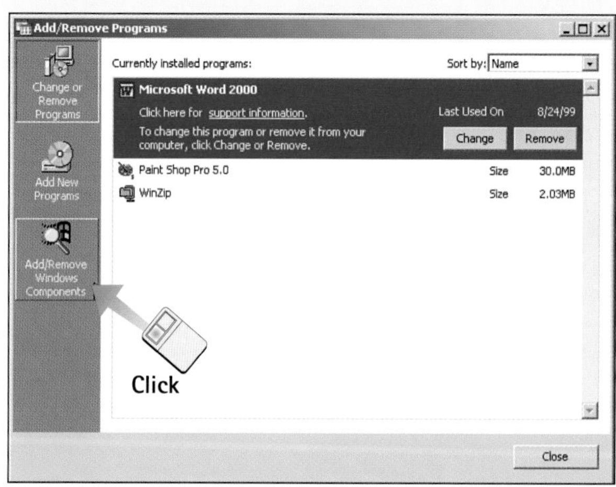

4 Select a Component

Select a component from the list of available components by clicking the check box next to it. Some components have subcomponents that you can choose from. If so, the **Details** button becomes active, and you can click it to see a list of subcomponents to choose from.

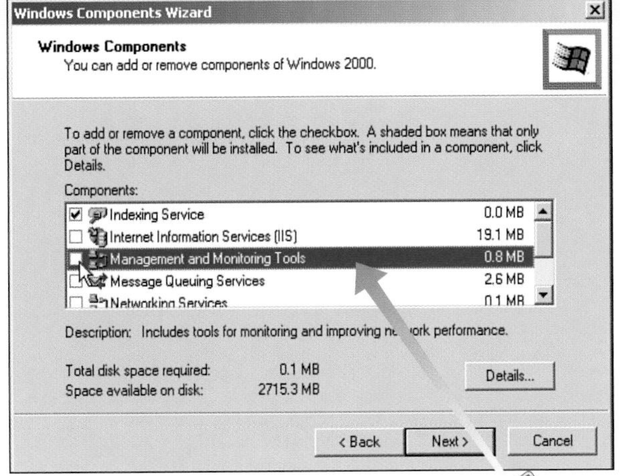

5 Next

After you have selected all of the components you want to install, click the **Next** button. Windows builds a list of files that need to be installed and copies them to your drive.

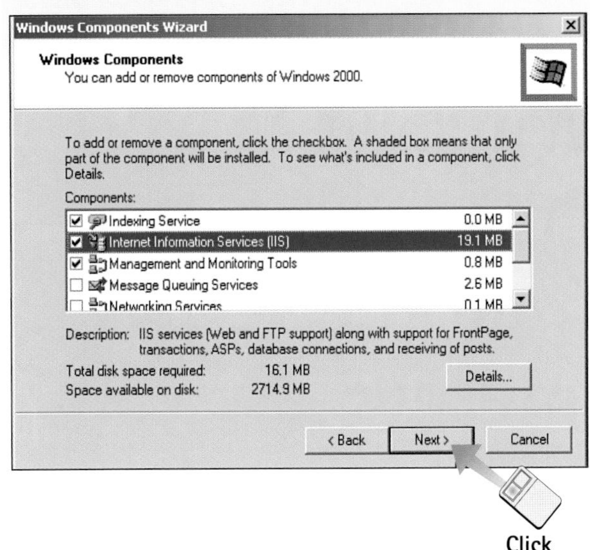

6 Finish

After Windows has installed the components, it lets you know that the process has been completed successfully. Click the **Finish** button to finish. Depending on the components you added, Windows might need to restart your computer.

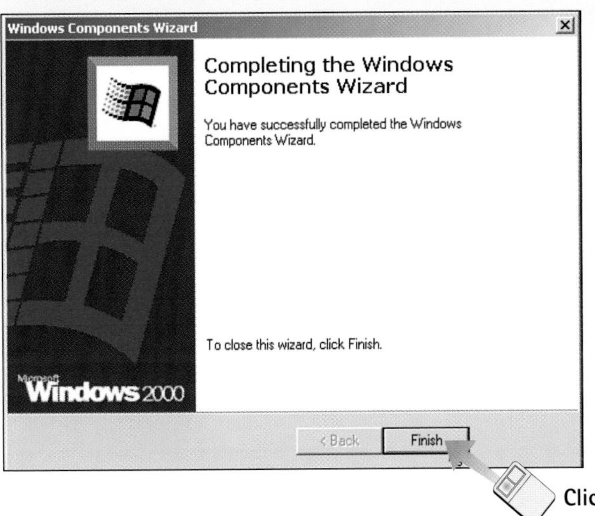

End

TASK 4

How to Add Windows Components from the Internet

Microsoft maintains a Web site that contains the newest versions of Windows components that you can download and add to your system. These components are updated versions of the components that come with Windows and new components and updates that Microsoft makes available.

Begin

1 Start Windows Update

Select **Start** and **Windows Update**. This launches the Windows Update Web site in Internet Explorer.

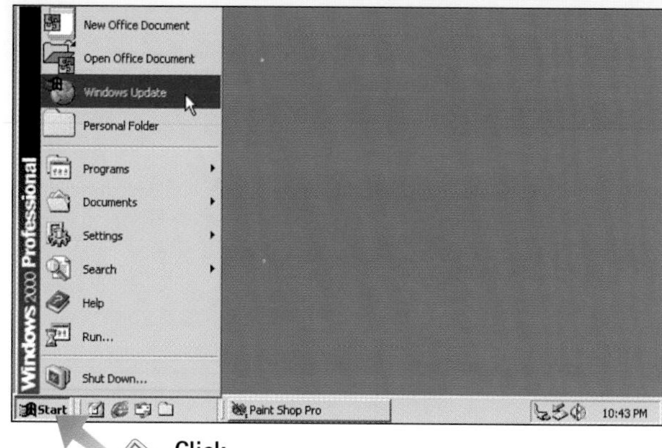

2 Choose Product Updates

Click the **Product Updates** link. Windows Update searches your computer for installed components and then displays a list of components that you can download and install.

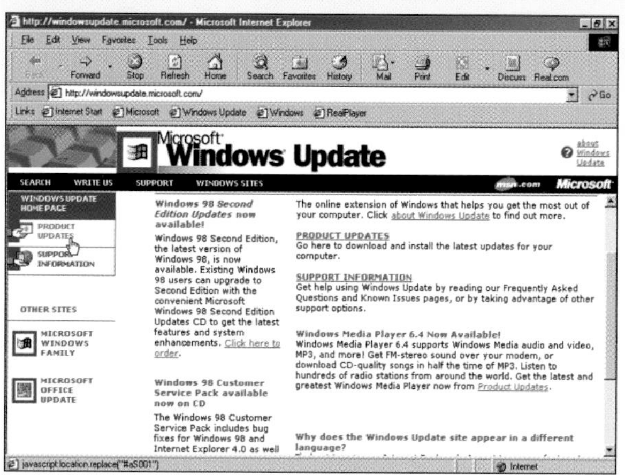

3 Choose the Components to Update

Choose the components you want to install by clicking the check boxes next to them. Keep in mind that you must download these components before they can be installed. For this reason, you might want to select fewer components and make multiple trips to the Windows Update site.

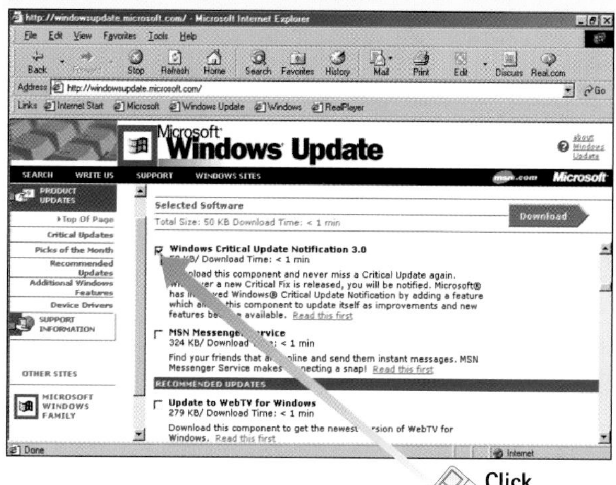

4 Go to the Download Page

When you have selected all of the components you want to install, click the **Download** button to go to the download page.

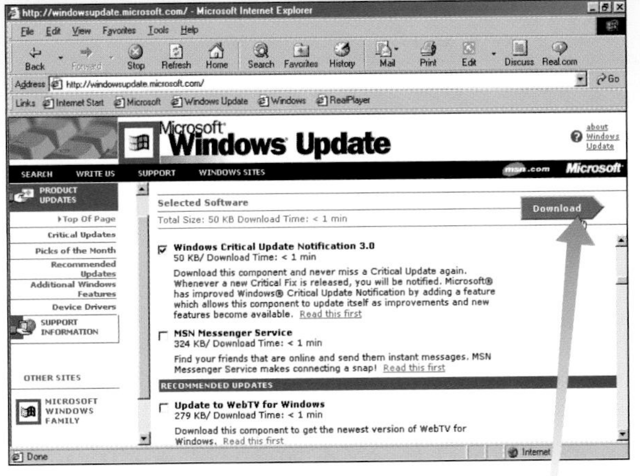

Click

5 Download and Install the Components

Review the list of components that you have selected. You can remove components from the list by clearing the check boxes next to them. When you are satisfied with your list, click the **Start Download** button to download and install the components.

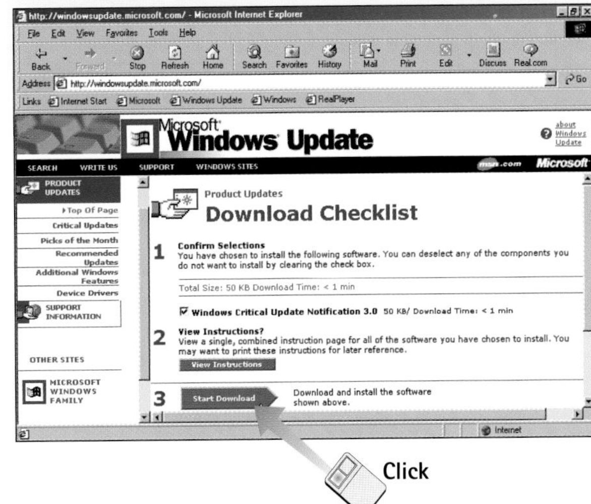

End

TASK 5

How to Find Out About Your Installed Hardware

Windows 2000 uses a tool called the **Device Manager** that lets you find out about all of the hardware on your system. You can see what is installed, what resources are used, and what devices might be having problems.

Begin

1 Open System Properties

Right-click the **My Computer** icon on your desktop and choose the **Properties** command from the shortcut menu.

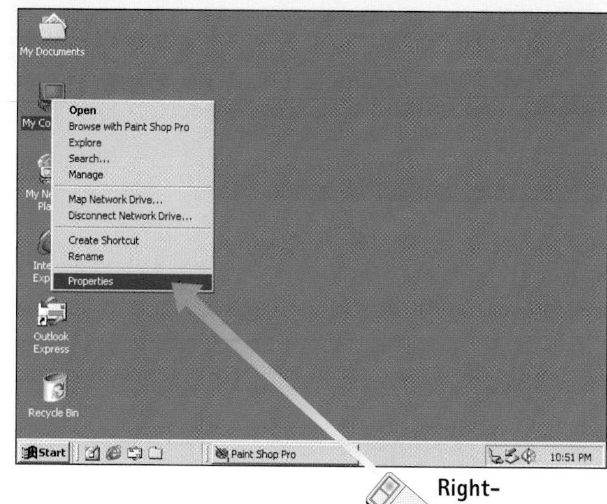

2 Switch to Hardware Tab

Switch to the **Hardware** tab by clicking it once.

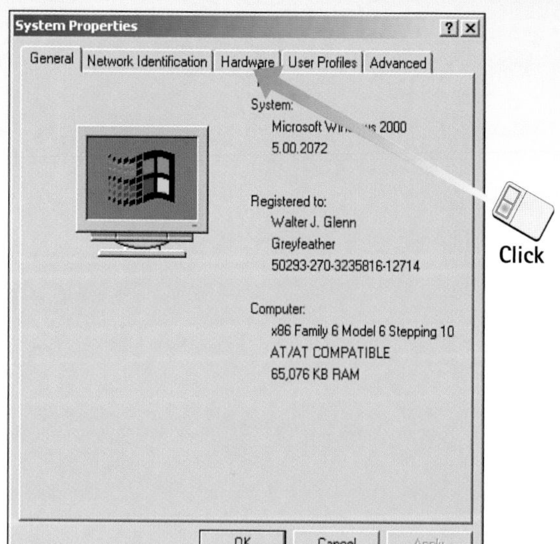

3 Open the Device Manager

Select the **Device Manager** button to open the **Device Manager** window.

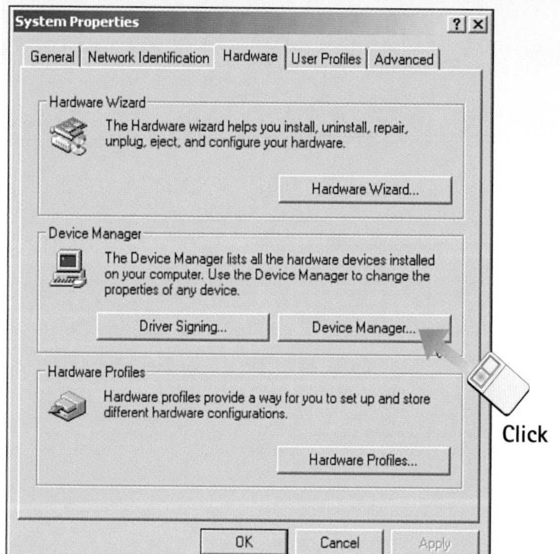

4 Expand a Category

The Device Manager shows a list of hardware categories for hardware installed on your computer. Click the plus sign next to a category to expand that category and show the actual devices attached to your computer.

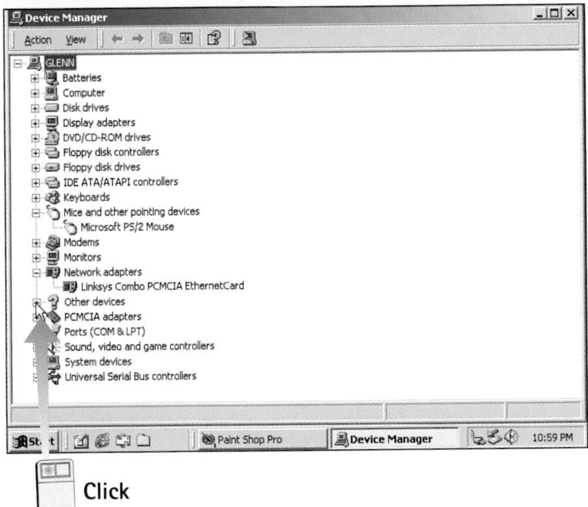

Click

5 Identify Problem Hardware

Devices that are having problems are identified with a little yellow exclamation point. Another type of symbol you might see is a red x, which indicates a device that is turned off for some reason.

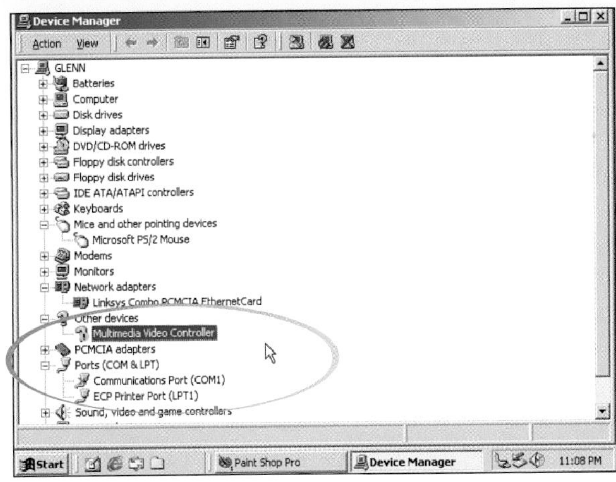

6 Open Hardware Properties

You can open a detailed properties dialog box for any device by double-clicking it. The dialog box tells you the device's working status and lets you disable the device. Other tabs let you reinstall software drivers and view the resources.

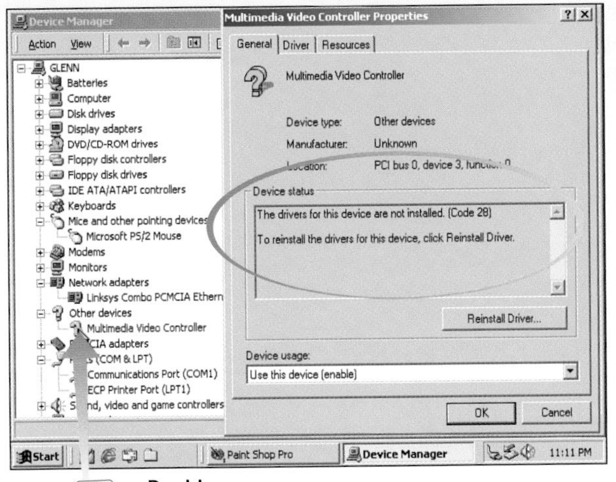

Double-click

How-To Hints

Reinstalling a Device

If you see a device that isn't working, try running the **Add/Remove Hardware Wizard.** Windows scans your system for devices and presents a list of what it finds. The malfunctioning device should show up in the list, and you can try to reinstall it.

End

Task

APPENDIX A

Installing Windows 2000 Professional

Even though the product itself is far more complex, the installation of Windows 2000 Professional is much simpler than installing previous versions of Windows. This is, in part, because the setup routine is smarter and can detect and configure more types of hardware for you. It is also due to the fact that Microsoft has taken a lot of the decisions out of the setup process.

There are several ways to go about installing Windows 2000 Professional. Perhaps the simplest method is to upgrade from another operating system, such as Windows 98 or Windows NT Workstation. In this case, Windows 2000 Professional takes the place of the old operating system. You can also install Windows 2000 professional while keeping an old operating system, such as Windows 98. This is known as a dual-boot configuration. When you turn on your computer, you are given the choice of booting to Windows 2000 Professional or booting to your old operating system. Yet another way to install Windows 2000 Professional is to install it on a clean system—one that has no operating system at all. This is the method you should choose if you build your own computer or if you decide to clear off your hard drive before installation. You might also use this method if you put a new hard drive in your computer.

In this part, you are introduced to each of these methods of installing Windows 2000 Professional. You are also shown how to create a set of setup floppy disks to use when installing Windows 2000 on a clean system.

TASK 1

How to Upgrade to Windows 2000

Upgrading is the easiest way to install Windows 2000 Professional. You can upgrade to Windows 2000 Professional from Windows 95, Windows 98, and Windows NT Workstation 3.5 or 4.0. To get started with the upgrade, all you have to do is insert the Windows 2000 Professional CD-ROM in your computer's drive.

Begin

1 Upgrade

When you insert the Windows 2000 Professional CD-ROM into your drive, a splash screen automatically appears along with a dialog box that asks if you want to upgrade. Click the **Yes** button to start the upgrade. If the splash screen does not appear, you need to open the CD-ROM and run the Setup program yourself.

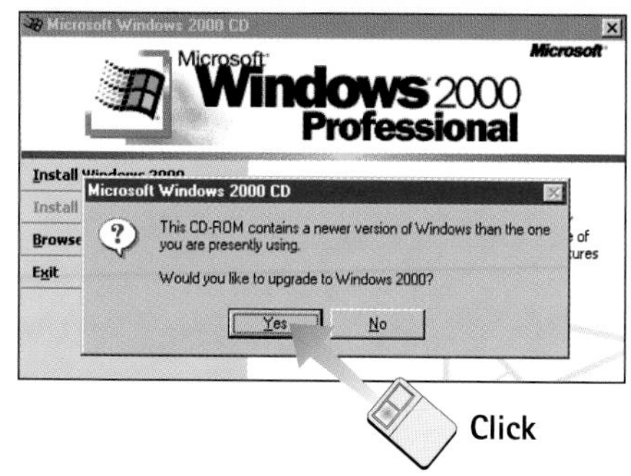

2 Choose Upgrade or Clean Install

If you choose to upgrade, your old operating system (such as Windows 98) is overwritten by Windows 2000 Professional. Settings you have made in Windows 98 and all of your software are preserved. If you choose a clean install, Windows 2000 is installed in addition to your old operating system. You can choose which to boot into whenever you start your computer. After you decide, click the **Next** button to go on.

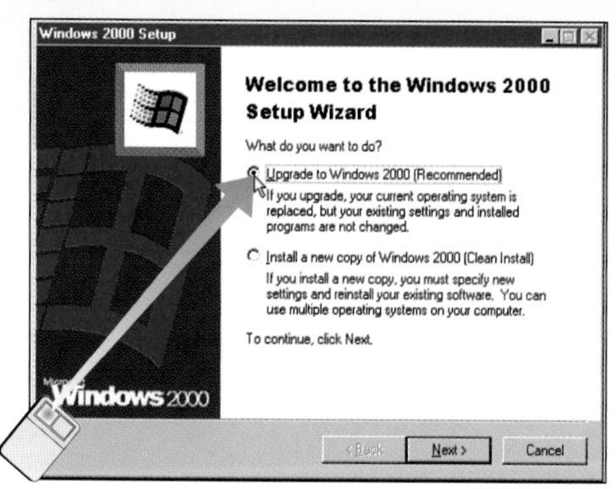

3 Accept the License Agreement

You must accept Microsoft's licensing agreement by clicking the **I Accept This Agreement** option before you can click the **Next** button to proceed with the installation.

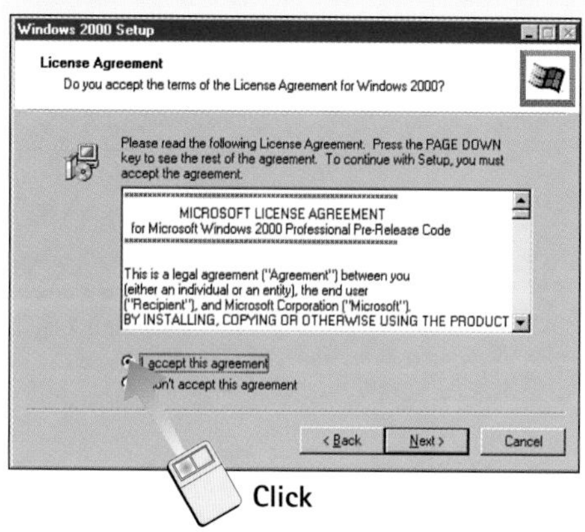

4 Let Windows Examine Your System

Windows setup now examines your system to determine what is already installed. Click the **Next** button to go on.

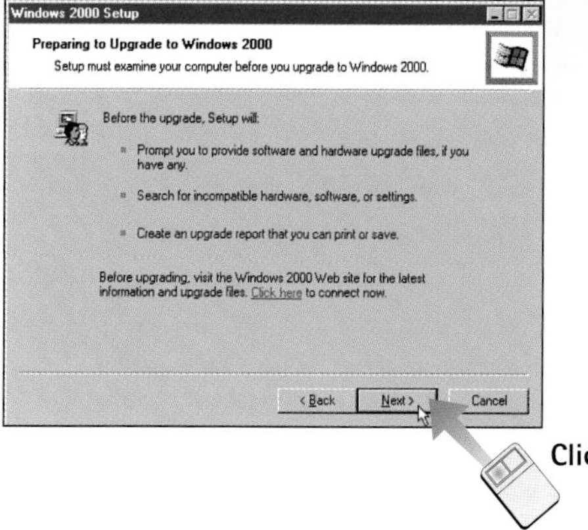

Click

5 Provide Upgrade Packs

Some software needs to be upgraded before it can be used with Windows 2000. If you have any upgrade packs, you can choose the **Yes, I Have Upgrade Packs** option and apply them during installation. However, it is better to choose not to apply them now and apply them after Windows setup finished. Should any problems occur after the upgrade, you will know that it was the upgrade that caused the problem and not the upgrade packs. Windows generates a report on what needs to be upgraded.

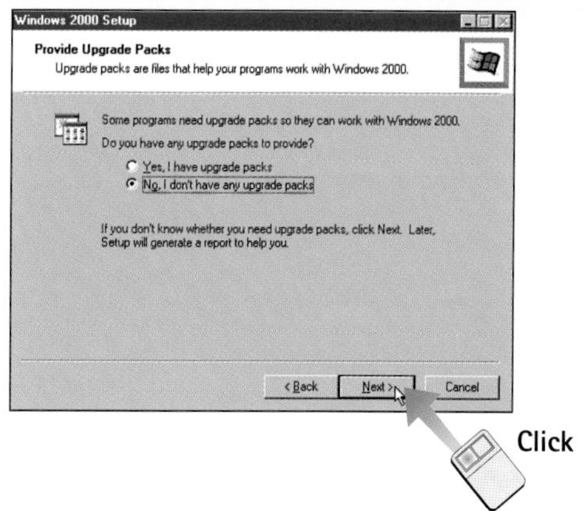

Click

6 Upgrade to NTFS

NTFS is a secure, robust file system used by Windows NT and Windows 2000. If you will only be using Windows 2000 on the computer, you are probably better off choosing to use NTFS. Windows 95 and 98 cannot use NTFS. If you are going to be keeping your old operating system, do not upgrade to NTFS.

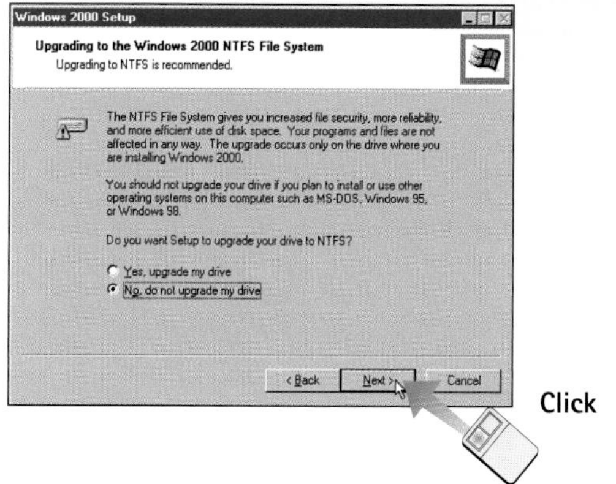

Click

7 Finish the Upgrade

Windows 2000 setup examines your system and prepares files for copying. This can take a few minutes. After it is done, you can view the upgrade report. After this, setup is ready to begin the upgrade. This can take a while and your computer will be restarted a few times. When done, you can start using Windows 2000 Professional.

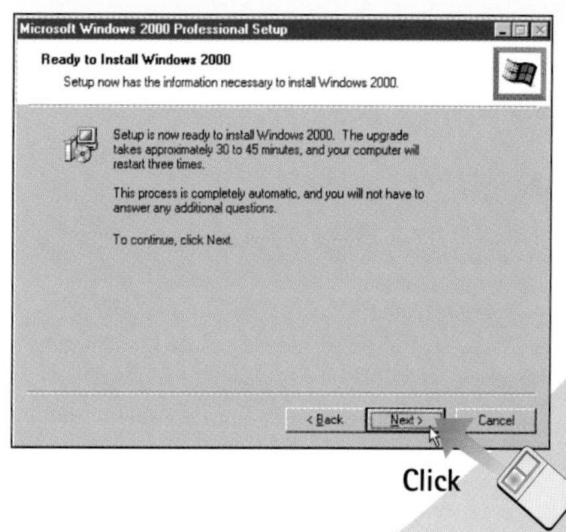

Click

End

TASK 2

How to Install a Clean Copy of Windows 2000

Installing a clean copy of Windows 2000 is a bit more complicated than upgrading. It requires that you have a blank, formatted hard drive and that you have a bootable CD-ROM drive or a set of four setup floppy disks. The procedure for creating the floppy disks is discussed in Task 3, "How to Create Setup Floppy Disks." To begin, insert the CD-ROM or the first of the four floppy disks into your floppy drive and start your computer. If you are using floppy disks, setup asks you for the second, third, and fourth disks before you get to make any other setup decisions.

Begin

1 Choose Setup or Repair

The first decision you are asked to make is whether you want to set up Windows 2000 or whether you want to repair an existing installation. For more on repairing, see Part 10, "Using the System Tools." To continue with setup, press the **Enter** key.

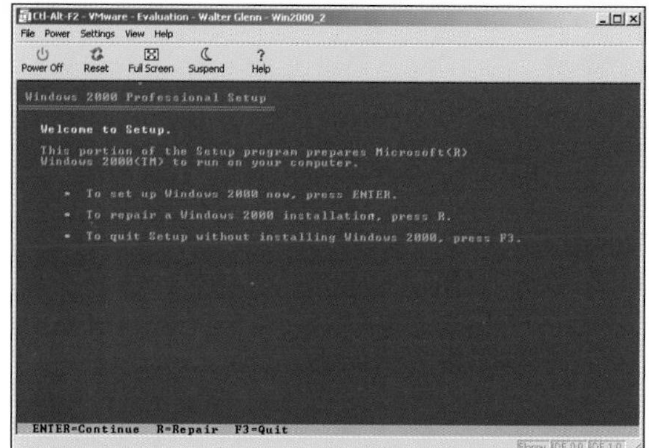

2 Read Hard Drive Warning

When you install Windows 2000 Professional on a clean hard drive, setup warns you that the drive is either empty or is running an incompatible operating system. If you are sure the drive is clean and you wish to install Windows 2000 Professional on it, press the **C** key to continue.

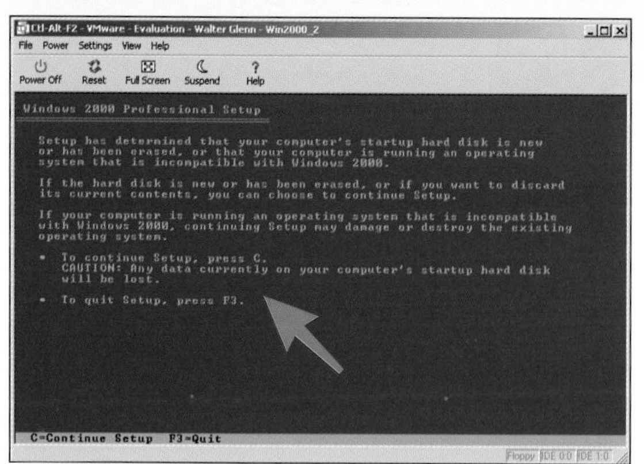

3 Agree to Licensing

To continue setup, you must agree to Microsoft's licensing agreement. Press the **F8** key to continue.

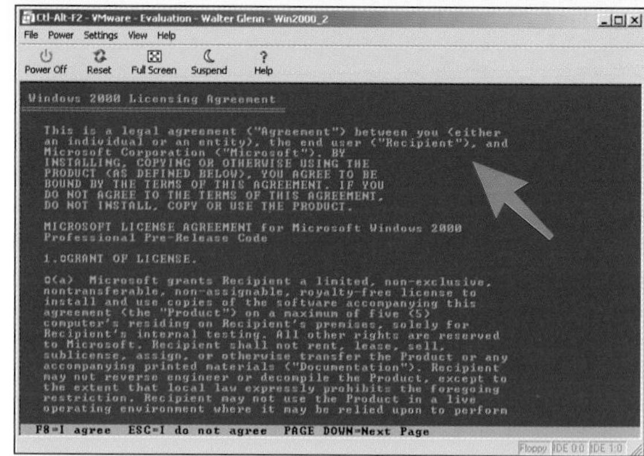

4 Choose a Partition

Next, you need to choose a partition on which to install Windows 2000. Highlight a partition using the up and down arrow keys. Select the highlighted drive by pressing the **Enter** key. You can also create and delete drive partitions.

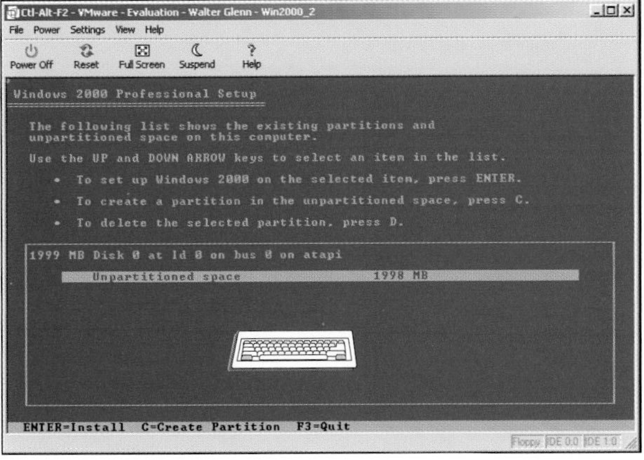

5 Format Your Drive

Next, choose whether to format your drive with the NTFS or FAT32 file system. NTFS is more secure, but only Windows 2000 and Windows NT recognize it. Windows 95 and 98 can recognize the FAT system. If your drive is already formatted, you also have the option of saving the existing format. Depending on the size of your drive, formatting can take a few minutes.

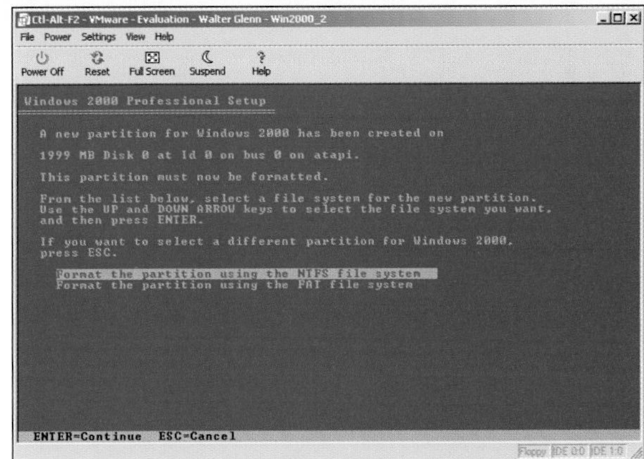

6 Copy Files to Your Disk

Next, setup copies files to your hard drive. This process can also take several minutes.

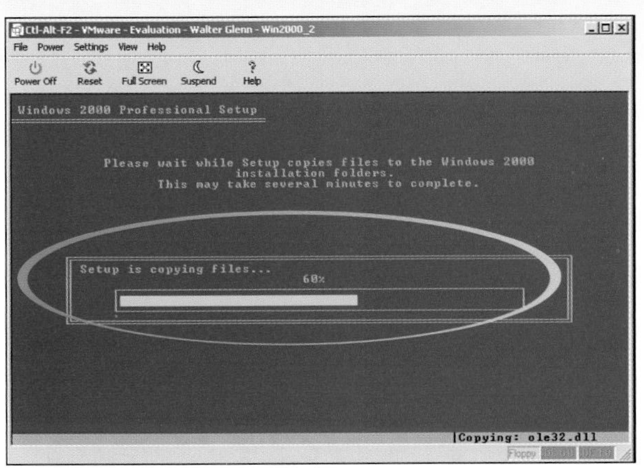

7 Restart Your Computer

Once all files are copied to your disk, your computer needs to restart. This happens automatically after 15 seconds, but you can also press the **Enter** key. Make sure you remove any floppy disks before you restart. When the computer starts back up, setup continues in a more familiar graphical interface.

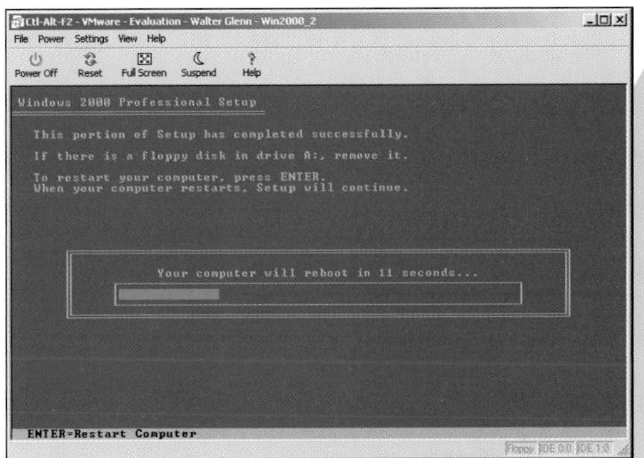

Continues

8 Look for Hardware Devices

After your computer restarts, setup initially spends several minutes looking for hardware devices attached to your computer. It is normal for your screen to flicker during this process. It is also possible that setup may need to restart your computer a time or two. All of this happens automatically—you can just watch.

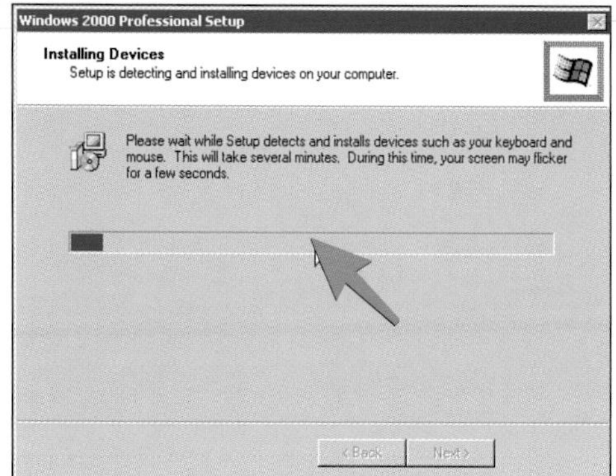

9 Customize Your Locale

Next, you are given the chance to customize your locale and keyboard input. The default is for the English language. When you're done, click the **Next** button to go on.

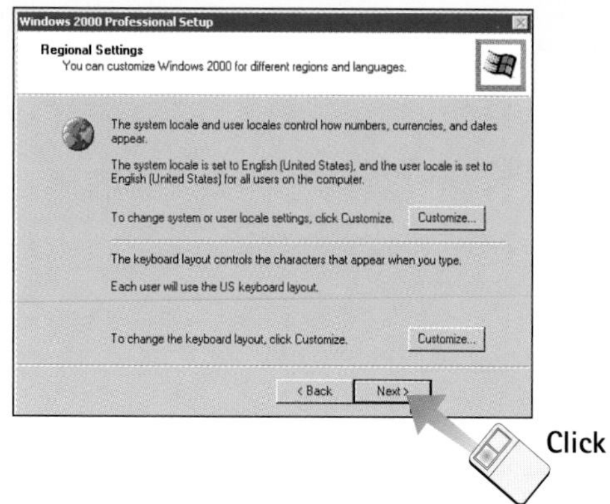

10 Enter Your Name and Organization

Type your name and the name of your company. If you want, you can leave the company name blank. When you're done, click the **Next** button to go on.

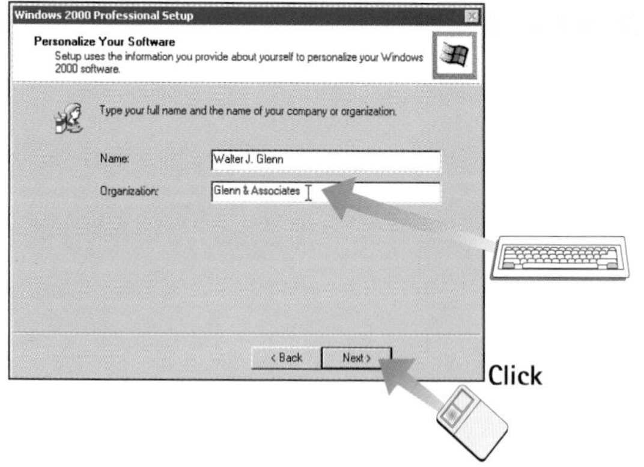

11 Enter Computer and Password

Type a name for your computer in the **Computer Name** box. Your computer will be known by this name on the network. Also, type in and confirm a password for the Administrator account.

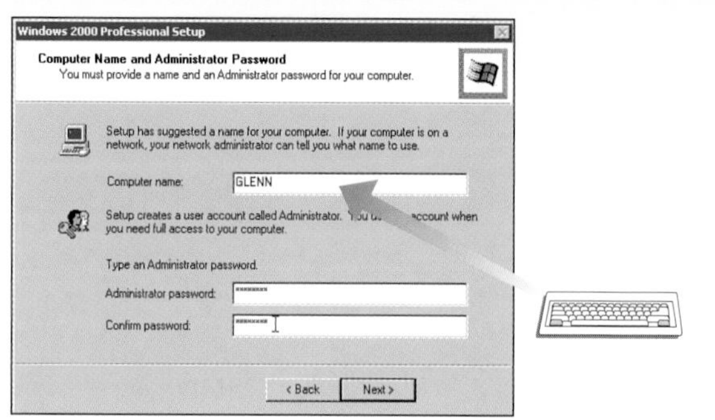

12 Enter the Date and Time

Next, you need to enter the correct date and time, if setup is not reporting it correctly already. When you're done, click the **Next** button to go on.

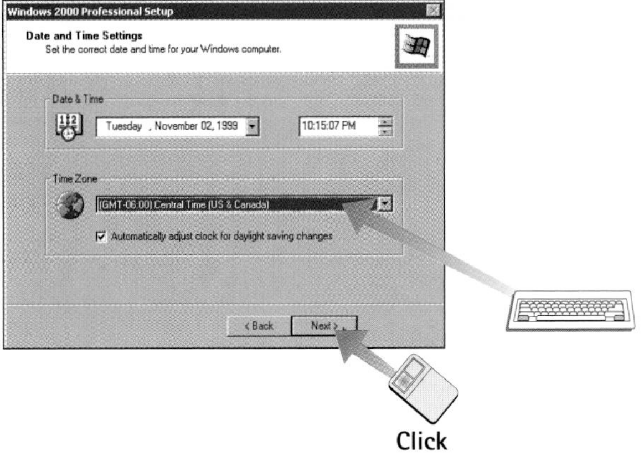

13 Choose Network Settings

Next, setup installs networking components for your computer. When it's done, you need to choose your network settings. Unless you know that custom settings are required, choose **Typical**. You can always change the settings after installation if you need to. Click the **Next** button to go on.

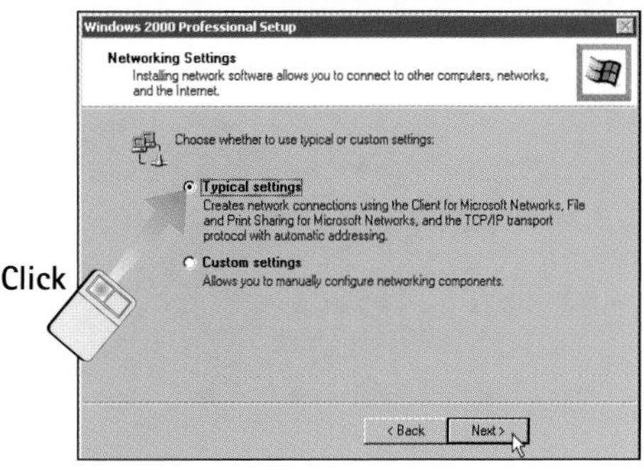

14 Join a Workgroup or Domain

If your computer will be part of a Windows networking domain, choose the **Yes** option. If not, choose **No**. Either way, type a name of a domain or workgroup into the box.

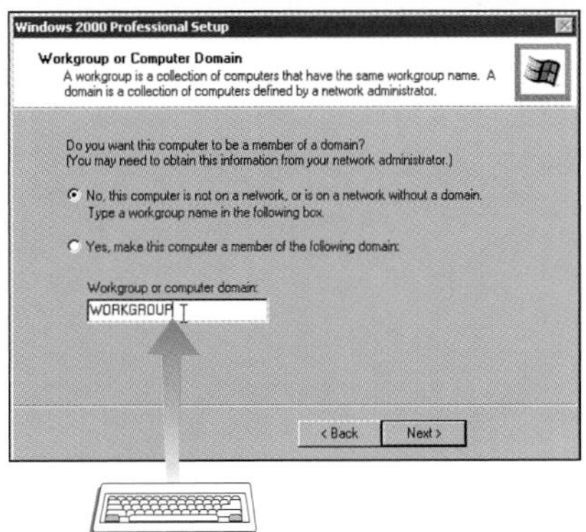

Windows 2000 Professional Setup
Workgroup or Computer Domain
A workgroup is a collection of computers that have the same workgroup name. A domain is a collection of computers defined by a network administrator.
Do you want this computer to be a member of a domain?
(You may need to obtain this information from your network administrator.)
No, this computer is not on a network, or is on a network without a domain. Type a workgroup name in the following box.
Yes, make this computer a member of the following domain:
Workgroup or computer domain:
WORKGROUP
< Back
Next >

15 Finish the Installation

Next, setup installs the necessary components to finish your installation. This process can take several minutes. When it is done, click **Finish** to restart your computer . When it comes back up, you're ready to start using Windows 2000 Professional.

End

TASK 3

How to Create Setup Floppy Disks

If you plan to install Windows 2000 Professional on a clean system (one without an operating system on it already), you need to create a set of four setup floppy disks. These disks are used to start your computer so that it can recognize your CD-ROM drive and other hardware and install Windows 2000. To make these disks, you need to insert the Windows 2000 Professional CD-ROM into a computer that has Windows 95, 98, NT, or 2000 installed on it.

Begin

1 Browse This CD

When you insert the Windows 2000 CD-ROM, a splash screen should appear automatically, presenting you with several choices. Click the **Browse This CD** link.

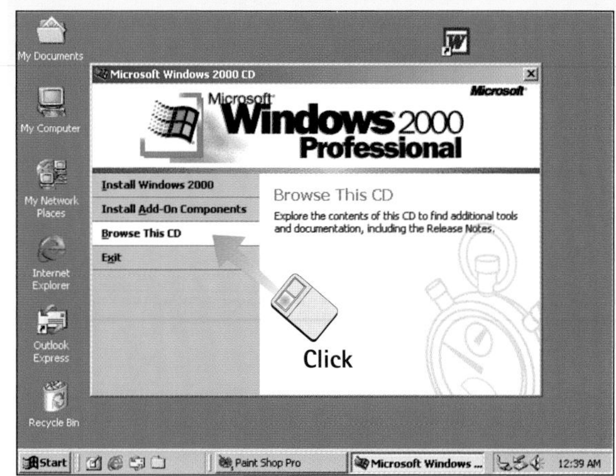

2 Open the BOOTDISK Folder

Double-click the **BOOTDISK** folder to open it.

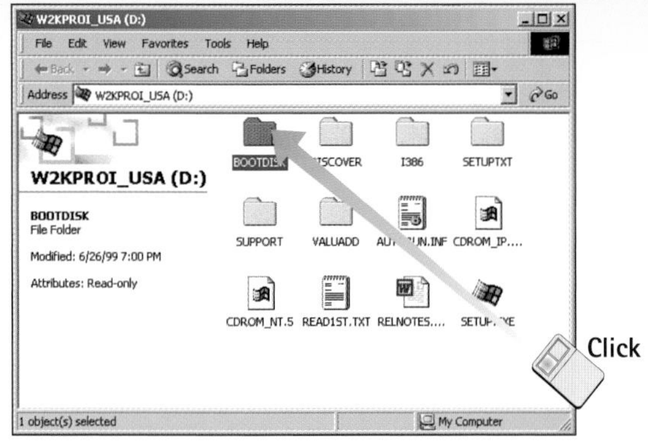

3 Start MAKEBT32.EXE

Double-click the **MAKEBT32.EXE** program to start it.

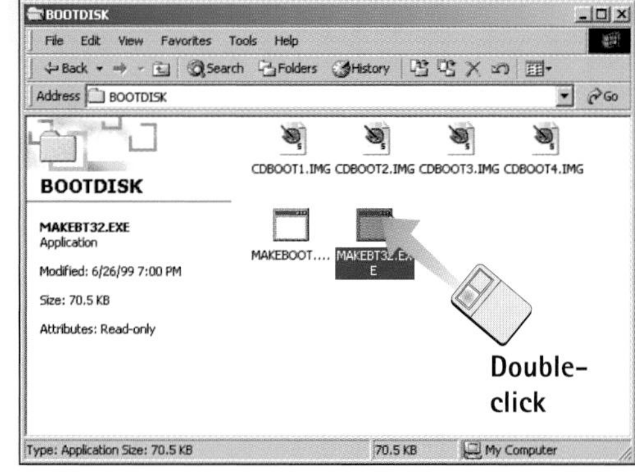

4 Type in the Floppy Drive Letter

Type the letter of the floppy drive you want to use to make floppies. This is usually **A**.

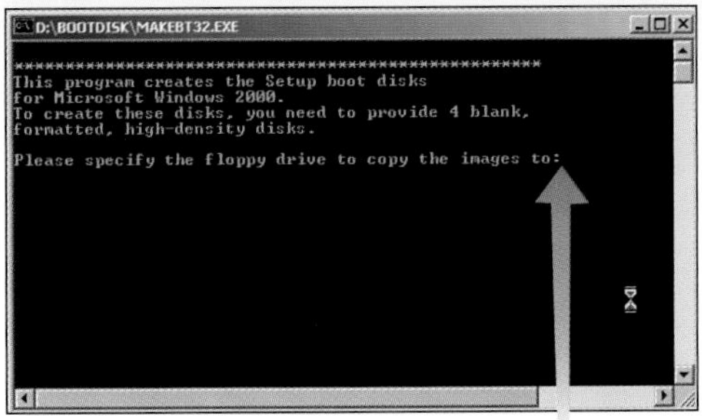

D:\BOOTDISK\MAKEBT32.EXE
This program creates the Setup boot disks
for Microsoft Windows 2000.
To create these disks, you need to provide 4 blank,
formatted, high-density disks.
Please specify the floppy drive to copy the images to:

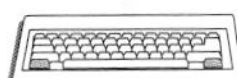

5 Insert the Floppy Disk and Press the Enter Key

Insert a blank, formatted floppy disk into the selected drive and press the **Enter** key. The program begins copying files to the disk, which becomes the first disk in the set. When finished copying, the program prompts you for the next disk and then the next. When the last disk is done, the program window closes automatically.

End

Index

A

B

C

E

F-G

H

I

J-K-L

M

T

U

V

W

How to Use *provides easy, visual information in a proven, step-by-step format. This amazing guide uses colorful illustrations and clear explanations to get you the results you need.*

Other How to Use Titles

How to Use Microsoft Word 2000
Sherry Kinkoph
ISBN: 0672315319
$24.99 US

How to Use Microsoft Excel 2000
Dan and Sandy Gookin
ISBN: 0672315386
$24.99 US

How to Use Microsoft Outlook 2000
Dave Johnson
ISBN: 0672315882
$24.99 US

How to Use Microsoft Access 2000
Jacqueline Okwudili
ISBN: 0672314916
$24.99 US

How to Use Microsoft Publisher 2000
Jennifer Fulton
ISBN: 0672315718
$24.99 US

How to Use Microsoft PowerPoint 2000
Susan Daffron
ISBN: 0672315297
$24.99 US

How to Use Lotus Notes 5
Dorothy Burke
ISBN: 067231505X
$24.99 US

How to Use Linux
Bill Ball
ISBN: 0672315459
$24.99 US

SAMS

www.samspublishing.com

How to Use Windows 98
Doug Hergert
ISBN: 1562765728
$24.99 US

All prices are subject to change.